Child Care
Administration
Planning Quality Programs for Young Children

Linda S. Nelson   Alan E. Nelson
Indiana, Pennsylvania

Publisher
The Goodheart-Willcox Company, Inc.
Tinley Park, Illinois

Library of Congress Catalog Card Number 99-057511
International Standard Book Number 1-59070-227-1
1 2 3 4 5 6 7 8 9 10   03 08 07 06 05 04 03

Library of Congress Cataloging-in-Publication Data
Nelson, Linda S., 1944-
    Child care administration: planning quality programs
for young children / Linda S. Nelson and Alan E. Nelson.
    p. cm.
    Includes index.
    ISBN 1-59070-227-1
    1. Child care services--United States--Administration.
2. Day care centers--United States--Administration.
I. Nelson, Alan E., 1943- II. Title.
HQ778.63 .N45 2003
362.71'2'068--dc21   2002040846

Introduction

Child Care Administration: Planning Quality Programs for Young Children was written to help you become a successful administrator of a quality child care program. It provides clear, step-by-step information about how to establish and operate both proprietary and not-for-profit programs. *"Director's Dilemmas"* throughout the text will help you to identify and develop strategies for dealing with real-life management situations.

Successful programs require careful planning long before the doors actually open for children. Part One of this book guides you through the process of determining the type of need that exists, obtaining financial support for the program, locating and preparing a facility, planning the daily program, hiring appropriate staff, and enrolling children.

Part Two of this text focuses on the management tasks required to operate a program. It provides information about how to develop leadership and organizational skills. Specific topics include an examination of special purpose programs, keeping children healthy and safe, and working with parents.

Providing quality care is complicated. It requires the combining of knowledge about child development along with thoughtful planning and organization. However, helping provide a positive child care experience can bring you the immense satisfaction of knowing that you have helped improve the quality of life for children and their families.

About the Authors

As a team, Linda and Alan Nelson work together with the goal of helping to improve the day-to-day quality of children's lives. Both Linda and Alan are active in numerous professional organizations, including the National Association for the Education of Young Children. They have given many presentations on family and child care-related topics.

Linda Nelson has taught at Indiana University of Pennsylvania for 33 years, where she is currently the Chairperson of the Human Development and Environmental Studies Department and Professor of Child Development and Family Relations. She is the author of grants in the Family and Consumer Sciences area and previously served as chair of the Home Economics Education Department at Indiana University of Pennsylvania. She has been a training consultant to child care and Head Start programs throughout Pennsylvania and has served as a guest speaker and workshop presenter at regional and national conferences.

Alan Nelson is currently Associate Professor of Child Development and Family Relations at Indiana University of Pennsylvania. For over 20 years, he was the Executive Director of the Indiana County Child Care Program, a Pennsylvania model program with services for over 600 children, ages infancy to 12 years old. He has served on numerous child care-related committees at the state level. Alan was also a cluster coordinator for two clusters of doctoral students at Nova Southeastern University. Prior to that, he worked as an elementary school guidance counselor. He was awarded the Friend of Home Economics Award by the Pennsylvania Home Economics Association (now, the Pennsylvania Family and Consumer Sciences Association).

Contents

Part 1
Organizing a Quality Child Care Program

Part 2
Administering a Quality Child Care Program

Chapter 18
Program Evaluation   381

Glossary   407

Index   415

The growing need for quality child care has resulted in a need for trained child care staff and administrators.

Chapter 1
Quality Child Care: Today's Growing Need

After studying this chapter, you will be able to

◎ explain the trends in society that have led to a growing need for child care services.

◎ describe the reasons quality child care is important.

◎ list the major characteristics of a quality child care program.

◎ describe the role of the administrator of a child care program.

◎ identify factors that influence entrepreneurial decisions in child care.

Throughout history, families have sometimes needed help and support in caring for their children. Fortunate families were able to count on nearby relatives, neighbors, friends, and older siblings. Many children grew up and stayed in the same community where their parents had lived their whole lives. Children played in safe neighborhoods. They knew that trusted adults were keeping an eye on them, 1-1.

As times have changed, families have also changed. Families now relocate more frequently. More mothers with young children are working to make ends meet. More families are headed by a single parent. Traditional support systems are not always available. New dangers threaten the safety of young children. The pressures of modern life make successful parenting more difficult than in the past.

Why Is There a Growing Need for Child Care?

Societal changes have brought an increased need for child care services. Unfortunately, the supply has not kept up with the demand. For many families, child care is simply not available. There is a shortage of trained individuals to staff child care programs. Several factors have contributed to the increased need for child care. These include

• the growth of single-parent families

• a shortage of skilled workers

• changing opportunities for women

• family economic need for two incomes

1-1 In this neighborhood, children can feel secure in knowing that caring adults are nearby.

Growth of Single-Parent Families

Today, more children are growing up in single-parent families. This has led to an increased need for child care. Current statistics reveal that one out of every four children will live with a single parent by age 18. Some children will spend their entire childhood with only one parent available to them. This lone parent must provide family income, nurturance, guidance, and basic care. Under the best of situations, single parenthood is hard work. It can often be stressful for both parent and child. Life becomes more difficult when poverty, custody battles, lack of education, and isolation from traditional support services are added. When these additional factors are a part of the family's stresses, the quality of life for children can be compromised.

Currently, one-half of all marriages will end in divorce. Many of these divorced couples have children young enough to require constant care and supervision. The custodial parent, typically the mother, often has to work outside of the home, creating a necessity for child care.

There has also been a dramatic increase in the number of single, never-married parents. Many of these parents are very young. They need help with child care in order to finish their basic education and to help them learn parenting skills. Lack of an education substantially increases the risk of poverty and instability for a family. Many communities and schools view the availability of child care as an essential service to help young parents stay in school.

Factors other than divorce, such as the death of a parent, result in a single-parent family. One parent's job transfer, commuter marriages, or a parent's need to care for elderly family members may cause family separations. Military commitments, job training opportunities, or parental incarceration may also separate families. Child care for these children can mean contact with additional compassionate, caring adults.

Shortage of Skilled Workers

The U.S. population is changing. The average age of U.S. citizens is rising. This means people are living longer and moving out of the workforce into retirement. Fewer young people are approaching adulthood and moving into the workforce to take the places of those retiring.

U.S. Department of Labor studies predict there will be a serious labor shortage in the near future. There simply won't be enough trained people to fill all of the jobs that will need to be done. At the same time, there will be young adults with little education, job skills, or training who will be unable to find work. Their opportunities will be limited to the most menial of jobs at the lowest wages.

Census statistics and school enrollments portray a reasonably accurate representation of the number of young people at each age level. These statistics indicate how many people are growing up, going to school, pursuing advanced education, or dropping out each year. There is concern that the coming shortage of skilled workers in many fields will harm the vitality of the U.S. economy.

In past years, most mothers of young children stayed at home to provide child care. Employers recognize these young mothers are a valuable labor source. However, without adequate child care, many mothers are unable or unwilling to return to work. Lack of quality child care programs and trained people to staff them are significant barriers. As employers begin to consider ways to bring mothers back into the workforce, child care has been identified as a major draw. Many employers are taking an active role in trying to make more child care available. Community organizations, such as chambers of commerce, service clubs, health care providers, and institutions of higher education, are examining the need for child care.

Director's Dilemma

You are deciding whether you want to open a new child care center. Everyone tells you there is a need for more services to families and children. Do you think they are right? Consider your family, the families of friends, and families in your neighborhood. Do you know any single-parent families with young children? Are you acquainted with young couples who both have careers? What kinds of child care arrangements are young families making in your neighborhood?

Changing Opportunities for Women

Historically, most women in the United States stayed home to care for their children. Many worked in traditionally female careers, such as nursing, teaching, or clerical work. There were few other choices available.

Today, women are employed in virtually every career field. The women's movement of the 70s, federal antidiscrimination legislation, and the need for women in the workforce brought about this change. Now there are expanded opportunities for jobs in fields that had been closed to women in the past. As women have found challenging and financially rewarding opportunities open to them, their interest in pursuing careers has increased.

More women are continuing their education beyond the secondary level. A woman who has spent time and money on education in preparation for a challenging career is less willing to give that up for full-time motherhood. If a woman takes time off to care for a young child, she may find there is no job when she is ready to go back. If she has goals for advancement, the opportunities can be lost by taking time out for child rearing. Women with high career aspirations desire quality child care, 1-2.

For today's women, interesting career directions have not come without a cost. Many in America still hold to the idea that women should be home with their children. They see women's careers as undesirable and unnecessary. There has been a reluctance to acknowledge the changing nature of families and work. This opposition to the added responsibilities of women has been partly responsible for the lack of organized effort on behalf of comprehensive child care.

For women with little education, job opportunities, even at a menial level, can be nonexistent. Since single mothers who cannot get jobs often receive public assistance, job training programs have been initiated. One goal of these programs is to help

1-2 Today, a large number of women with young children are in the labor force and need quality care for their children.

women become gainfully employed. If a trainee has young children, child care will be a necessary part of helping her participate in training. It will also support her efforts to find eventual employment.

The expanded need for child care services is directly linked to the movement of women into the workforce. As women develop interesting, satisfying careers, some are reluctant to risk losing opportunities by staying home when their children are young.

Family Economic Need for Two Incomes

Economic conditions have made it more difficult for young families to establish comfortable standards of living. Many of the new jobs created have been minimum wage jobs with no health insurance and few other benefits. Young families, especially those headed by individuals without special job skills or advanced education, find it difficult to survive financially without income from both spouses. Even when both spouses are working at minimum wage jobs, the family will still have an income level that is below the federal poverty standards.

Many Americans have dreams of home ownership, a college education for their children, adequate health and retirement insurance, a comfortable lifestyle, and financial stability. These have become increasingly difficult to achieve on a single income. For many young families, building a family life similar to what they experienced growing up requires the income of two working parents. The result is a need for child care while both parents work.

Two-career families often delay parenthood until their careers are well established. Today, it is not uncommon for women in their thirties to be starting their families. At this point in their lives, these "older" families have an established lifestyle and financial security that they are unwilling to jeopardize. Although the "juggling act" required to balance career and parenthood is difficult and stressful, these families feel it is worth it. They have contributed to the increased demand for child care services.

Why Is There a Need for Quality Child Care?

Currently, in the United States, the quality of child care varies widely. Regulations for child care services are different in each state. The current system of both private and public programs has resulted in many choices for some families and no room at all for others. A large amount of information now exists on the positive outcomes for children who attend quality preschool programs. Research indicates that the impact of good early childhood care and educational experience can be long lasting, 1-3.

The most widely reported research on the effects of preschool comes from a report called *Changed Lives* published by the High/Scope Foundation in Ypsilanti, Michigan. Children from lower-income families who were enrolled in a quality preschool program as early as the mid-sixties have been followed into adulthood. They have been compared with a similar group of children who did not attend preschool. Throughout the childhood and young adult years, the impact of the preschool program was clear. The children who attended preschool were more likely to

- score higher on school achievement tests

- have less need for special education classes

- stay in school until graduation

- get into less trouble with the law

- avoid becoming teen parents

- become gainfully employed as young adults

1-3 Good child care experiences can have positive life-long effects for children.

In general, attitudes toward school and skills for success in school were improved by participation in a good early childhood program. The data indicated that society can save almost seven dollars worth of later services for every dollar spent on preschool programs.

Other research has shown good programs also nurture creativity. They help children develop positive social skills. They also provide opportunities for children to develop thinking and problem-solving skills.

Concerned parents are looking for programs that provide positive experiences for their children. Many community and government officials are also convinced about the value of quality programs. *Custodial programs*, those programs that do nothing more than keep children safe, are no longer considered acceptable. Serious efforts are being directed toward improving the availability of good programs.

What Makes a Good Program?

Good programs for children have certain common qualities. They are planned to meet the needs of children. Each of the following characteristics is important in planning a quality program, 1-4.

Trained Teachers and Staff

Good programs have good teachers! Good teachers understand stages of child development and learning. They have had education that prepares them to work with groups of young children. Training in child development, family and consumer

Good programs have:
Trained teachers and staff
Low adult-to-child ratio
Small group size
Developmentally appropriate activities
Child-initiated activities
Clearly defined curriculum
Positive guidance
Parent involvement

1-4 Quality programs for children have certain important characteristics in common.

sciences (formerly home economics), or early childhood education prepares teachers to meet children's needs. They are better able to make decisions about program activities and guidance. They know where to go for information. Trained staff also understand that working with young children is a challenging job requiring careful thought and planning.

States vary in terms of the training required for different positions. Some states require four-year college degrees for teachers and administrators. Child development specialists and the major professional organizations in this field recommend this requirement. Other states require a two-year degree (Associate's Degree) for these positions. In some states, a combination of child development coursework and on-the-job experience is acceptable. In general, there is an increasing awareness that trained personnel are necessary for a good program. All states currently have some requirements regarding acceptable levels of staff education and/or training in their licensing requirements.

Developmentally Appropriate Practices

The program of daily activities is a central part of a quality center. The National Association for the Education of Young Children (NAEYC) is a professional organization of people who work in the child development field. It is particularly concerned with identifying characteristics of excellent programs for young children. NAEYC has developed a position statement that defines good programming as using *developmentally appropriate practices*. This means that equipment, activities, and guidance are carefully tailored to the developmental characteristics and needs of each group. The concept and position statement have received a lot of favorable publicity. They are being used as the basis for revised regulations and planning learning environments in several states.

Planning developmentally appropriate activities for young children requires the teacher

- knows age characteristics of the children in the group

- knows the types of equipment and activities preferred by the age group

- knows how to prepare the classroom and activities for optimum use

- knows how to plan concrete, "hands-on" experiences

- understands the progression of development, so activities can be matched to children's developmental readiness

- knows each child's unique characteristics

- knows where to go to get new ideas

- understands how to create a positive, supportive learning environment

A program that has a good daily program of developmentally appropriate activities requires careful planning. It doesn't just happen. There must be a match between what the children are ready for and the activities available to them. Teachers need to plan the room arrangement and select appropriate equipment. They have to plan the daily schedule, including special activities and group time activities.

A good program for young children will fascinate and challenge them. It will not bore or frustrate them. When children are in a quality program, they will look forward to the day's activities. They will end the day feeling successful and good about themselves. The children will take naturally to those activities that are appropriate to their developmental level, 1-5.

Child-Initiated Activity

Young children also benefit from being able to make choices and pursue their own interests, 1-6. Classrooms must allow many opportunities for children to set their own pace. This is a unique kind of teaching that is not common to classrooms for older children. Teachers must be able to recognize the differences that will exist within a preschool classroom. Children will have different background experiences. They will have different interests and talents. They will have different growth rates and varying attention spans. It is unrealistic to think they will all enjoy and benefit from doing the same thing at the same time.

Planning *child-initiated activities* allows children to have some control over their activities and helps them to feel responsible for their actions. They grow in their ability to plan activities and to make choices. Allowing them to control the amount of time they spend on a particular activity can encourage deep involvement and lengthened concentration.

By contrast, those programs that are heavily teacher-directed and tightly structured lead to a sense of frustration in children. They tend to feel powerless. It is important that children be given a block of "free-choice" time. During that time, children can choose among the activities the teacher has made available. They are helped to become "initiators" of activity instead of becoming individuals who only respond to the suggestions of others.

Positive Guidance

Good programs are also characterized by staff who use *positive guidance* when guiding children. There is an understanding that children need gentle guidance to help them grow.

1-5 These children are fascinated by activities geared to their developmental level.

1-6 Child-initiated activities allow children to explore and learn at their own pace.

Positive guidance helps children learn what behaviors are acceptable. It is matched to the age level and understanding of the children. This is in contrast to negative forms of guidance that focus on what the child does wrong. *Negative guidance* is often based on unrealistic expectations of children's behavior. It is often harsh and makes children feel worthless and incompetent. Shame, humiliation, embarrassment, threats, and physical punishment are examples of negative guidance.

In a good center, staff provides guidance based on each child's needs, rather than responding to children's behaviors emotionally. Children are not overwhelmed by rules. When limits are necessary, the children are given simple explanations that help them to understand the logic of the adult world.

Positive guidance is a "teaching tool" in the classroom. Children are always treated with a respect that helps them grow in self-confidence and self-control. Harsh, demeaning types of control and punishment have no place in the preschool classroom. They work against the goals of a quality program.

Parent Involvement

Young children's concerns focus primarily around their families. The family is the most important factor influencing them. Any program that wants to have a positive impact on children, must include parents. Parents and staff need to share pertinent information regarding the children.

Children benefit most when parents and staff communicate with each other. Teachers are often the first to detect special needs. Parents will know if a child has had an upsetting experience outside of school.

Good programs involve parents in many ways. Some have parents represented on the governing board. Others plan special activities for children and parents together. Parents can help with fund-raising activities and providing ideas for future planning. There may also be opportunities for parents to volunteer in the classroom or to attend parent education classes.

Parent involvement helps parents to feel they are an important part of the center. It allows for additional interaction between the staff and parents. Parents are more likely to share important information about their child if they feel comfortable with the teachers. They will feel a sense of commitment to the center if they understand its goals and methods.

What Will Be Your Role as the Director of a Center?

Directors of child care programs have certain responsibilities that are necessary to ensure the center can operate effectively. The difficulty in carrying out these tasks may ensure the center can operate effectively. The difficulty in carrying out these tasks may be affected by the nature of the center. Small centers with few classrooms are usually easier to administer than large ones. Centers that offer a wide variety of services to families will be harder to direct than less complex programs.

Perhaps you hope to open a center of your own. This can bring a great deal of personal satisfaction, but it may also entail additional work and commitment, 1-7. Some of the personal characteristics and resources needed to successfully own a center may be different from those needed when you work for someone else.

Administering a Child Care Program

A child care program needs a director who has a broad overview of the total program, whether it is large or small. It is the director who "holds things together" and understands how the different parts of the program relate to one another. A teacher focuses primarily on the classroom. The bookkeeper pays attention to the financial records. However, it is the director who must recognize how the budget relates to the cost of keeping the classroom in operation. It is also the director who must be goal-oriented and able to guide the program toward a successful future.

Responsibilities of the Director

In general, the responsibilities of a child care program director include

- providing leadership and overall organization for the program
- finding ways to provide adequate funding for the center
- choosing well-trained staff who can create a quality program for the children
- maintaining an awareness of community trends and family needs to plan future direction for the program

- communicating clearly with staff and being aware of how things are going throughout the program
- representing the program at various meetings and within the community
- evaluating and improving weak areas of the program.

You will learn about each of these areas as you study the chapters in this book.

Personal Skills and Abilities Needed to Be a Director

It is helpful to examine your personality

1-7 This director is proud of all the children and families her program has served.

in child care administration. In a small center, you may be handling the administrative tasks and working directly with the children. As your program grows, the administration becomes more complex. The administrative work may become a full-time position. You may have no direct responsibilities with the children.

Characteristics of a successful director include

- having good interpersonal skills that include a basic respect for all

- being knowledgeable about both child development programming and administrative responsibilities

- possessing leadership, problem-solving, and team building skills

- having the self-confidence to be an independent decision maker

- having the ability to organize

- being willing to take on responsibility

- being willing to work hard, even beyond actual working hours when necessary

- being flexible in adjusting to necessary, but unexpected, interruptions

The director has a unique role within the center. While working comfortably with staff, families, and outside agencies, the director must also be comfortable working independently, 1-8. As the "boss" of the center, you will find it necessary to develop personal friendships and relationships with people who are not involved with the program.

1-8 A child care center director has many administrative responsibilities.

Educational Requirements

Many young people start their education for child care administration in high school vocational and/or technical programs. There is a trend for these programs to provide supervised work experience in child care settings as a part of their program curriculum.

The competencies attained and the completion of coursework may support entrance into a junior or community college or a four-year college degree program. Strong knowledge of core early childhood competencies along with the work experience may prepare students to apply for the Child Development Associate credential. This credential is approved as acceptable preparation for a variety of early childhood related jobs according to state-mandated regulations.

The qualifications for being a child care

program director vary from state to state. They are determined by the licensing regulations. The number of children enrolled in the center may influence the required qualifications of the director. Programs with larger numbers of children and staff may be required to have a director with more education. Each state may also set different educational requirements for various types of programs.

Qualifications for directors of half-day nursery school type programs may be different than those for directors of full-day child care programs. Directors of infant/toddler programs may need different training than individuals planning to operate large programs with multiple age groups. You will need to find out what the specific requirements are in your state in order to plan your career preparation.

How Do I Open My Own Center?

You may have a dream of owning and operating your own child care center. You probably like the idea of being independent and working with children. If you plan to start your own child care business, you will be considered an *entrepreneur*. An entrepreneur is a person who is willing to take the risk that opening a new business involves. The entrepreneur also expects that the new business venture will be successful and earn a profit. In most new businesses, the owner also works as the manager or director.

Being an Entrepreneur

There are many successful entrepreneurs in the United States. However, there are also many individuals who consider opening their own program and decide against it, at least for awhile. They may prefer to work for other private or publicly funded programs. This is a decision you need to think over carefully. Successful entrepreneurs typically have a number of characteristics in common, 1-9.

Willingness to Take a Reasonable Risk

Starting a business involves the risk that it may not be successful. What will you have lost and what will you do if the center does not enroll enough children to continue to operate?

Knowledgeable About Child Care and Business Factors

Your chances of success are much greater if you know about what it takes to operate a successful center. Courses in child development, child care administration, and experiences working directly with children and families improve your chances. The risk of opening a center would be high for someone with no training in the field. However, your knowledge about child care administration will make the risk a more reasonable one. This course in administration will help you become familiar with the

1-9 Do you have the characteristics of an entrepreneur?

basic business techniques that are necessary to create a financially stable program.

Hardworking and Responsible

If you start your own center, you will quickly find out "being your own boss" is hard work. Entrepreneurs feel a need to be sure everything is going as it should. They keep a close eye on center activities. They may do the work of several people in order to save money. They may pitch in and help with menial tasks in order to get a job done. They take the responsibility of doing whatever needs to be done to keep the program functioning smoothly.

Goal-Oriented

A successful child care entrepreneur has a strong desire to start and own a child care center. If you are just thinking about starting a center because someone else thinks it is a good idea, you are less likely to be successful. Most successful entrepreneurs are very definite about their goals for center ownership within a specific time frame.

Self-Confident and Innovative

Entrepreneurs have belief in their own abilities to succeed. They are creative in finding new and better ways to create a successful program. They are not afraid to try out new ideas.

Advantages and Disadvantages of Entrepreneurship

There are both advantages and disadvantages to starting your own business. Many capable individuals decide that business ownership is not for them. As you study this course, your own goals for your career will probably become clearer.

There are several important advantages *to* owning your own program. They include

- *Independence and personal satisfaction.* Owning your own center gives you the freedom to create the very best center you can. As long as you conform to all licensing and regulatory requirements, you can bring your own ideas to the operation of the program. The decisions made about the program are your ideas. You can take pride in the success of the program. There is usually a deep sense of satisfaction in seeing families and children benefit from your program.

- *Profit.* As the owner of a program, you will receive any income left over after expenses have been paid. The time and effort you put into making the center successful will come back to you in the form of increased profit.

- *Job security.* As an entrepreneur, you are not subject to the whims or business practices of others above you. You cannot be fired, transferred, or forced to retire. As long as your center is financially healthy with a strong enrollment, you will have a job.

- *Status.* Business ownership is valued highly in the United States. As a program owner, you would have a social status above many others in the workforce.

There are also several important reasons why you may choose *not* to become an entrepreneur. Among the reasons are

- *Low or unpredictable income.* Child care is an expensive business to operate. Tuition must be kept low enough to attract families. Salaries must be high enough to attract employees. Supplies and equipment must be adequate to support a quality program. If the center has low enrollment for a period of time, the profit may be minimal.

- *Loss of investment.* As an entrepreneur, you will have to invest your own time and money to start the center. If the center is not successful, you may lose all of the money and effort you have put into it. Along with those losses, you would also have lost your job.

- *Hard work.* Most business owners work long hours and do whatever is necessary to get the business started. Successful child care centers usually offer care for more than eight hours a day. Your staff will only work part of that time. As the owner, you may find yourself finishing up menial tasks, required reports, and even, equipment repair. Hiring others to do these jobs would require additional cash outlay.

You will need to consider all these factors in deciding whether or not owning your own center is really for you.

Director's Dilemma

You have inherited some money from a deceased relative. You are trying to decide whether to use the money to open a new center. What should you consider before committing your money to this venture?

✪ Summary

Societal changes have increased the need for child care services. The rising number of single-parent families has contributed to this trend. Mothers have opportunities available to them for more diverse careers. Often, young families find two incomes are needed to provide them with adequate financial resources. Projections for the future indicate there will be a significant lack of educated workers. This means even more parents with young children will be taking jobs in the future.

There is a serious shortage of available quality child care services. Although the benefits of a good preschool experience are recognized, many families cannot find appropriate care. Government, communities, and employers are looking at ways to support the growth of new and expanded programs.

Good programs for children have many similarities. Teachers and staff have special training to understand children and their needs. Activities and equipment are carefully chosen to match the interests and abilities of the children. Positive guidance is warm and supportive. Successful experiences with adults, other children, and activities help children grow and learn.

The director must be familiar with all of the program. It is the director's responsibility to make sure all licensing and regulatory requirements are met. The director must plan for the future, guide the program toward financial security, and ensure quality care is being provided.

Individuals who decide to own and operate their own centers can be defined as entrepreneurs. Not everyone has the personality or resources to become an entrepreneur. Successful center owners must be knowledgeable about the field of child care and have confidence in themselves. They are willing to work long hours and to take the risk of investing their own money.

✪ Terms

custodial programs
developmentally appropriate practices
child-initiated activities
positive guidance
negative guidance
entrepreneur

✪ Review

1. Identify four trends in society that have led to the need for more child care.

2. Explain why the quality of child care varies widely.

3. List six long-term benefits that have been related to attendance in a quality early childhood program.

4. Explain why custodial care is no longer considered acceptable.

5. What is the purpose of NAEYC (National Association for the Education of Young Children)?

6. Identify four factors teachers must consider when planning developmentally appropriate activities.

7. Explain the difference between "child-initiated" and "teacher-directed" activities.

8. Explain why the director of a child care program must have a broad overview of the entire program.

9. Identify four areas of responsibility that directors of child care programs must address.

10. List three advantages and disadvantages of becoming an entrepreneur.

⚙ Applications

1. Invite several young working parents to your class to discuss how they made child care decisions.

2. Survey child care centers in your community. What ages do they serve? How many children do they serve? What are their hours of operation?

3. Interview an entrepreneur about the risks and benefits involved in opening a new business.

4. Talk with other students in your class to find out how many of them want to own and operate their own centers. How many of them want to become directors for already existing centers?

5. Find out what the requirements are in your state to become the director of a child care center.

You can determine the needs for child care in your community by talking with parents.

Chapter 2
Determining the Needs for Child Care

After studying this chapter, you will be able to

○ describe the factors that influence the need for child care.

○ discuss the various types of child care used by families.

○ identify information that will help you determine the types of child care services needed now and in the future.

○ describe the various methods of collecting information.

○ distinguish between the characteristics of the major philosophical approaches to programming in children's centers.

○ list the characteristics of the different types of child care services.

If you are thinking about providing a child care service, you must make sure there is a need for that care. While there is generally a child care shortage in the United States, a new program will not succeed unless it is used by the families in your community. A program will also not succeed if it does not match the specific needs of area families. For example, starting a half-day nursery school will not meet the needs of a working family. A child care center that is open daily from 9:00 AM to 5:00 PM will not help employees of a factory where the work day is from 7:30 AM to 3:30 PM. If a child care program is to be successful, it must provide the desired type of care in a convenient location at the right times of day. In other words, there must be a match between what families need and what you are providing, 2-1.

To determine the child care needs of your community, you must first identify those factors that influence child care needs. Next, you will need to determine how best to assess those factors in your community. Finally, you will try to match the identified needs with the various types of child care you might offer.

What Are the Characteristics of My Community?

Before you make decisions about the type of service you want to offer, you must study the community and local families carefully. Questions about location, hours, tuition, and type of services to offer cannot be answered until you have more information. Accurate information is essential if you are going to start a successful child care

2-1 Most centers must be open for at least 10 hours a day to meet the needs of working parents.

program. You will need to consider geography, the area's economic factors, and family characteristics.

Geography

Geographically, there are several factors you should investigate about your community. Start with a detailed map. Using your knowledge of the area, locate sites that will influence the demand for child care. Create a color key and use felt-tip markers. Identify the areas and sites discussed below.

Location of Major Employers

Mark the location of the main business areas and other major employers. Ask yourself the following questions:

* Where are the shopping districts or malls?

* Where are the large factories or office buildings?

* Where are the hospitals or nursing homes?

* Where are the grocery stores and schools?

These are the areas in a community where people will be working. Consider the hours when the sites will be open or in operation. Any child care service you start will have to match the hourly needs of the working people who will use your program. Check with your local chamber of commerce for facts about businesses and agencies in your community. That office may be able to supply you with additional information that would be helpful. Information such as population data, spending patterns, current and anticipated business activity, and local census data can give you useful information about your community.

Try to identify sections of your community that are growing or where new businesses are choosing to locate. These new businesses will be hiring people. Areas that are growing rapidly often attract young families. Young families often have child care needs.

Housing Areas

Locate the main housing areas on your map. Determine which areas are attracting young families. Homes priced for first-time buyers will attract families with young children, 2-2.

Director's Dilemma

You are the operator of several successful child care centers. The manager of a large office building has asked you to start a new center in the building for the people who work there. Many of the current employees are getting older. As they retire, the company wants to be able to attract and hire new, younger staff. What information do you need to collect before making a commitment to start this center?

Neighborhoods vary according to the average age and income of the residents. The typical cost of houses in a particular area can give you a clue about the incomes of the residents. Some neighborhoods attract dual-career families. Some areas are popular choices for commuters who travel daily to jobs in nearby cities. Other areas may be the choice of low- to moderate-income families. Economical housing costs can be very attractive to young families with children. These will be the housing areas on which to focus. You may be able to find out which schools are full and which ones have lower enrollments. This can give you a clue about the location of popular neighborhoods.

2-2 Identifying possible sites for a new center requires careful analysis of the area you want to serve. You may find a need for child care near a new apartment complex where young families with children will be living.

Locations of Existing Child Care Programs

As you collect information to help you plan for your center, it is useful to identify where other child care facilities are located. You may be able to find out what types of care are offered and whether or not the program has a waiting list. Check the yellow pages of the phone book for licensed facilities in your area.

Economic Factors

Child care is an expensive service to provide. Take into consideration the impact of economic factors on the ability of families to afford the cost of care.

Economy of the Area

Consider the overall economic conditions of your general location. Some areas are booming, while others are not. Some areas are characterized by high unemployment, low incomes, and depressed job opportunities. Other communities are growth areas with increasing demands for workers, the development of new shopping facilities, and a healthy housing market. It is useful to know if this is an area where new workers are likely to relocate. If it is a community that young families are leaving because there are no opportunities for them, you may want to consider whether there will be a market for a child care facility. The chamber of commerce can be helpful in providing you with information about the economy of the area.

Director's Dilemma

The director of a local center has told you there is no need for another center in town. She has not been willing to offer you any information or help. What can you find out about her center? What other sources of information can you use to find out about the need for additional child care facilities?

The employment picture is another factor to consider when deciding how to plan your center. What can you find out about the job stability in your target area? If you are planning a center you hope will attract the employees of a particular industry, you need to find out if that industry is doing well. Have the employees just had a recent contract settlement? Is there a strike looming? Does it appear the industry is growing, or is it laying off workers?

Identify the overall labor situation. Are new families moving to your area because of the availability of jobs? Do the new jobs pay high salaries, or are they mostly minimum wage jobs? Who are the major employers in your area, and what is the outlook for them? What are the major roads that people use to get to their jobs?

An additional area of concern is the availability of trained personnel in your area. Because salaries in child care are notoriously low, it is often difficult to attract personnel who do not already live nearby. Often, the people who work in child care have spouses who are employed. Usually, if the labor market is generally healthy, there will be talented people in the area who are interested in working in child care.

Family and Neighborhood Income Patterns

When considering whether or not to start a child care program, you must learn about the financial capability of the residents of the area. If you are planning a program that will be totally dependent upon tuition, you must determine if there are enough families who will be able to pay that tuition. In a lower income neighborhood, there may not be enough families who can afford the cost of care. A higher income neighborhood may be populated by older families with no need for child care. If your center is located where it can draw from families who represent a broader spectrum of income levels, you are more likely to have a clientele who can afford your program.

Family Characteristics

Planning a program to meet family needs requires knowledge about the families in your area. If you are accurate in determining their needs and wants, you are more likely to plan a successful program. Not every family can use the same types of services. If you have a clear picture of the variety of services that are desired, you can decide which of those services you can provide.

Ages of the Children

It is essential to have an estimate of how many children are likely to use a specific type of program. If you plan to open a preschool center for children ages three to five, but most of the families need care for infants or toddlers, you could have a problem with enrollment. If there is a large demand for before- and after-school care, but you are not planning a program for children in this age group, you will lose a possible source of enrollment.

Types of Care Preferred

Parents usually have definite preferences for the types of care they want their children to receive. Many parents prefer the small, cozy setting of a family child care home. Some families favor care from neighbors or relatives if it is available. For others, the stimulation and more extensive daily programs usually found in a center are desired. Some parents like to be involved in the center's program, whereas others do not have the time to do this. Some parents prefer large, multiple age centers so they can enroll all their children at the same location. Others don't mind having a preschool child at one building while their toddler is enrolled in a nearby family child care home. School-age programs are most likely to be chosen if they are located in the children's schools.

Hours of Care Needed

Some families need full-time child care. Others need care only on a part-time basis. Some parents are employed on weekends or evenings, but others may work varying shifts. If you can determine there is a clear indication of need for a center with weekend hours, you may want to consider this option. However, if there is almost no demand for weekend care, you could easily decide not to even consider offering it. Some centers are open 24 hours. Some centers, such as those in ski resort areas, may be open longer hours during peak tourist season. You must be sure the hours of the center match with the hours needed by parents who will use the program.

Special Services Desired

The needs of families vary. A program that can provide services to meet a variety of these needs will be popular. Some families might prefer to buy lunches, sign their children up for special lessons, or use occasional evening care for special events. If parents have no way to get their children from the school to the location of your after-school program, transportation might be a desired service. If you can provide bus or van service, the families are is more likely to enroll their children, 2-3. If a competing child care center provides transportation and you do not, you will probably lose children to the other center. On the other hand, if only one family requires this service, it may not be profitable for you to offer it. You will need to decide what special services your program should provide.

Parent education classes may be popular. Many parents often feel a need for more information about effective parenting. Trying to work and balance family demands can be difficult and frustrating. For many parents, having a chance to meet with others who are experiencing the same feelings, or whose children are the same ages, can be a helpful experience. Some centers sponsor parent education programs. For example, a parent educator could lead group discussions about various topics of concern with the adults, while the children, who are supervised by center staff, play with developmentally appropriate toys in the next room. The parents feel comfortable with their children nearby, while they have an opportunity to find support from other caring adults. Programs like this serve to introduce families to your center and staff. These same families might enroll for full-time care when it is needed.

Director's Dilemma

For several years, you have been planning to return to your hometown after you finish school. You would like to open a small child care center in the basement of a church. Many of your friends have told you they think this is a good idea. How can you find out whether your town really needs a child care center?

2-3 Transportation may be an essential need of parents.

There are a number of other services that can be offered to meet the needs of busy, working families. Some programs have cooperative arrangements with local dance or karate schools. Centers may link up with the local scouting and 4-H programs to provide these activities for the school-age children. Music lessons, gymnastics, tutoring, and meal catering can also be offered. Working families often have a difficult time scheduling all of the things they want for their children. Children's hours outside of child care are limited. A center that can help parents to provide lessons and special activities might be greatly appreciated, 2-4.

Financial Capabilities

Financial considerations include obtaining an estimate regarding whether or not interested families will be able to afford to enroll their children in your program. If your program will depend solely on tuition, you must be sure there are enough interested families who will be able to pay the fees. If your program will serve families who receive government support for part of the tuition, interested families must fall into income groups that are eligible for the subsidy voucher.

It is important to find out about the needs and resources of the families who are interested in using your service. If you plan an inappropriate program, or if the families cannot afford your program, you will have trouble recruiting enough children to maintain full enrollment. A successful program must be developed around the needs of the families you want to serve.

How Do I Obtain the Information I Need?

Determining information about the area in which you want to locate your program will require some detective work on your part. There are several ways in which you can obtain this data. These include

- doing background research on the area
- using questionnaires
- holding public meetings

You must decide what methods you will use to obtain useful information about family needs and preferences.

Background Research

You might begin your study by doing some background research. For example, identify the agencies or businesses within your community that are responsive to patterns and trends within your region. The local newspaper, Internet sources, school district personnel, the community planning agency, the regional Cooperative Extension office, and the local Chamber of Commerce all have an interest in the characteristics of the community and its families. Analyze the data from the most recent government census. It shows patterns of growth and decline in various geographic areas. The census also provides information on family size and economic data. Local health officials may be able to give you insights into the characteristics of their clients. Clergy can offer information about their denomination's membership. Neighborhood store owners also often have insights into the needs of families in their area. While it takes time and effort on your part to set up interviews, you can gain useful information by talking with others whose success also depends on knowing the community.

Directors of other child care services may also be willing to talk with you. Many good programs have waiting lists with names of children for whom there is no room. Caring directors find it frustrating to know that there are children needing care who cannot be placed in their program. Some directors would not feel threatened by the possible opening of a new center. They may be more than happy to help you get started. If there are several centers in a community and there is no waiting list, you may want to carefully consider whether your program will be able to attract enough children to be successful.

Getting to know other directors and maintaining friendly communication with them is a form of *networking*. A network or lines of communication with people who have similar interests, jobs, or goals can provide information and support. Network

---

Deciding Whether to Offer Special Services

If you are considering offering services other than basic child care, consider the following questions:

- How many families have indicated that they would use the services if it were available?
- Do other competing centers offer this service?
- How complicated would this service be for you to provide?
- What will it cost the center to offer the service?
- How much will have to be charged to participating families to cover the cost of the service?
- Can the service be offered in a way that is helpful to families, or will it add more stress?

2-4 Before making a commitment to offer a special service, you should ask yourself these questions.

contacts can serve as a source of new information, can help you identify trends, or may even help you avoid trouble. Keeping in touch with others who have the same types of responsibilities, frustrations, and concerns can give you new ideas and help you keep problems in perspective.

Questionnaires

A questionnaire is often a helpful tool in determining whether or not there is a need for child care services. When using a questionnaire, you can assess the needs of families and the type of services they are seeking.

Responding to a questionnaire is completely voluntary on the part of the family. Therefore, you must design a questionnaire that reflects concern for children and their families, sensitivity, and commitment to quality care. If parents feel that they will be criticized for their answers, or that they will be pestered for a commitment, they are not likely to respond. If parents feel that the questionnaire is too personal or too "nosy," you won't obtain much helpful information. Even families who need child care may be reluctant to answer a questionnaire if they know nothing about who is planning to operate the center.

The questionnaire must ask questions that will provide the information you need to know. Questionnaires must be written carefully so that the responses are meaningful. Questions should be clear, concise, and user-friendly so that parents are willing to answer them.

Most questionnaires ask for information related to the number and ages of children in the family. Information about parent work hours, type of care needed, nature of job and location of employer can provide knowledge about potential center location, hours, and tuition, 2-5. Many people will not answer questions that directly ask for their income level or what they are willing to pay for child care. However, if you know the number of wage earners in a family, the nature of their jobs, and their employers, you can usually figure out a rough estimate of the income of families.

When developing a questionnaire, you will need to think about the parents who will be answering the questions. It is usually not realistic to aim a questionnaire at a whole community. Instead, try to identify which families or groups of families are most likely to need your program. For example, if you want to set up a program primarily for the employees of a particular company, contact the company. They may allow you to enclose a questionnaire with the paychecks. If you are interested in serving a specific neighborhood, you may be able to distribute questionnaires through neighborhood religious organizations, clubs, or stores. These sources may also help you obtain the names, addresses, and phone numbers of families with young children, 2-6.

Director's Dilemma

You currently operate a successful center for 45 children. Your location is close to malls, the hospital, and major office buildings. Many of the parents who work in these locations must work in evenings, on weekends, or even through the night. Several of your families have asked you to consider keeping the center open through the evening, on weekends and possibly on a 24-hour basis. How could you decide whether or not to expand your hours? How could you find information about the number of families who might need care during these hours?

Sample Questions for a Questionnaire

We are considering opening a new child care center in your area. We need your help to decide if there is a need for such a program.

What are the current ages of your children?

_____ Under 1 year

_____ Between 12 and 18 months

_____ Between 18 and 24 months

_____ Between 2 and 3 years

_____ Between 3 and 4 years

_____ Between 4 and 6 years

_____ Between 6 and 12 years

Are you currently employed or in job training?

_____ Part-time

_____ Full-time

_____ Not employed or in job training

Do you use child care services? _____

If so, please identify the type of care and the approximate hours per week you use the child care service.

Type of care	Hours per week
Relative or neighbor	_____
Nannie	_____
Family child care home	_____
Group home	_____
Child care center	_____
Before- and after-school center	_____

Have you had difficulty finding child care? _____

Are you satisfied with your current child care arrangements? _____

What factors are important to you in choosing child care?

	Least Important			Most Important	
Distance from home	1	2	3	4	5
Distance from work	1	2	3	4	5
Cost	1	2	3	4	5
Hours of operation	1	2	3	4	5
Program structure and philosophy	1	2	3	4	5
Qualifications and skills of caregivers	1	2	3	4	5
Child's satisfaction with facility and caregivers	1	2	3	4	5
Caregiver-to-child ratio	1	2	3	4	5
The availability of financial assistance	1	2	3	4	5

Other? _____

Comments? _____

_____

_____

2-5 Your questionnaire might include questions like these.

Possible Sources of Information for Contacting Families

- Local chamber of commerce
- Local government extension office
- Neighborhood churches
- Neighborhood leaders
- Service or social clubs
- Employers
- Child care information and referral offices

2-6 These sources may help you identify families that might be interested in child care.

When deciding whether to develop a questionnaire, you will need to consider the costs. Postage; enclosing a self-addressed, stamped envelope; and printing costs can be expensive and need to be considered carefully. There may be other ways to distribute the questionnaires without using the mail.

Telephone surveys require an expensive use of time and effort. You will need to have some way of identifying potential families so you are not simply calling names out of the phone book. A list of questions prepared in advance ensures that you obtain the same type of information from every call. Follow-up calls to parents who have responded to an earlier written questionnaire may be more helpful than trying to obtain your initial information by phone survey.

Public Meetings

Sometimes it is helpful to hold a meeting for all those who are interested in child care. You may be able to hold it in the cafeteria of a business whose employees you hope to serve. You may also be able to schedule a meeting in a community center in the area where you hope to open a center.

The meeting should be organized so it will be convenient, both in time and location, for potential client families to attend. You can use the meeting time to find out if there is a need for child care and, if so, the kinds of programs or services families need. You may want to provide a questionnaire for this purpose. Be careful not to promise a specific opening date or tuition amount. Decisions about these items may have to be revised several times before your program is actually in operation.

How Do I Analyze Needs and Predict Future Trends?

The information you collect from your background research, questionnaires, and meetings can provide valuable information about the needs of families in your area. It is important to keep in mind, however, that not everyone who responded with interest will actually follow through by enrolling children in your program. Questionnaire responses cannot be considered a commitment for enrollment. Before your program is actually in operation, a family may have already found suitable care. The employment situation could change and child care may no longer be needed, or child care may be needed for different hours than what was originally indicated. It is probably safe to estimate that approximately one-tenth of the responding families may actually end up using your program.

Once you have assessed the specific needs for child care in a community, you can match those needs with an appropriate program. There are many types of child care programs and services that can be offered. The following discussion will describe these types of care.

What Are the Different Types of Care?

Child care and early education programs in the United States exist in many different formats. There are programs that operate for profit, and those that are organized as not-for-profit programs. Some programs depend financially on the tuition charged. Others receive public funds designed to assist low-income parents who would have trouble finding affordable child care. Programs may be privately owned, sponsored by religious organizations, community organizations, or the government. They can be organized by a group of parents or provided by an employer. In some parts of the country, parents have many choices when searching for a preschool setting for their child. In other locations, there may be very few options for parents, and child care may be extremely difficult to find.

Programs for young children can differ in a variety of ways. The number of hours the center is open each day, the goals of the program, the specific children who attend, and whether or not the program is based in a center or a home may vary. Within a community, there may be many different types of programs for young children. While each type of program has some specific characteristics, the basic components of quality programming and good care for children are basically the same. For the purpose of this discussion, the types of care will be classified as home-based or center-based. Special-purpose programs will also be described.

Home-Based Care

Many parents prefer care that is provided in a home setting, particularly for infants and toddlers. This is called *home-based care*. Homes are more likely to have a feeling of warmth and intimacy. Upholstered furniture, drapes, and good smells from the kitchen all create an atmosphere of nurturance. Home-based care is less likely to have an "institutional" feel to it. Types of home-based care include

- in-home care
- nannies
- family child care
- group homes

In-Home Care

Most parents of very young children would prefer having caregivers come into their homes to care for their children. This way, the child has one consistent caregiver, does not have to be transported outside on cold or rainy days, and is always in a familiar environment. If a family has several young children, in-home care can prevent the early-morning pressures of trying to get everyone up and ready to leave the house. The caregiver can take care of breakfast and early-morning routines in a more relaxed manner. Many in-home caregivers stay with a family until the children are all in school. They may become a life-long friend of the family. Parents often hope to find someone who will also prepare meals and do light house cleaning.

Most child care experts agree that when in-home care works well, it is highly desirable for families and young children. Unfortunately, the reality is that often it does not work out as planned. In-home child care is frequently provided by a neighbor or other adult who is searching for another job and is willing to "babysit" until something better comes along. The caregiver often has no training. If the caregiver is a young mother, she may also want to bring her own child along. With this type of care, there is no back-up. When the caregiver gets sick or can't come for some reason, the parent usually has very little time to make other arrangements. If the caregiver gets an opportunity for a better job, the parent may again be left with very little notice. The lack of training in child care, which is characteristic of most in-home caregivers, also means that the parent must be vigilant. Care in the child's own home does not mean that the caregiver will have the same values, guidance techniques, or willingness to attend to the child that the parents have. A caregiver without ideas for interesting activities may use the TV as daily entertainment for the child.

Nannies

In Europe, nannies have been a common type of child care for many years. Nannies are now also becoming popular in the United States. Nanny-training programs have been developed in schools and community colleges. A nanny provides the benefits of in-home care along with specialized training in the child development field. Placement agencies exist to screen both the family who is recruiting and the potential nannies. Good agencies review the qualities that the family wants, find suitable candidates, and review backgrounds and references. The agency also develops a contract that provides protection for both the family and nanny. The nanny usually lives and travels with the family, provides consistent care for the children, and receives a professional salary. These arrangements can work out quite well if both the family and the nanny view the situation with similar expectations.

Family Child Care

This type of care takes place in the caregiver's home. The family child care provider usually cares for several children who may be of varying ages, 2-7. Family child care is often used for very young children. It is also found in rural areas where there may not be enough children to keep a child care center in operation.

In many states, family child care homes are required to be licensed. They are inspected and held to state-determined standards. A voluntary registration system exists in other states. The number of children a family child care provider can care for varies according to state regulations.

There are several advantages to family child care. It provides a home-like atmosphere. The number of children being cared for is usually low, so that children get to know each other well. There are fewer children and adults for a child to get used to. Providers who see child care as their career frequently take advantage of training workshops, newsletters, and classes about children. Often, the parents and the provider's family become good friends. Family child care may also provide more flexible hours for parents whose work schedules vary.

2-7 This family child care home cares for six children of mixed ages.

Unfortunately, many caregivers are not aware of requirements in their states. They may operate without licensing or registration. They may, therefore, be unaware of any training opportunities that might be available. Frequently, they have very little education with no specific training in child care. This situation gives little help or protection to a family who is looking for child care. This contributes to the wide range of quality that is characteristic of family child care.

Some child care agencies administer a network of family child care homes. The agency helps the provider take care of paperwork, recruitment of children, and often links the provider with training opportunities and government food reimbursement programs. Large child care programs sometimes place young children in family child care homes and place older children in center care. Administrators are responsible for recruiting family child care providers and monitoring the quality of care in their homes. Because the homes may be spread out, supervision can be difficult. Finding providers who are skilled enough to be trusted when working independently with a small group of children can also be difficult. In addition to maintaining quality care sites, administrators must provide back-up if the provider is ill or unavailable. They must also be skilled in maintaining necessary records.

Group Homes

Group homes also typically are established in a private home setting. While regulations vary from state to state, group homes usually are permitted to enroll more children than a family child care home. Additional adults must be present in the home at all times. Licensing for a group home is often not as stringent as the licensing for a center. Group homes are frequently found in areas where there are not enough children to maintain enrollment in a fully licensed child care center. For many parents, a nearby group home can be a desirable choice. It provides a smaller group setting than a center and can offer the warmth of a home setting.

A disadvantage of the group home setting is that it is difficult to monitor. It is easy for providers to enroll more children than allowed. It is also possible for the provider to operate without sufficient adults in the setting. Because care takes place in the home, adequate supervision, which includes on-site visits to the home, is expensive in time and effort. As with family child care, some large agencies have a network of group homes that are affiliated with them.

Center-Based Care

Care for larger groups of children in settings that have been organized specifically for their use is classified as *center-based care*. Centers must be licensed by the state in which they operate. Good centers have a daily program of appropriate activities and trained staff members. Adequate equipment and healthful routines are provided for the children.

In most states, licensing regulations are very specific and have been developed with center-based care in mind. The amount of space needed, the qualifications of teachers, and the adult-child ratio are controlled by licensing standards that vary from state to state. Centers vary in terms of the hours that they are open and the services that they offer. However, they all provide a place away from home where a group of children stay while their parents are unavailable.

Child Care Centers

Centers are usually established with preschool children in mind. The typical entrance age is three years. Centers for infants and toddlers are also becoming more common. Most children leave this type of care when they enter kindergarten or first grade. Groups of children may be all of one age group, or there may be an age mixture within each group. While most will probably attend all day, some children may attend only part of the day.

The quality of care in centers varies considerably. Some state requirements for licensing are more strict than others. The level of staff training, the allowable adult-to-child-ratio, and group size can differ a great deal from state to state. The amount of space needed for each child, the equipment, the schedule, and the quality of planned activities can all affect the care provided.

Some centers consist of only one classroom of children, while others may have several classrooms serving many children. The number of children enrolled in a center will be determined by the ages of the children enrolled, the number of square feet in the building, and state licensing standards. The required number of adults in the center will depend on the ages of the children and the state-mandated adult-child ratios. In some states, maximum group size is also regulated.

Parents often choose center care because of the opportunity it provides for children to have an organized preschool experience. The center can help children get ready for school while, at the same time, they learn to play and interact with others, 2-8. Center care is reliable. The illness or absence of one staff member will not cause the whole

2-8 Center-based care provides children with an organized program and a chance to develop social skills while interacting with a group of others.

program to shut down. Many parents have become aware of findings that indicate that a good child care setting can have positive outcomes for the children who attend.

Some centers offer many options for parents. Full-day or part-day, weekend care, shift care, transportation, lunch programs, and opportunities for special lessons may all be available for parents to choose. Although some options require extra fees, for busy parents, not having to pack a lunch or pick their child up early for dance lessons can be a savings in time and effort.

Most parents value the peace of mind they feel knowing their children are in a program that is staffed by caring, trained adults. They seek programs that are licensed and well-supervised. Even parents of infants and toddlers frequently choose center-based care because of its stability and predictability.

Centers may be sponsored by not-for-profit organizations. They may receive public funds to help defray the costs for low- to moderate-income families. They may also be privately owned and operated for a profit. Funding sources will be discussed further in the next chapter.

Infant/Toddler Centers

The demand for center-based care for infants and toddlers is growing rapidly. Parents recognize the reliability of center care. They also expect the center will have a greater variety of toys and equipment than in-home care. Trained staff and developmentally appropriate activities are considered important and families look for those characteristics when choosing care. Licensed center-based programs meet basic standards of care. This provides parents with confidence that they have made a good choice for their children.

Infant/toddler center-based care is very expensive. To provide quality care, group sizes must be small. The ratio of adults to children must be low. Child development experts believe that, ideally, there should be one trained adult to every three or four children. This makes the cost of staffing high. The different characteristics of infants and toddlers result in a need to keep these two age groups separate. Toddlers are on-the-go constantly and are eagerly assertive. Infants, who lack the ability to walk or protect themselves, are no match for toddlers. Both groups require constant individualized attention from consistent caregivers, 2-9.

It is often difficult for parents to find quality infant or toddler care at a price they can afford. Health and safety issues are a major concern in infant/toddler care. It is also difficult for program directors to find and keep well-trained staff members who are committed to working with these younger children.

Before- and After-School Care

Recently, there has been significant growth in the numbers of school-age children enrolled in before- and after-school care programs. The typical school day does not always match the work day of employed parents. Growing concern over the well-being of children in self-care has led more families to recognize the value of organized school-age child care. Children in self-care are often referred to as *latch-key children* because they often carry house keys with them.

School-age care may be offered both before- and after-school. Relaxation and an opportunity to unwind are typically part of the program as well as breakfast or after-school snacks. Many centers also provide tutoring, a quiet place to do homework, crafts and games, 2-10. Some programs work cooperatively with scouts, Y's or other typical after-school programs so children will not miss out on other community activities.

Most school-age programs are linked administratively to centers that also offer preschool care. In many cases, they have developed because of the changing needs of school-age children who have been enrolled in a particular program since infancy or early preschool days.

As the demand for school-age care has grown, the number of programs offering that type of care has also grown. The public schools are beginning to react to the needs of modern day working families. Before- and after-school programs can now often be found right in the school where the children have spent their academic day. The schools may operate the programs themselves. In other cases, the schools have been reluctant to become directly involved, but have been willing to contract with a local child care agency to run a program for

2-9 This toddler is eager to play after her afternoon nap.

2-10 These school-age boys are ready for activities that are interesting and fun during after-school care.

them. The agency handles issues of licensing, liability insurance, staffing, and program development for the school district. During the summer, or on other days when the schools are closed, the program can expand to function on a full-day basis.

Drop-in Centers

Many families do not need care on a regular basis. Drop-in centers, that meet the need for occasional care, are becoming popular. They are often located near malls or fitness clubs. Parents can have a few hours to themselves while the children receive care in a pleasant, well-supervised setting. Resorts, hospitals or convention center areas are also places where drop-in centers may be found, 2-11.

While some children may be in the drop-in group on a fairly regular schedule, many will change on a daily basis. If the classroom is part of a larger child care center, the staff in it may also vary from day to day. For some children, this may cause no problem. For others, however, the changing personnel and children, as well as irregular attendance, may make adjustment more difficult.

As a director of a program that includes a drop-in classroom, you will need to be sure that enough staff are present to meet the mandated adult to child staff ratio. This means that some form of advanced reservation is necessary so you know how many children to expect. A registration procedure ahead of time allows you to collect emergency numbers and other important information before you assume care for the children.

Early Childhood Programs

NAEYC uses the term, *early childhood programs* in reference to all programs for children from ages birth to eight. The term covers full-day child care as well as

2-11 Some amusement parks have drop-in centers where tired children can rest or play while their parents try out the adult rides.

part-day programs. There is currently some confusion regarding the names for part-day programs. Among child development specialists, there is agreement that regardless of what a program is called, or how it is sponsored, quality programming is essentially the same. The kinds of activities, schedule, staff training, and guidance should be similar.

Nursery School or Preschool

Nursery schools have existed in the United States since the early 1900s. They are usually half-day programs and are chosen by parents who do not need full-child care. Most nursery schools use tuition as the main source of income. The types of programs found in nursery schools are generally play-based and consistent with the principles of NAEYC's developmentally appropriate practices statement. Preschool children, ages three to five, are the typical age served. This is why, the term "preschool" is often used interchangeably with the term "nursery school."

Laboratory Schools

Laboratory schools are those programs that exist for the primary purposes of training future teachers and studying children. They are affiliated with colleges, universities, vocational schools, high schools, community colleges, or other training and research institutions, 2-12. The programs are usually model programs where appropriate ways of working with children are demonstrated. Some lab schools are full-day and also serve a child care role for the parents. Others are operated only half-day and serve as a nursery school facility.

In many cases, the lab schools serve the children of families that work for the training program. Because of their reputation for high quality, many lab schools have long waiting lists. Much of the basic curriculum that is found in both child care and Head Start was developed in laboratory school settings.

Parent Cooperatives

Parent cooperatives use parents as assistants in the classroom. By volunteering their time, parents can reduce the cost of the care. Parent cooperatives are usually owned by a group of parents. They organize it, hire a teacher, make many of the toys, donate snacks, and work as assistants to the teacher. They also serve as a policy-making board for the program.

Parent cooperatives are often part-day programs. Because parents volunteer their time, a parent with a full-time job might have difficulty participating. Some cooperatives allow working parents to provide snacks, maintenance work, bookkeeping, or other services in place of direct work in the classroom.

Kindergartens

In many school districts, kindergartens are offered for five-year-olds. The programs are held in schools and staffed by school district teachers. The kindergarten year helps serve as a bridge for the child who is moving from the smaller, nurturing setting of child care to the more formal structure of the elementary school. Traditionally, kindergartens have been play-oriented. They have provided the next logical step in meeting the developmental needs of five-year-olds. NAEYC and child development specialists have been concerned over recent trends that have led many kindergarten programs toward a "pushed down" first-grade curriculum.

Some kindergartens are privately owned. Many are offered at child care centers as an alternative to the school program. Some school districts do not offer kindergarten at all. Kindergartens will be covered by state licensing requirements that may differ from those regulating child care for younger children.

2-12 Many college students learn how to be teachers of young children in laboratory child care centers.

Varying Philosophical Approaches

People do not always agree on what is best for children. Over the years, many have tried to find the perfect way to help children grow and learn. Varying ideas about children and how to help them have led to a number of different philosophies you might find in programs today. A program's philosophy is important because it affects

- the mission and goals of the program

- the role of the teacher in the classroom

- the choice of equipment and activities

- the daily schedule

- expected behaviors of the children

The director and staff must all share the same philosophy for a program to operate smoothly. Most trained adults find it impossible to work in a program that is in conflict with their beliefs about what is good for children, 2-13.

2-13 This staff works effectively together, in part, because they all have the same beliefs about what is good for children.

Developmentally Appropriate Practices

This book is based on NAEYC's recommended curriculum guidelines referred to as developmentally appropriate practices. It has been developed by child development specialists and early childhood professionals from the theories and research of the field.

This approach incorporates elements from the following philosophies

• maturationalist—children develop according to predictable biological patterns and increase in competence when the environment supports this development

• interactionalist—children learn through their interactions with the environment

• constructivist—children construct their knowledge of the world through having a wide range of concrete experiences in a variety of areas

All aspects of programs following this approach are planned to be both age appropriate and individually appropriate, meeting the needs of each child in the group. Programs based on developmentally appropriate practices are concerned about the development of the whole child-cognitive, social, emotional, and physical.

Montessori Schools

Most Montessori Schools are privately owned and operated. They follow a specific philosophy and curriculum developed by Dr. Maria Montessori in Italy around 1908. These programs use special equipment designed to help children develop their sensory awareness and cognitive skills. Daily activities include practical life experiences, such as table washing and shoe shining. The sensory equipment includes such items as letters covered in sandpaper. Children rub their fingers over the letters to develop a "feel" for the letter. Smelling jars are also found in the program. Children must match two sets of covered jars that contain items with common odors. For example, from the two sets of jars, the children must match the ones that have the same odor. As children progress, specific activities designed to prepare children for reading, writing, arithmetic, and geography are introduced.

The teacher is primarily an observer and demonstrator of the equipment. Each piece of equipment is to be used in a specific way. When a child shows a readiness to move on, the teacher introduces the child to a more complicated piece of equipment. Montessori teachers have specific training in this method. The Montessori approach has some similarities to NAEYC's developmentally appropriate practices. Both emphasize respect for each child as a unique individual. Both view children as eager learners. However, the two philosophies differ considerably in approach to the day-to-day experiences of the children.

Behaviorist Programs

Behaviorist programs have been developed from a psychological theory known as the scientific analysis of behavior or, more commonly, behaviorism. This philosophy focuses on observable behavior. It does not identify stages of development.

Children's learning is believed to occur as they have ever widening and more complicated interactions with the environment. Behaviors that bring about positive reactions from the child's point of view, are likely to be repeated. Those behaviors that have negative consequences for the child become less likely to reappear.

Programs following this philosophy have characteristics that include

- specific behavioral goals that focus on children's cognitive behavior

- teacher-directed and -controlled activities

- little time for free choice of activities

- minimal use of play as a teaching tool

- a reward system that encourages conformity to teacher expectations

Behaviorist teachers typically do not attempt to identify the underlying causes of any child's particular behaviors. They are focused on shaping each child's responses more closely toward the classroom's identified goals. The behaviorist classrooms are highly structured and teacher-controlled. Equipment is less varied than in other types of classrooms.

Research has indicated some successes with this approach, particularly in the field of special education. Research also suggests there may be some negative social consequences associated with this approach.

As the owner of a program, you must decide on the type of philosophy your program will offer. If you are hired to operate a program, the philosophy may have already been chosen by the owner or board of directors. Your satisfaction in working with children will be greatly affected by how comfortable you are in implementing the program's philosophy.

Special Purpose Programs

A number of programs exist to meet the needs of particular groups of children and families. These programs vary considerably.

Head Start

The Head Start program is sponsored by the federal government. It is specifically designed to provide a preschool experience for children from low-income families. It is usually a half-day program that includes breakfast and a hot lunch, medical and dental services, parent involvement, and an educational component designed to help prepare children for school. Home visits and parent participation in the center are a part of most programs. Children with special needs can also be enrolled in Head Start regardless of family income. Some programs operate on a full-day basis. Early

Head Start for children from birth to age three and Wrap-Around care for children needing full-day care because they have working parents are also offered by some programs.

The Head Start program has been successful in helping children from low-income families begin school with a greater chance for success. Unfortunately, the program is still not available to all children who are eligible for it. Proposed funding increases from the federal government and the addition of some state monies would help to provide some expansion of programs.

Sick Child Care

Most parents find their child care arrangements break down when their children are sick. Their usual center cannot handle children with illness. This has led to the growth of centers for sick children, 2-14. Some of these are housed in hospitals and staffed by nurses. Others are not. In general, they do not provide care for seriously ill children. Some resemble a hospital setting while others have made an effort to look like a nursery school. Overall, they play a role in helping parents who cannot be absent from work.

Sick child care centers usually charge a very high fee. Employers who cannot afford to have their employees miss work are sometimes willing to share the cost of the care. While there are not a lot of sick child care centers, they can usually be found in urban areas.

2-14 When a child is too sick to go to a regular center, parents may have to miss work so they can provide the care the child needs.

Information and Referral Services

Sometimes parents have trouble finding a program that meets their needs. At the same time, there may be providers who have available spaces that would be appropriate. Information and referral services do not operate centers of their own. They serve as resource centers to help match families with providers. Sophisticated I & R services utilize computerized listings of licensed programs. The family's address, employer, work hours, main route to work and other pertinent data can all be considered in identifying appropriate providers.

Many American families move around frequently. Finding child care in a strange city can be extremely difficult. Many employers help to support the cost of information and referral services because they help employees make an easier adjustment to a new location.

☼ Summary

Before you invest the time and money needed to open a successful center, you must become aware of the needs of the families in your area. You must have information about work hours, family income patterns, numbers of eligible children, and the types of services that parents prefer. Other helpful information includes locations of the major community employers and already existing child care programs. The more you know about a community and its families, the more likely you are to be able to open a successful program.

Child care is available in many different forms. Home-based care is usually used for young children and when a small group is preferred. Center-based care is most often used for preschoolers and before- and after-school care.

As the needs of families have changed, new forms of child care have become available. Drop-in care and sick child care are becoming more widely available. Families have also found that information and referral services can help them match their needs with appropriate services.

Many different kinds of programs are available, but it is important that they all provide quality care. Children from families of varying income levels can benefit from carefully organized, developmentally appropriate programs.

☼ Terms

networking
home-based care
center-based care
latch-key children
early childhood programs
laboratory schools
parent cooperatives
behaviorist programs

☼ Review

1. Describe the characteristics of a community of which you need to be aware before planning to open a child care center there.

2. Identify some of the special services that parents might look for when choosing a child care center.

3. List three methods of obtaining data about an area in which you might want to locate your program.

4. Name four types of home-based child care.

5. Why does the quality of care in child care centers vary considerably?

6. Why is infant/toddler center-based care expensive?

7. Where are drop-in centers often located?

8. What factors does a program philosophy affect?

9. List and describe the three philosophies that developmentally appropriate practices incorporate.

10. Identify five characteristics of a behaviorist program.

⊙ Applications

1. Check with your local chamber of commerce to find out what types of information about your community can be obtained through that office.

2. Conduct background research on your community to find out what types of child care services are currently available.

3. Find out if there is a nanny-training program near your area.

4. Develop a questionnaire you could use to find out what child care services have been used by the parents of children in your school district.

5. Visit a local child care center. Discuss with your class what you have seen.

6. Find out whether employers in your area provide help for their employees who need child care services.

Chapter 3
Planning a Budget

After studying this chapter, you will be able to

- identify various agencies that often serve as sponsors for child care programs.

- explain the differences between for-profit and not-for-profit programs.

- identify possible sources of money for your program.

- describe the types of expenses that are involved in operating a child care program.

- explain how to develop and analyze the program budget.

Any successful program must be financially sound. The director's job includes planning and monitoring the flow of money so bills and staff salaries can be paid. This includes identifying sources of income for the program. Many programs rely solely on *tuition*, the amount paid by parents for child care. Other programs may receive funding from sponsors.

The director must also develop the *budget*, or projected spending plan, based on expected income. Even the best program for children will not be able to survive if it cannot pay its bills. Since the budget is based on the income that you expect, it must be examined often to be sure that the income is not lagging. If income is less than expected, the budget must be adjusted to reflect the smaller income.

Directors may also be responsible for trying to find additional sources of money for the program. You may need to look into finding a sponsoring agency if your program needs additional support.

Will the Program Be Sponsored?

Many organizations care about children. Although they do not operate child care programs themselves, they may be able to help maintain a program. These groups may be willing to *sponsor* a program by making a commitment to provide on-going support. This support may be through donations of money, space, equipment and/or supplies. Some support may be in the form of services. Groups of medical, legal, or educational professionals may be willing to provide help in their areas of expertise. In return for the commitment, the organizations usually receive positive publicity for their effort. The group also gains satisfaction from helping to meet the child care needs of the community. Various components of state or federal government may also provide sponsorship.

Community Groups

Many programs receive support from groups within the community. The United Way has a long history of helping to raise funds for local child care. The YMCA/YWCA and Jewish Community Centers have also become active sponsors of child care, half-day programs, and school-age care, 3-1.

Programs sponsored by religious congregations provide much of the child care in the United States. Churches, synagogues, and other religious facilities often have available space that meets state licensing standards. These spaces may be offered rent-free or for a reduced rental as part of a commitment to the community.

Other local groups that may sponsor child care include

3-1 A local agency sponsors this child care program.

- community recreation departments

- health or fitness clubs

- service clubs or organizations

- apartment complexes

- shopping malls

With community sponsorship, additional spaces for children become available through local support.

Government

Federal and state governments provide sponsorship or partial sponsorship for programs in a variety of ways. Grants of money are given to each state to provide support for programs that serve families with limited incomes. The state determines which families are eligible for the subsidy and what the amount will be. The eligible family receives a *voucher* that represents the promise of the state to pay this amount to their child's program. The family must pay the remaining cost of care. Local governments may provide further sponsorship by accepting legal responsibility for the operation of the program. They may also make donations of space, items, or services to the program.

Specific departments of both state and federal government often sponsor child care services for their employees. Anywhere there is a large state or federal office building, there may be a need for child care. This not only includes the state and federal capitols, but also cities where there are regional offices. Branches of the military also sponsor child care for their personnel.

Colleges and Universities

It is common to find child care programs on college or university campuses. These centers are increasing in number. Offering quality child care helps the institutions attract faculty and staff who might otherwise accept jobs elsewhere. Some students enrolling in higher education also may have children. Child care may be an important factor in their decision to attend school.

Colleges and universities may also offer educational programs in Child Development and/or Early Childhood Education. An on-campus child care program can provide students with opportunities to work with children. These centers are often referred to as *laboratory center programs* because they give students direct experiences with a variety of children.

Public Schools

Public schools may also sponsor child care for several different reasons. One reason is to help teen parents continue their education. Providing a child care center at school meets their child care need. The schools usually include parenting classes. This arrangement allows young parents to be with their children during parts of the day, develop parenting skills, and complete their high school education.

A child care program may exist for use by the teachers and staff of the school district. If lack of available child care has been a problem for district employees, a district-sponsored center may help solve the problem.

Vocational child care programs and/or secondary level courses in the family and consumer sciences area may also sponsor full- or half-day programs that serve as laboratory centers. Students who are pursuing education in these areas usually have one or more courses where they must work directly with children.

Employers

Many employers are discovering that the lack of quality child care is a significant issue for their employees. There are growing numbers of employers who financially support child care programs for their workers. Some provide only partial support, with the employee paying part of the tuition. Others pick up the full cost of the care. Employer-sponsored care is found frequently in the health care industry, but other businesses are also beginning to offer it.

Many employers are discovering that there are advantages to offering child care as a benefit to their employees, 3-2. Lower absenteeism, less turnover in staff, and a

3-2 Employer-sponsored child care programs result in positive outcomes for children, employees, and employers.

more productive workforce are some of the positive outcomes of helping employees with their child care concerns.

Employer assistance to families with child care needs can take many forms. Some employers actually have a child care center at the employment site. Parents can visit their children during lunch time or breaks. Sometimes, a group of employers will work together to provide a child care center at a site that is convenient for all of their employees. Nursing homes and hospitals often work cooperatively because their employees have similar schedules. Employers may provide money to support an already existing community facility. They may also support child care through the provision of *vouchers*, which represent money that employees can use to help pay for care in a program of their choice. Assistance in finding available child care and parent education programs are also services that employers may provide. Government tax incentives have encouraged the growth of employer-sponsored child care.

Will the Program Be For-Profit or Not-For-Profit?

Child care programs can be divided into two categories. *For-profit programs* are operated to make a profit for the owners. *Not-for-profit programs* are legally organized to operate without making a profit.

For-Profit Programs

For-profit programs are usually privately owned centers. They may be owned by an individual or a group. Some owners may be actively involved in operating the center. Others may have provided money to help get the program started, but they do not help with the day-to-day work of the center. The tuition, budget, and operation of the center are coordinated to result in a profit for the owners. Many family child care homes, group homes, and centers are organized this way. They must meet all the licensing regulations that apply within their state. Legally, the programs are treated like any other profit-making business. The income is taxable, and the types of tax deductions available to any business apply to these programs.

The advantages and disadvantages of a for-profit program are similar to those of any business. Major advantages include making a profit and opportunities for independent decision making. Successful programs can result in substantial income. Owners can also feel the pride of operating a flourishing business. A major disadvantage to for-profit programs is they are usually not eligible for government and/or foundation grants. Opportunities for grants are minimal. Also, people may be less likely to give gifts to these programs because such gifts are not tax deductable. The program's financial success depends on its ability to make a profit.

Not-For-Profit Programs

Not-for-profit programs may also be referred to as nonprofit programs. They are usually organized as a community service. Legally, they are not allowed to earn a profit higher than three percent. This three percent can be used to provide a cushion for the program in case of unexpected financial problems. Any extra money earned after all expenses are paid must be put back into the program in some way. This may include purchasing needed equipment, giving staff bonuses, or improving the facility.

Not-for-profit programs are *tax-exempt*, meaning they do not have to pay taxes on purchases for the program. They usually receive some support from outside sources and are often eligible for government and foundation grants. Governance of the program is conducted through a formally appointed board of directors.

The status of a program has important implications. If you are considering owning a program or working as the director of a not-for-profit center, you will need legal advice to explore these differences.

What Are Sources of Income?

Because child care programs are expensive to operate, many programs must depend on a variety of sources of income. A financially secure program may depend on money from several sources. These may include:

- public funds

- private funds

- charitable organizations and foundations

- tuition

- fund-raising activities
- in-kind support

Public Funds

Various government agencies provide funds to support child care programs. Most of these are used to sponsor not-for-profit programs that provide care for low- to moderate-income families. State and national agencies representing child welfare, education, labor and job training, public health, and human services, often provide funds for child care services. When a family is determined to be financially eligible for support, the government agency pays a part of the cost of care. The family's *co-pay* is the amount still needed to pay the tuition and is the family's responsibility. This remaining tuition amount is paid directly to the child care provider.

Major sources of public money for child care currently include the "Child and Adult Care Food Program" and the "Child Care and Development Block Grant" voucher program. These programs are administered in varying ways by the states. Their availability and your program's eligibility for funds will depend on the political and economic situation in your state.

Private Funds

Some programs are supported financially by private individuals or private organizations. Churches are among the largest sponsors of child care programs in the United States. Resort areas, apartment complexes, and malls are examples of private organizations that sometimes provide money for the operation of children's programs.

Charitable Organizations and Foundations

Charitable organizations and private or community foundations, such as the United Way, and local service and/or fraternal organizations, may also provide money to help start or support a needed facility. As a director, you may be able to write a proposal for a grant to support your program or a part of your program. Some programs put together a financial package of money from several grants. The grants, along with tuition, can provide money needed to fully fund the programs.

Tuition

Tuition is the fee you charge for the child care service that you provide. It is paid by families, so their children can attend your program. Many private programs have no other source of income. The amount of the tuition must be high enough to cover the programs expenses, but not too high for families to afford.

Fund-Raising Activities

Many not-for-profit centers organize fund-raising projects to provide extra funds for their programs. Most states require a special permit to do charitable fund-raising.

Fund-raising activities usually will not result in enough money to keep a center in operation. However, the extra money raised may be enough to buy a new piece of playground equipment, or it may even provide a new addition to a building. Often, fund-raising projects are used to obtain start-up money for a new program. A project such as a car wash, fun fair, or spaghetti dinner can be an opportunity for staff and parents to have fun working together on a project that will benefit the children. However, fund-raising can be a lot of work that may have disappointing results.

In-Kind Support

In-kind support refers to items or services you receive from another source without having to pay for them, 3-3. For example, if a religious organization allows you to use its building for free, you are saved from paying the cost of rent and utilities. You are receiving a gift that is saving you money you would otherwise have to spend. The "in-kind" contribution refers to the value of the donation. If the rental of the space would normally cost you $500 per month, then over a 12-month period, you would save $6,000. This represents an "in-kind" donation of $6,000 to your program.

Some grants are called *matching grants*. This means that for every dollar you provide, the granting agency will match it with additional money. If you are able to raise $100 locally, a matching grant may be set up to provide another $100. Sometimes matching grants offer two or three times your basic amount. With some matching grants, the value of an in-kind donation can be counted toward the request for matching funds. With some grants, it cannot. However, even though in-kind donations do not involve an actual exchange of dollars, they do represent a monetary value to your program.

What Are the Typical Costs of Child Care?

A good program for children is expensive to operate. It requires trained, caring adults, a variety of developmentally appropriate equipment and supplies, and a building that is sturdy and safe.

The most significant cost of a program is determined by the number of adults on the payroll. The cost of staff salaries will be the largest part (60 to 80 percent) of your total budget. All states have licensing requirements that identify the ratio of adults to children in the center. The younger the children are, the greater number of adults you will need to staff the program. The more adults you need to run the program, the greater the operating cost of the program will be.

3-3 This computer was an in-kind donation from a company that updated its computer system.

States are also looking at the qualifications needed by teachers in child care. Research links the quality of programs to the type and level of training of the staff. Your program will have to pay salaries that are high enough to attract and retain well-trained personnel. If salaries are too low, good teachers will go elsewhere for employment.

While the largest portion of the child care budget is the amount needed to pay staff, additional expenses must also be figured into the cost of care. Rent or mortgage payments, utilities, purchases of supplies and equipment, insurance, food, licensing, and other administrative costs must also be considered.

What Do I Need to Know About Developing a Budget?

As the director of a successful program, you must figure out how much the program is going to cost to operate and how much income you will need. If you are not going to have enough income to cover your expenses, you will need to figure out how to increase income or cut expenses. This process of balancing income and expenditures requires that you plan a budget. A budget is a plan for the coordination of income and expenditures. It is how you will use the money that is available to you over a period of time.

Start-Up Budget

Often, programs are started in the middle of a year. Many programs open in August or September to correspond to the calendar dates of schools. In planning finances for the program, you will need a start-up budget to cover several months of preparation. This is money needed in advance of opening the center. It is used to cover *start-up costs*, expenses incurred before you receive any income from the program. See 3-4 for a list of typical start-up costs. Because the money necessary to support the planning and preparation of a new center is spent before you have any income from the program, it must be considered separately from the main budget.

If you plan to own your own center, you may have enough money saved to take care of the start-up costs. If not, you will have to find some other source of money for those early expenses. Banks may be willing to loan you part of the money needed, but they will rarely loan the entire amount. Government programs established to support the development of small business may also be a source of early support. Sometimes there is a general sense in a community that child care is needed. If that is the case, local service clubs, employers, or religious groups may be willing to provide start-up capital. Private investors are another source of funds.

When the proposed center is a not-for-profit, community-sponsored organization, grant funds may be available. Many government

Expenses That Must Be Incurred Before the Center Opens
Director hired (if not yourself)
Attorney fees
Rent/deposit paid
Facility cleaned, renovated, decorated
Equipment and supplies purchased
Utilities turned on
Expenses incurred in recruitment and hiring of staff
Expenses incurred in recruitment and enrollment of children

3-4 These are expenses that you must be prepared to cover before your program actually opens.

entities have funds that can be used for child care programs. Agencies that promote community development, human services, or the creation of new jobs may view your program as fitting in with their goals. If so, they may be willing to help fund the costs of getting started.

Be careful not to underestimate the costs of getting started. Setting up a new program for young children is expensive. Often it takes time for new centers to become completely filled. This means that you will have reduced income from tuition until enrollment is full. However, the expenses of operating the program will continue. Your start-up capital must include enough money to keep your program going until full tuition is being received on a regular basis.

Fiscal Year Budget

You will also need a budget that will guide your spending for the first year of operation. This is a *fiscal year*. It reflects a period of time during which a particular budget or source of grant money is in effect. The fiscal year may or may not be the same as a January-to-December calendar year. For example, if you receive a grant of money on July 1 and you have a year during which to spend the money, you will have use of the money until June 30th of the next year. This is your fiscal year. At the end of the fiscal year, you will have to account for your program's use of the money. Depending on the nature of the grant, you may lose any unspent money at that time.

Keeping track of your fiscal year is not difficult if you have a small program. Some large programs may have several grants for special projects. If the fiscal years for each of these grants are different, recordkeeping will be more complicated. Money that comes from the federal government may be budgeted over a fiscal year that runs from October 1st to the following September 30th. In some states, the fiscal year runs from July 1 to June 30th. Local government fiscal years may be different. You will need to consider where the largest portion of your money comes from and which fiscal year option to select for your program.

If you are using public money, at the end of your fiscal year, you will need to have an audit performed. An *audit* is done to examine the accuracy of your records and to verify your expenses. An audit is recommended by business professionals for all programs to close out the fiscal year.

Identifying Expenses

Developing a workable budget requires a careful analysis of projected expenses. The more accurately you can predict program expenses, the better able you will be to make wise financial decisions. You can have a wonderful program for children and families, but if you can't pay the bills, the program will have to close. The program

Director's Dilemma

A kindly benefactor has given a "one time only" donation of $10,000 to your program. You must decide how to use the money. If you purchase a new computer system, you will be able to increase the productivity of your current office staff. This will allow you to avoid hiring an additional bookkeeper. However, you would also like to show your appreciation to your staff by giving them each a holiday bonus. What factors would you consider in deciding what to do?

Director's Dilemma

As the first director of a new center, you are responsible for developing a projected budget for the first year of operation. Your center has been licensed for 45 preschool children. The director of a similar center in another town has offered to work with you in developing this first budget. What questions would you ask? What information would you need to bring with you to this work

cannot survive if it cannot pay its staff, the rent, or meet other commitments. It is a sad fact that many programs with directors who love to work with children flounder because those same directors hate to be bothered with "money matters."

Many of your decisions as director will influence the financial well-being of your program. Decisions involving money can also affect the morale of your staff. You may have to make a choice among several equally valuable options. Adding a new climber to the playground of one center, but not to another, may be accepted if the need is obvious. However, if the staff feels that you have favored one center over another, the decision could be one that causes problems. A decision to lower the quality of the food provided may save money, but may also cause families to leave your program for another. Choosing a cheaper grade of paper products may be a more acceptable way to save money. The purchase of a computer and administrative software may seem like an expensive idea. However, if it increases the efficiency of the office staff, it may save you the cost of hiring additional personnel. A good administrator must be aware of the impact of budget decisions on the quality and stability of the program.

If you are starting a new program, you will need to determine both a start-up budget, and a budget for the first year of operation. If your program has been in operation for several years, it will be easier to plan a budget.

When planning a budget for the upcoming year, you will need to estimate program expenses as accurately as possible. If your program has been in operation for awhile, you will be able to use information from past budgets. If you are preparing a budget for a new program, you will need to consider each category in the budget. How many staff persons will you need to hire and at what salaries? Will you need to travel to attend necessary meetings? Approximately how many miles? What amount per mile will you pay for travel expenses? What are the typical utilities costs for the building you will be using?

Preparing a budget always involves some "educated guesses." You cannot predict how much the prices for supplies or food will increase during the next year. You cannot tell if there will be extreme weather conditions that will require additional heating or air conditioning costs. Therefore, it is important to "nail down" as closely as possible, those costs about which you can be more accurate. Within any budget there are three different types of expenditures:

- fixed expenditures

- variable expenditures

- optional expenditures

Most centers have basically the same types of expenses. However, the actual dollar cost may vary widely. Costs are usually higher in urban areas than in rural areas. Care for infants and toddlers is more expensive than for preschoolers because of the additional staff required.

Fixed Expenditures

Fixed expenditures are those expenses to which your program is committed. Fixed expenses are predictable, and do not vary significantly throughout the year. Once you sign a lease, you are committed to paying the rent. Some items, like insurance, may be paid in one lump payment at the beginning of the year, or may be paid over several payments.

Variable Expenditures

Variable expenditures are costs that you will have to pay on a regular basis, but the amount may vary. The director usually has some control over variable expenses. When you use electricity, water, gas, and telephone, you will have to pay for those services. While the amount of those payments may vary somewhat from month to month, there are minimum payments that you can predict fairly accurately. Other variable expenses include supplies, field trip costs, food, payroll, equipment, and administrative costs. If the program does not have as much income as expected, the director will have to examine the variable expenses to see if there is some way to save money. Likewise, if there is more money than expected, costs in the "variable" category may be allowed to increase. Variable costs may have to be adjusted throughout the year if you have more or less children enrolled than you had expected.

Optional Expenditures

Optional expenditures represent your "wish list." They are expenditures for non-essential items or services. If you have extra money toward the end of the fiscal year, you may consider using some of that money for optional items. This may include such things as new software, additional playground equipment, or the hiring of a consultant for additional staff training, 3-5.

3-5 An elaborate playground like this may have to be built one climber at a time.

Anticipating Income

Anticipating income involves some thoughtful guesswork. If your program has been in operation for a while, you have an idea of what your income has been in the past. You already have knowledge about what percentage of the center has been full. When calculating income from tuition, it is important to remember your center might not always be fully enrolled. If your center is licensed for 45 children, but you only have 40 enrolled, you will be losing the tuition for five children. Most centers are not 100 percent full all the time. You need to know the community and have some idea about the direction of economic change that may affect your program. You also need to be aware of the market rate, or typical cost of child care in your area.

With new programs, however, you must try to project income without past experience. You will need to assume a new program will not have full enrollment immediately. It may take several years before that goal is reached. Therefore, when anticipating income, be cautious. Base your income projections on less than full enrollment tuition. This way, you will not have committed the program to expenses for which you cannot pay, 3-6.

If your program will have other sources of income, such as government or foundation grants or fund-raising activities, you will also have to consider the impact of this income. The grants may provide specific amounts, but fund-raising may be unpredictable. It is usually safer to underestimate income for your program than to overestimate it. It is easier to increase a budget than to decrease it.

The Budget Format

Your budget will include all the expenses you expect to have, but there are different ways to organize it. Some programs use the following budget categories: personnel, rent or mortgage, supplies and equipment, food, transportation, licensing, and miscellaneous. These categories work well for small programs. Larger programs will need to analyze costs in a different way. Typical budget categories shown in 3-7 allow the director to quickly identify what the food program is costing, what part of the total budget the administrative costs are, and what the direct classroom care for children costs.

When working with a complicated budget, it is a good idea to use *cost coding*. This means identifying each major budget category with a number code. In 3-8, the general category for Physical Plant and Maintenance is given the number 200. The separate items listed under this category could then be further identified by 200-level numbers.

After working with the budget for a while, you will be able to use the item numbers as a

Program Income	
Source of Income	**Amount Expected**
Tuition	
Fees paid by parents	_____
Registration fees	_____
Fees for Supplemental Services	_____
Tuition Supplement for Low Income Families	_____
Grant Funds (not-for-profit	_____
Fund-raising programs)	_____
Donations	_____
Total Anticipated Program Income	_____

3-6 A director must make an estimate of what the program's income will be for the year.

A Budget Format Organized Around Program Categories

Budget Category	Budget Item	Amount
100	**Administrative and general costs**	
	Salaries and fringe benefits	
	(Director, secretary, bookkeeper, etc.)	_____
	Audit and legal costs	_____
	Office equipment and furniture	_____
	Office supplies	_____
	Postage	_____
	Phone	_____
	Insurance	_____
	Travel	_____
	Advertising	_____
200	**Physical plant and maintenance**	
	Rental or mortgage	_____
	Utilities	_____
	Custodial salaries and fringe benefits	_____
	Custodial supplies	_____
	Maintenance on building/grounds	_____
300	**Classroom/educational costs**	
	Salaries and fringe benefits	
	Teachers, aides, substitutes	_____
	In-service training	_____
	Classroom supplies	_____
	Classroom equipment	_____
	Field trips	_____
400	**Food and nutrition**	
	Salaries and fringe benefits	
	Cooks, aides	_____
	Food supplies	_____
	Kitchen equipment	_____
	Food service supplies	_____
500	**Admissions and parent services**	
	Newsletters, parent handbook	_____
	Parent education classes/meetings	_____
600	**Transportation**	
	Salaries and fringe benefits	
	Driver	_____
	Vehicle rental or purchase	_____
	Maintenance	_____
	Operation (fuel and oil)	_____
700	**Health care**	
	Health Supplies	_____
	First aid kit, bandages, toothbrushes,	
	disposable gloves, antiseptic	
	Contracted health services	_____
800	**Other**	
	Miscellaneous	_____

3-7 The budget categories for a large program with several centers can be complicated.

Director's Dilemma
Your program provides transportation for children for an additional fee. You have charged the same fee for this service for several years. What budget items would you need to look at in order to determine the cost of this service? How could you tell if your cost to provide the service has increased?

shortcut for spelling out the whole name of the line. Each category can be further subdivided into additional, more specific items. If you are renting space in several different buildings, you might further divide the "210" category to show each facility.

Each of the lines in the 200 category (and all other categories) can be subdivided and given an identifying number as in 3-9. You can match up line items across categories. For instance, all the costs identified with Airport Center can be associated. You will be able to tell quickly if the costs for one facility are substantially higher than the costs for other facilities. This information can be helpful in making decisions for the next year.

How Do I Analyze the Budget?

The budget is a plan that you create. It is based on the amount of income you expect. If, throughout the year, income is less than what you expected, you will have to revise your budget so that you spend less. The budget you create at the beginning of the year should be flexible. Your actual spending pattern must be modified to reflect any change in the amount of income that you predicted. For example, if you expected to have enough income to purchase some new riding toys, you will have to delay that purchase if your income is less than you had anticipated. If income is greater than expected, you may be able to purchase additional items that were not originally on your budget plan.

When analyzing your budget, look at different components within your overall program. How much does it really cost to have a small group of infants? Are you charging enough for your after-school program? You can analyze the budget in two different ways to have a clearer view of the financial picture.

Line Item Breakdown of Budget Category
Physical Plant and Maintenance
200   Physical plant and maintenance
210   Rental
220   Utilities
230   Custodial wages and fringe benefits
240   Custodial supplies
250   Maintenance on building/grounds

3-8 Each subcategory in the budget should have its own number category.

Cost-per-Child Analysis

Doing a cost per child analysis will give you a clearer view of your financial health. A *cost-per-child analysis* is done by looking at each main age group in your center. Identify the costs of providing service to each group on a monthly or daily basis. Then divide this total by the number of children enrolled. Each day, it costs you a certain amount to provide your service. You must pay for teachers, classroom rent, supplies, utilities, etc.

Doing a cost-per-child analysis will likely show that the cost to provide care for infants or toddlers is usually higher than the cost of care provided to school-age children. This is because you must have additional adults hired to meet necessary adult-to-child ratio. School-age children will need more art and project supplies than toddlers, but the overall cost will be higher for the younger groups. Preschool groups will usually have longer hours in the center than will school-age groups, so the cost of the service will reflect that additional time.

Once you know what the cost is to keep each part of the program in operation, you can examine your tuition to see if it is enough to meet those costs. For example, you would probably find it necessary to have a higher tuition for infants and toddlers than for school-age-children. Preschool tuition would probably be less than infant/toddler, but more than that for school-age children. One flat tuition rate for all age groups would not suit the financial needs of your programs or of the families enrolled

Further Breakdown of Subcategories
210 Rental or mortgage
211 Office space
212 Airport center
213 Homer City Center
214 Ben Franklin School-Age Center

3-9 This detailed break down of expenses in subcategories gives the director important information about the financial picture of the program. Larger programs need a more detailed budget format to help in determining the amount of money needed in each category.

Calculating the Break-Even Point

Once you have figured out a budget estimate of income and expenses, you will need to see if you will have enough money to pay the costs of program operation. Your program must at least reach the *break-even point*, meaning that it must have enough money to cover basic expenses, if you hope to stay in operation. This part of managing is like juggling. If your income is not sufficient to meet expenses, you will have to figure out some way to increase income or cut expenses, 3-10. Each choice you make will have some impact on your program finances that may be positive or negative. You will have to decide which risks are worth taking or which choices are the best for your program. For example, a decision to raise tuition may cause some families to leave your program. Can you predict how many families you might lose? Will your tuition increase bring in the same amount of money with fewer children enrolled? If so, the empty spaces could then be used to recruit new children at the increased tuition rate. This will increase the overall amount of money available to your program. However, if you predict that the total income to the center would decrease, then the decision to raise tuition needs to be re-examined.

The break-even point represents your calculation of the number of children who must be enrolled in order to meet your program's expenses. If the number of children decreases, or your expenses increase, you will be forced to adjust tuition or find other sources of income.

Director's Dilemma
Your center has 45 preschool children enrolled. The program is open 50 weeks per year and has an annual budget of $292,500. Identify the amount of tuition per week you will need to charge each child in order to cover your costs. How will your income be affected if only 40 children enroll for the first year? What would happen to your income if 10 children enroll on a half-day basis? What strategies would you have to consider in order to "balance the budget"?

3-10 Preparing a budget can take many hours of work.

⊛ Summary

Tuition and fees from parents may be the sole source of income for many programs. Not-for-profit programs may have access to special grant funds or government money. Public money is available to some programs to help defray the cost of child care for low-income families. Other sources of income may include donations, employer sponsorship, or fund-raising activities.

A budget is a financial plan. It identifies the amount of income and expenses you expect for the year ahead. The director must make decisions that will ensure there is enough money to cover the costs of operating the program.

Among the program expenses are some over which there is little control. These fixed costs are predictable and will not vary throughout the program year. Other costs are variable. They can be controlled to some extent by careful management. Still other expenses are optional. When the money is tight, optional expenses can be eliminated. If extra money is available, these expenses can be incurred.

The budget may be arranged in different ways. However it is set up, it should show expected income and expenditures clearly. It should be organized in a manner that will allow for easy analysis of the different program components throughout the year or at a later date. Doing a cost-per-child analysis and determining the break-even point will assist you in making financial decisions.

⊛ Terms

tuition	matching grant
budget	start-up costs
sponsor	fiscal year
voucher	audit
for-profit programs	fixed expenditures
not-for-profit programs	variable expenditures
tax-exempt	optional expenditures
co-pay	cost coding
in-kind support	cost-per-child analysis
	break-even point

⚙ Review

1. What is a budget based on and why should it be examined often?

2. List six groups that may sponsor child care.

3. Why are employers discovering that there are advantages to offering child care as a benefit to their employees?

4. What is the difference between a for-profit and a not-for-profit program?

5. List six sources of income that can be used to fund child care programs.

6. What comprises the largest portion of a child care center budget?

7. As a director, if you are not going to have enough income to cover expenses, what do you need to do?

8. List three types of expenditures within a budget.

9. How is a cost-per-child analysis done?

10. What does the break-even point represent?

⚙ Applications

1. Look around your own classroom. Work with other students to identify all of the costs involved in operating your classroom. Discuss what would change if the school could not afford to fully fund your classroom.

2. Invite a child care director to discuss the budgeting process with your class.

3. Survey the child care centers in your area. Find out which ones are privately owned and which ones have sponsoring agencies. Who are the sponsoring agencies?

4. Identify some types of in-kind donations that community businesses might be willing to provide to a new child care program.

The first step in preparing a proposal or business plan is to meet with your staff to get ideas down on paper.

Chapter 4
Writing a Proposal or Business Plan

After studying this chapter, you will be able to

○ explain the purpose of a proposal or business plan.

○ recognize sources of grant money.

○ describe the various sections of a proposal.

○ identify characteristics of a successful proposal.

○ analyze the similarities and differences between a proposal and a business plan.

At some point in your work as a director, you may have to convince someone else your program is worth supporting. You may be trying to obtain a loan from a bank. You may be interested in starting a center for the employees of a large nearby hospital or business. You could be trying to get a grant of money from some government agency that would allow you to start a new service. The person or agency you are trying to convince to support you may not know anything about child care. There may be questions about whether you can do a good job. This is when you will find it important to know how to write a proposal or business plan.

What Is a Proposal? A Business Plan?

A *proposal* is a document explaining what you want to do, why there is a need to do it, why you think you can do it, and what kind of help you need. It must give the reader confidence you can actually do what your plan says you can do. A proposal forces you to think through your ideas or plans. When you actually put plans down on paper, you must be able to explain them in a way that allows other people to understand them.

The purpose of a *business plan* is to convince a bank or lending agency the program you want to start is needed and realistic and that you have the skills necessary to carry it out. Agencies that lend money to small businesses want to be assured you are familiar with the business aspects of child care. They must be convinced you will be successful enough to pay back the loan in a reasonable amount of time.

These documents are similar in many ways. They both represent your efforts to convince someone else to support your ideas and program by providing the needed financing.

Where Do I Find Sources of Grant Money?

A variety of sources of grant money may be available for your program. Government divisions, charities, local organizations, and foundations are all possible sources of funding. Funding sources often have a particular focus for their grants. Do some research to find sources of funds that match the type of program you offer.

Finding Funding Sources

You can find out about funding sources using several methods. The best place to start is probably your local library, 4-1. If you are near a college town, the campus library or grants office can be especially helpful. Directories exist that list various foundations and the types of projects they fund. Directories are also available that identify government agencies, their priorities, and information about funds available. If you find a government agency or foundation that supports projects of the type you have in mind, you can usually write or call for further information and guidelines.

If you have worked with a government agency or foundation in the past, you may already be on their mailing list for information about grants. In that case, you will probably receive announcements of funds availability in the mail. When an agency has funds to distribute, it issues a Request for Proposals or RFP. This is the official alert to interested persons. Some agencies issue an ITB which means "Invitation to Bid" or an RFI which is "Request for Information." While the phrase may be different, each means that grant guidelines or specifications are available and the agency is ready to review information from interested parties.

You may find out about funding from local sources. County and city governments usually have an office that is responsible for channeling money to programs that will meet the needs of local citizens. Community action agencies, Human Services offices, or United Way agencies may all provide support funds. Personnel in those offices may be able to alert you to other sources of funding. Local service and professional organizations, such as Zonta, Rotary, Business and Professional Women, or Kiwanis, may also provide funds.

Some child care agencies sign up for *subscriber services* that print newsletters on a regular basis to identify new grants that are available. Some report on government allocations that will result in more funding. Subscriber newsletters may also provide a condensed version of new information of interest to center directors. A number of these services are available. They usually are quite expensive. You will need to decide whether or not they are worth the cost for your program.

4-1 The library or Internet is a good place to begin a search for funding sources.

Many professional organizations publish newsletters that include information about available grants or other sources of funding. Some newsletters and journals are aimed specifically at child care directors and present information helpful in finding funds. You may have to be creative in reviewing funding categories to figure out whether there is some way your program needs and the goals and priorities of the funding agency can mesh.

Matching Your Project Needs with a Funding Agency's Goals

One of the secrets to successful proposal writing is to match the project you want to do with an agency that is likely to fund that particular type of project. You may have a perfectly good idea and a well written proposal, but if it doesn't match the goals of the foundation or agency to which you applied, it will probably not be funded. The same proposal, sent to an agency that matches in terms of goals, may be successful. For example, a funding agency whose goal is to improve teacher education, may provide money to build an observation booth. Consider the following factors when looking for an appropriate funding source.

Nature of the Funding Agency

Funding agencies always have some reason for their existence. There is some goal that they are trying to accomplish. The goal may be very broad, such as "to strengthen families" or "to improve society." Some goals may be more specific, yet still provide flexibility for a variety of projects. For example, grant money may exist for the purpose of creating jobs in a particular geographical area. Your program may be eligible for grant money, not because it is a child care program, but because its funding will result in more jobs for community residents. Other sources of funding may exist to support programs that will help children get ready for school, or to provide training for child care personnel. For instance, one agency had a need to provide training for its family child care providers. It received a large grant for the purpose of "improving the job skills of undertrained adult workers." The granting agency didn't really care anything about child care. It existed for the purpose of improving the employability of adults.

Your own specific needs will relate to your particular center, staff, or families. You want to develop a plan that can create a match between your agency's needs and the funding agency's priorities. You can determine whether or not this match is possible through a careful reading of the explanatory materials and guidelines the agency provides.

A request for guidelines from the agency you are considering will usually bring with it a cover letter and a general explanation of the purposes of the agency. These should be read carefully because they will give you clues that can help you

Director's Dilemma
You have been informed about a grant that is currently available. Money from the grant is to be used for the purpose of starting a before- and after-school center. The grant guidelines specify that the center must be located in an elementary school. Money will be provided to operate the program for two years. After that, no additional money will be available. What would you need to consider before deciding to submit a proposal for the grant money?

determine whether it is worth your time to work on a proposal. The cover letter usually points out any changes in the funding agency's priorities from the previous year. The introductory paragraphs often describe the purpose and reasons behind the availability of money. If there is no clear, logical way that your plans can meet the agency's goals and objectives, it is a waste of time and effort to prepare a proposal.

Funding Priorities

Within the broad goals of an agency, there will also be more specific objectives and priorities. There may be several goals the agency wants to accomplish, but not all will be equally important. If your project matches the top priority goal, you will have a better chance of being funded than if your project falls under the least important goal of the agency. Some guidelines indicate that the goals are listed in "priority order." You are most likely to have success if your project fits under the higher priority goals. This doesn't mean that a project under a lower priority goal won't be funded. It simply means that where only a certain amount of money is available, projects under higher goals will be funded first. The agency may distribute all its money before it gets to your project.

Available Funds

Funding sources vary substantially in the amount of money they have to offer. A government agency or foundation may have hundreds of thousands of dollars to grant, 4-2. A local agency may have several hundred. It can be very helpful to know the size of the grants that your funding source typically awards. If a funding source usually awards grants that request between $20,000 and $50,000, your proposal is

4-2 This building was completely remodeled with money provided by a foundation and donors interested in children.

more likely to be successful if it falls within this range. If your proposal requests $200,000, it is less likely to be successful. The funding source may not have that amount. It may prefer to fund four or five smaller grants rather than one large one. The opposite may also be true. Some agencies prefer to grant larger amounts. They may not want to be bothered by having to process smaller grants.

In general, it is a good idea to be aware of the typical size of grants provided by the agency. Sometimes it is difficult to find out that information. Small, private sources of funding may not publish a report of their activities. Large foundations usually produce a year end report in which the awarded grants are listed. Projects are described along with the amount of money they received. These reports are a good source of information regarding the types of projects that the agency funds and the amounts awarded. Try to make your proposal fall within the "ballpark figure" of what the agency seems to be willing to fund.

Eligible Agencies

The guidelines will also identify what types of programs are eligible for funding. Some grants are open to any type of agency. Others may be limited to not-for-profit agencies only. Some may be limited to projects that are sponsored by secondary schools or that are government-sponsored programs, such as a county child care program. Again, careful reading of the guidelines can help you determine whether your agency is eligible for funding. If it is not, there is no point in writing the proposal.

Other Types of Projects Funded in the Past

The guidelines may give you information regarding the types of projects that have been funded in the past by an agency. This is helpful in determining whether your proposal is similar to others that have been looked on favorably in the past. Any glimpse you can get into the priorities of the funding agency can help you figure out the best way to write your proposal—or whether to write one at all.

Restrictions Imposed by Funding Sources

If your program receives no funding from outside sources except tuition, you may have few restrictions other than those required by licensing. If, however, your program receives any money from government agencies, private foundations, or charitable organizations, you may have additional restrictions or guidelines to meet. These restrictions typically relate to areas of program participants' eligibility, use of money, and/or program philosophy or activities.

When planning the finances for your center, you must consider any restrictions that are tied to

Director's Dilemma

You have been made aware of some money that is available to expand child care services in your community. After you receive the guidelines, you discover that the grant is being sponsored by one of the local businesses. If you accept this grant, you must agree to allow the business to use your program for advertising purposes. You must also agree to purchase supplies from this business whenever appropriate. What things must you consider before deciding whether or not to accept this grant?

the receipt of money. You must decide whether these restrictions are ones that you will be comfortable implementing in your program, 4-3. Once you accept grant money with restrictions, you are legally bound to honor those restrictions. If you cannot accept the restrictions in good conscience, it is better to turn the money down.

How Do I Write a Proposal?

Most proposals contain similar information, 4-4. Guidelines from the funding agency may specify exactly how a proposal is to be set up and how each section is to be labeled. If this is the case, follow the guidelines exactly. If there are no guidelines , your proposal should include the following parts.

Cover Letter

This letter is usually prepared after you write the proposal. It is placed on top of the proposal and serves to identify what the proposal is. It should include reference to the RFP number. The letter should also be signed by an official of your agency who has the legal power to authorize the commitments contained in your proposal. This may be the director or perhaps, the chairperson of your board of directors. If your program is sponsored by a local government agency, you may need to have the signature of the responsible government official. The letter alerts the funding source that you are authorized to commit the organization to the proposal. This also ensures that one of your staff persons does not write a proposal that you don't know about or that you feel cannot be carried out by your agency.

Questions to Ask Yourself Before Accepting Money with "Strings Attached"

- How difficult will it be to meet these restrictions in my program?

- Are these restrictions consistent with the philosophy and goals of my program?

- Are these restrictions ones that I need to implement with or without the money?

- Will this additional money help to build a stronger program?

- Will money commit the program to something that cannot be continued over the long run?

- How much money will it cost to implement these restrictions?

- Is this money for one year only, or will it continue over several years?

- What will happen to the program when this money is no longer available?

4-3 It may be better to turn down grant money if you are not comfortable with related restrictions.

Cover Sheet

The cover sheet is the front page of your proposal. Its purpose is to give important information regarding the proposal document. It should include the title of the proposal and the RFP number. The name of the agency that is submitting the proposal (your program) should be identified along with its address and phone number. It is also helpful to identify a *contact person*, a person from your agency who is most knowledgeable about the proposal. If the funding agency needs more information, the contact person will be the one who is called. If the guidelines specify a certain format for the cover page, be sure to use it.

Abstract

Although the abstract appears at the beginning of the proposal, it should not be completed until last. The *abstract* is a summary of the proposal, providing an overview of the proposal to the reader. For that reason, it should be written once the proposal has been completed and the plan of action has been thoroughly formulated. Because this is the first encounter the reader will have with the proposal, it is particularly important to write it to grab the reader's attention and alert the reader to the need for the project. General goals of the plan should be identified, too. Specific details of the project plan are not necessary, but a brief description of how the problem will be approached should be included. It is also important to include either a budget summary or an indication of the total dollar amount requested in this section.

This section should serve to summarize the important elements of the proposal. It must be able to "stand alone." It may be reprinted in a report of the funding agency or, in some cases, be the only part of the proposal that is actually read by busy executives.

A proposal tells
- why there is a need for your project
- who will benefit
- what you want to do
- how you will do it
- what resources you have available
- how you will evaluate it
- how much it will cost

4-4 Proposals basically contain the same types of information.

Table of Contents

The table of contents identifies the location of sections of the proposal. It must also be completed after the proposal is completely written so page numbers are correct. It is important that the table of contents "walk the reader through the document." This means that it should be assembled to make it easy for the reader to identify the parts of the document and their locations. Each part of the proposal should be listed using exactly the same terminology as was used in the guidelines.

Introduction/Problem Statement

This section allows the reader to identify the need for your project. It gives a picture of the current situation, and it should also create, in the reader's mind, a belief that a project to address this need would be valuable. This is an extremely important part of the proposal because it establishes the reason for the request. All of the rest of the proposal will be linked to addressing this problem. If the problem appears trivial, there may appear to be no real reason to fund it. If the problem appears massive and overwhelming, the funding agency may decide that your program does not have the resources to deal realistically with it.

Including documentation in this section is usually helpful. If you have statistics that reveal a definite need for your plan, this is a place to include them. If you can obtain statements from experts, or from people who would benefit from the project, you may wish to include those also.

Be sure that your statement of the problem relates directly to the priorities of the funding source. If the goals of the funding agency are to increase the availability of child care, your problem statement should address the need for more child care. If the funding source is concerned about job opportunities, then the problem should relate to the need for more jobs. When concern with upgrading the skills of teachers is identified as a priority, then the need for additional staff training may be seen as a legitimate need that has led to the development of this proposal. A funding source concerned about the quality of daily care for children might be attracted to a proposal seeking money to buy more books and equipment.

Goals

The *goals* for your project identify what you are trying to achieve. They must relate back to the needs identified in the problem statement. The goals should be realistic. They should reflect what you can actually accomplish if you receive the grant money. For example, if you have documented the need for more child care, then your goal might be to create an additional classroom. If you have documented the need for more training for family child care providers, then a goal might be to provide opportunities for training for those providers. When goals are broken down to more specific levels, they are usually called objectives.

Target Population

The *target population* section describes who will actually be helped by your proposed project. These are the individuals whose needs are identified earlier in the proposal. You should specify how many children can be enrolled in your new classroom or center and describe the demographics, such as whether the children will be from a particular geographical area or whether they are children whose parents work for a particular employer. If this is a training proposal, you should indicate which staff members will be included. If the proposal is for family child care providers, indicate who will be invited to attend training sessions. You should indicate whether the training will be open to all providers in a geographical area or only to those who are affiliated with your agency. This section of the proposal will identify exactly who the proposal is designed to help.

Project Methodology

The purpose of the *project methodology* section is to describe clearly to the reader what you are going to do. It may also be called the "management summary" or "work plan." It should include your plan to meet the needs that you have identified in earlier sections. It is important that you have a clear image in your mind of what it will actually take to carry out the project. How much time will it take? How much equipment will you need to purchase? How long will it take that equipment to arrive? How many staff persons will you need to hire? How long will the hiring process take? If you have a complicated project in mind, it will be necessary to break it down into manageable steps in order to explain it clearly, 4-5.

Sample Time Line for Opening a New Classroom in Your Center

A time line may be included in a proposal to identify the sequence in which tasks will be completed.

Prior to Proposal Submission

- If outside funding is to be used, request guidelines.
- Begin writing of proposal or business plan.

Month 1-2

- Identify funding needed to cover the start-up of the new classroom.
- Conduct needs assessment to determine if the classroom is needed.
- Identify equipment needed for a new classroom.
- Identify staffing and budget needed to operate classroom.
- Meet with community groups or families to obtain input on proposal.
- Submit proposal or business plan.
- Upon approval of funding, begin active preparation for classroom.

Month 3

- Order equipment and materials for classroom.
- Advertise for new staff.
- Conduct interviews and hiring.
- Provide orientation and training sessions for new staff.
- Advertise for enrollment.
- Meet with interested families to discuss enrollment policies.
- Enroll children.
- Maintain all appropriate records on staff, families, and budget.

Month 4

- Hold an orientation meeting for families.
- Begin classroom activities with children.
- Evaluate start-up of new classroom.

4-5 A time line is a clear way to show how you intend to get everything done.

Once you have a clear picture of exactly what you will need to do to carry out the project, you must consider the best way to present that information. Instead of writing the steps in paragraph form, you might consider developing a *time line*, 4-6. This is a visual display of how you will complete the project. You may create a calendar or use indentations to identify different months and what parts of the project will occur in them.

Word processing capabilities allow you to create easily readable charts, graphs, and calendars that allow the reader to quickly understand what you are planning to do and how long it is going to take. You may also be able to set up a chart that identifies each task in the project and the length of time it is expected to take for completion of each task. In a project designed to open a new center, tasks might include site

Projected Time Line			
Month 1	**Month 2**	**Month 3**	**Month 4**
• Identify needed start-up funding			
• Conduct needs assessment			
• Indentify needed equipment			
• Identify staffing and budget needed			
• Obtain community input on proposal			
• Submit proposal or business plan			
• Upon approval, begin preparation for classroom opening.			
		• Order equipment and supplies	
		• Hire staff	
		• Advertise for enrollment	
		• Enroll children	
		• Establish	
			• Orientation meeting with parents
			• Open program

4-6 Visual time lines can be more interesting than paragraph descriptions.

selection, meeting licensing requirements, hiring staff, purchasing equipment, advertising, and recruiting children. It is usually impossible to open the center or to be in full gear on the first day of a project. Funding agencies know that it takes time to carry out the tasks that are necessary to set up the project. Your time line should reflect a realistic understanding of the time it takes to implement your plan.

Organizational Capability

This section referred to as *organizational capability* must prove your agency's ability to carry out the project. If you have never written a proposal, or if you are applying for funds to an agency with which you have never worked, you have no past history of success with that agency. You will need to prove that your program can actually carry out the plan that you are proposing. This section serves to convince the reader that you have the resources necessary to do the job.

A brief history of your agency may be a good starting point for this section. If your program has served the community well for a number of years, you will have a reputation for quality service and dependability. If your center or staff have been honored or recognized in some way, it can be pointed out in this section. The successful completion of other grants or special projects is also an indication of the capabilities of your staff or project team.

You must also identify the number of staff who will be assigned or hired for this project. This section should list their qualifications and job descriptions. If the project requires a number of new staff members or reorganization of existing staff, you may want to include an ***organizational chart***. This is a chart that shows how the staff positions are related to each other and what the lines of authority are in the organization. It can present a visual image of the organization that can be understood more quickly than a presentation of the same information in paragraph style.

A description of the facilities may also be needed in the proposal. If you already have a center with an available room, that is an important plus in a proposal to open an additional classroom. This fact should be pointed out to the reader. If you are planning to substantially expand the number of children to be served, the reader should know that restroom facilities are sufficient to handle the larger number of children. If you are adding children, your increased record-keeping responsibilities will be easier to accommodate if your program already has a computer and computerized records.

Any project is going to require additional resources. These resources may include space, personnel, time, and/or materials. When you already have some of those resources available, you are in a stronger position to carry out the proposal, 4-7.

Evaluation of Success

Most funding agencies will expect you to have some way of projecting how you are going to measure your success. The agency will not simply give you money without some plan for accountability. In determining a plan to evaluate the success of the project, go back to your goals. How will you know if you have served more children? How will you know that your teachers have received additional training? How will you know that you have achieved the goals that you outlined at the beginning of the proposal?

Usually, it is possible to determine the success of a project by determining if you have served the number of additional children that you projected. If your plan was to open a new center, did you actually open it? How many children are enrolled? What have parents reactions to the new center been? You may plan a questionnaire to be completed by parents of children in the new center. Can you document that the new center has reduced the number of children on your waiting list?

The evaluation methods you propose need

4-7 This program has a substantial number of professional staff already employed. It may be possible to reassign some of them to grant activities. A copying machine can be a valuable asset if you are trying to win a grant to produce a parent newsletter or to improve advertising materials.

not be expensive. In fact, they should not be unless you are proposing a major research project. They should be designed, however, so at the end of your project you will be able to clearly prove that you addressed the needs and met the goals that you identified earlier in the proposal.

Budget

The budget is the part of the proposal where you indicate what you are going to do with the money you are requesting. In writing a proposal, the funding source will want to know that you have a realistic understanding of what it will take to carry out the project.

The budget must be presented in a manner that is clear and straight forward. If the proposal guidelines give you a format for setting up the budget, follow it exactly. You must also be sure that the budget is consistent with what you have stated in the narrative section of the proposal. For example, if you are proposing to open a new classroom and hire the staff for that classroom, you will need to include staff salaries in the proposed budget. If you will need to buy new equipment for that classroom, or new computer software to maintain additional records, the cost of those purchases should be identified in the budget. You must be certain that you have requested enough money to carry out the commitments in the proposal.

Budgeting requires a realistic understanding of the costs of carrying out the proposal. Your request should not be padded unreasonably, but neither should it be held at an artificially low level. Once you have agreed to a proposal, you must carry it out for the contracted dollar amount. If you have under-budgeted, you will have serious problems meeting the commitments in the contract. For example, if your project includes sending a staff person to a conference, you may need to include an amount for airline tickets. Because you are probably unsure of exactly what discount tickets may apply or if any will be available at all, it is safer to request the full amount of an undiscounted ticket. Later, if a discount applies, you may be able to use the extra money for some other part of the project. If you don't have enough money requested initially, you may end up having to cancel the trip.

The budget included in a proposal must reflect your most accurate estimation of the true, undiscounted cost of carrying out the proposed project.

Appendix

The *appendix* of a proposal is a section where you can add a variety of items that lend credibility or support to your narrative. These are items that cannot be included easily in the body of the narrative, yet, may add important information that can support the funding of your project. You may include letters of support from parents or community leaders, resumes of staff persons, a proposed floor plan of the new classroom, printed articles about your program, or other helpful information. You may also wish to include a list of other funded projects that your agency has carried out successfully.

What Are Some Tips on Proposal Writing?

Writing a proposal the first time can be a difficult experience. This section outlines some tips to help you write a successful proposal.

Due Date

The guidelines may indicate that there is a specific due date for the proposal. If this is true, you must be very careful to plan your work time so that the deadline can be met. If your proposal arrives late, it may not be considered at all, even though it may be very worthwhile. If there are a large number of requests, a late proposal usually won't be reviewed.

Once you have identified the due date, it is a good idea to make a careful examination of your calendar. Make a checklist of each task that must be done to get the proposal ready. Mark the due date, then start counting backwards, 4-8. Figure out how many days it will take for the proposal to be in the mail. How many days will it take for the completed proposal to be copied and compiled? Must other people read and approve it? If your board of directors must read and take action on the proposal before it can be submitted, you will have to allow time for them to meet and review. Time must be allowed for draft copies to be prepared and revised, as well. After you have counted the days it will take to accomplish these tasks, you will be able to determine how much time you actually have left to write the proposal. Usually, you have less time to work on a proposal than initially appears at first glance. If you plan to write up until the very last minute, you will not have time for the other activities that are necessary in order to have a completed proposal.

Days Needed to Complete Writing of the Proposal	
Due Date: 25 work days from today.	**Work Days Needed?**
• How many days in the mail to the granting agency?	3
• How many days needed for internal program approval?	2
• How many days to copy/collate the proposal?	1
• How many days to prepare a good copy of the proposal?	2
• How many days needed for revisions?	3
• How many days needed for preparing the rough draft of the proposal?	3
• When must writing be completed?	11
Total	**25 days**

4-8 Consider all of the steps in writing a proposal, then count backwards from the due date to figure out how many days you will have to write the rough draft.

Some funding sources will accept proposals at any time. This will also be indicated in the guidelines. You will not have the pressure of meeting a deadline with this kind of a funding source. However, if your proposal arrives late in the fiscal year, the funding agency may have given out all of the money it has available. Your proposal may sit on a shelf waiting for more money to become available.

Consistency

One of the most important elements in successful proposal writing is *consistency*. What you say you are going to do in one part of the proposal must match what you say you are going to do in another part. For example, if you are planning to add a new classroom, you will probably need to hire additional staff and purchase some equipment. If you are projecting a need for three additional staff, then the budget must also show additional salaries and benefits for the three additional persons. The budget must also show the amount needed for equipment. If you are going to need extra office supplies to carry out the project, these too must be taken into account.

You may have various staff members help to write a proposal. It is important that one person, perhaps yourself, is responsible for putting it together. It should read as if it were written by one person rather than by a committee. Writing style should be consistent so the proposal is not disjointed.

A "We Can Do It" Attitude

In writing the proposal, you must convince the reader that your agency can complete the project successfully. You must convey the ideas that

- There is a problem.

- The problem can be solved, at least in part.

- We can do it, with the help of the funding agency.

You must present a picture of an eager staff who are enthusiastic about addressing and meeting the need that you have identified. Stress the strengths of your staff and agency. Avoid giving the impression the need or problem you have identified seems overwhelming. Stress the parts of the problem your agency can attack successfully. Write from a position of optimism. "This is a problem that we can solve!"

Use of Professional Terminology

Every field has its *jargon* made up of particular words, phrases, or abbreviations that are known to those who work in the field. A person who is familiar with the issues facing child care providers today will know what "developmentally appropriate practices" and the "trilemma of child care" mean. People who do not work in the field are less likely to be familiar with those concepts.

One of the challenges in proposal writing is to use the professional terminology appropriately. This way, the reader knows you are knowledgeable and up-to-date in your own understanding of the issues. If you don't understand a term, don't use it. Just throwing "jargon" into your proposal indiscriminately without careful thought, may actually harm your opportunity for success. You must demonstrate your knowledge of the field without over doing it.

Organization of the Proposal

The people who read and rate proposals may be dealing with large numbers of them. If they have many unanswered questions about your plan, they are not likely to take the time to search out the answers. They will simply rank your proposal lower. You must organize and write the proposal so that it is clear, logical, and easy to follow. Set it up so that it matches exactly with the format suggested by the funding agency. Even if you feel that a different sequence or order would be better, follow the style that the funding agency stipulates. Use the same terminology for proposal sections as are given in the guidelines, 4-9.

Make sure that you answer all questions posed in the guidelines, even if your response is that the question does not apply to your agency. Don't just ignore questions or topic areas. Address them in some way so that the reader knows that you didn't simply miss the question.

Necessary Sections in a Proposal

Frequently Used Name	Alternate Names
Cover Letter	Letter of Introduction
Cover Sheet	Title Page
Abstract	Summary
Table of Contents	Contents
Introduction	Problem Statement Statement of Need
Goals	Objectives Outcomes
Target Population	Audience Target Group
Project Methodology	Work Plan Management Summary Stategies Project Activities
Organizational Capability	Resources Personnel/Facilities History of the Organization
Evaluation	Measurement of Success Accountability
Appendix	Attachments
Budget	Cost Estimate

4-9 Be sure the categories in the proposal match the terms used in the guidelines.

Visual Appeal

Consider how the proposal will look to a stranger who is seeing it for the first time. It is true that first impressions are lasting. Your document must convey an image of professionalism and careful preparation at first glance. A sloppy proposal may contain good ideas, but it conveys an impression of carelessness. A visually striking presentation may not actually have the best plan inside, but it gives an sense of commitment, that will earn points. Thoughtful use of word processing and computer graphics can add to the visual appeal of your proposal. If you are part of an agency that plans to do extensive grant writing, you may need to consider how you can add these computer capabilities to your office.

Input from the Target Population

Government funding agencies have a particular obligation to be accountable to the general public. There is concern that projects and new initiatives should be ones that reflect the needs of those who will benefit from them. As a result of this concern, many funding agencies look favorably on those projects that have been developed with input from the target population. If your proposal for a new center was developed because of parent requests, be sure to point that out. If you have had a community advisory board who suggested the proposal idea, include that information in the narrative. If your proposal is for the upgrading of teacher skills through the provision of training workshops, you might include examples of requests from your teachers. A letter from an officer of your local professional organization might serve to support the need for additional training.

Coordination with Other Agencies

Another concern of funding sources is that many services designed to benefit children and families are fragmented and unconnected. Coordination of activities with other similar agencies is usually seen as a desirable element in a proposal. For example, training workshops for teachers' aides might be needed by your staff, but could also benefit the staff of the local Head Start program as well. If you are in a centralized location, you might coordinate training plans with those in other child care agencies as well. While it may not be desirable or feasible to cooperate on every proposal, partnerships with other agencies, nearby universities, regional professional organizations, or, occasionally, even competitors should be considered. They may result in successful proposals and the receipt of money for projects that you would not otherwise receive.

Director's Dilemma

Grant money is available to provide training for family child care providers. Your agency has never been involved in organizing training activities, but you do have some very good teachers on your staff. How can you find out if your teachers would be interested in earning some extra money by providing some training sessions? How can you find out if the family child care providers in your area are interested in training?

Proposal Rankings

Some guidelines will include a copy of the ranking scale or the categories on which the proposals will be ranked. This is helpful information. It allows you to carefully address every element on which you can gain points. When you know what you are being "graded on," it is easier to include those essential parts in your proposal. Sometimes certain types of project plans are weighted. This means that the points received for this type of information are actually multiplied by some number that indicates how much more important this category is than others in the proposal. You can boost the score of your proposal substantially if you pay particular attention to those categories that are more heavily weighted than others. For example, if your proposal can receive double points for the category that requests input from the target audience, then it is worthwhile to be sure you have gotten input from this group.

Proposal writing is a challenge. When you write a successful proposal, you can accomplish projects that might otherwise be beyond your grasp. You can use proposals to obtain money for projects that enhance your program and revitalize your staff. Proposal writing is always a gamble. You may put a substantial amount of time and effort into a project plan that does not receive funding. Project writing involves effort, hard work, creativity, and, often , time pressure. However, when the grant is successful, you have the opportunity to do something you couldn't do before receiving the grant, 4-10.

Director's Dilemma
Your staff has been very busy working on an expansion of your program. You have just been told that additional money is available, but the proposal will have to be written very quickly. Should you use staff time to work on a proposal when they are already very busy? How can you decide whether to write the pro-

How Do I Write a Business Plan?

If you are planning to start a private child care center as a business, you may have to look for a business loan. This will probably be necessary if you don't have enough money of your own or from investors to start the center.

Private, for-profit centers are usually not eligible for many of the grants from government agencies and foundations. As a small business, however, you may be eligible for advice and services that can help you to receive a loan. Government, at all levels, is interested in supporting the development of successful businesses, especially those that create jobs. A good place to begin is probably your local chamber of commerce. From there, you can receive advice that can help you track down the type of assistance that is available.

If you need to borrow money, you must develop a business plan. A business plan is a document written to convince a bank or other lending institution that you are a good risk for a loan. It must demonstrate your knowledge of the business side of child care. The primary concern of a commercial lending institution is that you will be able to pay back the loan on schedule. The business plan forces you to think through exactly how the business (in this case, a child care center) will be set up. Many people dream of owning their own business. The preparation of a business plan demands that you work out the actual details of that dream. Confronting the hard financial realities of your dream can be a real eye-opener!

4-10 The award of a small grant of money allowed this center to add new books to each classroom.

Similarities to Proposal Writing

In many ways, a business plan is like a proposal. In both cases, you must convince an outside reader that you are knowledgeable about child care. You must demonstrate an accurate understanding of the costs involved in your project. Your plan must be carefully prepared and consistent. Your budget must reflect consistency with the narrative part of your plan. The plan must have a professional appearance. Just as with a proposal, the visual presentation of the plan can serve to convince the reader of your careful planning and expertise.

Knowledge of the jargon of the child development field is probably less important in a business plan than is familiarity with the terms used by professionals in the business world. For example, rather than demonstrating your understanding of the "need of the target population" as you must do in a proposal, you will be demonstrating your understanding of the "demands of the marketplace." In a sense, these are the same. You are looking at whether or not there are people who need the service you want to provide. In a business plan you are looking at whether or not there are enough people willing to pay for the service in order to make it a profitable business.

Assessing Your Resources

It is absolutely essential that you convince the lending officer that you know what you are doing. Anything you can add to the plan to show that you are capable of operating a successful child care should be included. The lending officer will want to see your resume. Have you worked in a successful center? Have you taken courses in child development and child care administration? Have you had any administrative experience? Be sure to point out any experience or coursework that could add strength to the banker's image of you as a competent and proficient future administrator, 4-11

In a business plan, you should also identify other resources available to you. If you own a building that could easily meet licensing standards, you should point that out. If there are trained teachers who would be willing to come to work for you, that is also a plus. Can you purchase equipment inexpensively from another center that is closing? All these things can be viewed as resources. Of course, there will also be the question of how much of your own money you are willing to put into this new business. Most banks are not willing to lend more than 50 percent of the cost of the busi-

4-11 Before lending you money, the banker must feel confident that you have the ability and resources to make your business a success.

ness unless you are able to get a guarantee for your loan from one of the supportive government agencies.

Your business plan must also demonstrate that you have an accurate sense of what things cost. The banks have access to information on the typical costs of child care services. If your projected costs and projected income are way out of line, your entire plan will be questioned. You must also be realistic in regard to the length of time that it will take to open the center and attain full enrollment. The bank will not expect you to show a profit immediately upon opening. However, you must have a realistic estimate of when you can expect to begin to earn more than your expenses.

Areas to Emphasize

A lending institution is concerned that there will be a market for this new child care center that you are planning. You must prove that there is a need for the service. You will need to demonstrate that there is a shortage of care available. This might be done by finding out whether there are large waiting lists at existing centers. You might be able to circulate questionnaires, or talk with employers or union leaders to determine unmet needs of community families. You might also talk with the directors of other programs, particularly directors of not-for-profit centers who will be less likely to view you as potential competition. You may also want to point out anything that is unique and different about the center you are planning. There may be reasons parents would prefer it and move their children even though other centers are available to them. If so, you should point these items out in your business plan.

Be Realistic

Try to develop as realistic a plan as possible. Don't inflate either your estimate of costs or anticipated profits. If the bank sets conditions on the loan that you feel you cannot meet, look elsewhere. Banks are competitive. One bank may be willing to offer more favorable terms than another. Be aware, however, that the bank's terms will always be more favorable to the bank than to you.

Taking Your Plan to the Bank

It is usually a good idea to meet with the lending officer of the bank before you develop your business plan. Get an idea of the types of businesses this particular bank is likely to fund and find out if there is a special form for preparing your business plan. If you are going to a large bank with many lending officers, be sure you are talking with one who deals with businesses like yours. Some lending officers specialize in industrial loans, others specialize in working with retail businesses. If you work with a lending officer who deals with small businesses, your business plan is likely to get the careful consideration it deserves.

The lending officer should acquaint you with the bank procedures for approving your loan. You should also find out when the loan will actually be acted upon within the bank's approval process. If you must provide additional information, be sure that you have it there before the loan is actually processed. If you do not have the additional information turned in, there may be a delay in the approval date. This could delay the entire time plan for your center opening.

The lending officer should also help you determine the type of loan that you need. Most beginning businesses need a short-term loan that runs about five to seven years with which to purchase the equipment necessary to start the business. You may also need a long-term mortgage of 15 or 20 years, if you are planning to purchase a building. A short-term line of credit is similar to a charge account. With it, you have a certain amount of money available for unexpected, reasonably small expenses. You should work with the lending officer in order to determine the best package for your child care center.

Part of your success in getting a loan approved is dependent on your ability to create a working relationship with the lending officer. If the officer feels that you are knowledgeable, trustworthy, have a good credit history, and have been accurate in your preparation of the business plan, you are more likely to receive support for the approval of your loan.

☼ Summary

Finding financial support for your center or for special projects requires effort and hard work. If you are not wealthy enough to have all of the money you need to start and operate a program, you will need to look to outside sources for support. Your ability to present a clear, thoughtful proposal or business plan may make it possible for your agency to receive additional money.

Proposal writing requires that you identify a particular need that you want to address. Your proposal must convince the funding agency that the need is real and that your plan can do something about it. You will need to spell out clearly what your plan of action is. It will also be important to prove that your plan is realistic. Your budget and your plan must match each other.

The business plan is similar to a proposal. It is usually written for the purpose of securing a loan from a bank or other lending institution. The focus of the plan is to prove to the lending officer that you know enough about child care to run a profitable business. Writing a business plan forces you to think about the real costs and responsibilities involved in running a child care center.

✿ Terms

proposal
business plan
subscriber services
contact person
abstract
goals
target population
project methodology
time line
organizational capability
organizational chart
appendix
jargon

✿ Review

1. How are a proposal and business plan similar?

2. List four possible sources of grant money.

3. Why is the abstract of a proposal important?

4. In a proposal, to what must your problem statement be related?

5. What should a budget proposal reflect?

6. When writing a proposal, what three ideas must you convey to the funding agency?

7. Why should you avoid using terms you do not understand in a proposal?

8. Why do many funding agencies look favorably on those projects that have been developed with input from the target population?

9. Why is proposal writing always a gamble?

10. What contributes to the success of getting a loan approved?

⊙ Applications

1. Visit a library to examine directories that list sources of grant funding. Report your findings to the class.

2. Consider your own interests in the child care field. Write an essay describing the target population with whom you would like to work.

3. Interview a child development specialist to identify what jargon is currently used in the field.

4. Identify other community organizations that might have similar interests in working with you on a cooperative project.

5. Meet with a loan officer at a bank and collect information on what the bank expects in a business plan.

Chapter 5
Governance of Child Care Programs

After studying this chapter, you will be able to

- explain the purposes of licensing and other regulations affecting child care services.

- describe the role and responsibilities of a governing or advisory board.

- explain the relationship between the program director and the board.

- discuss accreditation as it relates to the quality of a child care program.

Many factors will affect the decisions you make in operating your program. You do not have total freedom to do whatever you wish. There are regulations that are dictated by licensing standards in your state. There are other requirements your program must meet because you are an employer or because you operate in a particular area.

Each state sets standards and regulations that child care programs must meet in order to operate. These requirements vary considerably. Some states set high standards, while other states do not. Some regulate full-day programs with one set of requirements and part-day programs with another. Some states exempt church-sponsored programs or Head Start programs, while others do not. You must become familiar with the licensing requirements in your state.

What Is Licensing? Why Is It Important?

Each state establishes regulations designed to protect children's health, safety, and general well-being while they are in child care. Programs that meet those requirements are granted a license. This license gives a program legal permission from the state to operate. Without a license, a program would be operating illegally. An illegal program may be fined, lose its insurance, and even shut down by the state. With a license, you can have confidence in knowing that your program meets the legal requirements of your state. The license assures parents, insurers, and the community that your program has met state standards.

What Licensing Regulates

The following aspects of child care may be subject to licensing requirements:

- number of square feet of space necessary in the classroom for each child enrolled

- number of square feet of space necessary on the playground for each child enrolled

- the ratio of adults to children in each age group

- training/education of the adults in the program

- nature of the daily program

- maximum group size

- type of equipment

- structural, health, and safety components of the building

- health exams and immunization status of children and staff

- criminal background checks on staff

These standards vary from state to state. Some states require a higher quality of care than others do, 5-1. In some states, programs that are only providing minimal quality care may be licensed. In another state, the same program might not be able to obtain a license. A license, in and of itself, does not guarantee that a program is of high quality.

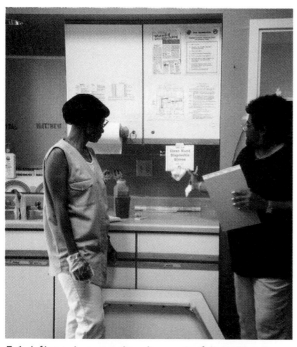

5-1 A licensing monitor inspects this center to ensure it is meeting required health standards.

Preparation for Licensing

Getting ready for a visit from a licensing monitor is a serious activity. It requires thought and preparation so you are sure your center is in compliance with regulations. While each state varies in its requirements, the following steps are typical of what you need to do:

- complete application and civil rights compliance forms

- update staff records to be sure they include TB test results, yearly physicals, evaluations, and required clearances

- update insurance information

- update children's records to be sure they include yearly physicals, immunizations, developmental records, emergency contacts, and record of parent contacts/conferences

- review plans for emergencies and evacuation, including notification of local authorities

- with staff, perform a visual inspection of center and playground

- review key areas of concern, such as plug covers, water temperature, required postings, etc.

Responsible Agencies

Every state has an agency or division that is responsible for the licensing of child care programs. Each state sets up its own organizational structure. This regulatory process and structure is not the same from one state to another. You must determine which agency is responsible for licensing in the state where you plan to operate your program. Regulation of child care in most states is under departments responsible for health and human services. Possible regulatory agencies are listed in 5-2.

While one agency will have responsibility for issuing the license, you may have to deal with several government divisions. Another division may be responsible for determining the basic safety and occupancy status of the building. A different office may have to inspect your kitchen facilities and food program. A half-day nursery school program may be subject to a completely different regulatory process from that of a full-day program.

Before proceeding with plans, you should become familiar with the licensing regulations in your state. Costly mistakes can be made if your plans don't conform to state requirements. Building renovations or hiring decisions that are not in compliance with regulations can create major problems. Exceptions or variances to the requirements are sometimes possible. This means that you may be able to obtain special permission to operate without meeting the licensing standards exactly. However, it is risky to count on a variance. You cannot assume that you will be able to convince officials your center should be exempt from certain standards. They may disagree with you and deny the exemption.

Local Ordinances

In addition to state agencies, child care programs may also be subject to local regulation. You will need to determine what city, township, county, parish, or other legally organized governance structures have jurisdiction over your proposed center. Typical local governing agencies include

- Zoning Commission

Director's Dilemma

You have operated a successful child care program in your home state. Now it has become necessary for your family to move to another part of the country. You know that your new location has a serious shortage of child care services. You would like to open a new center. How would you begin to find out the state and local regulations that would apply to your new center?

Regulatory Agencies
Department of Welfare
Department of Human Services
Department of Health
Department of Education
Department of Commerce
Office of Management and Budget
Office of Child Development
Office of Youth and Family Services
Department of Labor and Industry
Department of Environmental Resources
Department of Transportation

5-2 The agency responsible for licensing child care programs varies from state to state.

- Fire and Safety Commission
- Borough or Township Governing Bodies
- Local Planning Commission

Each of these types of agencies may have the power to impose restrictions on your program. They may also require compliance to regulations that are specific to your local community.

Zoning

Many communities have ***zoning codes.*** These are rules that specify the types of land use that are permitted. Size and type of building, nature of commercial activities, and number of occupants may all be regulated by the zoning codes. The outdoor play space may have to meet certain local requirements. The site plan may have to include a water and/or flood run-off plan. Zoning codes now may also require an examination of the environmental impact of your program. Scrutiny may also be directed toward the energy use and conservation efforts of your building plans. Size of the parking area and entrance-exit traffic flow may also be of concern if the building is located on a busy highway.

Fire and Safety Codes

Your local community may have its own fire and safety regulations. These may be more or less strict than the state regulations. The type and nature of wiring, plumbing, and heating in your building may have to meet these specific local standards. Building materials, sprinkler systems, and safety exits may all be subject to local as well as state regulation.

What Are the Legal Concerns and Obligations of Operating a Program?

As an agency that deals with the public, you must abide by federal laws that apply to your program. You must make sure that your program is in compliance with the following federal laws. You also must determine that you are adequately insured against any liabilities.

Federal Laws and Regulations

Several federal laws relate to child care programs. These include

- Civil Rights Compliance—Prohibits discrimination in hiring and program policies.

- Americans with Disabilities Act—Provides for building access for all persons (children, parents, employees) with disabilities and handicaps. This covers restrooms and fire/safety exits. It also prohibits discrimination in hiring or enrollment policies.

- Right to Know Act—Requires posted information regarding storage and use of cleaning materials or other hazardous chemicals.

- I-9 Illegal Aliens Act—Requires employers to see proof of employees' citizenship status.

- Department of Labor Fair Wage and Standards Act—Identifies minimum wage and employment conditions

Because new laws frequently go into effect and existing ones may change, you must be aware of current requirements that may affect your program decisions.

Liability Concerns

A major concern in the operation of child care programs is the need to provide a safe, healthful environment for children and staff. Strict adherence to licensing regulations is an important part of ensuring safety. As the director or owner/operator of a center, you are responsible for the well-being of the children in your care. It is generally accepted that young children cannot be responsible for themselves. Those who care for them must be aware of basic safety and health precautions. If a child is injured or becomes ill because of negligence or deliberate actions by your staff, you will be liable.

Careful adherence to all licensing and local safety requirements can provide you with some legal protection, 5-3. A center that is operating illegally would be at substantially greater risk for both civil and criminal legal action if an accident were to occur.

You must also be sure your staff is well-trained and careful about their responsibilities. Careless or poorly trained staff members are less likely to spot potential hazards. Alert supervision minimizes the likelihood of accidents. Liability resulting from an accident may be lessened if it is clear your center and staff have been diligent in trying to keep children safe.

Insurance Protection

No matter how cautious you and your staff may be, accidents can happen. Insurance provides protection against financial loss for your center. Your program will need to purchase certain types of protection by paying a premium. Often, insurance packages are offered to members of professional and child care trade associations. You may be able to save more on the insurance price than the cost of membership dues.

Director's Dilemma

You have been thinking about opening a child care center. After receiving the state licensing requirements, you realize there is more to this task than you realized. A friend tells you about a person who has been operating a center across town for several years. The center does not have a license. So far, nothing has happened. The person operating the center does not seem to be in any trouble. Your friend suggests you could open your center without a license. What do you think about this idea?

5-3 Posting the center's license lets parents know that your program meets licensing standards.

The insurance company that provides the policy may insist that your program adhere to additional requirements. These requirements are usually designed to minimize the chance that you will need to file a claim for insurance reimbursement. For example, some insurance companies will not insure a program if it includes family child care homes. The insurance companies know that family child care homes are harder to supervise. They present a greater risk for the company than a center would. Some companies may not insure a center if it has a swimming pool on the premises.

There are different types of insurance available. In some states, the licensing requirements dictate certain types of insurance coverage. You will need to consider which of the following is necessary for your program:

- liability—protects against financial loss due to successful lawsuit against program.

- property—protects against loss of equipment or building.

- child medical and accident–provides medical/hospital costs for individual child injury.

- disability—protects worker from lost income if disabled and cannot work.

- workman's compensation—pays wages of disabled worker who was hurt on the job.

- directors and officers—provides legal fee coverage in case of lawsuit.

- bonding—protects program against financial loss due to actions of officers or staff who are authorized to handle program money.

You must consider the characteristics of your program when deciding which types of insurance your program should buy. A center that is in a government-owned building or a rented facility probably will not need to carry insurance on the building. Insurance on the equipment, however, would be appropriate. Liability insurance is generally considered essential to protect you and your staff financially. Even though you have a highly competent staff and a safe center, accidents can happen. Someone can get hurt. A judgment against you or your staff could wipe out your financial resources.

What Are Governing or Advisory Boards?

Privately owned programs can be operated pretty much as the owners wish as long as they meet licensing standards and do not violate any applicable laws. Not-for-profit programs and those that receive government or charitable support sometimes require a more complex type of governance structure. This structure may be in the form of an advisory board or a governing board. An *advisory board* can study issues and make recommendations, but cannot require that those recommendations be carried out. A *governing board* is a legal entity that is authorized to actually operate the program. Decisions requiring legal and financial commitments must be made by the governing board.

When a program has a legal governing board, the director is an employee of that board. While, on a day-to-day basis, the director will make decisions for the program, overall policies that govern the activities and direction of the program will come from the governing board.

An advisory board has no legal authority to set policy, make commitments for the program, hire staff, or spend money. Its function is strictly to offer ideas and advice to the director. Many private programs have advisory boards to help the director gain insight into the concerns and ideas of community leaders or client families. Head Start programs have both a parent advisory council and an executive board. The first offers suggestions and ideas. The second has legal authority for the program. A comparison of the responsibilities of these two types of boards is given in 5-4.

Structure of a Governing Board

A governing board must have a formal structure. It is not just a group of friends who get together. Grant restrictions and/or program sponsorship may determine the size and membership characteristics of your board. Government grants usually require a board that has a substantial component of parents on it. Parents are the consumers of your child care services. They have a strong interest in helping to strengthen the program. Their ideas can also help to ensure that the program is responsive to the needs of local families.

Some boards have representatives from other community service agencies as members. This is helpful in providing links to other educational and family service organizations. The various agencies in a community often have common interests. Coordinated efforts among agencies can make it easier to help families obtain needed services.

Governing Board Responsibilities	Advisory Board Responsibilities
Legally incorporated	Study issues affecting the program
Has legal authority for the program	Make recommendations
Power to determine program policy	Advocacy for program
Employer of all staff	
Advocacy for program	

5-4 Governing boards and advisory boards both contribute to the center's operation, but they do not have the same responsibilities.

It is also helpful to have several recognized community leaders on your board. Their participation and personal reputation in the community serve as an endorsement for your program. Community leaders with expertise in the law, insurance, business, medical services, and/or child development programming can be valuable sources of support and information, 5-5.

New board member candidates are recommended by the nominating committee of the board. This committee tries to identify interested persons who are willing to serve. Geographic balance; political, social, or celebrity status; and the ability to raise funds and/or donate professional expertise all may be considered in selecting new board members. Additional candidates may be nominated at the election meeting. The full board then votes on the nominees. The nominating committee also prepares a slate of officers, or officer candidates, to present to the full board for election. Terms for both officers and board members are identified in the board bylaws.

Bylaws and Procedures

A legally incorporated board must develop a set of bylaws. These *bylaws* identify the official structure of the board. They also specify the rules by which the board will conduct its business. Typical bylaws include information on membership, officers, committee structure, meeting times, powers and responsibilities, and meeting procedures.

The board must establish bylaws in order to become incorporated. This may be completed before you are hired. If this is not done, you may have to provide advice to the board on how to develop a set of bylaws.

5-5 These board members spend their lunch time working on behalf of children in their community.

It is important that official business meetings of governing boards follow formal procedures. These procedures are designed to ensure both popular and unpopular positions and/or people are heard. They also provide for decisions by majority rule. Books on parliamentary procedure are readily available that describe these formal procedures. Because you will be working directly with a board that operates by these procedures, you should become familiar with them.

The bylaws also often identify a *quorum,* the number of board members who must be present to conduct legal business. If a quorum is not present at the meeting, certain types of official business cannot take place.

The decisions the governing board makes are important ones. See 5-6. They affect the future of the program and the well-being of the children and staff. For this reason, the board must operate under formal structure and procedures. Important decisions should not be made casually or by a small group of people with vested interests. Bylaws and parliamentary procedures help prevent this from happening. Formal procedures also protect your program against charges of unfairness or favoritism.

Board Committees

Members of the board are usually assigned to committees. These committees are smaller groups. They do the investigative work of the board and make recommendations for decisions by the full board. Each committee usually has a specific area of responsibility. Typical committees and their responsibilities are shown in 5-7.

The committee structure allows for a smaller group of people to deal with each aspect of running the program. If each member of the board was expected to be knowledgeable about the entire operation, few people would want to serve on the board. It would take too much time. This way, each committee has responsibility for studying issues related to one aspect of program functioning. The committees present recommendations to the full board. Usually, a board is inclined to approve the recommendations of its committees.

Legal Incorporation

Legal incorporation is necessary if your program is to exist as a not-for-profit agency. *Incorporation* affects how your agency will be treated by the law. It establishes that your program is eligible for tax-exempt status and certain types of government funding. Incorporation also provides legal protection for those persons who are willing to serve on your board. It will be necessary to work with a lawyer to accomplish incorporation.

If your program is *proprietary,* privately owned, and operated for a profit, you may not need to become incorporated. Your program will be legally organized differently. Legal

Governing Board Decisions May Affect the Following:

Obtaining and using large sums of money

Future directions of the program

Continued employment or hiring of staff

Center hours and tuition policies

Enrollment

Available services offered by the program

5-6 Important decisions are made by a program's governing board.

Typical Committee Structure	Responsibilities
Personnel	Determines personnel policies Makes hiring recommendations Suggests salary scale Conducts staff evaluation
Financial or budget	Reviews budget Monitors financial status Assists in search for funds Determines tuition and financial policies
Facilities	Recommends maintenance decisions Reviews decisions regarding rental or purchase Identifies future facilities needs
Program	Reviews program activities Knowledgeable about program philosophy Monitors program quality Considers unmet programmatic needs
Nominating	Identifies potential board members Nominates slate of officers Conducts elections
Executive - comprised of chairpersons from the above committees and the board officers	Meets on a regular basis to monitor program status Empowered to make decisions on behalf of the full board Can take quick action if necessary

5-7 Standing committees each have the responsibility to monitor and/or make recommendations regarding a particular part of the program.

advice is advised to ensure that your financial and legal structure are set up properly.

Relationship Between Director and Board

When your program has a board of directors, you are legally the employee of that board. Your working relationship with that board will vary according to how knowledgeable the board is about issues of child care. If the board members know little about child care, you will have to advise, guide, and educate them about your program. If your board is made up of individuals with expertise in related areas, the board may provide you with valuable assistance. At one time or another, you will be dealing with legal, personnel, medical, financial, and programming issues. A strong board can be a great help as you formulate policy and make decisions.

Some directors do little more than carry out the board's wishes. Other directors have boards that "rubber stamp" or automatically approve all their ideas. A board that has confidence in its director will not usually override that director's decisions. When a director's decisions are continuously reversed or overridden by the board, the board is indicating that it has little confidence in that director's ability.

Ideally, the board and the program director support each other. Each works for the benefit of the program. The director acts as a resource person, bringing ideas and plans to the board. The board offers suggestions and additional ideas. When a decision is reached, the director can be trusted to carry out the actions that the board has approved.

When this relationship is a positive one, board members and director feel good about their involvement with the program. Board members are recognized for the valuable role they play. The director feels that the board is supportive and trusting in the difficult role of administering a child care program, 5-8.

Director's Dilemma

The membership of your board of directors includes a substantial number of parents. The finance committee (which includes several parents) feels it is essential for the program to raise its fees in order to have enough money to operate and to improve the program next year. The committee will recommend the fee increase at the next board meeting. You agree that the increase is necessary, but you also know that some parents will oppose it. How will you work with the chairperson of your board and the finance committee to support passage of the recommenda-

What Is Accreditation?

It is sometimes very difficult for parents to tell a good center from a bad one. The reputation of a center often gets spread by word of mouth. If parents are happy with a program, they tell their friends. If they are unhappy, all of their friends will know.

Likewise, an excellent center may not have any way of sharing that information with others. *Accreditation* is a form of official recognition. This means that the program meets certain standards of quality. The program has also gone through a specified evaluation by an organization that represents the professional field.

Several organizations, such as NAEYC, the YMCA, The Child Welfare League, and the American Montessori Society, have accreditation programs. Of these, the most recognized accreditation program is the NAEYC accreditation program.

The National Association for the Education of Young Children (NAEYC) has an accreditation division called the *National Academy of Early Childhood Programs*. This division has identified the characteristics of high- quality programs. It also has developed a procedure to recognize those programs that are committed to the provision of quality programming. Those programs that successfully go through a three-part process receive the accreditation award. They are then permitted to identify themselves as accredited centers in advertising and for other professional recognition purposes. Programs that receive

Your Relationship with the Board Will Be Influenced by

How well you know the board members

The expertise of the board members

Relationships of board members to each other

Your past performance as director

Past history of the program

Vested interests of board members in decision

Commitment of board members to the program

Your skill in interpersonal relationships

5-8 You need to have a positive relationship with your board in order to do your best work as a director.

accreditation can be justifiably proud. The recognition represents approval by experts in the field that the program has achieved a high level of quality.

Academy Standards

The standards for NAEYC accreditation are given in a booklet called *Accreditation Criteria and Procedures of the National Academy of Early Childhood Programs* that is available through NAEYC. The booklet identifies the standards on which programs will be judged. The focus of these standards is on the relationships between children and staff, children and children, and staff and parents. An atmosphere where children and adults respect and care for each other is essential. Staff expectations of children's social behavior are realistic and developmentally appropriate. Children are encouraged to talk about their ideas and feelings.

Standards also address the need for a well-rounded curriculum providing activities and equipment to support each child's growing sense of self-esteem. Materials should reflect diversity. Activities and schedules grow out of the interests and needs of the children. A variety of developmentally appropriate choices must be available in both activities and equipment, 5-9. (Requirements for NAEYC accreditation are discussed in Chapter 18.) Programs receiving the accreditation are permitted to use the designation in advertising and press releases.

5-9 A variety of available developmentally appropriate activities is required in accredited centers.

⚙ Summary

There are many factors that affect how you operate your program. All states require licensing of centers. Meeting these licensing requirements is essential if your program is to operate legally. Licensing regulations vary from state to state.

Federal and state laws, as well as restrictions applied by funding sources, can also affect your decisions about managing the program. You must make sure your program can abide by these laws and restrictions.

The legal structure of your program will be determined by whether it is a not-for-profit or proprietary program. Not-for-profit programs must be legally incorporated and have a governing board of directors. The board of directors is legally responsible for the program and hires the director to operate it. Major decisions must be approved by this board.

A board of directors is not necessary for privately owned programs. Operators of proprietary programs can make decisions independently, as long as those decisions are legal and within licensing standards.

Some programs have advisory boards. The people on these boards can make recommendations, but have no power to determine decisions for the program.

A director of a program with a governing board will be both employee and advisor to the board. The director will be responsible for carrying out the directives of the board. At the same time, the director may have to educate board members about child care issues and principles. Relationships between the board and the director are best when they are supportive and trusting. If the board does not generally support the recommendations of the director, it may be time for that director to move on to a new position.

The accreditation process recognizes those programs that meet high standards of quality. Programs receiving the accreditation are permitted to use the designation in advertising and press releases.

⚙ Terms

zoning codes
advisory board
governing board
bylaws
quorum
incorporation
proprietary
accreditation

◎ Review

1. List five aspects of child care that may be subject to licensing requirements.

2. Before proceeding with plans, why should you become familiar with the licensing regulations in your state?

3. What do zoning codes specify?

4. Why is insurance protection important?

5. How are an advisory board and a governing board different?

6. When selecting advisory board or governing board members, what factors should be considered?

7. Why are the decisions that the governing board makes important ones?

8. Why is legal incorporation necessary if your program is to exist as a not-for-profit agency?

9. What does the NAEYC accreditation represent?

10. What is the focus of the standards for NAEYC accreditation?

◎ Applications

1. Identify the agency in your state that is responsible for child care licensing. Write for a copy of the licensing regulations and review them. Think of various public buildings. Would they be easy or difficult to bring into compliance with licensing regulations?

2. Invite an administrator from a not-for-profit center to speak to your class about funding sources for the program. Does the center have multiple funding sources? Does the center have special projects/programs that could not have existed without grant funding?

3. Obtain a copy of *Robert's Rules of Order* or another book about parliamentary procedure. Become familiar with the process of conducting a formal meeting. Have several classmates help you in role-playing a board of directors' meeting following parliamentary procedure.

4. Interview the owner/director of a private, for-profit center. Ask about the satisfactions and benefits of owning your own program. Find out what types of obstacles may have made it difficult to get the center started.

5. Observe a meeting of a board of directors of a child care program. Focus your attention on the process of the meeting. What is the role of the chairman of the board? The director of the program? The committee chairpersons? The other members?

6. Visit a center that has been awarded NAEYC accreditation. Ask the director about how the accreditation distinction has been meaningful to the center.

Chapter 6
Facilities for a Quality Child Development Program

After studying this chapter, you will be able to

- ○ outline factors to be considered when choosing a facility for a child care center.

- ○ identify the basic principles that must be considered in determining space utilization within a building.

- ○ list factors that influence the organization and arrangement of successful classrooms.

The choice of location for your center must be considered carefully. It is one factor that can influence whether or not your program is able to attract families who will want to enroll their children. The plan of the building can affect the smoothness with

6-1 The arrangement of this classroom would allow a teacher to supervise several activities at once.

which your program can operate. The nature of the space you select for your center can also be an important factor in creating an effective environment. Young children need an opportunity to move around freely, to explore, and to try out ideas of their own. At the same time, teachers must be able to keep a close eye on the children, supervise several activities, and communicate quickly with other staff members, 6-1. The size of the classrooms will determine how many children can be served in the facility. In turn, this has an impact on groupings, classroom management, and center income. These are just some of the many factors you must take into consideration when choosing a facility for a quality child care program.

What Do I Need to Know About Choosing a Facility?

You may already have a building in mind when you begin to plan your center. If you own a building or if space is donated, your choices may be limited. You will have to decide whether or not the building can be used as a center. You may be able to choose from among several sites, especially in city areas where more buildings are likely to be available.

Factors to Consider in Site Selection

Before making a commitment to open your center in a specific site, there are a number of factors to consider. Each building you look at should be evaluated in terms of the following factors:

- location
- licensing standards
- safety concerns
- room arrangement
- available utilities
- kitchen
- storage space
- accessibility
- security
- matching program type with space

Location

The location must be convenient for busy families. Even the "perfect" building will not attract parents if the center is too far out of the way. Main routes of traffic and primary business, shopping, or housing areas are factors to be considered in site selection.

Consideration should also be given to the overall arrival and departure patterns of families and staff. Some families may need to walk to the center. Others may come by bus, subway, taxi, or carpool. Some parents may arrive with an infant, toddler, diaper bags, formula, and a preschooler in tow. Their choice of a center will be influenced partly by whether or not the center is convenient for them. Your decision in selecting a building, should take this into account.

In rural areas, there may be very few empty spaces. Those buildings that are available may be in such poor condition that efforts to renovate them could be extremely expensive.

Licensing Standards

When choosing a site for your child care program, it is important to look at the licensing and space requirements for your state. Before signing any lease, rental, or purchase agreement, you must be sure that the building can either meet licensing standards as it is or can be renovated to meet those standards within a reasonable time and cost.

Each state sets its own standards for licensing. A building that would be approved in one state might not be approved in another. Although a facility may look attractive, if its ventilation, wiring, plumbing, and heating systems are inadequate or will not be in compliance with licensing standards, you might do better to look elsewhere rather than to become involved in major renovations. Some states specify such items as the number of sinks and toilets per group the center must have, the structure of the room housing the furnace, or the type of sink (three bowl) in the kitchen. Many states require that programs have a license before the doors can be opened to children. Therefore, the cost of renovations would occur before any income is received from the center.

Licensing requirements also dictate the amount of available space you must have and the number of children you can have in the facility. Child care experts recommend that there should be 50 square feet of available space for each child in a group. Therefore, a room for a group of 15 children should ideally have 750 square feet, or be about 25 feet by 30 feet in size. Most states do not require this amount of space per child, but the size of your group will be limited by the size of the space available.

It is important to remember that licensing requirements dictate minimal acceptable standards in each state. It is usually desirable to exceed those standards if possible.

Director's Dilemma

When choosing a site for a new center, you must decide between two possible locations. One is in the center of a city. The building has a series of small rooms and a large gymnasium. There is a park across the street. The other building has several larger rooms, is on the outskirts of town, and has a large playground and parking lot. What factors must you consider in deciding which site would be best for your program?

Director's Dilemma

You have been offered the use of an old restaurant building that is in the perfect location for your center. The space would be adequate for the number of children you plan to serve. The building has not been used for several years, so paint is peeling, plaster is chipped, and the odor of stale food and drink is strong. There is very little convenient storage space. What desirable features does this site probably offer? What are the drawbacks to using this facility?

6-3 A water supply in each room makes it easier for teachers to plan a variety of activities.

some provision for heating foods, making staff coffee, and clean-up.

Storage Space

Storage space is necessary in all centers. When evaluating a potential facility, consider the storage space it provides. A wide range of storage requirements must be met. Materials and equipment not currently being used in the classroom must be stored and available for later use. If teachers are to plan a variety of activities, they must have easy access to stored items.

Art supplies and food can usually be purchased more economically in large quantities. Without enough storage space, bulk purchases may not be possible. If the storage space is damp or too hot, problems will develop. Ruined paper supplies or spoiled food products will wipe out any savings that might have occurred from bulk purchasing.

Storage is also necessary for seasonal equipment such as sleds, snow shovels, or wading pools. Children love these activities, but during the off-season, provisions must be made for keeping them out of the way. Centers also have cleaning equipment and supplies that must be carefully locked away from the curious investigations of children.

Accessibility

Desirable sites for child care centers must be accessible to children and adults with disabilities. A federal law requires that all child care centers, public and/or private, must accept children with special needs. Efforts must be made to ensure *accessibility*, which means ensuring safe, easy access to and throughout the building. Doorways should be designed so wheelchairs can enter. Toilets can be modified to allow for easier use. Sturdy railings can be added. These considerations help the families of children with special needs feel truly welcome. It also provides support to your staff in their efforts to help all children fully participate in both indoor and outdoor activities.

Easy delivery of children to and from the center is an additional factor to be considered in making a site choice. Because young children must be escorted into the center, there must be some provision for temporary parking spaces.

Parents want a safe, easy way to bring their children to your center with minimal hassles. This is especially true in urban, high-traffic areas. Without provisions for parent parking, a staff member will have to meet children at their cars as they arrive and deliver them back to their cars at the end of the day. This type of arrival reduces the opportunity for parents and teachers to get to know each other and to communicate about the children. It is also more likely to create stressful separation anxieties for those children who need some additional parental support upon arrival.

Parking must also be examined in relation to your staff. Child care personnel usually do not receive high salaries. If they must pay for parking each day, they may choose to look elsewhere for a job. It is anticipated that the next decade will see a labor shortage. It will become harder to hire and keep well-qualified staff. Free, close parking is a benefit that will be greatly appreciated by the center staff.

Security

The security of buildings has become more of a concern in recent years. Children's safety can be compromised if the staff cannot continuously be aware of who is coming into the center. Some programs in high-risk areas may actually have to operate behind locked doors. All programs need to have limited access ways into the building so visitors will pass by a central reception area upon entering. Most programs will not experience the tragedy of someone coming in with the deliberate intent to harm the children. However, in our society with its high divorce rate, kidnappings by noncustodial parents and grandparents have, sadly, become more common.

Security also plays a role in the vulnerability of the center to robbery and vandalism. A center that must share space with other programs in the evenings or on weekends will be more difficult to protect. It is helpful when individual doors to the classrooms and offices can be locked. Outdoor lighting and visibility of the center can also discourage intruders.

Finding a building that will work well as a child care center is not easy. In establishing a new center, you may not be able to begin in a facility that has all of the characteristics you want. However, it is important to be aware of the "trade-offs" that you are making. If you choose a place that has adequate parking, but is on the outskirts of town, what will the impact be on your recruitment? If you choose a site where the nearest playground is three blocks away, what plans will have to be made to ensure adequate outdoor time? If the building has a water supply only in the bathrooms, how will that limit the creative art and water play activities provided for the children in the classrooms?

Matching Type of Program with Space

The type of program you plan to offer will influence space needs. School-age care usually requires large rooms. Larger groups, bigger children, and after-school physical activities require more space. Rooms for infants or toddlers can be small. Ideal group size for them is only three or four. Preschool classrooms frequently hold groups of 15 to 20. Rooms that are too small frequently result in more irritable behavior. Licensing requirements also must be considered. They usually have space-per-child requirements that must be met. It is desirable to have 50 square feet per child.

In addition to classroom space, the overall size and complexity of your program will influence the amount of office, bathroom, and storage space needed. If your center will serve only preschoolers and will need only one classroom, other spaces can be smaller. If you are planning a large, complex program, the administrative and service areas must be larger.

Director's Dilemma

A successful business executive in your city has decided to build a child care center for the company's employees. You have been chosen to design and operate this new center. What features would your "ideal" center possess? How would you begin to design the facility?

Few programs have the luxury of operating in a facility designed especially for children. Many different types of buildings have been successfully used for children's programs. Creative modification of a building can result in an excellent child care facility.

What Should I Consider When Modifying and Preparing a Facility for Quality Care?

Once you have chosen a site, your work has just begun. You now must figure out how to modify the facility to create the quality program that is your goal. You must decide how to use the rooms and hallways. The traffic from staff, families, and children moving into and through the center must be smooth. The arrangement of classrooms and offices must be logical. Size of rooms, location of doors and bathrooms, and the activities that will go on in the center must be considered. All of these decisions will require careful planning and a lot of hard work.

6-4 The "welcome" sign in this entry area helps to guide visitors to the receptionist.

The Entry Area

It may be helpful to pretend that you are a parent coming to the center for the first time. How will you know where to go? Who will know that you are there? Where will your child put coat and boots? Where will you pay your fees? See 6-4.

Whenever possible, it is best to have an entry area where parents and children can wipe off muddy boots, close umbrellas, and catch a breath before proceeding to the classroom. This reception area can serve to welcome families. The atmosphere here creates the first impression that families and visitors have of your program. Anyone coming into the center should have the feeling that children and families are respected. The choice of decoration, such as paint, art work, or wallpaper, should convey a sense of warmth and nurturance.

In a multi-classroom building where many people come and go, the security of the facility can be more easily controlled if everyone must come past a central reception area. Parents and visitors can be greeted, while those who are unknown can be prevented from roving through the center. Someone who has never been in the center before can be directed to the right location.

The Reception Area

The reception area is the perfect place to have a bulletin board with information parents need to know. The content of messages or cartoons should be positive, never sarcastic, disrespectful, or threatening. Items on the bulletin board, along with other aspects of the center, convey attitudes. They contribute to the overall feelings that people form in relation to the center.

Some centers provide coffee to parents. Others have magazines, a lending library, or an exchange box where parents can switch unwanted food coupons for ones they need. The overall atmosphere should be upbeat and helpful.

The Classrooms

Several factors are important when deciding which group to put into each available room. A good match between the room location and the characteristics of the groups can create a more workable, comfortable building. The size of the rooms, their access to fire or playground exits, and their water supply and distance from restrooms have an impact on these decisions.

Decisions regarding classrooms must be made after reviewing the ages of the children to be in each group. Keep in mind that the younger the children are, the smaller the group should be. Smaller groups of infants or toddlers need smaller rooms. Larger groups of lively preschoolers or school-age children will need more space to move around. If you have several groups that are similar in age, it is a good idea to have their rooms near each other. That way, sharing of equipment from one classroom to another will be easier. Any rooms that will house groups of children must meet state licensing requirements regarding size.

The location of the room within the building may affect its accessibility. Are there stairs to be climbed? Must you pass through one room to get into another? Where is the nearest bathroom and water supply? A parent who is carrying an infant and diaper bag in one arm while holding onto a toddler with the other hand, will appreciate a room with easy access.

Noise levels from one room to another also vary. Placing a lively class of four-year-olds beside a small group of infants won't work well for either group. This arrangement is likely to cause stress for both groups and their teachers, 6-5.

> **Considerations in Group Room Assignment**
>
> Before assigning groups to specific rooms, ask yourself the following questions:
>
> - Can the children in this group walk or must they be carried?
> - Can these children go up and down stairs independently?
> - Will these children be able to make it to the bathroom if it is not inside the classroom?
> - Will parents be carrying diaper bags or other items to the classroom?
> - Where will other groups of this same age be placed?
> - What types of materials and equipment will this group use? Where is the room located in relation to storage areas?
> - What is the best size room for this group?
>
> 6-5 Consider these questions when deciding which group to put into each room.

Floor Treatments

Young children in child care settings typically spend a lot of time playing on the floor. In some centers, they nap on mats on the floor as well. Children are also hard on floors. Spills occur frequently. Floor coverings must be chosen, not only for appearance, but for features that make them function well in child care centers. When choosing a floor treatment, you will want to consider such factors as

- licensing regulations

- the use or purpose of the area (eating, sand play, block building, napping, etc.)

- ease of clean-up and stain-resistance

- quality of construction and durability

- warranty

A basic choice is whether to use carpeting or some type of resilient flooring. Some centers even use a combination of both in each classroom. Each type has advantages and disadvantages, 6-6.

Carpet

Carpet, a floor covering made from natural or artificial fibers, lends warmth, interesting colors or textures, and sound absorption in a room full of children. Another advantage is that carpeted floors provide a warmer surface in areas where children are likely to be playing on the floor. This is desirable in cooler climates where surfaces may be cold. The carpet can help create a cozy invitation to participate in activities that involve sitting on the floor.

There are many different types of fibers, textures, and patterns available in carpeting. When considering carpet, the types of texture and fiber can affect both the durability and ease of cleaning. Carpeting designed for heavy use in restaurants and hotels usually holds up well, but may be rough on children's knees and clothes. These rough surfaces can cause skinned knees and brush burns as children play actively on the floor. Thick loops or shag carpet can be fun to play on, but may be difficult to clean. On a normal day, paints spill, food splatters, children get upset stomachs, and mud gets tramped into the building. Stain-resistance and washability are important characteristics to consider before purchasing carpeting.

Factors Influencing Floor Covering Decisions

- The covering should be easy to maintain, stain-resistant, and washable.
- Floor covering should be nonabrasive.
- Carpeting should not have large loops that snag and catch on children's clothing, shoes, or belt buckles.
- Rugs, mats, or runners that create a danger of tripping must be firmly secured to the floor or eliminated.
- Color choice is important.
- Consider the subflooring already in place.
- Carpet on the floors absorbs sound.

6-6 A variety of factors must be considered before purchasing floor coverings.

Some types of carpet require padding between the floor and the carpet. The padding adds insulation and makes the carpet bouncy to walk on. It helps to protect the carpet from the wear and tear of rubbing against the hard floor. Some types of carpet have a rubber type backing that serves the same purpose so no additional padding must be purchased.

Resilient Flooring

Resilient flooring refers primarily to linoleum, and vinyl or asphalt tile. Although each has its own unique characteristics, these floor coverings all wear well and are generally easy to keep clean. They can be damp-mopped after most days, or washed and waxed. Some new products don't require waxing to stay shiny.

Before making any decisions on resilient flooring, consider the amount of traffic and play the flooring will receive. Some products are designed for heavy use, while others are not. You must also examine the sub-floor, or the floor that will be covered by the new material. Not all resilient flooring can be used on concrete or basement floors, or on top of other resilient flooring. Frequently, old resilient flooring must be removed before the new can be installed. Again, products differ, but most are designed to be cemented or glued down.

Rolls of sheet type flooring in several different widths and squares of nine or twelve inches are the two main types of resilient flooring. Some products offer more cushioning and provide a softer, quieter surface. Many colors and designs are available.

Resilient flooring is generally cool to touch. In warm parts of the country, it can be more comfortable to sit on than carpeting. Its durability and ease of cleaning make it desirable for many areas of the center. It creates a harder surface than carpet, but is generally not abrasive, and will not snag children's clothing.

Color Choice

Color choice is important for whatever type of floor covering you decide to use. Current thinking is that neutral or natural colors are soothing to young children. Very intense colors, such as bright reds, purples, or oranges, over large areas, may be over-whelming to children. Very dark colors will show lint and dust. Light colors will show dirt. Pastel blues and greens are cool and soothing, while pale yellows and pinks give a warmer sense. Neutrals such as beige, gray, or gold are easiest to maintain. They also coordinate well with other colors in the room.

Many programs use a combination of carpet and resilient flooring in the center. The best choice for a classroom may be different from that which works well in a kitchen or bathroom. A careful choice of floor covering can enhance the appearance and functioning of your center.

Wall, Window, and Ceiling Treatments

Wall and ceiling treatments must be pleasing to look at as well as functional. The most common wall coverings include paint, paneling, and wallpaper. Paint is the quickest to apply and is less expensive than the other coverings. Latex, flat-finish paints are recommended for classroom use. Semigloss finishes are preferred in bathrooms and kitchens for ease of cleaning. Of course, no paint products containing lead should ever be used.

Decisions regarding wall coverings can affect the level of noise in the centers. Hard surface walls reflect sounds and seem to magnify them. Walls with fabric coverings or decorated with drapes and fabric wall hangings tend to absorb and minimize sound, 6-7.

Your building's ceilings may come in a variety of heights and shapes. While frequently unnoticed, ceilings can affect the lighting, temperature, and sound control within a room. Most ceilings are flat. If they are very high, as in an older building or warehouse, the ceilings can be lowered with a framework that holds sound-absorbing panels. This can help to make the room less overwhelming to the children and reduce the noise level. Light fixtures placed above translucent panels can provide overall room lighting. Open ceilings that show the interior construction of the roof can be dramatic, but they are costly in heat loss.

Color and pattern can be used to affect the appearance of the ceiling and its relationship to the rest of the room. Light, pale colors and/or small patterns will make the ceiling appear higher. Stripes or vertical patterns on the walls will make the ceiling appear even higher. To make the ceiling appear lower, use a darker color. Horizontal patterns on the walls also add to the impression of a lower ceiling.

When making decisions about the walls and ceilings, consider how they will look from the children's viewpoint. Pictures, posters, chalk boards and bulletin boards that are at an adult's eye level will be too high for children to look at comfortably. If you want them to notice the interesting things that have been put up on the walls, those things will have to be put at a level where the children can easily see them.

Windows provide light, ventilation, and views. Window treatments are visible from both inside and outside of the center. Be sure to select curtains or drapes made from flame-retardant fabrics. It is best to avoid plastic curtains. Even though they may

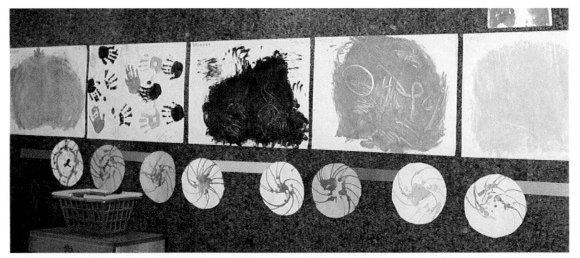

6-7 This center has one wall covered with squares of cork. The cork absorbs noise and provides a surface on which to display children's artwork.

be bright and inexpensive, they could become a hazard in case of fire. Keep in mind also that a heavy layer of dust on top of drapes or pictures can burn even though the fabric itself may be flameproof or retardant. Select window treatments that are washable.

Rooms where children are napping need to be darkened. Window blinds, shades, or drapes may need to be installed. Mini-blinds are inexpensive and used frequently, but old ones need to be replaced. (Recent research indicates that many older mini-blinds are covered with a lead-based paint that can disintegrate over time creating dangerous levels of lead dust.) Mini-blinds on the market after mid 1996 should be safe.

Lighting

The location of a center can make a difference in the kinds of lighting needed. Centers with windows facing the south will get more natural sunlight than centers facing other directions. If the center is located in a climate where there are long, cold, dark, dreary winters, special attention will need to be paid to the lighting.

Fluorescent lighting is usually found in public buildings. It is energy-efficient because it does not generate heat, gives off more wattage, and can last almost seven times longer than other bulbs. Once the lighting fixtures and bulbs are purchased, there is little expense in operation. The light produced by fluorescent bulbs is cool in tone as well as temperature. Because the light produced by this type of bulb actually flickers at a very fast rate, some research has linked it to headaches, eyestrain and dizziness. Some types of fluorescent bulbs are available that produce a full spectrum of light that is similar to sunlight. These bulbs are expensive, but may have some value in areas that experience many winter days. In consistently warm, sunny climates, the fluorescent lights can have a cooling effect.

Incandescent lighting comes from the normal lightbulbs found in homes. They are available in different brightnesses and they produce the warm colors of the light spectrum. These bulbs also generate heat. They can cause burns if a child touches one that has been on for a while. The bulbs are fairly inexpensive to replace, but cost more to use than the fluorescent types. Rooms in temperate climates with cold winters will have a warmer atmosphere with the use of incandescent lighting.

Lighting experts suggest that a combination of both fluorescent and incandescent fixtures will make a room most comfortable. The light generated by the incandescent bulbs can mask the flickering of the fluorescent lights.

Correct, adequate lighting is important in all parts of the building, 6-8. Eyestrain can cause weariness and irritability. Darkness can contribute to accidents.

Display Areas

An attractive, inviting center will have thoughtful displays of interest to both children and adults. Within centers, there will need to be facilities for display of many different types of items. Classroom teachers will want to put up children's artwork as well as other types of interesting or decorative items at children's eye level. Messages and flyers with information for parents to see should also be easily visible. Some bulletin or message boards will be needed for communication with staff.

Guidelines for Planning Lighting

Be sure there is enough light.

Light wall colors and furnishings will enhance the light. Dark colors will absorb it and make the room appear darker. Avoid too much bright light that can create a sterile, irritating environment.

Minimize glare.

Lightbulbs need shields to prevent direct glare. The lights should be moved if they are causing glare off a surface such as a refrigerator, mirror, or other glossy item.

Create even lighting throughout the room.

When one part of the room is noticeably lighter or darker than other parts, the contrast can be irritating. Dark areas of the room will usually be avoided by the children who may find them intimidating.

Eliminate shadows.

Shadows can cause problems particularly in hallways, stairways, kitchens, and work and reading areas. Be sure to plan lighting and wall switches so anyone coming into a room does not have to walk through dark areas.

6-8 Children and teachers will be more comfortable in rooms where the lighting has been carefully planned.

The display areas should be located where they can't be missed by the people for whom they are intended. Think about the routes that parents typically take when they are coming into the center. Place bulletin boards in easily seen locations at eye level. Information for staff is more likely to be seen if it is on a bulletin board designated for staff only. Trying to make one bulletin board serve too many purposes will be confusing.

Bulletin boards made of corkboard are relatively inexpensive and easily available. If they are painted to match surrounding walls or covered in matching fabric, they will also look attractive when not in use. Any bulletin board areas around infants and toddlers must be carefully watched. Dropped thumbtacks or pins can be serious hazards. For these rooms, you might want to consider the type of message board that uses magnetic or Velcro holders.

Children love to have their three-dimensional constructions, such as collages, block structures, and items made of clay, saved and displayed. Narrow tabletops or rolling shelves with flat tops can serve to display these creative works in the classroom or in the hall. Placemats or masonite can provide a working space that can be picked up and moved easily to a display area.

Display cases can be purchased for more elaborate displays. These work well for three-dimensional displays, but require additional time and effort on the part of staff to maintain. Unless you are sure that your staff has the creativity and time to keep the display cases interesting, they are probably not worth the expense.

Storage Space

The ideal building will have lots of storage space. Each part of the center has specific storage needs with specific storage requirements. The classroom, office, and kitchen each have items that must be stored, 6-9.

Storage areas for classrooms usually need a lot of shelves of different heights. Plastic bins of various sizes are useful. Large, unused commercial ice cream tubs can easily be labeled to hold items that have many small parts. Sturdy cardboard packing boxes can be covered with bright adhesive paper and used for dress-up clothes or other dramatic play props.

Classroom teachers rotate activities and materials. After an item has been available in the classroom for a period of time, it will be put back into storage. Some items, such as flannel board stories, are only used occasionally and then put away until those stories are told again.

Paper and art supplies must be kept in areas that will remain dry and free of insects. Extreme heat or cold can cause art supplies to deteriorate. Brightly colored papers will also be damaged by exposure to bright sunlight.

Food supplies should be kept in clean, dry areas. It is essential that food items be kept free of insects and rodents. Proper temperature is also important for the storage of food. A dangerous situation can exist if food is not properly refrigerated or kept frozen. Centers that have only small refrigerators or no freezers will not be able to take advantage of bulk purchasing savings or government food program availability of items requiring cold storage.

Children sometimes have medicines they must take throughout the day. You will need to

6-9 The storage space in this center is large and supplied with a large amount of shelving.

have some sort of lockable cabinet or shelf where these medications can be safely kept out of the children's reach. A chart for recording the time, date, dosage, and responsible staff member should be close by. No medication should ever be left sitting casually out on a shelf.

Office supplies are also not used all at once. They must be bought ahead for use when needed. Because the items stored in an office vary considerably, it will be necessary to have some type of cabinet that can be locked. Chemicals used for copying machines, expensive software necessary for computer operation, and tuition checks or cash will need to be kept in a secure place. File cabinets that lock are also necessary to ensure the confidentiality of family and personnel records.

Potentially hazardous chemicals such as cleaning fluids or pesticides must be stored with extreme caution. Cleaning and maintenance supplies must be stored in a safe, locked place where curious children cannot get into them. These items should be kept in areas away from food supplies. Chemicals that could react with each other if mixed, such as chlorine bleach and ammonia, must be kept well separated from each other. The storage area must be dry and protected from extreme high or low temperature. Cleaning equipment is often large and heavy. It should not be left in a visible area where curious children might be tempted to explore it. Check with your state licensing requirements and with state occupancy regulations regarding fire and safety to determine other standards that would apply to your center.

Paper supplies used in bathrooms and kitchens must always be on hand. These are lightweight, but bulky. If a cabinet is not available, high shelves, preferably with doors, can eliminate potential problems.

Most centers find it necessary to keep extra sets of children's clothes available. In a busy program, it is normal for children to occasionally spill things. Sometimes they have toileting accidents. A playtime in the snow can mean wet socks or slacks. Dry clothes help keep children comfortable. Extra sets of mittens, boots, and scarves make it possible for all children to participate in outdoor play even if they forgot to bring those items from home. Storage for these items does not have to be locked or elaborate, but there must be a place to put them when they are not in use.

Seasonal items, such as holiday decorations, or equipment used only in one season of the year, will require storage during the time when they are not in use. Some of these items may be big and bulky while others may be small and fragile. Some may be used outdoors, while others are indoor items. Appropriate storage will depend on the nature of the items.

The articles in storage are a financial investment. Most of them have probably cost money from your program. To replace them would cost additional money. It is important that these items be protected against theft or vandalism. If your center is in a building that is shared with other programs, it may be necessary to be more careful about keeping storage areas locked. If people have access to the center when none of your staff is present, locked areas will be necessary.

Outdoor Areas

Desirable centers also have provisions for outdoor play space. Outdoor activities are often minimal in many programs, yet they provide exciting learning opportunities for children and should provide for first-hand experiences with many natural elements of the outdoor environment.

Size and Location

Outdoor space should be divided loosely into zoned areas. Some of the areas to be included in the outdoor space are small and large muscle areas as well as wide open space for lively play. Spaces designed to promote dramatic play and sand play activities should be separated from the more active play areas. Gardens need to be out of the traffic patterns. Trike paths need to be away from climbers and swings. They may require a harder surface such as concrete or patio blocks, 6-10. Well-packed dirt paths may also work well for trikes, providing a less expensive surface.

Most experts recommend about 100 square feet of outdoor space per child. For a group of 15 children, this would be an area about 30 by 50 feet. The best location would be for the space to be right beside the center. A playground that is close is more likely to be used on a regular basis than one that is farther away. With a close playground, teachers can be encouraged to bring indoor activities out-of-doors and unexpected "potty" trips are easier to supervise.

Ideally, the center will have a covered porch to serve as a transition space between the classroom and the out-of-doors. A screened-in porch or patio area encourages year-round outside activities regardless of the climate or weather. A covered porch area also provides a protected area when the direct sun or wind are too intense to allow for comfortable outdoor play, 6-11.

6-10 This bike path has been designed to keep children out of the garden and other play areas. The little hill in the path adds a challenge for the riders.

Barriers that surround the play area are also needed. These provide a clear area where children can play freely without having to worry about traffic or getting lost. Most playgrounds have fences, but some also use hedges of thick bushes, or large flower box planters to surround the play area.

If several groups of children will be using the playground at the same time, it is a good idea to use partial fences or barriers to keep the groups separated. Even though many adults may be supervising, it is difficult to keep an eye on a large group of children. For both adults and children, smaller groups are easier to handle, even outside.

Often, children of different age groups will be using the playground. This makes supervision even more difficult. It is dangerous for younger children to play on equipment that has been designed for older children. Separate playground sections should be established to meet the play needs of the various age groups.

Surface Treatments

A variety of surface treatments make the outdoor area more interesting. Variation in surface textures and heights make an interesting play area, especially for the youngest children. Large grassy areas and trees provide a natural feeling. Children love to sit and play on soft grass. A spaded area allows for gardening.

Check to see that tree roots, vines, or other hazards are removed. Otherwise, children and/or staff may trip and fall. Often older playgrounds are completely paved over with cement. Many accidents have occurred on this type of surface.

The legs or posts of playground equipment such as climbers and swings need to be rooted in concrete. This will keep them from pulling out of the ground. The surface under the rest of the climbers can sometimes be left naturally, but may require impact resistant materials for insurance or licensing regulations. Some playgrounds use wood

6-11 A covered porch allows children to have some outdoor time when weather conditions would otherwise keep them inside.

chips, placed over sand and gravel. This provides good drainage and a cushioned surface.

Various impact-resistant surface materials are available for playground surfaces. These are expensive, but they can be worth the cost if older children will be using a part of the playground for basketball or similar sports. They are desirable, and sometimes required, under swings or climbers. These are the spots where children may fall. The impact-resistant surfaces are also usually designed to provide for water drainage. They are helpful in areas such as under swings where puddles tend to form.

Other factors will also affect your choice of surface treatment. Climate must be considered. Is it often rainy and muddy? Is it dry, dusty, or sandy? You will also need to consider whether or not you own or are renting the facility. Do you expect to be moving the center in the near future, or is this a permanent location? You will not want to install permanent outdoor equipment and surface coverings if you expect to be moving.

Outdoor Storage

Storage is a concern outdoors as well as indoors. Teachers are more likely to use equipment if it is conveniently located. An outdoor storage shed, treated to withstand the weather, might be necessary. It should be large enough to hold a variety of items such as trikes, sandbox toys, and wading pools. A shed that can also serve as a playhouse is desirable, 6-12. Large bins with locks can be built on porch areas. Canvas covers or tarpaulins can be used to protect outside tables or sandboxes.

6-12 This storage shed has a porch area where children can play.

No Outdoor Play Areas

If it is impossible to find a facility with access to an outdoor play area, special care should be taken to ensure that children have the opportunity to go on walks outside and to have vigorous, large muscle activity indoors. In some cases, a large gymnasium or classrooms that are big enough to be equipped with indoor climbers and wheel toys can provide some substitute activities. You must be sure what the licensing requirements regarding outdoor space are in your state. Some states will not license a center that does not have easy access to an outdoor space.

Eating Areas

Each center must be able to support the children's basic needs for food and rest. Child care for most children means long hours spent at the center. Not all of children's time is spent in play activities. Meals, naps, and bathroom time all must be accommodated within the center facility. In meeting these basic needs, it is important to provide comfortable, adequate spaces that are designed for children and operational for adults. Carefully designed areas help meet children's growing need to have some control over their environment. Yet, they also provide a setting that adults can easily supervise.

Eating areas may be in the classroom or in a separate room. Some centers have rolling carts to deliver food to each room. Others move children into a cafeteria or dining room area that is close to the kitchen. With either choice, it is important that adequate space is available. This helps prevent the accidents that occur when too many children are packed into too tight an area.

The atmosphere should be attractive and comfortable. Separate, small groups of children are more manageable than large cafeteria-style groupings. If you have a large group of children eating together at the same time, you can use some dividers to keep individual smaller groups.

The eating area should be simple to keep clean. Food in a child care setting is sometimes spilled or splashed. Close access to a water supply can make clean-up easier. Floors under the tables should have a hard surface that can be wiped up. If the center has carpeting, heavy plastic or vinyl runners can be taped down under the tables. Tabletops should also have a hard, smooth surface that will not be ruined by an occasional spill. Children can help adults with clean-up if the eating area is designed to simplify that task.

Facilities for Naps

Facilities for naps must have adequate space between cots or mats. This allows staff to move safely between cots when the room is dark. The spread of disease is also less likely when children are not face-to-face during naptime. The amount of space you must have between cots is dictated by most states in the licensing regulations, 6-13.

If children are to nap in their playroom, you will need to work out an arrangement that allows for easy storage of cots/mats when they are not being used. Lightweight stacking cots or mats that fold up or hang neatly on a rack help to minimize storage space. Classroom shelves on casters provide flexibility and allow for quick rearrangement of space to meet the needs of naptime.

Sheets, blankets and pillows used by the children need to be washed on a regular basis. If the center does not have a washer and dryer, some plan will be needed to ensure that the linens are kept clean. Some centers have a staff member who is paid extra to take care of the laundry. Others require that parents take the items home on

6-13 The napping area must be large enough so there is space around each cot or mat.

the weekend for laundering. Extra sets of bedding will be necessary for those times when children wet or become ill during naptime.

Restrooms

Licensing regulations identify the number of toilets and sinks that you must have in the center. The number of children you can enroll will depend, in part, on the restroom facilities that are available.

Ideally, each classroom will have its own bathroom, 6-14. This allows children to use the restroom as needed. It reduces the need for regimented bathroom times in the daily schedule. Since children basically stay in their own classroom, supervision by adults is easier.

Restrooms work best if they are designed with children in mind. It is more difficult for children to feel independent in restrooms where everything is adult size. Toilets and sinks come in different sizes. For very young children, small toilets are less threatening to look at and easier to manage, 6-15. If large toilets and sinks are already in place, the floor can be built up around them, or sturdy stepstools can help children to reach them easily. Soap and towel dispensers should also be brought down to a level where children can reach them. Toothbrushes should be hung on racks where air circulation will dry them between uses.

The temperature of warm water in the bathroom must be carefully regulated. Hot water creates a safety hazard for children who do not understand how to mix it with cold water or how to turn it off. Some states allow lukewarm water. Other states require that the hot water supply to the bathroom be turned off completely or mixer valves be used in all sinks.

Infant/Toddler Accommodations

Accommodations for infant/toddler care require some special consideration. Most experts feel that toddlers should be separated from nonwalkers. The world is such an exciting place that toddlers can't be expected to watch out for crawling infants on the floor. The more aggressive nature of toddlers requires that younger children be actively protected from them. Think about the environment from a toddler's point of view. The most visible part of a wall or divider is the first three feet above the floor. This is where to put interesting pictures, safety mirrors, and photographs of the children. Space above three feet is more visible to adults, but will be unseen by toddlers unless they are picked up.

6-14 This bathroom facility, with low walls for easy supervision, is built into a passageway between two parts of the room.

6-15 Small toilets and low walls can help young children feel more secure.

Very young children have immature immune systems that are just beginning to protect them from disease. They are vulnerable to many illnesses. Rooms that open directly into other classrooms or that are in high traffic areas are to be avoided if possible. This provides some protection from unnecessary contact with individuals who may be ill.

A nearby water supply is extremely important. Handwashing and sanitary diapering areas help to prevent the spread of disease. Caregivers may often change diapers and then work with children's formula or food. Easy access to soap and water helps to ensure that caregivers will remember to wash their hands.

Parents of infants or toddlers must carry many items with them. Diaper bags, bottles of formula or other food, a stuffed toy, and even a stroller are just a few of the items they may bring with the child every day. Ideally, rooms for these very young children will be easily accessible for parents who must carry everything. The center will need to provide some sort of storage shelf or bin for each family so that these necessary things can be kept in an orderly manner. Staff may need these items throughout the day. They must know where to find them easily and quickly. Each family will also need a small bin or other container for foods or medicines that need to be refrigerated.

Infants and toddlers need a great deal of individual attention. They need to be held and rocked. Several comfortable rocking chairs and soft, overstuffed furniture can help to make the setting feel more cozy. These items help to create a warm, home-like feeling. They are inviting to both children and caregivers.

Specific equipment such as cribs, high chairs, pull-toys, and stuffed toys must also be purchased for infant/toddler rooms. It is essential that the equipment used meets all safety specifications and is matched to the age of the children in the group. The toys that toddlers love will be too advanced for infants. Infants will be fascinated by items that bore the toddlers. Many toy companies now offer lines of equipment designed specifically for these younger children.

Isolation Area

Most states require that centers have a space where sick children can be kept away from others. This *isolation area* should be comfortable and not frightening. It must be located where a staff member can watch over the child. A room that is totally separate and used for this purpose is usually not necessary. A couch in an office may serve quite well.

Staff and Support Facilities

The needs of the staff in a child care center must also be considered. A large program will have a variety of staff members in different positions, often working on different schedules. Space provisions must be made to meet their needs. All staff will need secure places for their coats and personal belongings as well as a place to relax during breaks. Restrooms that provide privacy for adults are also necessary. Office staff sharing a large office may be more comfortable with sound absorbent room dividers. These dividers can also help to direct the traffic flow through a busy office. Classroom staff will need workroom space where they can prepare materials needed for daily activities. A water supply will be important in this area. In addition to the classroom areas, you will need to provide comfortable areas where each staff member can work.

Complex programs require a large amount of paperwork. Office space will be necessary for the administrative functions of the program. Large programs usually employ many staff, care for large numbers of children, and receive support from a variety of sources. The administrative responsibilities to keep such a program functioning smoothly require a team of people who do not ever work directly with the children, 6-16. Their work is primarily done in offices. This space, like the other areas of the center, should be attractive and comfortable. It should be set up so each person can work with a minimum of distraction from others. Some of the administrative work, such as conferences with parents or interviews regarding personnel issues, requires privacy. Some of the work requires close cooperation and communication among several of the staff. In setting up an office, consider which staff members will

- often work together

- need privacy to carry out their responsibilities

- require substantial storage space

- need to greet the public on a regular basis

6-16 This program secretary plays an important role in keeping the center running smoothly even though she does not work directly in a classroom.

In addition to the regular administrative staff, teachers also have paperwork to do. They have records to keep and activity plans to develop. Each teacher should have access to a desk for these responsibilities.

A workroom is an important asset to a center. Staff members need a place where they can work on "messy" projects such as making playdough. The workroom should have a water supply preferably with a laundry tub or utility sink, outlets, a sturdy worktable, and storage space. This room may also serve as the primary storage area for supplies.

Staff members also appreciate an area where they can get together to share information, work on group projects, or just relax. A staff lounge can provide this space. It is a perfect place for a staff bulletin board, reference library, coffee pot, a few chairs and a staff restroom.

Pleasant working conditions for staff are extremely important. Working in child care requires concentration, commitment, and long hours. Caring, concerned staff may be difficult to find. An environment where staff members feel respected and appreciated will help to meet their needs for recognition and support. It can be a major factor in encouraging stability and loyalty among personnel.

How Do I Set Up a Successful Classroom?

Classrooms that work well for young children do not happen by accident. Well-organized classrooms require careful planning. The result is classrooms that welcome children and support their development. Rooms that have been poorly organized are more likely to have discipline problems. Both children and teachers will be frustrated if the classrooms are not well-designed.

As the director, you are responsible for every aspect of the program. You need to be aware of the basic principles of classroom organization and planning. This allows you to be helpful and supportive to your teachers in their efforts to plan effectively.

Within each classroom, furniture and equipment will have to be arranged. This room arrangement has an important impact on classroom activities and children's behavior. Some set-ups seem to encourage involvement and self-control on the part of the children. Others do not. Most child care settings that work well have a number of things in common.

If you could look down on a room from above, you would see that the large classroom space is broken into smaller, *zoned areas* with each zone focusing on a particular type of play. The entire space is divided like a collection of smaller rooms, yet the barriers are low in height, so teachers can always see the children. At the same time, the children can always see the teacher.

The zoned areas can be created by using shelves and tables. Dividers and other equipment are used to break each room into smaller sections, 6-17. Equipment is not simply lined up along the wall with a wide open area in the middle. Each zone is sort of a mini-room of its own. The equipment is actually used to physically separate one area from another.

Director's Dilemma
A teacher has just been hired to help open a new classroom. She has designed a floor plan that has all of the equipment lined up against the walls. The center of the room is wide open. The teacher feels this will give children lots of room to move around freely. How can you help her to understand the value of zoned areas within a classroom?

6-17 The block shelves help to separate the block-building area from the rest of the room.

Zoned areas help children see what is available to them. Those pieces of equipment and materials that logically belong together are put into the same area. This type of arrangement also helps children organize their play ideas and helps them maintain self-control. They are less likely to be overwhelmed by large open spaces when that space is broken up. When there is no obvious, clear, straight path through the classroom, children will be less inclined to run.

It is helpful to sketch out several possible room arrangements on paper before actually pushing equipment around. Identify locations of doors, windows, electrical outlets, lights, and water supplies. Roughly estimate where the major areas could be placed. Evaluate possible layouts to decide which one might work best.

Good centers are all very similar in the types of equipment and play spaces that they provide for children. The following areas should be provided in each classroom:

- dramatic play area

- block-building area

- library area

- easel/art area

- table activities area

- science and nature area

- music area

- sand and water area

- open area

Dramatic Play Area

The ***dramatic play area*** is designed to encourage and enhance children's pretend play. It includes toys and equipment that have been used for many years to appeal to young children and to stimulate dramatic play, 6-18. This is one of the primary areas of the room. It should be large enough for several children to play together comfortably. The area should be located in a central, yet protected, area where traffic patterns will not cross through it.

This area is often referred to as the *housekeeping area* because it contains many replicas of familiar items found at home. New children to the center will often play in this area first. The child-sized kitchen equipment, such as sink, refrigerator, and range, remind them of home and help them to feel comfortable in the center. Older children will enjoy more realistic, elaborate props such as discarded coffee pots (without the cord), hair dryers, typewriters, etc. Some centers are adding a small file cabinet, desk, and calendar since many children's families have home offices.

The following items are basic to this area:

- child-sized kitchen equipment including sink, range, and refrigerator

- household phones

- dolls, doll buggies, and doll beds

- dress-up clothes

- dishes and plastic food

- a small table and chairs set

6-18 A selection of dress-up clothes help to interest children in the dramatic play area.

Items such as empty food containers or old kitchen utensils can often be added to this area. Care must be taken that sharp, heavy, or rusted items are not included. Items that have held real food must be carefully washed. Utensils and dishes in this area will need to be washed periodically. Children have a tendency to put these things in their mouths during play. Dress-up clothes will need to be replaced or washed regularly. (Hats should be avoided.) This is essential if there is reason to suspect a problem with lice or scabies.

Block-Building Area

A *block-building area* provides space that children can use for creating arrangements built out of blocks. The block-building area should be fairly large. Some experts recommend that it should be almost one-fourth of your classroom space. This will allow several children to build without interference from others. It should also be out of the main traffic patterns of the center to prevent anyone from accidentally knocking things over. A masking tape line on the floor about 18 inches from the shelves can remind children not to build too close to the storage units. This helps other children to reach remaining blocks.

There are many shapes available as part of sets or for purchase individually. Older children will benefit from a larger number and greater variety of block shapes. Enough blocks must be available to allow deep involvement and complicated building projects. The very nature of blocks helps children begin to see the mathematical relationships of the different shapes to each other.

Blocks should be stored lengthwise on shelves so that children can easily see what is available to them. Teachers often put silhouette cut-outs of blocks on the inner backs of the shelves so that children will know where to put away each type of block. The shelves can serve as dividers to separate this space from the larger room.

Teachers must decide how high they will allow children to build. They must also consider whether roofs on block buildings with children inside them will be safe. The age of the children, and whether or not the area is crowded may influence this decision.

Library Area

The *library area* provides children with a quiet space that contains an interesting selection of developmentally appropriate books. Whenever possible, keep this area away from the noisier areas of the room. Keep a selection of 15 to 20 books available that can be changed periodically as needed. Some centers have fluffy rugs and beanbag chairs. Others have a sofa or small table and chairs. A tape or CD player with earphones may also be added. This area should not only provide a variety of developmentally appropriate books, but also serve as a warm, cozy place for a child to snuggle up. Centers are very busy places. Children need a spot where they can get away from the group and have some quiet time to themselves.

If your center has a computer for the children to use, this may be a good place for it. Items like a fish tank or potted plants, that may be enjoyed quietly by one child at a time, are frequently here. If electrical items are in this area, your staff will need to keep a close eye on them during use. It is also important that the books, CD's, computer games, and tapes that are available have been screened by the teaching staff. Materials should be multicultural and should be appropriate in content and attitude for young children.

Easel/Art Area

Every classroom should have an ***easel/art area*** for creative art activities and easel painting. Easel painting should be available to the children every day, 6-19. It gives them a chance to explore dimensions of color, as well as to try out different kinds of paints and papers. Working with paints can be relaxing for children. Painting should be available throughout the free play time so children feel invited, not pressured, to be creative. If two easels are available side-by-side, two children can have a social experience while painting.

The easels and supplies should be located close to a water supply. Because paints sometimes spill, and creativity is sometimes messy, the room arrangement should help make clean-up as easy as possible. Easels should not be placed on carpeted areas unless some washable surface can be put down under them.

Centers should also have a wide variety of art supplies such as paste, scissors, water colors, and clay available. These may be kept on a nearby shelf for the children to use when they wish. A table with a washable surface in this area can be used for various projects. Care must be taken that all materials used are nontoxic.

Table Activities Area

A ***table activities area*** is necessary in each classroom for special activities, mealtimes, or general daily use. Several tables may be in the same area, or separate tables

6-19 Easel painting and play dough are regular activities in the art area.

may be in different parts of the room. Many of the manipulative toys, such as small building blocks, puzzles, or stringing beads, may be used on a table or on the floor. Different shapes and sizes of tables and chairs are available. Generally, the rectangular shape seems to be the most versatile. A teacher seated on one side of the table in the middle is close enough to help all of the children at the table. A small round table is a pleasant addition to the housekeeping area.

Lower tables and chairs are needed for younger children. Some tables are available with adjustable legs that can be raised if needed for older children. Chairs designed especially for toddlers are also available.

The tables must be sturdy and have smooth, washable surfaces. They should be stain resistant so spilled food or messy creative projects will not be a problem. Rounded corners and edges are an important safety design feature.

When tables are placed on a hard, washable floor surface, spills are easy to clean up. If tables are on carpeted floors, you should put a sturdy plastic or vinyl runner under them.

Science and Nature Area

Some centers have a special *science and nature area* where interesting science items are available for children to explore. Prisms, magnifying glasses, an aquarium, live plants or animals, eye droppers, scales, and displays of rocks or leaves are all examples of the types of things found in this area. Items on display should be easily seen at eye level. A table or shelf may be used, but it should be in an easily visible spot where children passing by will stop for a look. A nearby shelf of related science books and a close table for related activities can help bring science into the mainstream of the classroom.

Music Area

Rhythm instruments, tape or CD players, and, possibly even a piano are usually found in a *music area*. An electrical outlet will be necessary if records and tapes are to be used. Autoharps or other musical instruments, such as a guitar or recorder, may be used to provide musical experiences.

Sand and Water Area

The *sand and water area* allows children to participate in activities involving sand and water. Sand and water play are mainstays of child care programs. While not always presented in the same way, all good centers make some provision for them to occur. These activities are soothing and can be used in various ways by the different age groups.

Some centers have sand or water tables. These usually have casters on two legs so they are easily moved. They also come with a cover and a plug in the bottom for ease in cleaning. If a water/sand table is not available, these items can be provided in galvanized or plastic tubs, photographic trays, or dishpans. Whatever you use must, of course, be watertight. Even the sand works better for play if it is damp.

A selection of toys for use in the water and sand will be necessary. Spoons, small shovels and pails, squeeze bottles, measuring cups, floating and sinking toys, and other items make the play more interesting. These objects should be available on a nearby shelf.

The sand and water areas should be near the water supply. This will make it easier for the staff to set up these activities. These activities also need to be placed on a hard surface. Water spilled on a carpet can take a long time to dry. Sand spilled on carpet is difficult to clean up. Place some sort of waterproof covering under these activities if the floor is carpeted. Be sure that no electrical items are near the water and sand play areas.

Open Areas

The *open areas* in a classroom must be considered carefully. Every room needs an area that can be used for lively movement or full group participation. Usually, however, large, wide-open spaces or obvious pathways do not work well in the center. Too much open space invites running or chasing around aimlessly. An area where shelves or tables can be easily moved aside may work better than totally open space. Some classrooms set up indoor climbers, wheel toys, rocking boats, or other large muscle equipment in open areas, 6-20.

The room arrangement may need to be changed throughout the year. If trouble seems to always break out in one particular part of the room, moving that zone to another location may eliminate the problem. If a group has a large number of children who really like block-building, that area may need to be enlarged. If children seem bored because of long, indoor winter days, a new room arrangement could help to renew interest. There are some basic guidelines for room arrangement that can help you in planning, 6-21.

The arrangement of space in the classroom can have a significant effect on the behavior of the children. A room that is well-arranged is like a magnet for children. They will be drawn to the activities and toys that the teachers make available. A poorly designed room will usually have more running, fights over space, and more accidents. It will create additional stress for the children and will be more difficult for teachers to supervise.

6-20 This center has a large room used exclusively for large muscle activities.

Guidelines for Room Arrangement

- Separate quiet areas from noisier areas.

- Keep messy areas, such as art, near a water supply. Areas where electrical equipment, such as tape players will be used, should be placed near outlets and away from water supplies. Unused outlets must have plug covers. Long extension cords should be avoided because they can cause children to trip.

- Arrange the dividers so there are no "runways."

- Put the block-building area where there will not be much traffic passing through it.

- The block-building and dramatic play areas should be large enough for 4 to 5 children to engage in in-depth building and/or play activity.

- Make each area distinct, but don't let it have a feeling of isolation, or the children may be afraid to use it.

- Zone the room so space is well divided, but avoid the cluttered feeling that results from too many little areas.

6-21 These guidelines can help you and your teachers create a successful room arrangement.

⚙ Summary

When choosing a building for a child care center, several factors must be carefully considered. The location must be convenient for families. The building should not be too difficult or expensive to bring into compliance with state licensing standards. It should be free of asbestos and lead-based paint and be designed so it can be kept secure from unauthorized persons. The building must be accessible to people with disabilities and it must be suitable for the types of services to be offered. Programs for older children require larger rooms than those for infants or toddlers. Adequate utilities and storage space must be available.

Modifying or preparing a building for use involves attention to the various areas of the center. Classroom, office, work areas, and restrooms must all be designed for optimal use. Children, parents, and staff will all appreciate a carefully designed center.

Each classroom should be divided into zoned areas. Each area is designed to encourage a specific type of activity. There is a lot of similarity in all quality centers. They typically have similar room areas that include dramatic play, block-building, easel/art, library, and table activities. Science and nature displays and activities, music, sand and water play, and lively large muscle activities must also be accommodated. General guidelines for room arrangement should be followed.

⚙ Terms

accessibility	block-building area
carpet	library area
resilient flooring	easel/art area
fluorescent lighting	table activities area
incandescent lighting	science and nature area
isolation area	music area
zoned area	sand and water area
dramatic play area	open areas

❂ Review

1. List five factors to consider before making a commitment to open a child care center on a specific site.

2. What type of standards are dictated by licensing requirements?

3. How can child care centers be made accessible?

4. Why would a school-age program require a larger room space than an infant or a toddler program?

5. List five factors to consider when choosing a floor treatment for a child care center.

6. What type of paint is recommended for classroom use?

7. What type of lighting do lighting experts recommend for child care centers?

8. How much outdoor space do experts recommend per child?

9. List four factors to consider when setting up an office.

10. How can zoned areas be created?

❂ Applications

1. Ask a real estate agent to take your class through an available building that could be used as a child care center. Write notes about the floor plan. Identify how the rooms could be used in the center. Determine what types of modifications might have to be made to meet licensing standards.

2. Make arrangements to visit several different centers. Look at the general floor plan of the center. Look for the zoned areas in the classrooms. What types of items are used for dividers between the areas?

3. Work with a partner to design an ideal center facility. Indicate where all of the various parts of the center are. Label each classroom according to the age group that will be using it. Show the design to other classmates to get their reaction. Review the designs of others to get more ideas.

4. Ask the director of a modified facility and a director of a program in a building built especially for child care to discuss their buildings with your class. Find out how the directors participated in the design of their centers. How much opportunity did they have for input? What were the challenges each faced in the development of the facility?

Chapter 7
Choosing Equipment and Supplies

After studying this chapter, you will be able to

- identify the criteria you should consider when choosing equipment for your center.

- plan the equipment and supplies needed for the center.

- outline strategies for obtaining needed equipment and supplies.

The equipment and toys in a child care center will be used by many children. They must need to withstand more rough play and continuous use than the toys and equipment used in most homes. For this reason, good quality children's toys and equipment are essential. They can also be very expensive. The toys and equipment that you purchase are an investment in your program. Carefully chosen items are worth their cost. They will last for many years, 7-1.

You will probably not be able to buy everything you would like for the center right away. It is more realistic to plan a list of "start-up" equipment in the same way that you planned a "start-up" budget. Decide what you will need to equip the center with the basic items needed for opening day. Additional items can be purchased later when more money is available.

What Should I Look for When Choosing Equipment?

It is easy to be an impulse buyer when shopping for children's toys. Many items are colorful and cute. They are appealing to the adult eye. Unfortunately, a lot of the toys and

7-1 This puppet show stage can be used by children of different ages. It will provide hours of creative play for many years to come.

137

equipment on the market have limited value in a child care center. There are several principles that can guide you when making equipment and toy purchases.

Developmentally Appropriate

Toys and equipment in a classroom must be developmentally appropriate. This means that they must be matched to the abilities and ages of the children who will use them. It would be a mistake to expect rattles and pull toys to interest a group of four-year-olds. However, infants and toddlers would find those same toys fascinating. The complicated puzzles and board games that challenge school-age children would be frustrating to the average preschooler.

There are many items in the classroom that are appropriate for all of the children in the center. Dolls, easels, puzzles, and books are standard preschool items. However, you will need to examine each carefully. Some doll clothes are easier to fasten than others. Easels are of differing heights. Puzzles can be found with only four freestanding pieces or with 20 small, interlocking pieces. Some books have large, clear pictures and simple prose. Other books have elaborate plots and fewer pictures. You must consider the ages of children who will be using the items. Then decide on the size and level of difficulty that will be developmentally appropriate for the group.

When you are deciding what to buy for the center, you might want to visit another center to see what items the children there prefer. Experienced teachers who are trained in working with young children can provide good suggestions. There are also many books available that describe ages and stages of development. These can be helpful in matching equipment to the needs and interests of the children.

Catalogs from the major equipment suppliers can also give you ideas about which items are available for different age levels. Be careful not to assume that everything in a catalog is appropriate for your particular group. Some suppliers have a good reputation for producing toys that are developmentally appropriate for young children. Other suppliers do not. You may want to check with other directors for their recommendations.

Safe Design and Construction

Safety in design and construction are of primary importance in evaluating a piece of equipment. When judging the safety of a toy, consider the following points:

- What is the toy made of? Will it splinter? Shatter? Rust?

- Does the toy have small pieces that could be swallowed by a young child?

- Are painted items covered with nontoxic and lead-free paint?

- Are there electrical components? If so, is it Underwriter's Laboratory approved?

- Is it sturdy?

- Can fingers be pinched in it?

- Is it made so parts fit together well and any exposed bolts are covered?

- Is it easy to keep clean?

- How is it designed to be used? How else might a child use it?

- Is it developmentally appropriate for the age group who will be using it?

Some toys that are safe for older age groups may not be safe for younger children. Four- and five-year-olds are not likely to swallow small pieces of building toys. A two-year-old might. A toddler could easily fall off of a climber that is perfectly matched for the abilities of a kindergarten group. It can be a real challenge to determine the right pieces of equipment for your center.

Able to Be Used in a Variety of Ways

Developmentally appropriate programs encourage children to think and act in creative ways. Teachers support imaginative uses of equipment and the exploration of objects and ideas. Much of the equipment chosen should be able to be used in a variety of ways by the children. A yellow riding toy that looks like a bus and says "School Bus" on the side can't be used for much else. A plain riding toy without much detail can become anything the child wants it to be.

Adults tend to like replicas with a lot of detail. Children like toys that are plain and nurture more imaginative play. The wooden climbers, housekeeping equipment, riding toys, and blocks found in well-equipped centers have been designed to encourage a variety of creative play ideas.

The same items that stimulate creative play are also important in meeting the needs of a diverse group of children. Not every child will have the same abilities in playing with a particular toy. Some children will be able to make elaborate block buildings, 7-2. Others will only want to stack the blocks up in a pile. Some will make elaborate landscapes in the sandbox, while others will push the sand into heaps. Some will create complicated scenarios in the dramatic play area. Others will simply imitate the actions of a parent. No matter what level they are playing on, the children can all feel good about their play. There is no right or wrong way to play with sand, water, and blocks or to pretend. Younger and older children can all be successful in these types of play.

It is important that your center have toys and materials that allow each child to

7-2 Children's block-building becomes more elaborate as they get older.

experience success in play. It is unrealistic to expect that each will be interested in the same things or will use the equipment in the same way. A three-year-old and a five-year-old with widely different abilities can play happily in the sandbox, water table, block, or housekeeping areas.

Durable

Choose toys that will stand up under heavy use. Fragile toys will not withstand the normal play of a group of young children. Wooden toys should be made of hard woods such as maple or oak. Plastics or vinyls should be thick enough so that holes can't be easily poked in them.

Children like to figure out how a toy works. They are fascinated by toys that can be taken apart and put back together. Movable parts, such as wheels or doors, should work smoothly as designed. Parts that don't work properly are frustrating and may lead to destructive behavior. A well-designed and constructed toy will last longer and provide more satisfying play than an inferior one.

Toys That Reflect Diversity

Children's feelings about themselves and others begin to develop during the preschool years. Their sense of self-esteem and their sensitivity to the feelings and needs of others are affected by their early experiences.

The toys that you choose for the center should include items to which all children can relate. Books and toys should be ones that include interesting stories and pictures of children of different races, sexes, ethnic groups, physical disabilities, and religions. The ideas in the books or pictures should convey respect and dignity. They should not be ones that depict or reinforce such sex-role stereotypes, such as girls always being passive, while boys are shown in active, more interesting roles. Your choice of dolls, flannel board figures, puzzles, stories, and board games should also include children of various ethnic, racial, and religious backgrounds. Selection of all toys and equipment should take into account the need for a diverse array of materials in the center.

When the toys and equipment in the classroom reflect the diverse nature of our population, all children can feel "at home" in the center. Children can find dolls and pictures like themselves. They feel welcome and valued in the center.

Director's Dilemma

A local elderly person has crocheted several dolls for your program. The dolls all have pale skin, blue eyes, and blonde hair. How would you respond to the person's donation? How could you make sure that your program has multicultural dolls available for the children?

Equipment for Children with Disabilities

Children with disabilities will often need some special equipment or modifications to allow them to participate fully in center activities. Swing seats with high backs, extra support, and safety belts are available. Additional railings on lofts can allow an unsteady child to climb the stairs to the top. Some children may need to wear protective helmets all the time to prevent head injuries from falls. Soft sided blocks provide the experience of building with large blocks, but are made of vinyl-covered foam to protect children who fall or bruise easily.

Equipment can be examined in catalogs specializing in items for children with special needs. One of the major preschool equipment companies has developed a special division devoted solely to producing apparatus to support full inclusion of all children into the activities of the center. Some modifications are easily done, such as replacing buttons on doll clothes with Velcro closures.

Many children will come to the center with their own personal items. Wheelchairs, walkers, hearing aids, breathing aids such as nebulizers, or other necessary items usually are supplied by parents. You need to work with parents to be sure that children have what they need during their time in the center. Staff must also be trained in the proper use of all equipment.

Avoiding Toys That Promote Violence

Some commonly available toys are not appropriate for the center. By their very nature, toy guns, knives, whips, grenades, etc. promote violent play. The play associated with these items always becomes rough and aggressive. Even the costumes of popular superheroes, usually with capes and masks, lead to chasing, racing around, and out-of-control behavior. Although many children have these toys at home, they should not be available in the center.

What Equipment Do I Need to Get Started?

Buying equipment for the center requires a great deal of thought. Your decisions will affect the quality of your program, the enthusiasm of your teachers, and the behavior of the children. A well-equipped program provides more interesting things for children to do. Teachers are encouraged to plan a greater variety of activities. Experts support the idea that during free play, children should have five choices of activities/areas available to them. Behavior and morale problems stemming from boredom are less likely to occur in rooms with lots of interesting things to do.

Equipment for the Children

Quality programs usually are similar in the type of equipment that is available to the children. While buildings and room arrangement may differ, each classroom is zoned. Each zone or area of the classroom requires certain pieces of basic equipment.

Be sure to choose a selection of toys for each area. Don't put a lot of money into blocks if you will have nothing left for the dramatic play area. Don't buy expensive dolls if there will be no money for books or riding toys. Make sure that each area is attractive and interesting for children. The activities that occur in all areas are valuable and provide different types of learning experiences. Remember that each year your center operates successfully, you will be able to add additional items to the classrooms.

Director's Dilemma
The owner of an old nursery school is planning to retire. She has offered to sell you all of her equipment and supplies for your new center. Should you buy? What things will you need to consider before deciding to make the purchase?

Classroom Equipment

Each zoned area should have enough equipment to make it interesting and attractive. See the chart in 7-3 for a list of toys and equipment for each area. It is very important to have duplicates of small toys, such as telephones, doll carriages, and plastic animals, 7-4. This encourages children to talk or play with each other. It also prevents fights over sharing.

Basic Equipment for a Preschool Classroom	
Dramatic Play Area	**Art Area**
Child-sized kitchen equipment including stove, sink with plastic pan for water, refrigerator	Easels—at least two
	Powdered tempera paint and powdered laundry soap for thickening
Doll beds – including those big enough for a child to climb into, as well as doll-sized	Finger paint
	Table with washable surface and chairs
A variety of girl and boy dolls including some with multicultural features. Some should be washable while others should be soft, cuddly types (also washable by adults).	Shelves to hold materials
	Long-handled brushes with various widths of bristles
Doll clothes and storage dresser or chest	Plastic paint jars or buckets that fit easel paint holder
Doll carriages—one big enough for a child to sit in	Children's right-and left-handed scissors
Doll high chairs	Smocks to protect children's clothing
Child-sized rocking chair	Nontoxic paste and white glue
Child-sized ironing board, toy iron, clothesline and clothespins, mops, brooms	Variety of papers—newsprint, construction paper of manila and assorted colors
Child-sized pots and pans, dishes, coffee/tea pot, eating utensils	Finger paint paper, rolls of brown wrapping paper, art tissue paper (Buy enough paper so children can use it freely.)
Selection of women's and men's dress-up clothes and provision for storage, such as a chest or child-sized clothes closet	Art clay and playdough
	Selection of washable, nonscented markers, crayons, colored chalk, stamps for printing
Props for other types of dramatic play, i.e., post office, health clinic, grocery store, beauty shop, restaurant, pet store, etc. These props should be in storage and added to the classroom when appropriate.	Rolling pins, cookie cutters
	Selection of wallpaper sample books, pieces of fabric with different textures, cellophane in various colors, and colored pipe cleaners
Small table and chairs	Drying rack
	Shelves—large enough so children can see what materials are available for use

(continued)

7-3 This list shows that a variety of items should be purchased for each area of the center.

Basic Equipment for a Preschool Classroom (continued)

Reading and Listening Area

Selection of 15 to 20 classic books—supplemented by regular visits to local library. Let each teacher choose some books for classroom to match planned activities or themes.

Comfortable chairs, couch, or pillows

Small table and chairs

Display shelf for books

Tape, record, or CD player

Computer and printer with developmentally appropriate software

Block-Building Area

Set of unit blocks matched to the age and number of children in group (Older preschoolers need larger number of blocks and more diversity in available shapes.)

Small vehicles that will fit on unit block-sized roadways

Plastic or wooden people, animals, shrubbery, and trees proportioned for play with blocks

Small road signs

Enough shelves to hold blocks lengthwise and for use as dividers to separate this area from the rest of the room

Table Area for Manipulative Toys

Selection of wooden, inlay puzzles varying in difficulty from 4 to 20 pieces

Peg - Boards with pegs at least 1 inch long

Stringing beads and laces with a variety of shapes and colors

Table-sized building blocks

Dollhouse, furniture, and miniature people

Miniature construction sets of interlocking, plastic units

Matching games, nesting items, color cone

Indoor Large Muscle Items

Rocking boat

Indoor climber

Selection of riding toys—trucks, cars, fire trucks, tractors, trains, planes, etc.

Balance beam

Miscellaneous Classroom Items

Water or sand table and accessories

Puppets and puppet stage

Soft, washable, stuffed toys

Rhythm band instruments—maracas, tambourines, rhythm sticks, sandpaper blocks, traingles, bongo drums, jingle bells, cymbals

Woodworking equipment - workbench with vise and clamps, screwdrivers, pliers, rasp, hammer, file, saw, nails in various sizes and types—kept in sorted containers, sandpaper, safety goggles

Adult-sized rocking chair

Cots or mats for children's naps

Additional tables to seat 6 children (18 to 22 inches high depending on size of children)

Chairs—one for each child and staff member, (10 to 14 inches high depending on size of children)

Bulletin boards at children's eye level

Aquarium, pet cage

Clock

Telephone

7-3 (continued)

7-4 Duplicates of small toys encourage play among children and help to prevent fighting.

7-5 Climbing equipment often becomes the setting for dramatic play.

Play Yard Equipment

Outdoor play yards should be an extension of the classroom. The equipment and design of the yard should provide opportunities for a variety of types of play. While much of the emphasis is on large muscle play, the yard can provide new ideas for dramatic play, art, science, block play, etc., 7-5. The outdoor play space should be roughly divided into zoned areas. Areas may include

- space for climbing
- space for riding toys and trikes
- a dramatic play area
- a flat area for block-building
- a protected, shady area for tables, easels, etc.
- space designed for sand, water play, and gardening
- open space for free movement

Quiet areas should be separated from areas where more lively play will usually occur. Differences in elevation, for example, a small hill, can add interest.

A storage shed can be used to protect smaller items that are not permanently installed. Some items might be kept outside during certain seasons, then used indoors when outdoor play is not possible. For example, large, hollow blocks are often moved indoors if space permits. Easels, art supplies, and doll equipment are also frequently moved, 7-6.

Manufacturers are constantly developing new outside equipment that can be viewed in catalogs, in showrooms, or at conference exhibit areas. A list of traditional outdoor equipment needed for a group of preschool children is give in 7-7.

Cubbies

Cubbies, a commonly used term for lockers that hold children's coats and possessions, are frequently found along the sides of the hallways. If the classroom is large enough, they may be placed inside the room near the door. Ideally, there will be a separate cubby for each child.

In child care, most items must be shared, yet, young children need a place in the center they can call their own. The cubby is a place for keeping treasured items and for storing creative work. It also holds coats, hats, and boots.

Cubbies or lockers can take up a fair amount of space. However, they have many advantages. First, they provide each child with a personal space. A cubby, identified with a child's name, gives a sense of ownership. The cubby can be a private spot in the hustle and bustle of the center. The child knows special items brought from home can be safely left in the cubby. Precious art work can be placed there so it doesn't get mixed up with someone else's when it is ready to go home.

Most commercially-available cubbies/lockers are about 50 inches high and are sold in units of 2 to 5 cubbies each. The most common design has each individual locker divided into

- a top shelf to hold a tote box or other items

- a large middle section with hooks for hanging coats or bookbags

- a bottom shelf, slightly deeper, for a child to sit on, with space underneath to store boots

The cubbies are typically about 11 inches deep on top, with the bottom shelf section about 14 inches deep. This design makes the unit more sturdy. Each unit should be attached to the wall for safety, 7-8.

Cubby units are expensive to buy, but those made of hard wood will last for many years. They

7-6 The water table in this center is moved outdoors on warm days.

Recommended Outdoor Equipment
Wheeled toys
Age-appropriate climbers installed in concrete
Several large wooden packing boxes
Set of large hollow blocks
Sandbox with protective cover and sand tools
Gardening equipment and digging toys
Heavy-duty swing set installed in concrete
Medium-size wagon and wheelbarrow
Watering cans, pails, large painter's paintbrushes for water painting
Tubs for water play and a variety of plastic tubes, short pieces of hose, etc.
Balls
Play tunnel

7-7 Outdoor equipment should be usable in a variety of ways.

7-8 The cubbies not only hold coats and other items, they also give children a space of their very own in the center.

7-9 A local volunteer created this cubby arrangement.

are also items with a relatively simple design. You may be able to find someone with the woodworking skills to make the units for you, 7-9.

If you cannot afford cubbies, you will need to figure out some other way to provide private, personal space for each child's coat and other important items. One center with little money used a separate folding chair labeled with each child's name. Boots went underneath, coats were hung over the back, and the seat served as a shelf for artwork and other special possessions. While not as attractive or orderly as lockers, the chair arrangement worked adequately until the center had money to purchase commercially-produced cubbies.

From a teacher's point of view, cubbies are valuable also. When each child has a cubby, belongings are less likely to get misplaced. It is easier to keep the room organized when items can be quickly placed in a child's cubby, 7-10. Messages to parents are also not as likely to be lost if they are attached to or placed in the cubby.

It may not be possible to buy cubbies when you are first opening your center. However, they are a worthwhile purchase to consider for the future.

Tables, Chairs, and Shelves

Every classroom needs a selection of tables, chairs, and shelves. The number of these items you need will depend on the size of the room and the number of children enrolled.

Tables and chairs vary in height and shape. Tables designed for preschoolers vary from 18 inches to 22 inches high. Three-year-olds need the lower tables, while four- and five-year-olds need the taller ones. Chairs for three-year-olds should have the seats 10 inches from the floor. Four- and five-year-olds are usually ready for a seat height of 12 to 14 inches. Toddler chairs, especially designed for stability, are also available and are usually purchased in heights from 5 to 8 inches, 7-11.

Some tables are designed to be used with others, while some are designed for stand-alone use. Whatever shape you choose, the table tops should be hard enough to withstand vigorous use. They should also be easily washable and made of a material that is stain-resistant and nonporous. Rounded corners on tables can help to prevent injury if a child bumps or falls against them.

Some chairs and tables have legs that can be adjusted for different heights. This is a desirable feature if you anticipate different ages of children using the equipment over the years. The chairs should be designed so they are sturdy and don't tip easily. Stackable chairs are convenient if you expect to move them often or get them out of the way.

Shelving units are also necessary equipment in a center. They are used to hold and organize items. Most teachers also use shelving units as room dividers. The units separate one area of the classroom from another, yet are low enough to allow for easy supervision.

Shelving units come in many shapes and sizes. You probably need a variety for your classrooms. Some are perfect for holding books, while deeper ones may be better for storing blocks. Shelves on casters are easy to move. If you use a space that is shared with other organizations, shelves that fold together and lock shut will protect your items.

Nap Equipment

Full-day programs require equipment for children to nap. Many half-day centers also schedule a rest time. Cots or mats are used by most programs to provide a clean, comfortable place for children to lie down. They may also be necessary to meet licensing regulations.

Cots are resting surfaces held off of the floor by a frame with legs. These are available in 4- to 12-inch heights. Consider the ages of the children who will be using the cots when deciding what height to buy. The sleeping area is usually made of a washable, woven vinyl or similar fabric stretched across the frame. This surface can be easily wiped off. Canvas coverings are also available. Check to be sure they are easily

7-10 Individual tote boxes can be used for each child's belongings.

7-11 These toddler-sized chairs are designed to prevent accidents that might occur because of young children's limited skills in balance and coordination.

washable. Cots for young children are designed to be lightweight and stackable. This provides for out-of-the-way storage. Cots are a good choice if your center has drafty or cold floors.

Folding *mats* provide a padded, vinyl resting surface that is sold in one- or two-inch thicknesses. These mats are placed directly on the floor. They work well in classrooms where the floors are warm and not drafty. Mats sold through companies that specialize in child care products are usually designed to fold into thirds or fourths. They are lightweight and can be moved or stacked up easily. Before buying, be sure that the mats are sturdy and will not tear. They should also be easy to wipe clean.

Cots and mats available today are flame-retardant and often mildew-resistant. You should check for these characteristics when choosing nap equipment. Fitted sheets and blankets, sized for the cots and mats, are used in many centers. If your center provides these items, you will need to make plans to have them washed regularly. Some centers require that parents provide blankets, small sheets, and pillows. Parents are required to take these items home weekly for laundering.

Audio-Visual Equipment

Almost all centers have some type of audio-visual equipment in each classroom. The most common items found are tape, CD, and/or record players. These items are used frequently by teachers.

Some centers are also purchasing video tape cameras and players to tape interesting activities in the centers. Parents often enjoy seeing tapes of their children at play. Demonstration tapes can also be for use in community or training presentations. Centers that are vulnerable to vandalism may use video cameras as part of their security system.

Still cameras are frequently found in the center. Also, digital cameras used with computers are becoming popular. Children usually love to have their pictures taken. Interesting bulletin boards and other projects can be developed out of photos taken in the center. Some programs have even provided simple cameras for the children themselves. Before any pictures or tapes are taken in the center, photo permission forms should be signed by the parents. These should be kept on file.

Equipment for Other Parts of the Center

Besides the classrooms, there are other parts of the center that must be equipped before you can operate. The office areas must be ready to handle program inquiries and enrollment, as well as to maintain all records. The kitchen area must be ready for food preparation and storage. Facilities for storage should be set up for efficiency so inventory is easy to track and staff can find what they need. Maintenance equipment must be ready as soon as children are in the center.

Office

The office of a child care program must be equipped with standard office equipment. The larger your program is, the more complex your office tasks will be. Additional office equipment will be needed. A small program might only need one desk, chair, shelf, file cabinet, and computer. A more elaborate office will need workstations for several people. Tables, computers, a copier, and a phone system become essential in a large, complex program. See 7-12 for a list of office equipment.

Time and money will be saved if your office staff has the equipment necessary to carry out responsibilities. Trying to add long rows of figures without a calculator, or submitting handwritten reports may cost you time and accuracy. Well-organized, accurate and professional-looking reports, newsletters, and financial records are important. They contribute to your program's reputation as a careful, conscientious, professional operation.

Director's Dilemma
You are preparing to order office and art supplies. Several catalogs have been used to make up a list of needed items. Before ordering, you discover that a local business also carries similar products. What do you think would be the advantages to ordering the items from the local business? What would be the advantages to ordering from the catalog? What would be the disadvantages of both?

Kitchen

Another area that must be equipped is the kitchen. If your center will only be preparing snacks, the kitchen will not need much equipment. However, if you are preparing hot lunches and full breakfasts, more extensive equipment will be required. A list of possible kitchen equipment is given in 7-13.

As with the office equipment, the larger your program is, the more kitchen equipment and supplies you will need. You must determine whether you can get along with regular household equipment or if you will need to invest in commercial-type appliances. Commercial quality equipment is considerably more expensive, but it may be necessary for large quantity meal production.

Storage

Every center needs a storage area for items that are not in current use. Items in storage must be visible, organized, and easily reachable if they are to be used by the

Office Equipment	
Desks and chairs	Locking cabinet for supplies
Shelves	Mailbox system
Files cabinets with locks	Bulletin board
Phones	Bookshelves and bookends
Computer and printer	Calculator with print-out tape
Copier	Paper shredder
Chairs for visitors	Key holder for organizing keys
Garbage cans	Scissors
Paper cutter	Supplies (stationery, tape, paper clips,
Desk lamps	etc.)

7-12 Basic office equipment is essential for use in organizing and administering a center.

Kitchen Equipment		
Large Appliances	**Small Appliances**	**Small Equipment**
Range	Toaster	Bottle openers
Refrigerator/freezer	Can opener	Jar opener
Dishwasher	Griddle	Dishes
Washer and dryer (possibly)	Blender	Pots and pans
Microwave oven	Mixer	Utensils
	Coffee maker	Sealable storage containers
	Food processor	

7-13 The size and amount of kitchen equipment needed will depend on whether your center will be offering food service.

staff. Clear plastic boxes, for instance, make contents easily visible. Labels on boxes and shelves will encourage children and staff to return items to their proper location. Some centers have tall, narrow, vertical shelves to hold such awkward items as saucer sleds, trays, or poster board. Large, heavy cardboard boxes can also become holders for picture files or packets with flannel board stories. An outdoor storage shed will be necessary for trikes and wagons. For a center with many records, extra file cabinets will be required. If confidential records are being kept, locking cabinets will be necessary.

Maintenance Equipment

Specific equipment is also necessary for keeping the center clean and in good repair. See 7-14. This list may be fairly simple if your center is relatively new and maintenance free. While you will need cleaning supplies, your equipment expenses in a new center may be relatively minor.

If your building is an old one, however, you may have to purchase more expensive equipment. Floor polishers may be necessary if your floors are covered with tile or linoleum. A carpet cleaner may be desirable if your rooms are all carpeted.

Maintenance Equipment and Supplies	
Large bucket on wheels	Brooms and mops
Simple tool set	Supplies (rags, papers towels, and toilet paper)
Vacuum sweeper	Soap and cleaning/disinfectant solutions
Spray bottles	Replacement bulbs
Toilet bowl brushes and plunger	

7-14 This list of maintenance equipment identifies what is needed to keep the center in clean and sanitary condition.

If you are responsible for the outdoor area, you may have to make more extensive purchases. Will you be responsible for lawn care or snow removal? If so, you will need to purchase a lawn mower, snow shovels, etc.

Do you have to take care of general maintenance on the building? For work that must only be done occasionally, you may wish to simply hire someone to take care of it. This could be less expensive than buying all the maintenance equipment and hiring a custodian yourself. It is also possible to hire a janitorial service. They would provide all equipment and supplies used in maintaining the building. The cost of these supplies would be built into the fee charged by the service provider.

Director's Dilemma

Sales representatives from various equipment and supply companies have been urging you to buy their products. You don't really know anything about any of their companies. How could you find out more information about each company's reputation and the quality of their products?

How Can I Get What I Need for the Center?

Setting up a center for the first time can be a daunting task. The amount of equipment and supplies to be obtained represent a major financial commitment. You must analyze various ways of obtaining what you need. Some ways will be more expensive than others.

There are three ways to obtain the items you'll need. Some types of equipment are best purchased from companies that specialize in the development and manufacture of preschool equipment. Many items are not difficult to find and can be purchased in your community. Finally, some items that are useful in the center can be made for you.

Using Major Suppliers

Some companies specialize in the manufacture of toys and equipment designed especially for child care centers. They offer items that are basic to a good program, yet are not easily available from local sources. For example, the calibrated unit blocks needed for preschool settings cannot be found in most typical retail stores. Reputable companies produce developmentally appropriate, durable items that can endure the hard play of many children. The suppliers guarantee their products and provide replacement if an item is defective. Some of the items you should consider purchasing from a specialized company are listed in 7-15.

Some suppliers buy equipment and supplies from a variety of sources and make them available through one catalog. If you are dealing with a company with which you are not familiar, consider the purchase agreement terms carefully. Can you return the items if they are not satisfactory? Are the descriptions of the items the same as in the catalogs of other companies? Compare the price of an item from one catalog to another. Is the price different? Why? Sometimes an item looks the same as one available from another source, but it may actually be an inferior copy.

Items to Buy from Major Suppliers	
Child-sized tables and chairs	Rocking boat
Wooden riding toys	Doll carriages
Wooden climbers	Speciality shelves for blocks and books
Housekeeping area items (stove, refrigerator, sink)	Tricycles
	Sturdy dolls
Unit block set	Multi-cultural dolls and books
Hollow block set	Equipment for children with special needs
Coat cubbies	Playground items
Water table	Workbench
Miniature people and animals	Train set

7-15 Items designed to be sturdy enough for use by many children every day are available from companies who specialize in equipment for group care settings.

Major suppliers will add you to their mailing lists upon request. Many of them also set up exhibits of their products at national or regional conferences. You can also visit other centers to examine their equipment and supplies.

Using Local Sources

Many of the items you will need for your center can be purchased locally. You can shop at discount stores, flea markets, and outlet centers. Garage sales and thrift shops can be economical sources for some items. Most of the items listed in 7-16 can be purchased in your community.

Items to Find Locally	
For the Classroom	**For the Office**
Child-sized pots and pans	Office equipment
Child-sized dishes and utensils	Office supplies
Dress-up clothes	Furniture
Scarves, tablecloths	**For the Kitchen**
Doll clothes	Pots and pans
Bulletin boards	Storage containers
Some art supplies	Dishes and utensils for meals
Magnets	Appliances
Toy cash registers	
CD, Tape and/or record player	
Soft items (pillows, stuffed toys, etc.)	
Tools and wood for woodworking area	
CDs, books, tapes	

7-16 An alert shopper can find many appropriate items for the center from local sources.

Compare prices and quality when making decisions. You may be able to obtain donations of items for your program. One high school teacher who was opening a child care center in her family and consumer sciences program recruited help from her high school students. She made up a list of items that families were likely to have, such as books, dolls, colorful magazines, and old clothes. She included the list with a letter asking for donations to help get the center started. Many items needed for the program were obtained this way.

Items That Can Be Made

It may be possible to have some items made for your program. For example, one industrious group of vo-tech students started a small business making sturdy outdoor climbers. Several of these were sold to a local child care program. An item made locally may cost more than one purchased through a catalog from a company that makes large quantities of the item. Price consideration is necessary before making any commitments.

Doll outfits, dress-up clothes, easels, puzzles, playhouses, and cubbies are items that can be made for the center. These items can often be made by volunteers. Parents, teachers, club members, or retirees may be willing to make equipment or supplies for your center, 7-17.

Keep a "Wish List"

Be sure to keep catalogs on hand. Have a "wish list" of items you would like to have for the center. Sometimes extra money becomes available that you did not anticipate. If you are funded by grants, money that is not used by other projects may become available. Your program may receive a special appropriation or donation. Often this money has to be spent very quickly.

When you have catalogs and an idea of needed items, you can prepare orders very quickly. If you have to request catalogs, survey teachers, and then prepare orders, the process will take longer. You are more likely to make mistakes and order things you don't really want if you are caught by surprise.

7-17 This rocking horse, made by a volunteer, has been a favorite for many years.

⚙ Summary

Equipment for the center should be developmentally appropriate. There must be a "match" between the age and interests of the children and the toys that are available to them. Toys and equipment must be safe and sturdy enough to allow for vigorous play. Items that may shatter, splinter, pinch, or be painted with lead-based paint should not be purchased. Exposed bolts should be covered so they cannot scratch or snag children's clothing.

Most equipment in the center should be designed to be used in a variety of different ways. Children of different ages, abilities, and interests need equipment that can be used according to their needs. A variety of multicultural dolls, books, puppets, and pictures help each child to feel welcome in the center. Multicultural materials also help children in developing positive attitudes toward diversity.

Equipment for the center should be durable. The items in a center will have frequent use by many children. The equipment should also be easy to clean and maintain.

Centers need a variety of equipment and materials for each area of the classroom. Spending all of the budgeted money on one type of equipment will mean that other areas might be shortchanged. A basic selection of toys for each area is necessary to get started.

It is also necessary to buy equipment and supplies for the office, kitchen, and entry areas of the center. Maintenance supplies, equipment, and storage facilities must also be considered.

Several reputable suppliers of equipment for child care programs offer sales through catalogs. Some items designed especially for use in child care programs should probably be bought from these suppliers. Some suppliers specialize in art or office supplies. Many items that are available locally may not be suitable for programs with large numbers of children. You will need to consider which items are best bought locally and which will need to be purchased from specialty vendors. Garage sales, flea markets, and donations are all possible sources of auxiliary items for your center. You may be able to find someone who can make some items for you.

Always maintain a supply of catalogs and a list of needed equipment and supplies. Sometimes extra money becomes available. It may have to be spent quickly. Being aware of what your program needs can allow you to make purchasing decisions quickly.

⚙ Terms

cubbies
cots
mats

○ Review

1. Why are good quality children's toys and equipment essential for a child care center?

2. List five questions you should ask yourself when judging the safety of a toy.

3. Why do children tend to like toys that are plain?

4. How many choices of activities/areas do experts recommend are available to children during free time?

5. Why should duplicates of some toys be available?

6. Why do teachers value cubbies in a child care center?

7. Why are adjustable legs on tables and chairs a desirable feature?

8. Besides the classrooms, what other parts of the center must be equipped before you can operate?

9. List three ways to obtain the items you'll need for a child care center.

10. Why should you keep a "wish list" of things you would like to have for the center?

○ Applications

1. Visit a preschool classroom. Using the equipment list in 7-3, what item would you suggest the program purchase to add to the classroom?

2. Identify 15 different pieces of equipment you would like for your center. Use catalogs from at least two major suppliers of child care equipment. Compare these 15 items to see what they cost, whether they are exactly the same or made differently. Do you think these differences in items would matter? Compare the total cost of buying from each catalog.

3. Using your knowledge of your community, create a list of items you could obtain locally. Also, create a list of items that could be made by someone or some group that you know.

The staff you hire for your center will have an impact on the children and your program.

Chapter 8
Selecting Appropriate Staff

After studying this chapter, you will be able to

- ❂ develop an organizational structure.
- ❂ determine staff needs.
- ❂ prepare job descriptions.
- ❂ recruit qualified job applicants.
- ❂ interview and select qualified staff members.
- ❂ develop an orientation plan to help new staff members begin work successfully.

The quality of your program will be determined, in large part, by the skill of your staff. Well-trained teachers are essential to a successful program. Child care is a *labor-intensive* field, meaning "people power" is the most important part of the program structure. Without a good staff, your program cannot be a quality center for children.

Facilities and equipment alone are not enough to provide for children's needs. Your budget will reflect the major role of the staff. Staff salaries will likely utilize 65 to 90 percent of a typical center's budget.

What Kind of Person Do You Want to Work in Your Center?

Staffing the program is one of the most important parts of the director's job. It takes time. Good staff may be hard to find. Hiring top-notch employees is a process that involves both careful screening and intuition.

Desirable Characteristics of Persons Working with Children and Families

Working with children and families requires a special type of person. Each staff member's personality will have an impact on the program. An encounter with an irritable, critical individual can set the tone for the day for other staff, children, and family members. It can also cause parents to consider whether this is a place they want their children to be. Those who think only of themselves and convey a sense of self-righteousness cannot give the warm care and support that children need. They also can create an unpleasant atmosphere for other staff. For a successful, happy program, select staff members who have the following characteristics:

- kindness

- nurturance

- gentleness

- nonjudgmental

- tolerant of differences

- accepting of mistakes

- mature judgment

- sense of humor

- knowledgeable about children's development

- enthusiasm for learning

- open to new ideas

- positive sense of self-esteem

- honesty and reliability

Kindness

Children need to be treated with kindness. The world can be a scary place. Children feel secure with adults who treat them kindly, 8-1. Adults who are tender in their interactions with children are usually kind in their dealings with adults also. They go out of their way to reassure and help others. This characteristic is a necessity in the personality of anyone working with children and families.

Nurturance

Being able to nurture others and help them grow and develop is another necessary characteristic of program staff. It requires being able to support children in their efforts, to applaud their successes, and to soothe them in their disappointments. Adults who are nurturant are able to leave their own problems outside the door. They can give love and warmth that children need whenever it is needed.

Gentleness

Staff members must treat children gently, both physically and emotionally. Washing a toddler's face, helping a child get into a heavy snowsuit, or soothing injured feelings should all be done with gentleness. Not only are children appreciative of the sensitivity and often more willing to cooperate, they also have a role model to guide them as they interact with others.

Nonjudgmental

Each individual has a set of values and beliefs that guide behavior. It is sometimes difficult to accept others whose values and beliefs are different. Working with families requires the ability to avoid criticizing or judging others who may view the world differently. A staff member who is always critical of others and behaves with a superior attitude will quickly be avoided by others.

8-1 Children can trust adults who are kind to them.

Tolerant of Differences

Staff must also be aware of the need to maintain a tolerance of differences. The center is a busy place with many people. It is common to have a mix of such factors as personality types, clothing styles, food preferences, attitudes, and lifestyles in the people who visit or work in the center. Children's families may be quite different from those of the teachers and staff. You will want to select staff who are able to work comfortably with a diverse array of families, children, and other center personnel, 8-2.

Accepting of Mistakes

Children are beginners in every aspect of life. They are just beginning to know how to control their bodies, interact socially with others, solve problems, and learn all they will need to know. A good staff member encourages children and supports their efforts to learn. Everyone makes mistakes occasionally. Adults also need to work in an atmosphere that is relaxed and free from fear of criticism.

Mature Judgment

Every day, teachers are required to make decisions about how to handle situations in the classroom. For example, they must help children learn to deal with conflicts and take turns while playing with others. Teachers must know when to give extra love and support to a child who is upset. Staff members must also be able to judge how to handle conflicts with other

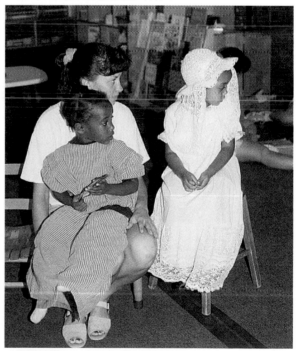

8-2 Staff in a child care center must be comfortable and supportive of all children.

staff. Mature judgment includes knowing when to stick up for yourself and when to back off.

Sense of Humor

A kindly sense of humor is helpful to anyone working in the center. It helps children to relax. It also helps them to know that the adults here are fun, they are not just waiting to pounce on mistakes. Gentle humor can help defuse confrontations between children and adults as well as between the adults themselves. It can help everyone keep the day's events in perspective and minimize stress, 8-3.

Sarcasm, a tendency to ridicule, laughing at others, and/or using a joking style to embarrass or attack someone are not examples of gentle humor. They are hurtful and destructive, and are characteristics to avoid when hiring staff members.

Knowledgeable about Children's Development

Teachers must have an education that provides a good working knowledge of children's development. This allows them to plan activities that are developmentally appropriate and matched to the needs of each individual child and the group as a whole. Teachers who possesses this specialized training are able to create a quality day-to-day experience for the children. Current research clearly shows that trained staff provide a better program for children than staff with no training. All staff members need to have knowledge about the developmental characteristics of the children in the center. Everyone who comes in contact with the children should have some understanding of their needs and behavior patterns.

Enthusiasm for Learning

Good staff members are always eager to learn more. They find the world an interesting place, full of new things to explore. An office staff member who is enthusiastic about mastering a new computer system is an asset to your program. The aide who wants to know more about children's development may have the potential to become a teacher. Teachers who are always looking for new ideas and learning more about child development pass that enthusiasm for learning on to the children. The children, in turn, model themselves after these important adults in their lives.

8-3 A good sense of humor is an important asset for staff members

Openness to New Ideas

As a director, you are aware of the need to be alert to new ideas for your program. The staff you hire should also have an openness to new ideas. This may be as simple as a willingness to try a new room arrangement. It may involve acceptance of a move to a different classroom. In a growing program, change is inevitable. Children grow old enough to leave the program and new ones arrive. Staff may change. The needs of the program, in terms of adding new classrooms or providing additional services, may require that all staff members need to adjust to changes and try new ideas. The staff member who approaches new ideas with confidence and enthusiasm is pleasant to work with and helps others. The individual who complains to everyone and resists change is a negative influence that can stall or make progress difficult.

Positive Sense of Self-Esteem

Many of the characteristics already discussed are related to *positive self-esteem,* or the knowledge that you are a good and worthy individual. Positive self-esteem supports your sense that you can be a successful person and that what you think and do matters to others. Being able to relax with a gentle sense of humor, having an openness to new ideas, and the ability to deal with others in a nonjudgmental, tolerant, and accepting manner, are all linked to a positive sense of self-esteem. Staff hired for the center are more likely to possess all of the other characteristics if they have a positive view of themselves.

Honesty and Reliability

Anyone hired to work in the center must be honest and reliable. You must be able to depend on staff to be at work on time. They must complete records carefully and

honestly, 8-4. Some staff are responsible for handling money. Others maintain the waiting list for enrollment and interact with parents. Some positions may require filling out time sheets for wage calculation. Teachers must be role models for the children and staff in their classrooms. The center cannot function effectively if some staff members are deceptive and dishonest. Parents will not choose a center if they are aware that essential staff are not at work on time. Honesty and reliability are essential requirements for all jobs in the program.

One of the most important tasks of your job as director is the selection of staff. You must consider the positions that you need for the center. Then develop a plan for how to find the appropriate individuals for each position.

How Do I Develop an Organizational Structure?

Before you make a commitment to hire anyone, you must consider how your program will be organized. If you have a small half-day

8-4 This staff member is trusted and relied on by the director of the program.

nursery school program, you may need only one or two employees, 8-5. If your program is large and will involve many employees, a more sophisticated level of organization will be necessary.

In a small center, one person may handle several sets of responsibilities. For example, you may be a teacher/director. Some of your duties will be teaching duties and others will be administrative in nature. In larger programs, there may be several people who handle strictly administrative tasks. A totally different group of employees will be working with the children in the classrooms.

Organizational Structure

Program staff can be grouped under three categories: classroom staff, administrative staff, and support personnel. *Classroom staff* are those people who work directly with the children. Staff in each classroom can be viewed as team members. The teacher is the leader, organizer, and planner for that team. Many classrooms have an assistant head teacher, who helps with decision making in the classroom and can take over if the head teacher must leave. There may also be several aides. They play a valuable role by providing assistance that helps the classroom run smoothly.

Administrative staff are those employees with organizational and planning skills who provide direction for the total program. They seek funds, pursue licensing, recruit and enroll children, and handle other managerial duties. Administrative staff do not usually work directly in the classroom.

The third group includes *support personnel*, which includes secretaries, bookkeepers, receptionists, cooks, van drivers, and maintenance staff. Their work provides essential support to program activities. They help others do their jobs.

When organizing your program, it is helpful to map out an *organizational chart*. This chart gives you a visual image that indicates job titles and the lines of authority within your program, 8-6. The organizational chart tells you how many job classifications there are in the program. It also shows which staff positions are responsible for overseeing others. Employees can see how their positions fit into the overall organization. In general, positions on the higher levels of the chart involve additional responsibility and training. Typically, those positions that are higher on the organizational chart are characterized by the following:

- require more training and/or experience
- demand more planning and organizational abilities
- include greater responsibilities
- have more authority
- have more flexibility in when and where the work is done
- are responsible for lower-level positions
- have higher salaries

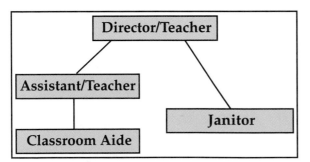

8-5 An organizational chart for a half-day program is very simple.

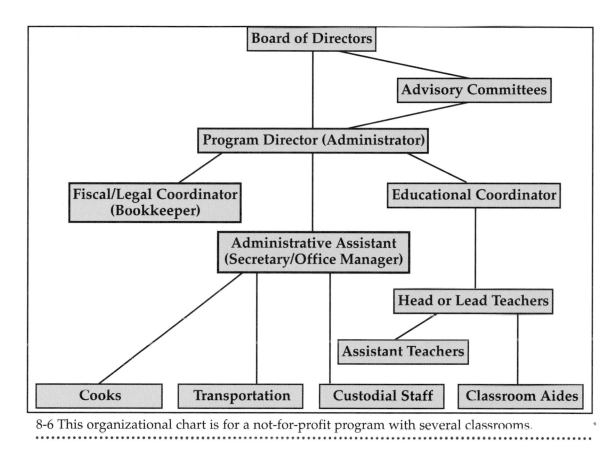

8-6 This organizational chart is for a not-for-profit program with several classrooms.

Those positions that are near the bottom of the chart usually require little training or decision making. They also earn the lower salaries.

Factors That Influence Your Organizational Chart

There are a number of factors that will influence your program's organizational pattern. Each of these must be considered when deciding the best way to organize your program.

Size of Program

The size of your program plays a basic role in how your program is organized. In small programs, each element is usually simpler to operate. There are fewer children to be enrolled, a smaller staff, less recordkeeping, and a less complex budget. Tasks that would each require one staff member in a larger program may be consolidated. Each person may be able to fulfill more than one task. You, the director, may handle staffing, enrollment, and budgeting. Some directors serve as teachers if there are part-day groups. The bookkeeper, secretary, and receptionist duties may also be combined in small programs.

Larger programs are more complicated. The staff must be larger to provide care for larger numbers of children. Although the individual teacher's job does not change much as the program gets larger, there will be a need for more classrooms and more teachers. Recordkeeping on bigger numbers of children and staff takes more time. With larger numbers of employees, you will need additional help to provide training, monitor classroom programming, deal with concerns and problems, and conduct regular evaluations. There may be a need for additional staff in middle management or supervisory roles to whom you can delegate these tasks.

Program organization should be designed to group components of the program logically together. Bigger programs will need more staff in each area, although the areas of organization may be the same as in smaller programs.

Types of Services Offered

The types of services offered will affect the organizational structure of your program. If you offer only full-day child care, your organization will be simpler than if you also offer before-and-after school care and infant/toddler care.

If your center provides transportation, has affiliated family child care providers, and offers parent education classes, these will need to be shown in the organizational chart, 8-7. You may choose to make a separate division for each program component. If so, you must create a clear chart that shows which position will be the primary staff member in charge of each component. If you have several small components that can be supervised by one person, the chart should indicate these areas under one position.

Sponsorship

Sponsorship can also determine the nature of your organizational chart. Most private, not-for-profit programs receiving government or foundation support money must have a board of directors who are the actual employers and legal decision makers for the program. This board will need to have a separate, top line on the chart indicating the board's power and responsibilities. The director will have a direct line to the board, and the rest of the staff will be positioned in clusters according to job categories underneath the director.

The owner of a proprietary center may also serve as the director. This individual has the decision-making power for the program within licensing and other legal regulations. A privately owned program may have an advisory board. Since this board has no real power except to make recommendations, it does not appear in the body of the organizational chart. It may be acknowledged off to the side and connected to the owner by a broken line.

8-7 When a program provides transportation, additional staff will usually be needed.

State Regulations

State regulations may require one supervisor for a certain number of classrooms. For example, one supervisor may be required for every five preschool classrooms. The regulations may also require separate supervisors for various components of the program. Because regulations are usually so different for family child care providers than for preschool classrooms, having one person supervise both may be too difficult. In that case, separate positions might need to be created. This would be reflected in the organizational chart.

Skill/Training of Available Employees

When your program is able to attract well-trained, highly skilled personnel, the need for training and frequent supervision may be less. These staff members can carry out their job requirements independently. One supervisor may be able to handle responsibilities for several program components. However, if your program has been unable to attract highly competent individuals, the need for closer supervision and additional training will exist. In this situation, you may need to hire another supervisor to ensure additional training is provided and monitor the daily activities of those individuals.

The organizational chart is a quick, easy way to describe the personnel structure of your program. New employees can see where they fit in the program structure. Supervisory personnel can see which positions they are responsible for supervising. It clarifies the "chain of command" for your program. In a large, multi-service agency, the organizational chart will be an essential tool to help determine the most efficient structure for your center.

The organizational structure you plan will determine what positions you will need to fill. Every program for children will have classroom staff. Your structure may include supervisors, teachers, assistant teachers, classroom aides, and/or volunteers. The organizational chart will also show what administrative support staff is needed.

Job Descriptions

The next step in staffing the program is to identify the responsibilities of each job category. All jobs in the program need *job descriptions* that spell out the duties as well as the qualifications and experience needed for each job classification. Job descriptions help clarify in the director's mind the purpose for each job. Jobs in the same job category, such as head teacher positions, will be identical or very similar, 8-8. This is because each of the head teachers handles basically the same responsibilities and require similar training. The job description also identifies other positions that report to the head teacher and specify to whom the head teacher is responsible. As the program grows or changes, job descriptions might have to be changed according to program needs.

The job description also helps a potential applicant decide whether to apply for the position. Anyone reading the job descriptions should be able to tell how that position fits into the organizational structure. It may also include a salary range for persons in that position category.

Job Description — Head Teacher

Qualifications: B.S. degree in Child Development, Early Childhood Education, or related field that includes a minimum of 18 hours of coursework relevant to work with children and families or an A.A. degree that includes 18 hours of coursework in child-related studies and two years of successful experience in child care.

A Head Teacher in the child care program is responsible for supervising the total program of the individual classroom.

Responsibilities:

- **Responsible to the Program Director.** Head Teachers are responsible for conducting the program in the classrooms in accordance with the policies established by the Board of Directors and interpreted by the Program Director. The Head Teachers are to inform the Program Director or appropriate coordinator of the needs of the children, parents, and classroom staffs. They are to suggest improvements and discuss problems. The Head Teachers are to help maintain the budget control as established by the Program Director.

- **Supervision of Staff.** Head Teachers are to participate in the interviewing of Aides and Assistant Teachers and in the assignment of classroom staff responsibilities. They are responsible for scheduling the hours of the classroom staff, assigning duties, and sharing information with the classroom staff. Head Teachers should meet frequently with their classroom staff members both individually and as a group to discuss plans and problems. Head Teachers will participate in the evaluation of their classroom staff members and will be evaluated by the Program Coordinators.

- **Development and Implementation of the Daily Program.** Head Teachers organize all aspects of the daily program. They are primarily responsible for the preparation of materials and the organization of developmentally appropriate activities. They will have a large part in the establishment of program goals and the ongoing process of program evaluation.

- **Primary Responsibility for Children.** Head Teachers will have the primary responsibility for the welfare of the children who are in the care of the center. They should know all the children in their classroom well. They should be aware of the special needs of the children and plan for ways to meet these needs. They should cooperate with the appropriate Division Coordinator to arrange for consultant services for those children needing them.

- **Responsible for Health and Safety Decisions Within the Classroom.** Head Teachers maintain healthy and safe classroom practices, use universal precautions, and are prepared to respond appropriately to emergency situations. Head Teachers have and maintain CPR and First Aid certifications.

- **Maintenance of Facilities and Equipment.** Head Teachers are responsible for seeing that their classrooms are in order and that equipment is kept in good condition. They are responsible for keeping the Director up to date on equipment and supplies needed to carry on the daily program.

- **Maintenance of Records and Reports.** Head Teachers are responsible for keeping time sheets and vacation information for their classroom staff. They are to maintain lists of needed equipment and supplies, classroom attendance, and daily plans. They are to contribute to records involving the children in their classroom.

- **Interpreting the Program to Parents.** Head Teachers are responsible for working with their Division Coordinator in interpreting the program to their classroom parents. They share responsibility with the Coordinator for giving parents information about their children. They are responsible for keeping parents informed about the center calendar and special events.

8-8 A sample job description clearly indicates the duties and responsibilities of any head teacher's position.

Clear explanation of duties is essential. Persons being hired for the staff are entitled to know what duties are expected of them. Evaluation of staff work is linked to the performance of assigned duties. If there is no clear understanding of what a job entails, there may be problems later. For example, all teachers in the program will have basically the same types of responsibilities. The teacher may be expected to

- plan the classroom activities and daily schedule

- set the classroom atmosphere

- provide expertise in determining the appropriate guidance

- plan the schedules of the aides in the classroom

- order classroom supplies

The job description for head teacher positions should identify those basic responsibilities for which they are accountable. The job description for a head teacher, as shown in 8-8, identifies all of the duties required of someone in that position. The job requires the ability to apply specific training about working with children. It also requires decision-making and organizational abilities. In comparison with the responsibilities of a classroom aide, 8-9, the head teacher has a much more complex job. Normally, the additional training and responsibilities should be expected to result in a higher salary and status within the program structure.

Job Description — Classroom Aide

Qualifications: High School diploma or G.E.D. is required for this position. Aide must also have personal qualities, interests, abilities, and potential for effective functioning in this position.

A Classroom Aide in the Child Care Program is responsible for carrying out the duties as assigned by the Head Teacher and/or Assistant Teacher. Aides are responsible for sharing ideas and suggestions in a manner supportive of the Head and Assistant Teachers.

Responsibilities:

- Responsibility to the Classroom Head Teacher and Assistant Teacher. The Aide is directly responsible to both the Head Teacher and Assistant Teacher. Aides carry out duties and assignments in accordance with instructions. They are responsible for informing the Teachers of observations on the needs of the children.

- Implementation of the Daily Program. The Aides assist classroom teachers with daily activities and routines. They may conduct special activities in line with interests and abilities. Aides may be assigned some kitchen duties and clean-up duties as well as activities directly with children.

- Responsibility for Children. Aides with the help of another Aide may supervise groups of children for brief periods upon direction of the Teacher. Aides may give special attention and help to children needing it.

8-9 An aide's job description indicates that this position requires less education and has less complex duties than that of the head teacher.

Job descriptions take time to develop. They are essential, however, to ensure that the responsibilities of each position are clearly identified. Small programs may function quite well with an "everybody pitch in to get the job done" philosophy. However, in larger programs, confusion over responsibilities is likely to occur. Some important tasks may not get done at all because no one feels responsible. People may be spending time on tasks that are not matched to their expertise or salaries.

Whenever a position becomes vacant, examine the job description. It may need to be changed to reflect changes in your program and the expertise of your staff members. It should be updated periodically.

Adult-to-Child Ratios

Each state determines the *adult-to-child ratio,* the number of adults who must be in the classroom with the children. This ratio usually varies according to the ages of the children in the group. NAEYC encourages adult to child ratios of

- infants—1 adult to 3 children

- young toddlers—1 adult to 3 to 5 children

- two-year-olds—1 adult to 4 to 5 children

- three-year-olds—1 adult to 7 children

- four- and five-year-olds—1 adult to 10 children

- school-age children—1 adult to 12 children

The younger the children are, the more adults will be needed. States may also regulate the total group size of each age group. This can also affect the number of adults who must be present. When the center is open for longer than an eight-hour day, additional staff will be needed. Overlapping shifts in the classroom may be necessary.

Director's Dilemma

Your center has an opening for a head teacher. One of the assistant teachers eagerly applies for the position. You know this person has all of the academic qualifications for the job. You also know that her work as an assistant teacher has not been very good. She seems to have a poor attitude and will be very angry if she does not get the promotion. How would you decide whether to give the position to her?

How Do I Find Good Staff?

The search for good staff persons requires a thoughtful recruitment process. Finding qualified people and attracting them to your program can be a difficult task. Because salaries in the child care field are notoriously low, many talented and qualified people leave the field. Teachers often move into administrative positions. Many programs are plagued by high turnover rates among staff members. Even relatively stable programs will find it necessary to recruit new staff members at some time.

Established programs should look first within their own staff for employees who are ready to move up into higher positions. This has the advantage of providing an incentive to hard-working, loyal employees. The possibility of moving into a position of increased prestige, responsibility, and salary can be an encouragement to a staff member. Of course, this still leaves the director with the problem of filling the spot left vacant by the promoted employee.

Let qualified people know that you have an opening. Post the job description for the position, including the qualifications that are necessary. Indicate to employees the procedure for applying for the position. Also notify parents and board members of any openings.

Develop an overall recruiting plan based on the position you have available. Positions requiring higher levels of education and experience in child development and/or early childhood education may be harder to fill. You will need to advertise more widely. This will also be more expensive, 8-10. Positions requiring less specific training and experience can usually be filled from local candidates.

If you are planning to hire someone for a position such as classroom aide or cook's assistant, very little formal training may be expected. There may be a number of people in your community who could fill the job adequately. Ads in the local paper, notification of the local employment office, and word-of-mouth, may be sufficient to attract applicants, 8-11. Notices in church newsletters, community bulletin boards, or local radio announcements can also be helpful.

Recruitment of personnel for the positions requiring higher levels of specific training may be more difficult. You may be trying to attract the interest of someone who lives in a different community. A large multiservice program with many children enrolled might find it worthwhile to pay the higher cost of advertising in a national newspaper or professional journal. It is also popular to post job advertisements on the Internet.

Most regions have a major metropolitan newspaper with a large classified ad section. Advertisements in this paper would reach a broader population than would a local paper. Regional papers focusing on nearby suburbs or geographic areas can also help to alert possible applicants about the position. Identify colleges that offer programs in the fields you need. Their career services offices are set up to help match their graduates with job prospects. A recruitment letter sent to the academic department along with a copy of the job description could be helpful.

You could also advertise in the newsletters or journals of the professional organizations. Local chapters of NAEYC and other groups often have their own newsletters in addition to those of national organizations. Many of these professional organizations also have job boards listing openings at their meetings and conferences.

Advertisement for the director of a large, complex child care program.

Director needed for employer-sponsored child care program. Duties include all administrative aspects of operating a large, multiservice program for 500 children, ages 6 months to 12 years with a budget of over $1 million. Master's degree in child development, early childhood, related human service field and coursework, or training in administration required. Five years of administrative experience in child care, Head Start, or related human service field necessary. Competitive salary and benefits. Send resume to New Software Inc., Box 11701, Rochester, NY 14666. We are an equal opportunity employer.

8-10 Because of the specific nature of the requirements for this job, this ad might be found in national newspapers or the journals of a professional or trade organizations aimed at child care professionals.

Examples of Help Wanted Ads:

Teacher position for three-year-old group in full-day child care program. Four-year degree in child development or early childhood required. Two years of successful work experience with children preferred. Send resume to ABC Child Care, Box 162, Indiana, PA 15222 by July 10th. Equal opportunity employer.

Custodian needed for child care center. Must be over 18 and have prior experience in cleaning and maintenance. Must be available to work evenings. Call 555-4422 for application. We are an equal opportunity employer.

8-11 These ads are similar to those found in local newspapers.

The ad you write to recruit applicants for a vacant position needs to include essential information about the job. This includes

- title of the job

- brief description of duties

- educational qualifications

- experience

- address or phone number for response from interested individuals

- statement of compliance with federal laws

The content of your ad should be consistent with the job description, but it will not be as long and detailed. The ad for a teaching position with its education and experience requirements will probably be longer than the ad for a support position, such as janitor, which may have fewer requirements. Complete sentences are not usually used since the cost of advertising is normally related to the number of words in an ad.

The wording of your ad can affect the number and type of responses you receive. Give clear information about the type of applicant you want. If a certain qualification is definitely important, and you will not hire someone without it, then use the terms *required* or *necessary*. Individuals without the specific qualification will be less likely to apply. You may also word the ad to indicate that persons with education or experience in a related field may be considered. This will usually increase the number of responses. If a qualification is not absolutely needed, use the terms *desired* or *preferred*. Individuals with related or similar backgrounds, but with some variation from the specified qualification, are more likely to respond to this type of ad.

You will also need to state the type of response you expect from applicants. Applicants with advanced education will usually send you a *resume*, a summary that includes name, address, phone, educational background, professional certifications, work experience, honors, special talents, and the name and addresses of references. This may serve as the initial application.

Some applicants will not have a resume to send. If you are requesting a completed application from each interested individual, you must plan how the applications will be distributed and returned. Most directors prefer to have applicants write to the program requesting that an application be sent to them. It can then be filled out and returned by mail to the center. If you need to fill a position immediately, you may list a phone number. The possible applicant could be asked to come to the center to fill out an application and have an interview. Many phone call inquiries, however, can take up a great deal of staff time. Likewise, inviting potential applicants to come to the center for an application is time-consuming for your staff. Most centers prefer to mail applications to those who request them. Applications are usually accepted by mail or dropped off in person. Those persons invited for an interview on the basis of a resume should fill out an application form at the time of the interview.

Government Employment Regulations

It is essential that your advertising and recruitment plan is in compliance with Civil Rights legislation. This requires specific efforts to attract job applicants from all minority groups. As an equal opportunity employer, you must include on job descriptions, applications, and ads a statement that guarantees compliance with the 1964 Civil Rights Act, 8-12.

All your employment practices must be in compliance with applicable state and federal laws designed to ensure fair hiring practices. These laws are occasionally amended or changed, so you must check with your state's employment agency to determine the current status of the legislation.

Regulations on Hiring

Several major federal laws will affect your hiring practices. The Civil Rights Act of 1964 and its amendments prohibit discrimination in hiring on the basis of race, color, sex, age, disability, or national origin. A statement to this effect must appear on employment applications and job advertisements.

Affirmative action plans designed to ensure recruitment strategies that will result in a diverse pool of applicants may also be required. Strategies include publishing ads in journals or newspapers with a large minority readership, or contacting colleagues who might know qualified minority individuals in the field. With luck, your job announcement will reach appropriate persons who will decide to submit applications for the position.

It is best to take applications for one position at a time. This avoids confusion for both you and the applicant. If another position is open, have interested applicants fill out a second application for this specific position. After a position is filled, keep all of the paperwork relating to the top candidates. Keeping clear track of applicants for each specific position creates a paper trail that provides protection for your program in case of a legal challenge to your hiring practices. Each new position that opens should result in a completely new search and pool of applicants.

How Will I Select the Best Applicant?

The screening process you develop to identify the best candidate will involve several steps. First you must obtain or create an application form that gives you important information on the candidate. Next a group of top candidates are invited for interviews. Following the interview, these candidates' references, backgrounds, and application information must be verified.

> **Sample Compliance Statement**
>
> This agency is an equal opportunity employer. We employ persons without regard to race, creed, color, religion, sex, national origin, or disability.

8-12 This compliance statement or a simplified version must appear in all literature representing the program.

Director's Dilemma

You have interviewed several applicants for a position as a classroom teacher. The choice has been narrowed down to two candidates. One applicant is a recent graduate with a child development degree. She has had some experience with children through her training. She was comfortable with your program's philosophy and had a strong academic record. The other applicant has had less formal academic training. She has worked in another child care center. Although not familiar with philosophical concerns, she is willing to learn. The first applicant only wants to work in the area for a year, then leave. The second applicant is a local resident who is more likely to stay with your program for a long time. What should you consider in making this decision?

The Application

The application form you use should be developed to provide you with essential information about the applicant for the position. It must also comply with all applicable laws regarding nondiscrimination. A typical application form is shown in 8-13.

Some information may be asked only if it relates clearly and directly to a candidate's ability to perform a particular job. For example, a person whose medical status includes a tendency to unexpectedly lose consciousness could not work safely in a classroom. The same person might, however, be a valuable employee in the type of position where constant alertness is not necessary.

Screening the Applicants

Once you have received applications or resumes for the vacant position, you must screen the applicants. This process is an initial sorting of the applications. Some candidates may clearly fit the qualifications you have identified in the job description. You will definitely want to consider them further. Other applicants will clearly not match the qualifications at all and can be dropped from further consideration for that particular job. A few applicants will have different qualifications from those you had identified. Their unique training and/or experience, however, may still lead you to consider them as viable candidates.

You should identify the number of candidates you want to interview. Interviewing is a time-consuming process. You will likely not be able to interview every applicant for every position. The initial screening is done on the basis of the applications or resumes in order to determine which candidates would best fit the job. Once you have completed the screening of the applications, you can proceed to schedule interviews.

The Interview Process

The purpose of the interview is to give you and the applicant a chance to get to know each other better. You are trying to find the person who will best match the job description and demonstrate the characteristics desirable in a child care staff member. The interview allows another way to obtain additional information about the individual.

Several people should assist you in conducting an interview. The staff member who will supervise this person directly should be included in the process. If you are interviewing for an aide's position, the head teacher and/or program supervisor of

Job Application
Child Care Program

_____
Date

_____   _____
Name   Social Security Number

_____   _____
Present Address   Phone

_____

I certify that I am 18 years of age or older, as required by (insert your state's licensing requirement if applicable).

_____   _____
Signature   Date

Position(s) applied for _____

What method of transportation will you use to get to work? _____

Would you work:

Full-time?_____   Part-time?_____

List days and hours available to work _____

_____

List any friends or relatives working for us (names). _____

_____

Please list all child care experiences that can be documented (other than caring for your own children).

_____

_____

Are there any other experiences, licenses, certifications, or skills that you feel would especially qualify you for work with our organization? If so, describe.

_____

_____

(Continued)

8-13 This type of application can be used for positions at all levels in the organization.

Record of Employment

List below all present and past employment, beginning with your most recent job.

Name and address of employer/phone #	Dates employed	Describe work done	Starting and last (or current) salary
1.			
2.			
3.			
4.			

Record of Education

School	School name/address	Course of study	Years attended	Degree
High School				
College				
Other (Specify)				

Any special awards or honors received? _____

_____

Names, addresses, and phone numbers of three references (not family members).

1. _____

_____

2. _____

_____

3. _____

_____

The facts set forth in my application for employment are true and complete. I understand that if employed, false statements on this application shall be considered sufficient cause for dismissal. You are hereby authorized to make any investigation of my personal history and financial and credit record through any investigative or credit agencies or bureaus of your choice.

I understand that I have the right to make a written request within a reasonable period of time to receive additional, detailed information about the nature and scope of any such investigative report that is made.

Signature of applicant _____

Please note that we are an equal opportunity employer.

8-13 (continued)

that classroom should be a part of the interviewing team. If the position is a higher-level, supervisory one, the other supervisor(s) who will work with that individual should participate. For the higher-level positions, it is also a good idea to have a member of the personnel committee from the board of directors present. The actual recommendation to hire goes to the board for official approval. Directors or owners of small, private programs with only a few employees may want to include a parent representative or local child development expert in the interview process. Very large programs may have a personnel specialist on staff who handles procedures for hiring.

Before actually interviewing applicants, develop a form on which you can rate each candidate, 8-14. This can help you document each candidate was evaluated on the same criteria. Do not write during the interview, however. Evaluate the candidate immediately following the interview.

The interview is a stressful time for the applicants. Each one wants to make a good impression. Each one is hopeful about being offered the job. Your responsibility is to ensure the interview is conducted in a fair, considerate manner. You are looking for the person whose training, experience, and personality best match the responsibilities of the job.

The interview should be conducted in an atmosphere of respect for the candidate. Not every person you interview will be the right one for the job. However, each should be treated with the same consideration you would expect him or her to show the children. Trick questions, high-pressure tactics, and condescension will not help you find the best applicant.

Before interviewing any of the applicants, you must think about how the interview will be conducted. Planning and organizing the interviews ahead of time will result in more accurate information. The interview should be held in a comfortable office or conference room where there will not be interruptions. Check the lighting, temperature, and ventilation ahead of time.

The types of questions asked and the level of the response expected will vary somewhat according to the nature of the position. A teacher candidate should be expected to know more about planning, guidance, and age characteristics than an aide candidate should. A potential secretary or bookkeeper will probably know little about the teaching aspects of the center. However, this person should be expected to pass a keyboarding test or answer questions related to financial recordkeeping.

To compare responses fairly, be sure the same questions are asked of each candidate. Avoid questions that can be answered with a simple yes or no. Some candidates may bring a *portfolio*, which is a container including samples of the individual's previous work. You should review this carefully. It can give clear examples of this person's competencies.

Try to ask questions that will give you some insight into how the candidate feels about children and families. Questions about how a candidate would handle different kinds of situations can tell you about his or her ideas on discipline and guidance. Be careful not to telegraph the answer you prefer. A question like, "I think children should have time to choose their own activities, don't you?" tells the candidate what response you want.

There are certain questions you cannot ask on the application or during the interview. The law forbids the asking of questions that could be used to discriminate against a candidate on the basis of race, color, sex, age, disability, or national origin. See 8-15.

Criteria for Ranking Interviewed Applicants for Teacher Position

Name of applicant _____

Date of interview _____

Criteria	Score (1 = poor, 3 = adequate, 5 = excellent)				
1. Education meets job criteria.	1	2	3	4	5
2. Experience meets job criteria.	1	2	3	4	5
3. Expressed attitudes about children are consistent with program philosophy.	1	2	3	4	5
4. Classroom observation indicates ease and warm rapport with children.	1	2	3	4	5
5. Comments and answers indicate knowledge of children's development.	1	2	3	4	5
6. Personality seems to include characteristics desirable in individuals working with children.	1	2	3	4	5
7. Ability to organize and implement a developmentally appropriate classroom.	1	2	3	4	5
8. References.	1	2	3	4	5

Total _____

Comments: _____

_____

Signature of interviewer _____

8-14 All candidates for a position should be evaluated according to the same criteria.

One of the most difficult aspects of hiring staff for a child care center is trying to find individuals with caring and compassionate personalities. Working with children and their families requires special characteristics. Some of these qualities are very difficult to discern in an interview. Somehow, through the selection process, you must try to identify whether or not an individual has these characteristics, 8-16. For any position that involves classroom work, you might want to have the candidate spend time in the room with the children. Allow at least 45 minutes to an hour for this part of the interview. This will give the individual time to interact with the children and will allow the head teacher time to assess the candidate's direct involvement. You can stop by periodically to observe. Classrooms with an observation booth are helpful, but be sure the candidate knows that it is there.

At the end of the interview, give candidates a chance to ask questions. Individuals applying for higher-level positions should have a basic knowledge about how child care programs operate and usually have some questions. These may include questions about services, clientele, sponsorship, and their role in the overall structure of the program. Most applicants want to know what the position will pay and what the benefits are. Even if they don't ask, you should let them know when the final selection for the position will be made. Let them know whether they will hear from you by letter or phone. Do not make an offer on the spot. You will need to evaluate the individual in writing on the rating scale and consult with others who participated in the interview. If it is decided this is the right person for the job, you can call after the review process is completed.

At the end of the interview, no matter how it went, you should thank the person warmly and politely for their interest in your program. You or a staff member may give the person a tour of the rest of the center.

Information You Can Request on a Job Application
Name, address, phone number
Educational background
Work experience
Licenses, degrees, certification
Special training or job skills
References
Philosophy on child care

Information You Cannot Request on a Job Application
Age, weight, or height
Marital status
Children or plans to have children
Race or religion
Political affiliation

8-15 Job applications must not include questions that would violate the Civil Rights Act.

Typical Interview Questions for a Teacher Applicant
Why are you interested in working in the child care field?
How did you hear about the opening in our program?
What kinds of work have you done with children in the past?
What kinds of things do you like to plan and do with children?
What do you think a good center should do for children and families?
What special talents or abilities could you bring to the program?
How would you handle a situation like ...? (pose a discipline problem)
What kinds of things do you think young children need?
What do you think would be the "perfect" day for the group of children in your care?
What would you like to be doing five years from now?

8-16 Questions like these give you more information about an applicant than simple yes or no questions.

Plan to inform candidates of the decision no later than two weeks after the interview. This is courteous. You don't want your preferred candidate to take a position elsewhere because there has been no word from your program. Likewise, candidates who are not selected should not be delayed in their job search because they are waiting to hear from you.

Criminal Background Check

Concern about child abuse has led most states to enact laws designed to protect children in child care. Several well-publicized cases of reported sexual abuse in centers has resulted in the passage of child protective legislation. These laws are for the purpose of ensuring the safety of children in child care settings. Anyone convicted of a crime against children or named as the perpetrator of a founded report of child abuse cannot be hired.

Before you begin to hire staff, be sure you know the laws of your state. Most states require a criminal history check of every new employee. This is usually carried out by the state police. FBI clearance and a Child Line clearance may also be necessary. When a job applicant is from out of state or has moved around from job to job often, these clearances are particularly important.

Employers may also require an employee disclosure statement from applicants. This is a sworn statement signed by the applicant. It affirms that the person has not been convicted of child sexual abuse-related crimes. It also clearly states that the employee will be dismissed if the criminal background check indicates a conviction. Your state may require that provisional employees awaiting clearance must work within eyesight of a permanent employee at all times.

The potential occurrence of child sexual abuse in a center must be taken seriously. It is your responsibility to ensure that the children in your care are safe. Criminal background checks require additional paperwork. They take time, effort, and money. However, they help you to protect children against someone who may be intent on harming them. Some states impose substantial fines on programs that employ staff without adequate clearances.

Director's Dilemma

You have interviewed several applicants for a position as a classroom aide. One particular woman seems to be the strongest applicant. She appears to possess the qualities that will make her an effective member of the classroom team. Before you offer her the job, you discover that her husband has been arrested for child sexual abuse. How should that affect your decision about the position?

References

Another essential part of the employment process is the checking of references. This is a time-consuming task that directors sometimes try to avoid. Licensing requirements usually mandate that letters of recommendation be on file for each employee. You should have a minimum of two written references verified by a follow-up phone call. Many directors find that a call to previous employers and references can give a more accurate picture of the potential employee.

When requesting written references, you may simply ask for a letter. Those responding can be as brief or lengthy as they prefer. A questionnaire with categories to check and a section for comments may result in additional details. Reference forms can be relatively simple, yet still cover the information you need, 8-17. See 8-18 for a more complex form using a rating scale.

Making the Final Selection

When making the final selection, you should use all of the information you have available. This would include your own rankings of the candidates as well as the rankings of the other staff and board members who participated in the interview. In private programs, this might have included other staff, parents, or a child development consultant. Talk with the others to find out the reasons behind their rankings of candidates. Discuss each person's interpretation of the references. If you all agree on the best candidate, the decision is made. If there is disagreement, you should continue to discuss the candidates and the best match for the job description until the group can come to a consensus. Ultimately, you, as the director, will have to make a decision that will be consistent with the rankings and acceptable to yourself, the staff who must work with the individual, and the board with its legal responsibility for hiring.

All candidates should be notified in writing regarding the decision. Unsuccessful candidates should be thanked for their interest. It is also helpful to briefly indicate the particular background or expertise, such as previous experience with the same age group, that made the successful candidate the best match for the job.

The successful candidate should be given information about the starting date and salary. You should set up an appointment to meet with this person as soon as the job has been officially accepted. State employment laws differ in regard to the need for a *contract*, a legal agreement signed by the new employee and you, as the director of the agency, that commits each to the terms specified in the agreement. These terms usually include starting salary, starting date, commitment to personnel policies, and an ending date when the contract expires.

Employment at will refers to hiring an employee without using a contract. This means that the employee or the program can terminate the employment at any time. No reason is needed. This type of employment condition exists in most states as long as your program does not use a contract or personnel policies that state otherwise. It is a good idea to have your personnel policies examined by an attorney or employment specialist to ensure that you have the employment situation that is most beneficial to your program and acceptable to the board of directors. Because of changing labor laws in many states, you will also need current information regarding appropriate papers that need to be signed by you, as program director, and by the newly hired employee.

Compensation

Federal and state laws affect the wages and benefits that you can offer a new employee. Minimum wage legislation sets the minimum amount that an employee can earn on an hourly basis. As a director, you have no control over wages mandated by minimum wage legislation. If the minimum wage is raised by law, you must increase your salary scale accordingly. In turn, you will also have to adjust your budget and, possibly, the tuition charged to families.

Sample Reference Form Usable for All Program Positions

Child Care Program
Address

_____ has applied for a position with our child care program and has given your name as a reference. We would appreciate you answering some questions about this person and making a general statement as to how you think he or she might perform in this capacity.

1. How long and in what capacity have you known this applicant?

_____

_____

_____

2. Are you related to this person?_____   If yes, what is the relationship? _____

_____

3. In the space below, give a general statement concerning this person especially regarding his or her fitness and a/an _____

_____

_____

4. Would you employ this applicant as a/an _____

Yes _____No _____

Signature _____

Date _____

8-17 This reference form is simple and easy to fill out, yet it gives you some basic information to back up an employment application.

The salary offered to the new employee should be comparable to prevailing wages for similar positions in your area. It will also depend on what your program can afford to pay. You should also consider the experience and education of the new employee.

As an employer, you will be required to provide some benefits to your employees. Both federal and state laws will affect what these benefits are and how much they will cost your program. Full-time employees may be entitled to more benefits than part-time employees.

Before a New Employee Can Begin

All new employees must complete necessary paperwork before they can be officially hired. This ensures that your program has all of the information needed for local, state, and federal records.

Sample of Reference from Previous Employer or Instructor

_____ has applied for a teacher position with our child day care program and has given your name as a reference. We would appreciate your opinion of this person.

How long and in what capacity have you known this applicant?_____

Are you related to this person?_____If yes, what is the relationship?_____

Please rate the candidate on the following characterisitics:

	Low		Average		Excellent
1. Maturity of professional judgment	1	2	3	4	5
2. Ability to work effectively with a diverse group of children and families	1	2	3	4	5
3. Knowledge of children's ages and stages of development	1	2	3	4	5
4. Sensitivity to children's needs	1	2	3	4	5
5. Ability to work independently	1	2	3	4	5
6. Honesty and reliability	1	2	3	4	5
7. Ability to work as a member of a team	1	2	3	4	5

Would you hire this person to teach your own children? Yes _____ No _____

Comments: _____

_____

Signature of interviewer _____

Date _____

8-18 This reference form gives more specific information about a candidate. It is valuable when considering an applicant for an position working directly with children.

It is easier to obtain this information from applicants before they are actually on staff. Once they are working on a daily basis, completing forms and getting physicals will be difficult to schedule. For licensing purposes and for your records, however, this information is essential. It must be on file. Whenever you offer a job to someone, you must make it clear that these forms must be completed before work can begin, 8-19.

The United States Department of Justice through the Immigration and Naturalization Service requires completion of an "I-9" form by applicants for

Information Needed from New Employees

- Completed application form
- Current health appraisal
- Proof of negative TB test
- Information in case of an emergency
- W-4 form for income tax purposes
- Criminal background clearance
- Proof of educational status
- Reference letters
- Form I-9

8-19 New employees should have all documentation on file and all paperwork completed before beginning employment.

employment. This form, known as the Employment Eligibility Verification Form, is used to verify eligibility for employment in the United States. As an employer, you must examine evidence of identity and employment eligibility.

Conditions of Employment

Certain conditions of employment must be met by new employees. These conditions are usually determined by state licensing regulations. Employees must typically be free of contagious diseases or conditions that could threaten the children in their care. Their criminal background checks must be cleared. Any required drug testing must have been completed. Their claims of education and experience must be truthful. Employees should be aware that deceit in any of these areas is grounds for dismissal.

Probationary Period

As a protection for your agency, it is a good idea to have a *probationary employment period*, a time to get to know the new employee before you make a permanent commitment. New staff must demonstrate their ability to work within the philosophy of your program. A staff member who promises positive guidance yet uses harsh, humiliating discipline is not meeting this condition of employment.

Typical probationary periods run from 90 to 180 days. It could be a longer or shorter period of time if you prefer. New staff who successfully complete the probationary period and are moved to permanent status are frequently rewarded by a slight raise in salary.

How Can I Help New Staff Get Off to a Good Start?

Remember what it was like starting a new job? No matter how much advanced preparation you have, it is still hard to begin a new position. As the director, you will want to find ways to help new employees become oriented to their jobs. Each staff member needs to feel welcomed as a valuable addition to the team.

The Need for an Orientation Plan

Most people come into a new job wanting to do well. They want to be recognized as individuals, and they want to be viewed as competent. They need to feel that they are liked and that they

Director's Dilemma

One of your bus drivers has to quit. She is urging you to hire her son as her replacement. Several staff members have indicated that the son has a problem with alcohol and drug abuse. How would you handle this situation?

belong. As each of these needs is met, the individual becomes more comfortable and confident. Commitment to the new job grows.

It's a good idea to have an organized ***orientation plan,*** a plan that includes both formal and informal ways to help new staff become acquainted with the center and their role in it. An organized plan helps to ensure that you don't accidentally forget to tell someone something important!

Much of what you need to tell or show new employees is general information about the program or agency. Other information is specific to the particular job or classroom to which the new person is assigned. Along with deciding what information to give, you will need to decide how to present that material.

Introducing a New Staff Person

You can help new employees feel more comfortable in the center by making sure that they have been introduced to the other staff who will be working near them. In a large agency, it may not be possible to introduce a new person to everyone. Help each new staff person meet a core of acquaintances who know their way around the program. Introductions may be made at a staff meeting, training session, or informal picnic, if convenient. Refreshments and a time for informal conversation can show the new person that the center staff are warm, caring, and interesting individuals, 8-20.

Providing a Mentor

It is helpful to the beginner to have a more experienced staff person assigned as a ***mentor,*** a person who serves as an advisor, a role model, and a friend. Success in a job requires that a new person develop a sensitivity to the routines, personalities, and priorities within the work setting. The mentor can provide knowledge of "the way things work" that can smooth the way for a successful beginning for the new employee. Sometimes, this relationship simply develops on its own. Usually, however, it is a good idea to ask a specific staff member to take on this role. The mentor should be someone who can warmly welcome the new employee. The mentor must also be an individual who possesses the qualities that contribute to success on the job and in interpersonal relationships. A troubled and unhappy staff member with a negative attitude would probably not be a good mentor.

As the director of the program, you should not take on the task of mentoring new staff yourself. You are responsible for hiring, monitoring, and evaluating this new employee. If the person does not work out well in the job, you may also be responsible for terminating

8-20 An informal gathering is a comfortable way to introduce a new employee to the rest of the staff.

employment. These functions of your job do not mesh well with the mentor's role as a listener, advisor, and friend.

Explaining Procedures and Goals

As a part of the interview process, you should have discussed briefly the purpose and goals of the child care agency. The new employee will, therefore, have a basic idea of the mission of the organization. At the beginning of employment, it is helpful to review both the goals and the basic philosophy of the center. You may do this personally with each employee to ensure there are no misunderstandings, 8-21. In a larger organization, you may delegate this duty to a staff person in charge of personnel.

Each new employee must understand the basic procedures that are a part of the job. If the new employee will be closing the center at the end of the day, it is essential for that person to know the center security procedures. Should the temperature be turned down? Are the porch lights left on? Is there an alarm system to be set? The staff member must also be familiar with policies regarding release of children, emergency procedures, and location of phones. Whatever responsibilities this staff member must handle should be carefully explained.

Most programs also have various procedures regarding employment. The paperwork necessary to request a vacation day or the procedure for using a sick day must be explained. Each program will have unique information that must be given to the new employee. You may want to include the following:

8-21 This director is going over important information with an enthusiastic new employee.

- goals and philosophy of the program

- description of the agency

- organization of the center and the new employee's place in the organization

- floor plan of the center including exits

- samples of forms used for various paperwork

- center phone numbers

- hours of operation and yearly calendar

- procedures to follow in case of an emergency

- names of authorized adults permitted to pick up each child

Consider information a new employee would need to know to become comfortable and competent in the center.

Tour of Facilities

If your center has only one room, a tour of that room will be brief and simple. You will need to identify locations of storage areas, and point out the basic organization of the room arrangement. If your facility includes many classrooms, offices, and storage areas, a tour of the space will be more important. The location of exits, bathrooms, fire extinguishers, maintenance items, the copying machine, telephones, employee parking area, and refrigerators will all need to be pointed out.

The relationship between one classroom and another is also useful information. If the new staff person is assigned to a room of three-year-olds, the location of other predominately three-year-old rooms should be known. This will facilitate sharing of developmentally appropriate equipment. It will also let the new person know where to go for help or advice.

☉ Summary

The number of staff you will need to hire will be determined by the size and nature of your program. A very large program will need classroom teachers, office personnel, and support staff such as janitors and cooks. Before hiring anyone, you must think through the organizational structure of your program. Consider how the staff will be organized. An organizational chart can be developed that shows lines of responsibility. It will help you determine what positions you will have to fill. State licensing requirements must be met regarding the number of adults who must be assigned to each classroom.

A recruitment plan is the method you use to make sure potential employees know that your program has a job available. Your plan should consider potential locations for advertisements that are likely to be seen by those you want to attract. Your plan and hiring practices must be in compliance with state and federal anti-discrimination hiring legislation.

Potential employees must be carefully screened and interviewed before working with children. This will include checking references, health appraisals, and criminal background clearances.

New employees must complete all paperwork necessary for your program records. A probationary period gives you additional time to make sure that the new employee will be able to carry out the job. An orientation plan can help a new employee get off to a good start. It should be planned carefully so the individual has all the information needed to function as a full member of the staff.

☉ Terms

labor-intensive
positive self-esteem
classroom staff
administrative staff
support personnel
organizational chart
job descriptions
adult-to-child ratio

resume
portfolio
contract
employment at will
probationary employment period
orientation plan
mentor

⦿ Review

1. Explain what is meant by the statement "Child care is a labor-intensive field"?

2. List the three categories under which program staff can be grouped.

3. How is an organizational chart useful?

4. What is the function of a job description?

5. What often determines an adult to child ratio in a classroom?

6. How does the Civil Rights Act of 1964 and its amendments affect hiring practices?

7. What is the purpose of an employee disclosure statement?

8. What is the purpose of a probationary employment period?

9. What is the purpose of an orientation plan?

10. How can a mentor be helpful to a new staff member?

⦿ Applications

1. Look at the help wanted classified section from the Sunday edition of a large metropolitan newspaper. Find ads that are for jobs in programs for children. You might find these listed under headings such as: child care, preschool teacher, child care aide, administrator, director, etc. Examine how each ad is written. What does each ad tell you about the job? In which of these jobs might you be interested?

2. Invite a center director to speak to your class about the interviewing process. Find out what types of questions are asked. Is the applicant asked to spend time in a classroom? How is the interview for a teaching position different from that for a staff support position? Does the director conduct the interview alone or do others participate? What suggestions would the director have for other new directors regarding the hiring of staff?

3. Role-play an interview situation to fill a teacher's aide position. Assign the following roles: the director, the classroom head teacher, a member of the personnel committee of the board, and the applicant. Demonstrate how the interview would proceed from greeting the candidate to saying good-bye. Continue the role-play to include the discussion of whether or not to hire the candidate. After the decision has been made, ask the rest of the class why they agreed or disagreed with it.

Chapter 9
Marketing and Planning for Enrollment

After studying this chapter, you will be able to

○ plan an advertising and public relations strategy for your center.

○ develop registration and enrollment procedures.

○ determine appropriate group placements.

○ establish procedures that will help children and parents adjust to the center.

As you begin a new program, consideration must be given to how you will let people know that your center exists. You must think about ways to attract families who will enroll their children. How do you want people to view your program? How do you see your center's place within the community? How many children must you enroll in order to meet your budget commitments? How can you help ease children's adjustments to the center?

The choices you make regarding each of these areas influence the way people view your center. You want your program to have a reputation for knowledgeable programming, fair policies and procedures, and sensitive caring for children. The center's reputation will affect your program's stature in the community and, in turn, your enrollment.

How Do I Let People Know About My Program?

The term *public relations* refers to an awareness of and a positive attitude toward a business or program. It includes those activities that help to make people aware of your program. Public relations activities also help promote positive feelings about your program in the general community. There are two goals to keep in mind when planning public relations strategies. One goal is to advertise your program to people who may be interested in enrolling their children. The other goal is to create a favorable impression of your program within the community.

Building enrollment quickly is important. The tuition is necessary to help your program become financially stable. On the other hand, your reputation in the community is built over a longer period of time. A good reputation helps to ensure that your program will continue to attract new families. Your program will benefit when it is viewed as an asset to the community. A good "word-of-mouth" reputation can ensure community support when times are tough.

Director's Dilemma

You are planning to open a new center. You believe it will primarily attract families who are employed at a nearby office building. You also feel that families living within a two-mile radius will possibly enroll. What kinds of advertising can you do to reach these two groups of families? What kinds of advertising would not be appropriate?

Advertising for Enrollment

In order to build enrollment, you must make sure that the people who need your program know about it. Successful advertising results from identifying the groups that are likely to want your services. Your primary advertising should target these groups.

Forms of Advertising

You may wish to use different types of advertising. These include brochures and flyers, newspaper ads, radio or TV ads, informational meetings, etc. Each of these has specific advantages and benefits. Most also may have a cost that you will need to investigate before making a commitment.

Brochures and Flyers

Brochures and flyers are both pieces of printed information, usually run off in large quantities, that can be given out to interested individuals. Brochures usually have several pages, while flyers are more likely to be a flat piece of paper, folded or unfolded. Because brochures have papers folded and stapled, they are more expensive to produce. If color photographs are added, the price will be higher. Flyers are simpler to prepare. However, they will not be able to contain as much information as a brochure. Trifolds are flyers made of single sheets of paper, folded into thirds lengthwise. Desktop publishing capabilities and copy centers make it relatively easy to produce professional-looking brochures and flyers for your center.

Brochures and flyers can be left, with permission, in such places as doctor's waiting rooms, grocery store bulletin boards, reception areas of various public or religious buildings, and other locations where interested parents might pick them up. Local employers may be willing to enclose them in paycheck envelopes or to post them in employee cafeteria or lounge areas.

Newspaper Advertisements

Local newspaper ads can be a very effective way to advertise the opening of a new center or an enrollment period. Informational meetings, open houses, presentations by special guest speakers, can all be easily announced this way. The cost of your ad is usually determined by the amount of space you want, whether or not you need help in preparing your ad for publication, and the number of times you want the ad to appear, 9-1.

Radio and Television Advertisements

Ads on broadcast media may be worthwhile for your center if the cost is not too high. Local radio stations and local cable TV stations have made broadcast advertising less expensive. These stations cover a small geographic location, so your program would not be wasting money by advertising to areas far away from the center's location.

Child Care
St. Mary School
430 Church Drive, Riverton, PA

4-year-olds
   Monday, Wednesday, Friday

3-year-olds
   Tuesday, Thursday

Mornings - 9:30 to 11:30 or
Afternoons - 12:30 to 2:30

Call for information
555-924-2220

9-1 This newspaper ad is attractive and catches the eye of the reader.

It may be possible to develop a series of public service announcements with useful information for all parents. A final statement such as, "This announcement has been brought to you by —Child Care Program" can alert parents to your program's existence. This type of announcement may be broadcast at no charge since stations must devote a certain amount of air time to public service announcements.

Direct advertising of your center on broadcast stations should be considered after finding out about the costs. The cost of the ad may limit you to a 15-, 30-, or 60-second time slot. This will require a carefully developed script to ensure that you are including information about the qualities of your program and how to contact the center.

Informational Meetings

Group informational meetings are most successful when you are targeting a particular group rather than a whole town. Inviting all the employees of a large employer, the residents of a major apartment complex, or the members of a particular religious group or social club to an informational meeting allows you to direct your presentation to the needs of each group.

You may have a series of several meetings held at different places and times, so anyone who is interested will find a convenient meeting. If you are planning a large group meeting or open house that is for the whole town, it is still a good idea to send specific invitations or flyers to those groups or individuals who are most likely to be interested. This will help to build attendance.

Writing Advertising Materials

Materials that you prepare to advertise your program should be easy to understand. They should clearly explain information a potential client (family) wants to know.

The following information should be included:

- age range of children served

- location and phone number

- statement of program philosophy and goals

- special services or programs offered

The publicity materials should reflect respect for children and their families. A cartoon of a frazzled teacher with an "out-of-control" child may be cute, but it does not present an image of competent teachers. Be careful about how you choose to portray your program to people who are not familiar with it. Materials that go out to the public should be professional in appearance and content.

There will be some information that you may not want to put in your brochures. Tuition costs or hours of operation may change occasionally. It would be expensive to reprint the flyers when these changes occur. You might include a one-page insert that could be pulled out and revised if needed. Interested parents could call for current prices, hours, and availability.

Match Advertising to the Market

You can use your advertising dollars wisely by figuring out where your target families obtain information. For example, an advertisement in a large metropolitan newspaper could be very expensive. Although it might be seen by many people, it will also cover a broad geographic area. Many people who will read your ad might live too far away to have any real interest in enrollment. A similar ad in a small, regional paper that serves nearby neighborhoods would be a better choice.

Consider the services that you plan to offer. For families with older children enrolled in a particular school, information could go to the home with school reports. Pediatricians, pharmacies, and grocery stores may be willing to display posters or flyers also.

Building Your Program's Reputation in the Community

Public relations efforts should support the idea that your program is an asset to the community. When you or other representatives of your center participate in community activities, you help local residents get to know your program. They see you as an active contributor to the well-being of the area.

Such community service activities as writing an "advice to parents" column in the local newspaper or sponsoring a booth at a local fair to distribute parent education materials can serve two purposes. Helpful information is made available to all parents, and those parents who need child care will become familiar with your program.

Effective directors try to expand their influence into the community. Volunteering to be a guest speaker at a local service club can help community leaders learn more about good child care. Getting to know other human service agency directors can help you to keep them up-to-date on your program. Many directors make an effort to communicate and cooperate with heads of other agencies. This means that a conscious attempt is made to establish good working relationships. Willingness to help on another agency's fund-raising project can mean additional volunteers when your program needs help.

Join local business and economic development groups. Organizations such as the chamber of commerce like to feature new community services. They can provide public relations support by featuring your program in one of their newsletters. These groups also often develop brochures designed to encourage new businesses to move into the area. The brochures typically feature all of the businesses and services that are available in the area.

Another way to increase the visibility of your program is to get to know the family editor of your local paper. Send information about your center's plans for NAEYC's National Week of the Young Child or other recognition activities going on that may be of interest to families. Invite photographers and/or reporters to cover special center activities. Children from your center singing for a group of senior citizens, a center anniversary open house, or a special board meeting to honor a long-time board member, all make good human interest stories for the paper. They also make your center better recognized in the community.

Your personal reputation in the community reflects on your program. Are you viewed as honest, mature, hardworking, and compassionate? Are you and your staff seen as individuals who can be counted on to work for the good of the community? Is your staff aware that their public behavior reflects on your program's reputation? Simple things like answering the phone with courtesy can be important. Greeting visitors, answering questions, and helping parents find services they need can all affect the image of your program.

One essential part of building your program is to be sure you are meeting the needs of community families. For example, operating an infant program is often not profitable. You may not be sure it is worth providing this service. However, in most communities, there is a serious shortage of good infant care. Families who enroll their children in your infant program become familiar with your center. They are likely to continue enrollment for the entire length of time that their children need care, 9-2. In this respect, one part of your program becomes publicity for another part.

Director's Dilemma

You have been operating a center for several months. Things are going reasonably well, but you feel that many people don't know about your center. What things could you do to make the community more aware of your center?

9-2 When parents are satisfied with their child's infant or toddler care, they will probably stay with your program as their child gets older.

A full enrollment in your preschool classes can lead you to think about offering an after-school care program. As the preschoolers grow older, their families' child care needs will change. As with the infant program, most families would prefer to stick with a center that is working out well for them.

Many young families have not given much consideration to the idea that they will some day need child care. It comes as a surprise when they realize that quality child care may not be easy to find. The reality of the need to return to the workforce and having to leave their child in the care of others can be difficult to handle.

When parents first approach your center, they may have very mixed feelings about leaving their child in the care of someone else. They want good quality care, but they also want it to be convenient and inexpensive. It is helpful for parents to be given some information on the qualifications of the staff. The program's license should also be displayed where parents can see it. As they begin to explore various child care options, they may begin to realize that finding the right place for their child is a more complicated task than they expected.

How Can We Make the Center a Welcome Place for Parents?

Consider all the ways that parents may first make contact with your center. Then begin to look at each of those contacts from the parents' point of view. Would they feel welcome? Would they feel like intruders? Begin to work on making each point of contact a comfortable place for parents.

Telephone Inquiries

Most parents will make their initial contacts with the center by phone. The attitude and helpfulness of the person who answers the phone will make the initial impression on the family. In a very small center, where you are the director-teacher-secretary, you might need an answering machine to handle routine calls. A pleasant message promising to call back later in the day when you are not with the children, will reassure parents of your priorities.

Larger programs will have a receptionist/secretary to answer the phone. You must be sure that this person understands the importance of tone of voice in greeting callers. The phone should be answered with a pleasant, "hello", the name of the center and, "May I help you?" The receptionist will be able to handle many routine calls for information. This can save you and other staff members valuable time.

One way to keep track of calls is to develop a log sheet that is kept by the phone. It should be divided into columns so that basic information about the call can be quickly recorded. Information to be kept should include

- date and time of call

- name and number of caller

- nature of call

- any further action to be taken regarding the call

- action completed

A log like this can help to ensure that if a caller has been promised a program flyer, that it has actually been sent. Sometimes promises made over the phone are forgotten. This causes ill will and leads callers to think you don't care about them. With a written log, you can be sure to return calls, look up answers to questions, or send out information.

The receptionist should also have an up-to-date list of appointment times. If a parent wants to come in to discuss enrollment, an appointment should be set up as quickly as possible with the appropriate staff member.

Above all, the person answering the phone should speak clearly and courteously. Parents may be reluctant to make that first call when exploring child care options. They need to hear a welcoming voice, 9-3.

Make a First Visit Easy for Potential Clients

There are many ways that the center can convey signs of welcome. One of the easiest ways is to simply have clear directional signs to help parents know where to go. Entering a strange building with no directory can be overwhelming. Standing in the middle of a hallway, helplessly looking around, is not a positive experience. Signs and arrows that point to major offices and classrooms can ease entry into the building.

A bright bulletin board placed by the entrance can serve as a warm greeting. The smiling face of the receptionist is another welcome sight. An environment with the cheerful hum of busy activity, perhaps with the smell of cookies baking, can all assure the parent that this is a happy place to be.

9-3 A pleasant voice on the phone can help parents feel that they are welcome to visit the center.

What Do I Need to Do to Register and Enroll Children?

The process of enrollment management includes several different steps. Attention must be paid to developing smooth procedures for *registration*, a written expression of interest telling you that parents are seriously interested in having their child attend your program. The *enrollment* process occurs when the center has an opening for the child and the parents make a commitment that the child will attend.

Your center may have a long *waiting list*, a list of children who are registered but waiting for an opening to occur. If so, you will also have to develop policies that will allow smooth, rapid movement from waiting list to center placement. Because of the priorities of sponsoring or funding agencies, this may not be as simple as "first come, first served."

It is also necessary to consider the appropriate group placement for each child enrolling in the center. While children are often placed in groups based on their ages, if you have several classrooms of the same age group, you must identify the group where the child and parents will feel most comfortable.

Keeping track of the reasons families leave the center can also give you valuable information. Hopefully, most of those who leave will do so for reasons that have nothing to do with your program. However, you need to know if a family withdraws its child because of inconvenient center hours or a concern about the experience its child is having.

Registration Procedures

When families register their children with your program, they are telling you they are interested in enrollment. Your program has not guaranteed it can provide care. The parents have not promised to enroll if space is available. Registration merely indicates a family has begun a process with your program that may lead to enrollment.

Some families who register are eager to enroll as soon as possible. Other families may be planning for child care at some point in the future. Still other families may be signing up for space at several centers. They may be on several waiting lists and will decide where to go later. Many things can change families' plans between the time they register and when their children officially enroll. You cannot assume a lengthy registration list will automatically mean full groups.

Develop a registration form that covers information you need to know about the child and family, 9-4. It should include such basic information as

- name, birth date, and address of the child

- type and hours of care needed

- name of parent or legal guardian

- any special circumstances, such as referral from another agency

- other siblings already enrolled in the program

- date when care is needed

Although similar information is needed by all centers for the registration process, you will need to develop a form that fits your center. For example, if a certain

---

Child Care Center
Sample Registration Form

Child's name _____ Birth date _____

Date when care is needed _____

Name and address of parent(s) or legal guardian_____

_____

Phone _____

Employer's name and address _____

Do you need full-time or part-time care?_____

Days of the week when care is needed: Mon. Tues. Wed. Thurs. Fri.

Hours when care is needed: _____

Other children enrolled in the center: _____

Are you eligible for any subsidy or voucher from any source that will provide full or partial payment

of tuition? Please explain. _____

Parent signature _____

Date _____

A nonrefundable registration fee of $xx must be included.

9-4 A registration form must provide the information you need to put the child's name on the waiting list.

employer helps to sponsor your program in return for spaces for employees' children, you will need to know if a member of the family is employed by that employer. If your program has several centers in nearby towns, you will need to ask in which center location the family is interested.

If a family is eligible for subsidized care, a financial disclosure statement may also be completed or attached at this time. If your program receives a subsidy for child care, incorporate subsidy guidelines into your enrollment management procedures.

Because staff time and effort are necessary to process registration materials, some programs charge a registration fee. This may discourage some well-intentioned families from registering for your program. On the other hand, it may prevent registrations from families who have little intention of actually enrolling in your program.

Waiting List Management

No matter the size of your program, you may have more children registered than you can enroll. In such cases, you will need to develop a waiting list. A waiting list is made up of children whose families have completed the registration process. They are ready to enroll as soon as a space is available.

If you operate a large center, you will have to develop procedures to keep your waiting list up-to-date. Even if your program is small, the following suggestions will help you manage your waiting list.

Determine whether your program will operate on a simple first-come-first-serve basis. In a small program, this policy is usually the fairest and easiest. However, if your program receives support money in the form of grants or subsidies, waiting list procedures may be more complicated.

There may be priorities that must be applied to the applications. For example, government subsidy money is usually used to support working families whose income is within a particular range. Among those financially eligible, first priority may be given to single-parent families. Priority may also be given to families where a parent is in job training. Children with special needs who have been referred from other human service agencies often are given priority status. If your program is sponsored by a particular employer, employees may have first chance at spaces, 9-5. Only when the "priority" children have been enrolled, will others be able to fill empty slots.

Many programs also feel that it is important to give preference to families with other children already in the program. It is very difficult for parents to have one child in one center and another child somewhere else. If the family finds another center that will enroll all of their children, you may lose the whole family.

Your program's ability to move a child from the waiting list to enrollment in the program may also depend on other factors. If you have several centers, the location preferred by the parent may influence the time when a child can be enrolled. You may have a space in one classroom, but not another. There may be available spaces in a group of four-year-olds, but no "slot" for toddlers. If a family has a preference of location, group, or teacher, time on the waiting list may be lengthened. A family who is willing to take any classroom where there is space may be able to enroll more quickly.

9-5 This child was enrolled as soon as there was an opening because her mother worked for the business that sponsored the program.

Some centers in large cities have waiting lists with 400 or more children on them. In these programs, waiting list management is very complicated. It is essential that you develop procedures that can guide this process. The procedures must be fair. They must be easily explained to both parents and staff.

Careful waiting list management is important to both families and your center. A parent who is ready to start a job usually needs child care quickly. The availability of child care may make the difference in whether or not the parent can take the job. At the same time, empty spaces in your program mean lost income. Financially, it is important that you keep enrollment as close to capacity as possible in order to maximize income.

As children move to the top of the waiting list, it may be helpful to offer a parent education meeting on children's readiness for group situations. If parent meetings are not feasible, printed information sent home may help parents to determine if their child is ready for the group experience. Some children may be old enough for enrollment, but not ready emotionally to adjust to the situation. While most children do adjust in a few days, some children are overwhelmed and distressed continually. Some children may adapt easily to a small family child care setting, but not to a larger center classroom. You need to talk with parents to help find the right placement for each child.

Enrollment Procedures

Develop formal policies and procedures for the enrollment of children. These procedures allow parents to know what services they will receive. The parents, at this point, make a commitment to send their child to your program. This allows you to plan group placement. It also signals you to make preparations for the new child to enter the program.

The actual enrollment of children represents a commitment from both your program and the parents. Your program is committed to provide care during specific times. The parents make a commitment to abide by program procedures and to pay for the child care service. Enrollment procedures should clearly spell out the obligations of each side. Fewer problems will develop when parents understand this commitment.

Begin by developing an enrollment form, 9-6. The enrollment form should request specific information needed for your program. Some of the information you may want to request is

- name, address, phone number, and birth date of the child

- name, address, and phone number of parent(s) or legal guardian

- emergency information, such as the child's allergies, chronic health conditions, and family doctor or pediatrician

Director's Dilemma

A mother calls to enroll her child in your center. She tells you that there is a job she can have if she can start right away. Your center is full and there is a waiting list. You know that there probably will be no openings for several months. How would you handle this situation?

Child Care Center
Sample Enrollment Form

Child's name ———————————————— Birth date ————————————

Parent(s) or legal guardian's name ————————————————————————

Address ———————————————————— Phone ————————————

Parent(s) or legal guardian's employer ————————————————————

Employer address ———————————————— Phone ————————————

Date when care will begin ——————— Full-time ——— Part-time ———

Days and hours when care will be provided ——————————————————
   (See schedule for days when program is closed.)

Emergency information

Name, address, and phone of child's doctor: ——————————————————

——

Name of person to contact if the parents are unavailable in case of an emergency: —————

——

Allergies or chronic health conditions: ————————————————————

——

I give my permission for my child to be treated by the doctor or hospital in case I am unavailable
and an emergency need for medical care occurs.
                Signature——————————————— Date ———————————

Names and phone numbers of persons authorized to pick up child from the center:

1. ———————————————————— Phone ————————————

2. ———————————————————— Phone ————————————

3. ———————————————————— Phone ————————————

How will your child be transported to the center? ——————————————————

Names of other siblings enrolled in the center: ——————————————————

Child's likes and dislikes, fears, etc.: ————————————————————

For office use:
Fee ——————— **Person responsible for fee payments** ——————————————

              Address, phone ————————————————————

Fees are payable each Monday for the following week.

9-6 Enrollment forms include the service the center will provide and the amount that the
parent will pay for the service. Parents should have a copy of the enrollment form.

- names of persons who are authorized to pick the child up from the center

- name of person who will be responsible for paying the fees

- amount of the fee and payment information

- times and dates of care (list any dates when the center will be closed)

- starting date for child

- name, address, and phone number of employers

- general information on child such as likes, dislikes, fears, etc.

- other siblings enrolled in the center

In addition to the above, parents may also need to supply the program with additional information. Children's health status obtained on a physical exam may be necessary. Proof of immunization is required by many states. Signed photo release forms should be requested if you anticipate taking any pictures in the classrooms.

Required forms or information are usually easier to obtain at the time of enrollment. Once a child begins to attend the program, both parents and staff are likely to overlook incomplete information. This can create problems later when a need for that information occurs.

Parents must be assured that the information they provide will be kept confidential. You must develop procedures that ensure confidentiality. Only those staff whose work requires them to have access to the information should be able to see it. Staff should be cautioned to never allow files or paperwork regarding families to be left out on desktops. When not in use, files should be kept in locked file cabinets. All computer records on families and children should be coded so unauthorized individuals cannot get into the files. Parents should also be assured that they have the right to look at all the information on file about their child at any time.

Eligibility for Subsidized Care

Many programs participate in the state provision of *subsidized care*. This means families who meet certain guidelines can receive child care for a reduced fee. The state or other agency, through various formulas and financial mechanisms, pays the remainder of the child care cost. If your program is part of this subsidized care program, you will need to let families know about this benefit.

In some states, each program is responsible for determining which families are eligible for the subsidy. Family eligibility is determined upon application to the program. In other states, a centrally located, independent office makes that determination. An eligible family may receive a voucher that can be used as partial payment at any approved center.

If your program participates in subsidized child care, you will need to identify state procedures to certify eligible families. You must identify personnel who will be responsible for verifying the eligibility. The impact of subsidy eligibility on the family's place on the waiting list must also be determined.

Special Needs

When a child with a special need is enrolled, communication with parents is essential. Parents can provide specific information regarding their child. They can help staff become informed about care and safety procedures. Parents often have the special equipment their child needs during the day. If they don't have it, you may be able to help them arrange for needed items or you may purchase some from center funds. Many educational and charitable organizations exist to help meet children's special needs. They may provide special training, educational materials, or additional equipment items, 9-7.

As the program director, you must be sure that your staff has access to information, equipment, and support. Every child needs to participate in center activities as fully as possible. Establish procedures to ensure children's safety and to help provide them with successful experiences. Sensitive and well-trained staff will welcome all children and work to help them have a positive experience.

How Do I Determine the Best Group Arrangements?

As you begin enrollment, consider the assignment of children into groups. In planning group assignments, many factors must be considered. These include such factors as age, personality, the child's previous experiences in group care, special needs, and existing openings. Try to match each child up with a group that is compatible. This can make the adjustment process easier for children, parents, and staff.

When children first enroll in your program, you must decide where to place them. If your groups are based strictly on age, the decision is easy. A three-year-old will go into a three-year-old group. A toddler will go into a toddler group. However, if there are several overlapping age groups, the decisions may be more difficult.

Begin by considering your state's licensing requirements. These requirements often specify the following:

- number of children allowed in a given classroom based on room size

- maximum group size

- age range of children in a group

- adult-to-child ratio based on the ages of the children in the group

- qualifications of teachers based on age range of children in group

9-7 This oxygen tank is stored where staff can reach it quickly if a child with lung problems needs it.

The regulations will affect the number of children who can be placed in each group. This, in turn, affects where you have an opening and which child on the waiting list matches the mandated group characteristics.

Ideally, children should be placed in groups where they can feel comfortable quickly. Information from parents will help you to determine the best group for each child. When matching children with groups, the following should be considered:

- the age and sex of the child

- personality characteristics of the child

- personalities of other children in the group

- style and personality of the teachers and staff

- developmental level of the child

- previous group experience of the child

- special needs of the child

Current research indicates that a child with special needs should be placed in a group with other children of the same chronological age. This helps to give them role models of children their own age and helps to build their self-esteem.

Ages of Children

You must decide whether to have mixed ages in each group. If you are starting a small center, it may be necessary to have a mixed age group until enrollment increases. Once you have enough children to have separate classrooms for three-year-olds, four-year-olds and five-year-olds, you may decide to create separate groups based on age.

There are advantages and disadvantages to both types of groups. Usually, *chronological groups*, groups of children of similar age, are interested in similar activities. They have similar developmental characteristics and similar needs. This makes planning for same-age groups somewhat easier. However, within any age grouping, there is wide variation in children's development. Teachers still must plan to meet the needs of each child as an individual, 9-8.

Vertical grouping occurs when mixed ages are present in a classroom. This type of grouping is also called family grouping since the varying ages in the room are closer to what children would experience in their own homes. This means a wider age range and obviously different age characteristics and individual needs within the group. Teachers must be especially careful to plan the types of activities that allow all children to be successful. A unique benefit of vertical grouping is that younger children get a chance to learn from older ones. Children, as they get older, have the opportunity to help younger ones.

In a large center with several classrooms, you can determine which type of group seems to work best with your teachers and program. In a program with only one classroom, vertical age groups usually occur automatically. The exception to this

9-8 These children quickly formed friendships with each other.

might be a half-day preschool program aimed specifically at children who will be attending kindergarten the following year.

Hours Care Is Provided

Grouping decisions may also be influenced by the hours when particular children need care. If you have several who all need care early in the morning, they could be in the same group. If the "early " children are spread out throughout the building, you will need a staff person in each classroom. If all of the "early" children are in the same room, you may need fewer staff until later in the day.

Group Characteristics and Cost

There is an important relationship between the types of groups you create and the cost of your program. That cost is tied directly to the number of staff you must have to operate the program. Any decision that increases or decreases the number of adults needed, will have an impact on the budget.

When considering the most cost-effective way to structure your groups, review licensing requirements. Mixed age groups, for example, may require adult-to-child ratios based on the youngest child in the group. A decision to group older and younger children separately may result in a need for fewer staff.

You may decide that a particular grouping pattern is worthwhile even though more costly. Keep in mind that state regulations represent minimal standards. A decision that results in higher standards, for example, more adults in the group, may be desirable. It will also be more expensive.

How Can I Help Children and Families Adjust to Child Care?

Entering child care can be an exciting adventure for children and their parents. It is a milestone in growing up. As with any major life change, the emotions felt by parents and children are likely to be both positive and negative. For children, there is the pleasure of finding new friends and toys. At the same time, children usually experience *separation anxiety*, fears about being away from their parent, 9-9. They also may have doubts about finding friends, and a general anxiety about their ability to cope with this new experience.

For parents, there is also the joy of seeing their child take a major step toward independence. When parents are happy with their choice of program, they are usually pleased at the opportunities for play and learning their child will have. Yet, for parents, this is a difficult time also. They often feel guilty for leaving the child. If the child has not been in child care before, the caregiving parent may feel a great sense of loss at not being with the child all the time.

Well-trained and caring staff should understand the mixed feelings of both children and parents. They know that a quality program includes helping families adjust to this important step in their lives. The friendly support of staff must be available to help each family make this transition.

Helping Parents Help Their Children

Sometimes, parents don't know how to help their children get started in the center. Some parents might tell their children, "If you're not good, the teacher won't like you!", or "Just be quiet and don't cause any trouble." These kinds of comments frighten children. Rather than help, they make the child's adjustment to the center more difficult.

Center staff can help by preparing a list of suggestions that will help parents know what to say and do to help their children. They can encourage parents to understand that this new transition can be stressful for the child. They can assure parents that the staff will have concern and compassion for their child.

Teachers can also help parents understand their own feelings about child care. Most parents

9-9 Most children experience separation anxiety. A sensitive, well-trained teacher can help children handle this new situation.

have mixed feelings about leaving their child at a child care center. There is relief at having a few hours without the responsibility of caring for the child. However, there is also a sense of loss and guilt over leaving the child with someone else. For some parents, this can be quite overwhelming. A caring teacher can help to reassure the parent that these feelings are normal. Staff are also important in helping the parents see clearly that their children are being cared for well. If the parent is comfortable with the situation, the child's adjustment to the center may be easier.

Families approach the start of child care with mixed feelings. There is relief that a good child care program has been found. However, there is also the realization that their child is taking a significant step away from the family and into the larger world. Most parents view a good preschool setting as a positive experience for children. Yet, parents often feel guilty about leaving their child in the care of others.

The family may also be experiencing other major changes. Child care is often needed because a parent is starting a new job or job training. This also can be a cause of stress and worry for the parent. Following a divorce, the single parent may seek child care. The child will already be facing dramatic changes in his or her family structure.

The staff of your program should be prepared to accept the concerns of parents and children. Sensitive help and understanding can ease the separation anxiety that both parents and children may experience, 9-10. Smooth entrance of children into the program helps to build your center's reputation. Parents talk to other parents. When one family feels good about the child care decision they have made, they will tell others. When a teacher compassionately helps children adjust, the parents become supporters of the center.

Develop procedures that support and enhance children's adjustment to child care. Compassionate entrance procedures into the program can result in happier, more comfortable children. It can be the best advertisement for your program. These entrance procedures should include: parent orientation, a home visit, if possible, a gradual entrance for the child into the classroom, and on-going reassurance and communication between staff and parents.

Parent Orientation

New families should be reassured that they have made a wise decision in choosing your program. They need to know that the program has a well-trained staff. They should feel that their children will be nurtured and kept safe. This may be done through an individual home visit or through a group meeting.

Home Visits

It is often a good idea for teachers to visit with parents and children in their own home. These are referred to as *home visits*. This allows the family to get to know the teacher within a familiar environment. Meeting the teacher in the center can be intimidating to parents and children. For parents, meeting the teacher as a visitor to their home may be more comfortable. Parents can be given needed information about the classroom and center operation as well as see that the teacher is a kind and caring individual.

The child is aware that the teacher and parents are getting to know each other. Children also like to show teachers their room, pets, special toys, or a favorite play area. When entering the classroom, the child will see the teacher as a familiar face and a friend. Children are likely to feel more secure because they have already met the teacher.

For the teacher, home visits can give greater insight into the child's home and family life, 9-11. The teacher can help the child by mentioning information related to the home visit, such as "How is your bunny today?" or "I liked the pretty blue color of your room." The teacher can also be more aware of the lifestyle and concerns that parents may have.

Home visits are a valuable way to get to know parents and children. They can also be costly in staff time. If there is any concern about the safety of a staff member during a home visit, it is essential that at least two staff members make the visit together. It may also not be feasible to make a home visit because of time, safety, travel distance, extended bad weather, or parent unwillingness.

Group Meetings

If several families enroll at the center at the same time, a group meeting may be appropriate. This ***orientation meeting*** gives new parents in the program a chance to learn more about the center. They also have a chance to meet other new parents and to get to know the staff. Orientation meetings are usually held in the fall, but they may be held anytime a new group of children have started at the center. You may plan only one meeting, or several as the year progresses. Orientation meetings often form the beginning of a series of parent education programs.

Any orientation meeting needs to focus on helping parents feel comfortable with the center, the staff, and each other. Refreshments are important in setting a relaxed tone. Name tags help people get to know each other. Slides of center activities, or a brief video showing quality

9-10 Playing in the "post office" is fun, but sometimes this boy misses his parents and needs the support of a caring teacher.

9-11 A home visit involving an activity, such as putting a puzzle together, gives the child, parents, and teacher a chance to get to know one another.

child care, can also be useful in holding parents' interest. If information must be presented in lecture form, keep it brief. Use handouts or posters to emphasize your points. It is important that this first meeting be relaxed, fun, and interesting. If it is not, parents will be reluctant to return to other meetings.

The parent orientation meeting serves several purposes. It should

- introduce parents to their child's teacher and classroom

- help parents understand the program philosophy

- give parents the daily schedule and examples of typical activities

- explain basic procedures and policies regarding attendance/health

- describe fee and payment policies

- identify additional services that may be available through your program

- help parents understand changes they may see in their child's behavior

- give parents information on how to help their child cope with separation anxiety

- reassure parents and answer questions that they may have.

Programs can do other things to support parents. Some centers have developed a parent handbook that answers many questions. A lending library of books on child development and parenting can be helpful. Other centers plan ongoing meetings for parents. Help in arranging carpools or finding additional needed services can create the sense that the center is a place for parents as well as children.

Gradual Beginnings

There is more to enrolling children than just getting parents to "sign on the dotted line." You must also develop procedures for helping children enter and adjust to the center. For some children this will be an easy process. For others, it will be more difficult.

Child development experts recommend a gradual entrance into the center program. Children need a chance to visit the classroom with parents before being expected to stay. During this short visit, they can look around and meet the teacher. They can discover the locations of toys, bathrooms, and cubbies. Children should be reassured that the staff of the center is kind and caring. They also should see that parents and staff respect each other.

Whenever possible, plan another short visit or keep the first day of attendance brief. Allow the child to bring a security object such as a stuffed toy, pillow, blanket, etc., to help with the transition from home to center. Be sure your staff is trained to provide sensitive support for each new child. Even though your center is a wonderful place, new children and their parents may feel some separation anxiety.

Children's feelings of nervousness, fear, loneliness and, even sadness must be respected. It is unrealistic to think that new children will walk right in the first day without a twinge of concern, 9-12. Children deserve to be treated as you would want to be treated in a new situation. Gentle support and encouragement provided by well-trained staff can help children adjust to the center.

Happy, well-adjusted children are your best advertisement. When children like the center, parents tell other parents. They are also likely to keep their child in your program for as long as the child needs care. A poor center is often like a revolving door. Children may be enrolled and withdrawn from the program quickly as parents discover the program is not what they want.

Parent Reassurances and Communication

Part of helping parents feel comfortable with your center is maintaining communication with them. When parents feel at ease in talking with the center staff, important information can more easily be passed back and forth.

Parents must be kept informed about how their children are doing. Parents who feel guilty or anxious about leaving their children, need to know that the teachers understand their concern. When the staff can share interesting parts of a child's day, the parent knows that the child has been carefully supervised. Parents may also often feel that they are missing significant milestones in a child's development. Communication between staff and parent can help minimize some of that feeling of loss.

Communication works positively in both directions. Staff shares information with parents. Parents share information with staff. Much of what happens at home affects children's behavior in the center. Ideally, parents will inform the staff when something significant has occurred in their children's lives. Likewise, staff should share significant classroom events with parents.

In cases of divorce or separation, noncustodial parents may feel uninvolved with the center. Even though they may be actively involved at other times with their children, they are usually not included on the center's mailing list, or they may not see invitations, notices, or newsletters sent home with the children. Many centers ask the custodial parent for permission to include the noncustodial parent and grandparents in center communications and activities. Of course, this decision is made by the custodial parent and must be respected. When approved, however, it gives the noncustodial parent a better understanding of the child's daily life in child care.

9-12 Children often experience an adjustment period during the first few days at a center. Caring staff can make this transition easier for children and their parents.

Communication between parents and staff is particularly important when the children are young, 9-13. Information is needed on naps, bowel movements, formula or food intake, and general mood. Young children can't use words to describe how they feel. Caregivers and parents often have to be detectives to determine whether a child is ill or simply tired. Many centers develop a simple form for communication with parents. Teachers then simply check off information that parents need to know on a daily basis.

You should also consider other forms of communication with parents. When you have a variety of contacts with parents, each can find what is most useful. Many families like to receive the following:

- newsletters and parent handbook

- monthly menus

Good Things to Know			
Child:			
Setting	**Date/Time**	**Event**	**Comments**
Play area	9/25 11:15 a.m.	Kasey pulled herself into a standing position in the play gym.	First time we have seen this at the center. Has she done this at home? Way to go, Kasey!

How the Day Went

Child:

Feeding: _____

Sleeping: _____

Toileting: _____

Self-care: _____

Caregiver: _____ Date: _____

9-13 These are forms of communication that can help to reassure parents about the care their children receive.

- schedule of classroom activities

- notice of special events for children and families

- center open house

- parent-teacher conferences

Sometimes special efforts must be made to include items or events that will appeal to fathers. Many of the parent materials and/or meetings tend to be oriented toward mothers. Involving fathers in center activities can help them learn about their children's development and provide an enjoyable time. Everything you do to help parents feel comfortable with your program will build their commitment to your center. Every time your staff compassionately helps a child and parent adjust to child care, your program gains a satisfied family. More information on parent involvement is discussed in Chapter 17.

☼ Summary

Marketing your program successfully means letting people know that it exists. You must determine ways to advertise your program to the families who are most likely to enroll. You must also be concerned about the long-term reputation of your program within the community.

Registration and enrollment procedures should be developed that support the smooth entrance of children into the center. These procedures must be clear and easy to explain. They must also take into account the priorities of funding sources and group limitations imposed by licensing.

The size, age range, hours of needed care, and number of adult staff needed can all vary. These factors also can determine how expensive a group is to operate. Decisions regarding placement of children in groups are important. They can affect the ease with which a child adjusts to the center. They can also affect the cost of operating the classroom.

Procedures that help both children and adults adapt to child care should be carefully considered. Sensitive handling of separation anxiety can help ease adjustment. On-going communication with parents and a gradual entrance for children are essential components of a good beginning. Helping families adjust positively to child care helps build their long-term commitment to your program.

☼ Terms

public relations
registration
enrollment
waiting list
subsidized care
chronological group
vertical grouping
separation anxiety
home visits
orientation meeting

☼ Review

1. What are the two main goals of a public relations campaign?

2. List four types of advertising that could be used to let people know about your program.

3. List three items that should not be included in written advertising materials and explain why.

4. Describe some ways directors can expand their influence into the community.

5. In what ways can you make it easier to welcome visitors and potential clients to your center?

6. What factors may affect a child's placement on a center's waiting list?

7. What is the difference between the registration process and the enrollment process?

8. Compare *chronological groups* and *vertical groups.*

9. Give an example of a gradual beginning for a child entering the center as a new enrollee.

10. Name four types of communication that you can use with parents.

☼ Applications

1. Design an advertising flyer to interest potential students in this class. Briefly identify the goals of the course. Include a description of the class and the main areas that you study. Include all the necessary information an individual would need to know to enroll in this class.

2. Plan and staff an informational booth with your classmates at your local county fair, shopping mall, or other locations where young families might be. Prepare posters, banners, etc., that will attract young families to your booth. Obtain brochures and articles from professional organizations or prepare your own, that describe what to look for in quality child care. Also prepare or obtain printed materials on how to help children adjust to child care. Distribute these to interested families. Be ready to explain the information and its importance to anyone who might stop to collect materials on these topics.

3. Obtain permission to attend a parent orientation meeting at a program for children. Observe the process of the meeting. Write your reactions to the following questions after the meeting. Discuss your reactions with your class. Were any special measures taken to help parents feel welcome and at ease at the meeting? What topics were discussed? Were parents helped to get to know each other? Was the meeting a pleasant experience for the parents? If you were a parent, would you want to go to another meeting?

Chapter 10
The Daily Program

After studying this chapter, you will be able to

- define the role of program philosophy in program planning.

- explain the elements of a developmentally appropriate curriculum.

- discuss the decisions made when planning a daily schedule.

- recognize the value of the various activities in each time slot.

- relate how a positive atmosphere contributes to each child's emotional support and well-being.

Good programs for children require careful planning. A carefully thought-out daily plan is essential to a quality program. Well-trained teachers understand the importance of the daily program in providing a successful and satisfying experience for each child in the classroom.

What Role Does Your Program's Philosophy Play in Program Planning?

This book is based on a program approach known as developmentally appropriate practices. It was developed after a careful consideration of children's age characteristics. Guidelines help teachers match the classroom environment, schedule, and activities to the children's readiness and needs. Teachers are expected to plan a program that is developmentally appropriate for each child.

The guidelines help teachers identify *objectives*, which are goals for what they want the children to gain from their experiences. This further helps teachers think about planning activities that help children reach those objectives. By focusing on children's needs, likes, and abilities, teachers are guided as they plan an environment to meet these needs and provide support for children in accomplishing the developmental tasks of early childhood. This approach, based on developmental appropriateness, helps teachers avoid activities that are too

Director's Dilemma
A parent is considering enrolling his child in your center, but he is afraid the child will be bored. How would you reassure him that the child will have a busy, productive day?

easy and boring for the children, 10-1. It also aids in preventing the planning of activities that are too challenging and frustrating for the children. Teachers whose planning is based on age-related characteristics and needs also use the guidelines to identify the best ways to guide and support children.

What Needs Must Be Met Through the Daily Program?

Trained staff are aware of the age-related characteristics and needs of their classroom group. Through careful observation and conversation with parents, they must also develop a knowledge of each child's individual needs. Teachers should understand the patterns of growth in the physical, social, emotional, cognitive, and language areas of development.

Plans for each day's program should include activities that will support development in each of these areas. For example, an obstacle course might be set up to help children develop better large muscle coordination, 10-2. Buttoning a doll's dress aids small muscle coordination. Playing with dolls while involved in socio-dramatic play contributes to the children's social skills. It also helps children explore new ideas and relate the play to real-life experiences. Planning for all areas of development is not difficult when the room is well-equipped for its age group and when the teacher understands the needs of the children. However, it does take deliberate care and effort to ensure that all areas are included.

The following sections of this chapter identify the elements of the program that should be available for children. Suggestions for creating a developmentally appropriate classroom are included.

10-1 This three-year-old is deeply absorbed in figuring out how scissors and a paper punch work.

What Should Be Included in the Daily Program?

As the director of the program, you may have to help your teachers plan an appropriate schedule. This schedule must be based on the needs and developmental levels of the children in each group. It should reflect knowledge of young children and an understanding of the activities needed on a daily basis.

Child development specialists have identified the elements that should be included in the daily schedule of each classroom. Most good preschools have daily programs that are very similar.

Free Play

Free play is the heart of the preschool day. It is also frequently the most misunderstood. Many people consider free play to be a waste of time, or they think that it is a frivolous activity to be allowed when there is nothing better to do. Both of these viewpoints reflect a lack of information about how young children learn.

Young children are bombarded with sights, sounds, and experiences all the time. Play activities, particularly dramatic or pretend play, give children the opportunity to make sense out of all their varied experiences. The *free play time* is the time of the day when children can make choices about the things they want to do. It is a time when they can work on those things that have meaning to them, 10-3.

Children can master new skills and integrate new information with previously known ideas through play. Children who are tense or experiencing stress can choose soothing activities. Children who have had an emotionally upsetting experience may choose to use the dramatic play props to recreate the experience in a safe, controllable setting.

10-2 All of these toys are fun to use, and they help to develop large muscle coordination.

Another important component of generous free play time is it allows for child-initiated activity where children have the opportunity to decide what they want to do and to control the amount of time they spend with it. They have a sense of control over their lives that they cannot get when a teacher controls access to every activity. This promotes a sense of initiative. Children who have some control are more likely to feel a sense of responsibility. They are helped to become "self-starters" in a world where too many people sit back and wait for something interesting to happen.

There are great differences in the needs and abilities of a group of preschoolers. A schedule that minimizes free play assumes that all children are ready for and interested in the same things at the same time.

One mistake that teachers often make is to assume that free play "just happens." Simply telling the children to "go play now" or "find something to do" will not lead to a productive free play time.

Teachers must plan free play carefully. A valuable free play time must include teacher planning in the following areas:

- allowing a substantial block of time in the daily schedule (usually 45-60 minutes)

- planning a room arrangement that has zoned areas and a variety of equipment

- creating attractive, inviting set-ups within the zoned areas

- providing interesting special activities or special props for dramatic play

- encouraging an atmosphere that conveys approval of play

- allowing materials to be used in a variety of ways

- including creative art and reading of stories as part of the choices

- providing opportunities for both individual and small group activities

- allowing for both active and quiet interests of children

Teachers control the framework of the free play time. The activities, time, available equipment, and general atmosphere are all established by the adult. Within this framework, children can make choices and pursue activities that are of greatest interest to them.

Story Time

The preschool years are wonderful times to help children learn to love and enjoy listening to books. There are many outstanding classics that have been written with young children in mind. Books can help children understand themselves and others better. They can help children make sense out of the complex adult world. They can also provide sheer pleasure.

Many classrooms have several different story times throughout the day. Full-day programs should have a story time in both the morning and afternoon. Books should also be available for informal reading times during free play or quiet times as well.

10-3 Free play time gives children practice in making choices about how to use their time.

Some teachers have a large group story time for their entire group. Other teachers have found that breaking the large group into two or three smaller story groups is more successful. With the smaller group format, stories can be chosen with the interests and abilities of that particular group in mind. It is almost impossible to find a story that is appropriate and interesting for both three-year-olds and five-year-olds.

The amount of time devoted to story time will vary. Older children like more complicated stories and can sit and listen for longer time periods. Younger children, whose books are mostly pictures, will enjoy the experience more if it is kept shorter.

Young children are beginners at the skills of listening to stories and enjoying books. A story time that is too long or a book that is too complicated will frustrate and bore them. This can lead children to avoid stories later on.

Story time should probably be about 15 minutes long. It may be lengthened or shortened according to the nature of the story or the interests of the children. Often teachers use puppets, flannel board stories, or fingerplays during this time, 10-4. Especially popular are stories that involve a lot of movement and physical activity on the part of the children. A 15 minute story time that includes several fingerplays, a flannel board story and/or a good book may hold the children's interest for much longer than the basic 15 minutes. On the other hand, a long book with few pictures may hold the attention of some for the full time, but may not be appropriate for all.

Music and Movement

Music and movement activities can also be planned for the entire group of children. As with story time, many teachers prefer to break the large group into several smaller groups. This makes the activities less intimidating for cautious children.

Music activities help children become familiar with another aspect of the world. Music provides another form of communication. It can convey feelings and emotion that are difficult to express in words. Music can be relaxing for a tense child. It can stimulate the interest of a bored child. Through music, children learn songs of their culture as well as basic elements of tone and rhythm.

Movement activities help children become more confident with their bodies. They learn how their bodies move and what their bodies can do. Confidence and coordination can be improved by lively opportunities for movement, 10-5.

Often, teachers will plan story and music times together. As long as there is enough variation in the segments, children can remain interested. When planned alone, music and/or movement should probably be about 15 minutes. It may occasionally go longer if children are interested, or it may be cut shorter. Some children may want to stay for more songs, while others are ready to move on.

10-4 This story area allows teachers to create interesting story times using puppets and flannel board figures.

10-5 Music activities involving movement help to maintain children's interest.

Teachers often incorporate music and movement activities into other times of the day. Singing a song while pushing a child on the swings can be a delight for teacher and child alike. Using music to soothe children who are ready for nap is also a helpful technique. Movement activities done outside can provide greater freedom for the children to investigate how their bodies move.

Snack and Mealtimes

Snacks and/or mealtimes are an essential part of the day. A busy schedule at the center will require a lot of energy on the part of the children. When they are hungry, children are more likely to become irritable and difficult.

Some centers have formal "sit-down" snack times. All children are expected to join the group at the table. At other centers, the snack is simply offered from a cart. Children who are hungry can select the food they want and eat it at a nearby table.

Snacks typically take about 15 minutes out of the schedule. This time may be lengthened if the teachers also use it for story time or other small group activities.

When a snack is offered informally, it may be available for about 20 minutes. With this type of arrangement, children must be alerted in time to get the snack before it is removed.

Breakfast is one meal that works well when offered informally. Some children will have had breakfast at home before coming to the center, while other children will not. When the cereals, toast, or other breakfast foods are available for 30-45 minutes, you can usually cover all of the children who arrive at different times of the morning.

Most teachers are strong advocates of providing breakfast for children. They recognize that hungry children are less likely to be ready for the day's activities. With breakfast, children feel cared for and energetic.

Lunchtime in most centers is a sit-down meal for everyone. In full-day programs, children will need this nourishment in the middle of the day. It should be a pleasant time for eating and comfortable conversation. The schedule should be structured in such a way as to meet the needs of children who eat fast and those who eat more slowly. Provision for children to move to a story group or to table activities as they finish eating can allow for individual eating patterns.

An additional snack planned for mid-afternoon can help both parents and children have an easier reunion at the end of the day. Busy families often find that the dinner hours are the most difficult times of the day. The children are eager for their parent's attention at the same time that the parents are frantically trying to get dinner served. The afternoon snack can help children be less hungry during this difficult transition time. When the parents have a little "breathing room" in getting home from work and preparing dinner, the whole family benefits from the more relaxed atmosphere.

You may need to remind teachers that meals and snacks in the center should be relaxed, informal times. Eating is a social experience in addition to providing nourishment. A calm time for comfortable conversation can help children develop their language and social skills.

Nap Time

Children who attend full-day programs will need a nap or rest time in the afternoon. Many children arrive at the center in the early morning. They are exhausted by early afternoon.

The length of the nap time will be determined by the needs of the children in the group. Young preschoolers may need a full two hours of sleep to feel refreshed. Groups of five year olds may need only 45 minutes to an hour of rest time. Quiet reading of books or working puzzles on individual cots may meet their needs.

Nap time may be a time when teachers' and children's needs conflict. After a busy morning, teachers may be anxious to get children to sleep. Some children, however, may not be able to sleep or may not need as long a nap as teachers would like. As the director, you will have to work with your teachers to ensure that the decisions made about nap time are child-centered decisions.

Outdoor Time

All children need time to play outside. The sunshine and fresh air help to give them a feeling of well-being. Typical childhood activities that can be disruptive indoors can be allowed outdoors. Running, jumping, and yelling are all part of normal outside fun. They must be limited indoors. Outside play provides natural opportunities for the large muscle, more rough and tumble activities of childhood, 10-6.

Director's Dilemma
You notice that one of the new teachers has planned a schedule that does not include any outdoor playtime. When stressing the need to add outside time, what would you tell her?

10-6 These children are enjoying the thrill of "flying through the air."

10-7 Outdoor play can also provide a time for quiet thinking and exploration of nature.

Research has indicated that children in child care centers do not get to spend as much time outdoors as children who are cared for at home. A deliberate effort must be made to ensure that outside time is planned into the schedule on a regular basis, 10-7.

The outdoor schedule will depend on the climate and daily weather patterns of your center's geographic location. Where seasonal weather patterns vary a great deal, the amount of time spent outside will have to be adjusted as the weather gets colder. In climates where the weather is consistent, the amount of time scheduled for outside may be similar all year round.

There may be several outdoor times in a day, or one longer time. The decision about how much outdoor time to schedule may depend on the following:

- weather

- age of the children

- location and ease of accessibility to outdoor play space

- availability of a protected, shaded space

- ability to make a variety of interesting play activities available outdoors

- accessibility to restrooms and a water supply

If the outdoor play area is nearby, it may be easy to go out in the morning and afternoon. When the playground opens right off the classroom, children may be free to choose indoor or outdoor activities during free play, 10-8. If reaching the outdoor area requires a substantial walk, scheduling of outdoor time cannot be as flexible.

When the outdoor play area is difficult to reach or must be shared with other groups, teachers may need to find additional ways to provide outdoor experiences. Walks, hikes, field trips to parks, or community recreation areas help to meet the need for more vigorous activities, 10-9.

10-8 These children have an inviting array of activities right outside their classroom door.

Group Time

All children need to have the opportunity to learn what it is like to be a part of a group. Most classrooms have several times of the day when the children come together for large or small group times. The very nature of group activities tends to make them "teacher-directed" times. Care must be taken that group times do not become too long for the children to handle, 10-10.

Smaller groups are usually easier for children to handle. You may need to remind your teachers that children are beginners at learning how to be members of a group. If the activities planned are lively, children may be able to stick with them longer. If there is little waiting time for a turn, there will be less frustration. When group activities are carefully planned to be developmentally appropriate, children will find them more interesting.

In general, group time should not be longer than 10 to 15 minutes. If there is a small group table activity that moves to a large group music activity then back to small group story time, a longer period may be appropriate. However, in this case, there are actually three separate times linked together.

The only way to determine what is right for a group is to try out the schedule and see how it works. The appropriate length for a group time will be influenced by each of the following:

- ages of the children in the group

- nature of the group activities

- temperament and attention span of the children

- other elements of the schedule around the group time

- the teacher's skill in keeping children actively participating

10-9 Field trips help children become familiar with their neighborhood and provide ideas for later dramatic play.

10-10 Watching popcorn pop can hold the attention of children.

Group times should be scheduled so that children feel successful about their participation. If the times are too long, children will act up, and teachers will feel frustrated. When children like the group time activities and feel good about them, they will want to come back for more.

Bathroom Time

Ideally, there is a bathroom located within each classroom. This will remove the need for a formal bathroom time except to ensure that children wash their hands before eating. If there is a center bathroom, it must be shared with other groups. It will be away from the classroom. In that case, a specific bathroom time must be scheduled.

Of course, children must always have access to a toilet when they need it. Younger children may need more frequent bathroom times than older children. On warm days, when children drink more liquids, additional trips to the bathroom will be required. Bathroom time before nap time is also important to prevent embarrassing accidents while children are sleeping.

Another thing to consider is the location of the playground. If it is some distance from the center, it is best to schedule a bathroom trip before going out. Otherwise someone will have to be available to help the children go back inside to the bathroom if necessary.

Are There Some General Principles to Follow When Planning the Schedule?

There are some basic principles for teachers to follow when planning the daily schedule. These principles can serve as guidelines in helping to plan interesting days in the centers. Because each group of children is different, there is no one "right" schedule.

Predictability

Young children like predictability. A daily schedule that is pretty much the same from day to day provides security for them. They like to know what is coming next. They also use the schedule as a way of telling time. It is not unusual to hear a teacher saying, " Your mom will be coming right after snack and story." Children who are familiar with the order of the schedule usually have an easier time of moving through the transitions of the day.

Flexibility

A schedule or classroom plan should not be rigid. Trying to make the minutes of every day work out like every other day is unrealistic. Each day is not like every other day. Some days, the children will be deeply absorbed in activities just when the schedule calls for change. On other days, the children will be ready for a change long before the schedule calls for one.

Flexibility in scheduling also includes taking advantage of unexpected opportunities. One group of children had an exciting day when a giant crane was brought nearby to raise the beams for a new building. The teachers used the unexpected event to stimulate interest in a variety of building- and construction-related activities. It would have been foolish to have ignored the unusual experience in favor of "business as usual."

Variety

Many activities in the center are available in some form almost every day. Water play, easel painting, block building, and dramatic play are usually available on an ongoing basis. However, even these favorites can become boring if there are not some interesting changes in how they are presented. Children's interest can be renewed by changes in each of the following:

- location of set-up in the room

- props that are added to the activity

Director's Dilemma

The teacher of the four-year-old group has the easel and paints available to the children every day. However, it is always set up in exactly the same way and place. Few children bother to paint anymore. They seem to be bored with the activity. Suggest some ideas that she could use to renew the children's interest in easel painting. How could she bring some variety to this basic activity?

- basic arrangement or set-up of the activity

- related activities that stimulate renewed interest

Children like to repeat favorite activities. Providing some elements that are new and different can stimulate children's interest and creative use of materials, 10-11.

Balance

Planning a day-long program can be a challenge. A schedule that works well for a half-day program cannot simply be stretched out for a full day. An hour-long free play cannot simply become three hours of free play. Both children and teachers become bored if the schedule is not balanced.

Think of riding on a swing when looking at your schedule. The schedule should move back and forth between different types of activities. These activity segments should provide a balance for each other that keep the day more interesting for both children and adults.

When planning the daily schedule, you must consider the appropriate balance among the following types of activities:

- active times versus calm times

- time for individual activities varied with time for group activities

Water Play	
Change the Setup:	**Change the Props:**
water table	boats
basin	dolls
galvanized tub	floating and sinking items
buckets	bubbles and straws
flat trays	plastic bottles
sink	spoons
outdoor puddles	measuring cups
Change the Atmosphere:	**Supportive Teacher Behaviors:**
play music	accept and approve of water play
add food coloring	encourage new ways to use toys
move the play outside	provide time
change the location in the room	change props and introduce new ones

10-11 There are many interesting ways to set up water play.

- child-initiated activities balanced with time when the teacher plans and directs the activity

- rest times balanced with lively times

- indoor times varied with outdoor times

A good program is never boring. Activities that are allowed to go on too long or several activities that are too much alike will lead to problems in the classroom. An interesting program with a carefully planned daily schedule can eliminate many potential discipline problems.

What Does a Daily Schedule Look Like?

A daily schedule shows the sequence of activities that the staff will follow throughout the day. It should incorporate the elements of good planning identified above. While most schedules have times included on them, teachers should view these times as tentative. For example, if the story time is scheduled for 20 minutes, but the children are very restless, a wise teacher would shorten the story and move on to a more lively activity. It is a good idea to follow the same sequence every day so that children learn to predict what is next. However, it is also necessary to adapt the actual amount of time devoted to a program element to meet the needs of the children.

Full- and half-day programs should not vary in the program elements. When planning a full-day program, however, each element should not simply be made longer. An hour's free play time is long enough for most children whether they are in a half-day or a full-day group. Rather than extending the times for the various parts of the program, it is better to repeat an element later in the day. For example, in a full-day group, you should not have a two-hour free play time in the morning. Instead, plan an hour's free play in the morning and another in the afternoon after nap.

Scheduling elements that are too long will bore children and encourage rowdy behavior. Elements that are too short will frustrate the children. They may develop a tendency to avoid deep involvement in play because there is not enough time. Teachers should develop a schedule that works well in the morning and then plan which elements to repeat in the afternoon, 10-12.

Within both full- and half-day schedules, it is important that the children have interesting activities from which to choose. Free play time in both types of schedules should include at least five real choices that children can make. Free play that does not provide enough to do will not work well in either type of program.

The schedules for children may also have to be adjusted according to the ages of the children in the group. Five-year-olds can often enjoy a free play time of an hour and 15 minutes. They may also be ready for longer group and story times. Three-year-olds may become disorganized and frustrated after a free play time of 45 minutes and a story time of 10 minutes. Schedules for infants and toddlers must also be designed for their age-related characteristics. Infants need a

Director's Dilemma
One of your teachers has just moved from a half-day group to a full-day classroom. What would you tell her about planning a full-day schedule? How is it both the same and different from planning for a half-day?

Half-Day Program	Full-Day Program
9:00 Arrival and free play activities	7:30 Quiet activities for early arrivals
10:00 Cleanup, bathroom, handwashing	8:30-9:15 Breakfast available
10:10 Snack, roll call	9:20 Group story and welcome
10:30 Story time	9:35 Free play activities
10:45 Outdoor free play	10:35 Cleanup
11:25 Music/movement	10:45 Music/movement
11:40 Finger plays, quiet activity	11:00 Outdoor free play
11:55 Preparation to go home	11:45 Bathroom, handwashing
	12:00 Lunch
	12:25 Story time, small group quiet activities
	12:50 Bathroom, handwashing, preparation for nap
	1:00 nap
	3:00 Wake-up, bathroom, handwashing
	3:10 Snack
	3:25 Story, music
	3:35 Free play and preparation to go home

10-12 All programs need a balanced schedule to keep the day interesting for the children.

setting where the schedule fits their patterns. Toddlers may enjoy slightly more routine, but time periods will all need to be shorter than those for preschoolers.

What Are Developmentally Appropriate Activities?

Developmentally appropriate activities refer to activities that are a good match with the children's age-related characteristics, abilities, and needs. All activities in the center should be developmentally appropriate. Which specific activities are appropriate will vary somewhat as the children grow and change. In general, developmentally appropriate activities have the following characteristics. They

- require little teacher assistance; the children can do them independently

- can be done in a variety of ways so all children, regardless of age or ability, can experience success

- encourage creative thinking and allow children to explore an item or activity

- do not create competition among children nor subject them to time pressures

- recognize the interests and concerns of each age group

- allow teaching through informal interactions rather than through formal teacher-directed lessons

- are *concrete experiences*, meaning they provide experiences that children can touch, hear, see, taste, or smell

- avoid use of workbooks, coloring pages, or other patterns that reflect only adult creativity

- introduce children to their environment in concrete ways

Programs that are committed to developmentally appropriate practices avoid activities that have traditionally been taught to older children. Pushed down first grade plans and lessons are not used. Instead, the emphasis is on helping preschoolers learn the things that preschoolers need to know, and helping them learn in the ways that preschoolers learn best.

What Kinds of Guidance and Discipline Are Best for Young Children?

The general atmosphere or tone of the center tells you a great deal about whether or not this is a good place for children to be. A visitor's first impressions of a classroom should be positive ones. Rooms that convey a feeling of harshness and stress send a message that something is wrong. Good teachers know how to create a climate that is warm and supportive for children, 10-13. Staff members who lack training or commitment often resort to guidance methods that are not based in sound child development practices.

Teachers who are successful in using developmentally appropriate guidance methods pay attention to a number of things:

- typical age characteristics of the age group with which they are working

- the individual needs of each child in the group

- what the theories say about common developmental tasks and patterns

- appropriate expectations of children's behavior

- specific situations that occur on any given day

- a range of interesting experiences each day

10-13 This teacher's positive expression lets the child know that he is welcome at the center.

Successful teachers behave in ways that are predictable to children. However, the behavior should never be rigid and unfeeling. Effective teachers know what is fair to each child is measured by what each child needs. Well-trained staff use a variety of positive guidance strategies that are aimed at helping children learn to think about and control their behavior.

Teacher Behaviors That Minimize Problems

Many potential behavior problems can be avoided by careful planning. Daily programs that are developmentally appropriate are designed to match the interests and abilities of young children. A balanced schedule, a variety of activities, and lots of opportunities for child-initiated activities will appeal to virtually all children.

A safe atmosphere where children feel secure to explore and express thoughts and ideas will stimulate their willingness to cooperate. A relationship with adults that is caring, warm, and respectful will nurture children's self-concept and confidence. When children grow in commitment to a relationship, their willingness to "work at it" also grows. When children feel good about themselves and positive about their teachers, they are less likely to engage in disruptive and destructive ways.

Teachers' actions and attitudes influence children's behavior. Successful teachers know how to minimize the likelihood of negative behaviors in the classroom. See 10-14.

Using Positive Guidance

Much has been written about the value of using positive guidance in the classroom. For most teachers, it is a skill that must be learned. Like learning a new language, it is only mastered by deliberate practice and a belief in the value of its usage.

Positive guidance is based on the idea that children are more likely to listen if guidance is given in a positive rather than a negative way. Adults take the time to stress what children are allowed to do rather than what they are not allowed to do. Children are helped to understand what behaviors are acceptable instead of being faced with an endless string of "don'ts."

Young children are beginners at understanding rules. They aren't familiar with the reasons adults think some behaviors are acceptable and others are not. They are trying to get a sense of their own independence just at the time when their behavior often brings them into conflict with others. Also, they get tired of being "little" and being "bossed around" all the time. When directions are stated positively, children are less likely to feel their control of their behavior is being threatened or challenged. They are more willing to go along with the teacher's requests and guidance.

Positive guidance is an effective strategy in the classroom for the following reasons:

- Children are less likely to be resistant to teacher directions.

- Children feel they are retaining control of their behavior.

- It is usually more precise and gives children clearer instructions.

- It is respectful of children's feelings and is less "bossy."

Teacher Actions That Decrease Behavior Problems

- Review the daily schedule to see if there are persistent "trouble spots" that can be eliminated by schedule rearrangement. Allow enough time for children to become deeply absorbed in their activities, but not so much time as to become bored.

- Review the activities to determine that they are developmentally appropriate and that there are a variety of things to do.

- Provide many opportunities throughout the day for children to make choices.

- Make sure there are sufficient opportunities for active play.

- Plan activities that will allow each child to experience success in numerous ways.

- Get to know children as individuals and build a personal relationship with each one.

- Examine the room arrangement for areas that are not used much or where trouble frequently occurs. Rearrange the room to make it more usable by the children.

- Always give children advance warning before expecting cleanup or switching to a new activity.

- Anticipate particular combinations of children that lead to behavior problems. Assign a staff member to "stay close" to help the children find compatible ways of resolving disagreements.

- Take the time to talk to children about why they must do or not do certain things. Children need to be helped to see the logic behind adult decisions and behaviors.

- Help children to become aware of the feelings of others and the impact of their behavior on others.

- Remember that behavior has two parts: actions and feelings. Teachers must be sensitive to the feelings behind behaviors although, at times, they may have to stop behaviors.

- Start the group (or enroll a new child) gradually at the beginning of the year. Avoid having a whole classroom full of new children arrive at once for a full day. Give each child a chance to get to know the teachers and the routine in a small, more easily controlled group.

- Be careful about your own tone of voice, body posture, and general health status.

- Teachers who feel and look cranky usually convey that attitude to children.

- Set few limits, but be clear and firm about those that are important to maintain the safety and well-being of the group.

10-14 There are many things a teacher can do to prevent problems in the classroom.

- It provides a model of effective communication among adults.

- It helps children to know what they are allowed to do.

There are other components of positive guidance that are important to know when working with children. These include the following:

- Avoid the use of embarrassment or humiliation of children to control their behavior.

- Respect the misbehaving child even though behavior must be stopped or changed.

- Avoid the use of value-laden labels like *brat*, *little doll*, *babyish*, *selfish*, etc.

- When talking or referring to children, avoid ridicule and sarcasm.

- Never talk about the children in front of them.

- Always refer to families and other staff members with respect.

- Never use physical punishment or techniques that hurt the child physically or emotionally.

- Avoid the use of "star charts" or other methods that compare one child with others. Every child needs to be a winner!

- Respect each child's efforts as well as successes.

- When discipline becomes necessary, it should "fit the crime." For instance, a child who throws sand may not be allowed to play in the sandbox for the rest of the day.

Hopefully, you will be able to hire staff members who are familiar with and committed to the use of positive guidance. If not, you will need to make it clear that this is the type of guidance that is expected in the classrooms. You may need to provide access to training sessions if your staff does not use positive guidance successfully.

☼ Summary

A good daily program for young children must be carefully planned. It grows out of knowledge about the developmental needs and characteristics of young children.

A daily schedule should include times for free play, stories, music and movement, outdoor time, and group times. It must also include consideration of meals and snacks, and bathroom and nap times. These elements are characteristic of quality, developmentally appropriate classrooms.

Children need both predictability and flexibility in their daily program. When planning, teachers should consider ways to keep the schedule balanced and the activities interesting.

The emotional tone of the center should be a positive one. Good teachers create a climate that is warm and supportive for children. Specific techniques of positive guidance are used to help children grow in self-control.

☼ Terms

objectives
free play time
concrete experiences

☼ Review

1. How do the guidelines of developmentally appropriate practices influence the daily program for children?

2. Identify the areas of development that should be addressed in planning daily activities.

3. Why is free play an important component of the daily program, and what amount of time should be allotted to a free play session?

4. How can you vary story time for the children?

5. What factors should determine how much outdoor time to schedule?

6. Identify four general principles to follow when planning a daily schedule.

7. Describe a daily schedule that is well-balanced.

8. What are the differences between planning for a half-day program and planning for a full-day program?

9. What is meant by having a "safe atmosphere"?

10. Explain the concept of positive guidance.

☼ Applications

1. Visit several programs serving preschool children in your community. Watch to see which activities the children seemed to enjoy. How did the teacher prepare and set them up? Did the teacher add special materials or props? Make a notebook of activity ideas that were successful with the children. In class, discuss the activities and why you think they are developmentally appropriate for preschool children.

2. With three or four classmates, identify a typical behavior problem that occurs in preschool settings. Develop two versions of the situation to role-play for your class. In the first, show a teacher who does not see the problem developing. What happens before the teacher gets things under control? In the second version, show a teacher who is aware of the situation before it becomes too involved. Demonstrate how the teacher's alert, early use of positive guidance can keep the problem from getting out of hand.

3. Develop two daily classroom schedules for full-day programs. For one schedule, assume that all of the children arrive at the same time on a bus. For the other, assume that the children arrive at various times between 7:00-9:00 AM. How would these differences affect the elements of the schedule?

4. Make a list of locations within walking distance that would make interesting field trips for the children. What types of concrete experiences would the children have on the trip? What information might they learn about their community through the field trip? What kinds of props would you need to set up a dramatic play area where children could incorporate what they have seen on their trip into their dramatic play?

Chapter 11
You, the Director–A Complex Role

After studying this chapter, you will be able to

○ prepare yourself for a professional leadership role.

○ recognize those tasks that all administrators must perform.

○ identify those responsibilities that are unique to child care settings.

○ relate how leadership skills will enhance your ability as a director.

○ define a commitment to a professional code of ethics.

As the director of a child care program, you will find that your responsibilities are different from everyone else's in the program. While others will have a definite work schedule, your hours may change according to the work that must be done. While the teaching staff may worry about having the right colors of construction paper for tomorrow's project, you may be making decisions that could affect the ability of your program to pay all the staff salaries.

What Does a Director Have to Do?

As the director, you are the leader of the program. It is your vision and problem-solving skills that will determine the future directions of the program. The efforts of other staff members will relate to their part of the program. The director, however, must be knowledgeable and concerned about all aspects of the program. It is the director who must have a broad view of the scope and activities of the total program. It is also the director who must be aware of broader forces in society at large that will impact the program.

As the director of a child care agency, you must be able to

• have a broad overview of the entire scope of your program

• understand how decisions in one part of the program may impact other parts

• make decisions that may be unpopular with others who consider only their own point of view

- work whatever hours are necessary to get the job done

- keep in mind the long-term goals of your program

- create an environment where all feel respected and appreciated

- stay up to date on new ideas and information relating to child care

- be aware of the strengths of your program and areas that need to be improved

- direct others on the staff so that they are helped to do their work effectively

Success depends on your abilities. These abilities include solving problems, supporting a quality daily program, planning for the future, directing others, and paying the bills.

Management Responsibilities

Management books, written for those in business, identify basic, essential tasks that must be performed by those in administrative positions, 11-1. The following five tasks must be considered as an essential part of the job of any director.

11-1 The director's responsibilities are different than those of any other member of the staff.

Planning

Planning, as a function of your job, involves setting goals for the program and identifying methods or strategies for reaching those goals. It involves considering what the priorities of the program should be. Where should your agency be headed? Do you want to expand? Will you add new age groups? Is your program as big as it should be? Should you consider buying a building, or is renting a facility a better option?

The task of planning also involves figuring out ways to meet your goals. How will you move your agency closer to accomplishing those chosen goals? What factors can you control? What factors are beyond your control? Can you change those elements that work against the achievement of those goals? Planning requires bringing your knowledge of future trends together with your understanding of the capabilities of your program.

Controlling

The *controlling* function of management includes regular monitoring and evaluating your program as well as taking action, when necessary, to maintain and improve its quality. It is the part of your job that requires you to know what is going on throughout your whole program. Only when you have accurate, up-to-date information, can you make wise decisions. Controlling means keeping track of such things as

- average daily attendance in each classroom

- food inventory and purchases

- location of equipment

- number and ages of children on the waiting list

- current status of program income

- amount of money spent or committed at each point throughout the year

- deadlines for reports

- work assignments and schedules for employees

- new opportunities for your program

Controlling also includes using these types of information to make adjustments or changes to your program. For example, if one of your classrooms usually has a lower attendance than others, you would want to figure out why this is so. Based on your information, you may decide to adjust the enrollment in this group. If one staff person is continually late, you need to be aware of the problem. You must consider how this affects your program and what you can do to solve the problem. Everything you do to keep your program on track is a part of the controlling function of a director.

Organizing

Organizing is defined as determining an appropriate arrangement of time, people, and space, in a plan that will support the achievement of goals and the efficient operation of a quality program. A director is responsible for determining how to carry out the work of the program in the best way. You must decide how many people you will need to staff the office. You must plan the number of head teachers, assistant teachers, aides, cooks, etc., you will need for the size of your program. You must also figure out which staff members are responsible for which duties.

In your position as director, you will be aware of all the work that must be done to keep the program functioning smoothly. It will be impossible for you to do everything yourself. You must consider how to organize your staff into work groups so all staff members know where they fit in the program. Identify those responsibilities that must be done by you alone. Decide which tasks can be more efficiently delegated to others. Identify which staff persons will be responsible for supervising and guiding others. Write clear job descriptions for position categories.

There is no one "right" way to organize a child care program. Decisions will be affected by the size of the program, the ages of children being served, the level of training of your staff, the additional services you provide, and licensing regulations. As director, you must look at your program and creatively come up with an organizational structure that works well.

Staffing

The function of *staffing* refers to the recruiting, hiring, and retaining of the skilled individuals needed to operate a quality program. This function requires that job categories are well-defined. Appropriate staff must be found, encouraged to apply, and hired for the program. Orientation and ongoing training must be planned and provided.

Personnel policies must be clearly spelled out. These policies will guide decisions that define the relationship between the employer (your program) and the employee.

Staffing is an area where the interpersonal skills of the director are important. You will be communicating expectations to new employees. You must also be able to evaluate fairly. If necessary, you may have to dismiss those employees who cannot perform their responsibilities in a satisfactory manner.

As the director, you may also have to help develop working relationships among staff who are not comfortable with each other. Helping staff to work cooperatively with each other, with you, and with parents can be a very difficult task. Many directors discover that the staffing component of their job is one of the most demanding in time and effort.

Directing

Directing is the part of your job that involves providing leadership for your program and influencing others to successfully meet their responsibilities. This may include helping to educate board members who have limited training in the child care field. It may also involve keeping the program on track in working toward the long-range goals. Identifying problems, motivating personnel, and determining policies are all parts of the directing function.

Clear communication is necessary for successful leadership. This includes communication between you and the program's staff as well as communication with those outside of your agency, 11-2. Careful communication within a program should include

- clearly worded policies and procedures that minimize problems

- acknowledgment and recognition for those who put forth special effort

- clear, concise written memos

- a willingness to listen to concerns without becoming defensive

- an openness to new ideas

The director of a program also must consider ways to make things happen. Goals and plans will not be met if specific strategies for reaching them are not developed.

Many agencies have wonderful goals written down on paper. The day-to-day program continues to plod along as it has always done. Defining deliberate steps to achieve goals is often the hardest part of leading the agency. What specific things must happen in order to move the agency forward? What obstacles are in the way of this forward movement? Are there other ways to achieve goals or remove obstacles?

What Management Style Works Best?

The way you view your staff affects your leadership style. If you see them as competent individuals who work hard because they care about their work, you will treat them one way. If you view them as having no commitment to their jobs and only doing the minimum neces-

11-2 Clear communication, whether verbally or in writing, helps to ensure that what you are saying is not misunderstood.

sary to get by, you will treat them another way. Douglas McGregor, professor and author of management books, theorized that these two perspectives on human nature lead to two very different styles of management behavior called Theory X and Theory Y.

Theory X and Theory Y

The "Theory X" type of manager basically believes that employees have no real commitment to their jobs. They work only for money and have no loyalty to the agency or to meeting the goals of the agency. They will not willingly seek out additional responsibility except for additional pay/rewards. This results in the manager having to "keep an eye on them." Decisions are all made by the administration. Staff are expected to do as they are directed. Their input is not sought nor valued in the decision-making process of the agency.

The "Theory Y" manager, on the other hand, believes that staff will become committed to the agency's goals. If staff have had a chance to add their thoughts and ideas during the goal-setting process, they will feel valued. They are more likely to work independently to help achieve those goals. Personal satisfaction and a sense of accomplishment become as important as money in motivating staff to work hard. Even when a supervisor is not present, staff will continue to function effectively.

This perspective on human behavior results in a management style that seeks ideas and suggestions from staff. Input on goals and strategies are sought. Staff are treated with respect and encouraged to work independently. Creative ideas are encouraged.

Research indicates that employees in Theory X and Theory Y organizations will behave differently. Those working with a Theory Y manager are more likely to take responsibility for their own actions and to have feelings of commitment to their agency.

Within any organization, you will have staff members of various abilities, training, and motivation. Some will eagerly work hard, while others will not care. Some will be anxious to share their expertise, while others will not.

In general, it seems that the Theory Y style of management is more compatible with the values and the humanistic nature of a child care center. In quality child care, the director strives to create a place where children feel valued, respected, and nurtured. It makes sense that the program staff should be treated in a manner that reflects those same values.

What Leadership Skills Will I Need?

Many of the skills associated with being an effective leader can be learned. Recent studies indicate that interpersonal skills and the ability to communicate clearly are important components of leadership along with the ability to help a group function effectively. A good leader provides recognition for the concerns and efforts of staff. Various points of view are weighed before making a decision. There are many resources available to help you develop these skills.

Interpersonal Skills

The term, *interpersonal skills,* refers to your ability to get along with others and to help them feel at ease. It is an essential component of leadership. Many business leaders identify good interpersonal skills as one of the most important characteristics they desire when hiring new employees. Among the interpersonal skills that are helpful for leaders are helping others feel at ease, listening, and empathy.

Helping Others Feel at Ease

A good leader helps other people feel at ease. Even in situations where you might not feel completely comfortable yourself, you need to be able to help others. As a director, other people look up to you. Your willingness to smile and greet others warmly can help them feel welcome in a new setting. Read a book on etiquette. As you feel more confident in business and social situations, you will find it easier to make others comfortable.

Listening

A leader should also be a good listener. Staff, parents, and children all need to feel that you are concerned about what they have to say. When talking to them, listen intently. With children, get down on eye level for a conversation with them. Pay attention to their body posture and emotions as well as their words.

Sometimes individuals simply need to express their feelings about a situation. A technique called *reflective listening*, in which you repeat a person's statement back again only using slightly different words, may be helpful. This lets individuals know that you have heard their concerns. It also provides an objective response that helps them clarify situations where they might have mixed or confusing feelings. For example, a teacher complains that a parent is always late picking up her child. A reflective listening response might be, "You sound upset that Mrs. Smith is often late." Teachers usually understand the parent's problems, but will still be appreciative of your recognition of the frustrations those problems cause for staff. A child might come crying to you because another child grabbed a toy. Your reflective listening response could be, "It makes you angry when someone grabs a toy away." You could also then help the child consider how to deal with the problem by talking with the child who grabbed the toy.

There are times when you must be more actively involved in a conversation. If a staff member has alerted you to a problem that must be solved, you need to discuss the situation further. You will need to find out the details of the problem. The staff member may also have some good ideas about how to solve it. Careful listening can give you a more accurate understanding of the situation.

Empathy

Empathy is the ability to understand how others feel and to recognize their point of view. Even though you may not agree with them, your recognition of their feelings, attitudes, or concerns affects your interaction with them. When you are empathetic toward someone else, your behavior toward that person is more likely to be patient and sensitive. Research indicates that effective leaders usually have a strong sense of identification with the concerns of others and a caring attitude.

While you may empathize with someone, you must also be able to make objective decisions regarding your program. Sometimes your decisions may be in conflict with the requests or feelings of others. Letting them know that you understand their disappointment or anger will not make those feelings go away. It also will not make others agree with you. However, it often does help staff to be a little more accepting of decisions and assures them that you recognize their attitudes as valid.

Communication Skills

The ability to communicate clearly with staff, families, children, and those outside of your agency is important. Others don't have access to the same information that you have. You can't assume that they understand an issue, task, or decision just because you have thought about it carefully.

Consider which decisions require group input. Then decide who the appropriate group members should be. For example, if you are considering the purchase of new playground equipment, you may want input from the teachers. They probably have ideas regarding the equipment that would be appropriate for their groups of children. If your decision relates to a change in program operating hours, you should discuss those possible changes with parents as well as members of your staff.

Some decisions, such as which night to hold a community open house, may actually be made by group consensus. There are decisions that must be made by you with advice and information from others. Still other decisions must be made by you alone. Where to purchase new carpet may be a decision made by you based on bids and/or previous experience with a vendor. What color of carpet to purchase may be a decision that includes input from those staff members who will have the new carpet in their rooms.

One way to enhance communication in the center is to be open about the decision-making process. Not every decision will please everyone. You are bound to have personnel who would have liked to have had a different decision. Administrators who are effective communicators do not give in when difficult decisions must be made. However, they are willing to share the overall scope of the decision with those who are affected by it. They seek input from those who work directly in the decision area. They consider the pros and cons of different strategies. They also explain the rationale of the decision to those affected. In that way, staff understand the factors involved in making the decision, even though they may not agree with the outcome.

As a communicator, there is often news that you simply need to tell to the appropriate person. More complicated material must be carefully written down. Many items, such as the date of a staff party, must be shared with the entire staff. Other information, like a personnel evaluation, is confidential and should not be generally available. You may need to discuss a topic directly with a staff member or parent as well as to put that information in writing.

Consider how and when you will communicate. Where will you locate bulletin boards for staff or for parents? Does each staff member need a mailbox? Can the head teacher of each classroom pass information on to the staff or families of that room? See 11-3. Do people need advance notification to prepare for a meeting or event? Is this a particularly bad time to interrupt a teacher? How will staff at other sites receive information in a timely fashion?

It is also important to remember that body posture and expression also convey information to others. A director who rolls his/her eyes at the mention of a particularly difficult parent is quite clearly indicating an attitude toward that person. Anyone around will be aware of that attitude. You must be particularly careful to serve as a role model for positive, respectful attitudes in all forms of communication.

11-3 Parents in this center can read messages attached to the children's cubbies each day when bringing the children to their classrooms.

Conflict Resolution

You can play an important role as mediator and peacemaker in the center. Sometimes people simply need a way to express their feelings, then they can get on with their jobs. Others need to feel that their presence makes a difference in the center and that things would not go quite as well if they weren't there. Occasionally misunderstandings need to be cleared up, situations clarified, or conflicting points of view examined objectively. You can be helpful in each of these situations. You can also help staff to keep things in perspective. A staff member who counted on using a particular piece of equipment for a project may be very angry at another teacher for using it without signing it out. You can help resolve the situation while at the same time keeping it from becoming a major dispute between staff who must continue to work together. The same conflict resolution approach you hope to teach children can be helpful with adults. Steps include

- clarifying the situation

- expressing feelings verbally

- exploring possible solutions

- considering ways that the problem can be avoided in the future

Occasional conflict cannot be avoided. It is bound to occur in situations where people spend time together. As the director, you must stay out of the middle of such conflicts while also trying to help resolve them.

Group Leadership Skills

Many issues can be handled more successfully by pulling together a group of people with various points of view, expertise, ideas, and concerns. The make-up of the group can influence its effectiveness. Consider individual temperament and skills when establishing a group. The group is more likely to be successful in reaching its goal if members have compatible personalities and complementary skills. Your role becomes that of supporting the group as it works. There are some specific things you can do to help that group function effectively. These include

- arranging for a meeting site and time that is convenient

- creating a room arrangement that allows each group member to see all others

- making sure the room is well-lit and the temperature is comfortable

- educating group members about the responsibilities of being a participant in the group decision-making process

- providing background information on the issue and an agenda prior to the meeting

- organizing the agenda so group members have a chance to get to know each other

- having some refreshments available

- helping the group to clarify its goals

- providing resources that will help the group have the information it needs

- clarifying or summarizing various points of view

- helping the group form an action plan to achieve group goals

- obtaining a commitment from group members regarding who will complete work that needs to be done before the next meeting

- providing child care or transportation if needed

There are many times when you will need to organize staff or other adults into a group that can work cooperatively on a particular problem or task. There are also times when you must make a decision independently and take responsibility for the results of that decision.

Decision-Making Skills

As a director, you will be called upon to make many decisions, both easy and complicated. Easy decisions usually have fairly obvious answers. There is little at stake, and there will be few negative outcomes if the decision is wrong. For example, a decision on what color of stationery to order might stimulate some interesting conversation. Overall, however, it is not a particularly important decision. A decision regarding whether or not to open an additional center could be very costly. If you do not open the new center, someone else may. Your program could lose enrollment and income to this competing center. On the other hand, if you decide to open the new program, you will have to commit money, time, and effort to getting it started. If enrollment is too low to keep the center open, the decision will have been a costly one. Resources will have been used unsuccessfully. Other aspects of the original program may have been weakened by the use of resources to establish the new, unsuccessful one. Successful decision makers usually follow a specific set of steps when making a complicated decision.

Clarify the Decision to Be Made

It is important to clearly identify the decision you must make. Often, decisions are defined too narrowly. This leaves you with few alternatives. Don't focus right away on a single aspect of the decision, such as, "should we open an additional site on the north side of town?" Instead, keep the basic problem you are trying to solve clearly in mind. If the problem is a demand for more child care spaces, then your decision can include looking at a wider range of possible options.

Consider Your Program Goals and Values

Re-examine the goals for your program. The *goals* define future directions and/or desirable achievements for your program. What are you trying to help your program accomplish? Do your long-range goals include expansion to meet all the child care needs of the area? Is one of the long-range goals to achieve national recognition as a top quality program? Has a goal been to provide better equipment for the classrooms? Do your program goals need to be reconsidered because they are out of date? If your goals were identified when the program was started, expansion might not have even been a possibility. If your program is successful and now several years old, a goal to enlarge the program might be appropriate.

Values represent beliefs about what is important. Program values represent the common beliefs you hold, as well as those held by the board members and the staff regarding what is significant as the center accomplishes its activities. For example, when high-quality care is valued, decisions about staffing, equipment, and activities are made with that value in mind, 11-4. A decision to open a new center would have to include consideration as to whether or not the resources exist to establish a high-quality program.

11-4 In support of valuing language development, this center encourages children to have conversations with each other during meals and snack time.

Identify the Various Choices You Have

Consider all the possible options that relate to your decision. When you have kept the decision fairly broad, there will be more possible alternatives than when the decision is a narrow one. You may want to brainstorm with others who can help identify various possibilities. The decision regarding the creation of additional spaces for children might be determined by finding a workable strategy for providing those spaces. Establishing a new center is a possibility, but so is adding additional space for classrooms onto your old center. You might also consider starting only preschool classrooms, as opposed to beginning a larger program that would cover all age groups. You must also consider that adding additional spaces in any way could be beyond the current resources of your existing program.

Examine the Pros and Cons of Each Option

Every alternative you consider when making a decision will have benefits and drawbacks. You don't want to make a decision without having considered as many of the pros and cons as you can identify. It takes time to weigh the benefits and the costs of each option that is a part of your decision. For example, a decision to expand the program will involve significant costs. You must obtain cost estimates that are as accurate as possible regarding the alternative ways of expanding your service. The costs of building or buying a completely new center, adding to an existing building, or renovating existing but underutilized space will be quite different. When matched against the financial resources of your program, these costs give a more accurate picture of the impact of your decision.

Review sources of requests for service. If they represent families who would find your current center inconvenient to reach, your decision will have to include the element of location. Renovation of current space might be the least expensive option. However, if the families who are requesting care will not travel to that site, you must consider those options that include space within easy access for them.

Consider the Worst Possible Outcome if the Decision Is Wrong

When making a decision, you must identify the worst possible outcome if you make a poor choice. What is the risk to your program if everything goes wrong? Will your program be able to survive? Will your program have to go out of existence? This is the harsh reality of making a major decision. Before borrowing money, signing long-term agreements, or making commitments on the part of your staff, appraise the impact of the decision on the well-being of the existing program. If your program already has substantial money available, you may be able to undertake a building or renovation effort without much risk. If there are no other child care facilities available and you have a firm estimate that there is enough demand to ensure full enrollment, the opening of a new center is less shaky. If your program can survive the worst possible outcome of a decision, then the option of going ahead becomes more reasonable.

Make the Decision

After considering which option will result in the greatest possible outcome with the least amount of risk, make your decision. You may decide that a small amount of risk is worthwhile in order to move your program toward its goals. You may also decide that a particular option is too risky for further consideration. Sometimes, even after much deliberation, there is still an element of uncertainty. This is where your knowledge of other directors' decisions, the past history of your program, and your analysis of the future trends can have an influence. Ultimately, you must make a decision. Making no decision is the same as making a decision not to act at all.

Some days it will seem as if you have a million decisions to make. Often you may feel that you are being forced to make these decisions without all the information you would like to have. This can be frustrating and exhausting. However, it is also an essential component of your role. You bring to the director's position all your education, experience, and vision for the future of the program. No one else on your staff will have the same broad perspective on the agency that you have.

Time Management Skills

There are many books and articles written about ways to manage time more effectively. Most administrators find that there are always more things to do in a day than there is time to do them. Some directors shut themselves in their offices to work on paperwork all day. They may be surprised to discover that their staff members feel unappreciated and unsupported. Others may spend a great deal of time talking with personnel and maintaining an "open door" policy. As a result, reports, proposals, and records may not be completed by their deadlines. A director who is unavailable to talk to parents may miss the warning signs that changes need to be made in the program.

There is no one perfect system for organizing your time. You will need to try some management strategies to find out what works best for you. You may find some of the ideas presented in 11-5 helpful.

You may be able to create other strategies for organizing time. If your job keeps expanding as your program grows, it may be time to consider reorganizing your

Helpful Ideas for Managing Your Time

- Organize your tasks so all of the papers and information you need to complete a particular job are together.

- Prioritize your responsibilities so you clearly identify which tasks are the most important

- Maintain a calendar that covers several months. Mark due dates for important projects or reports. Mark a reminder a week or so in advance of the due date so you won't forget about it.

- Handle each piece of paper once. As you review mail, decide immediately what to do with it.

- Decide which responsibilities should be delegated to other staff. Which tasks are the ones that only you can do? Which are the ones that could more efficiently be handled by someone else?

- Organize phone calls by using a duplicate message book so that calls don't get lost. Maintain a record of what action is taken regarding calls. If you are working on a detailed project or in a meeting, have a message taken for you and call back later.

- Keep a list of things that need to be done, so you don't forget.

- Plan time each day when you can be available to talk to parents and/or staff. Organize time so that it occurs when staff and parents are free to talk.

- Identify those tasks that must be done on a regular or daily basis and those that are done on other regular patterns.

- Save time for your own professional growth and renewal. Read a professional journal, go to a conference, or even visit with another director to share ideas.

11-5 Time management skills can help you get more work done.

administrative staff and revising job descriptions. A new organizational structure may be needed.

How Can I Persuade Others to Support Our Program?

A stable program depends, in part, on the good will of others—other agencies, community leaders, government officials, and satisfied families. Activities that help people get to know you and your program can build support. There are strategies you can use to help others see your program as a valuable asset to your community.

Cooperation with Other Agencies

Most communities have various agencies that are trying to provide services and help to families. Many human services agencies receive financial support from the same government program. Charitable organizations may be linked in with national foundations and may have similar operational guidelines.

These programs usually have much in common. They need support from others in the community who share similar values and concerns. They need willing volunteers to serve on their board of directors. Also, there is always a need for help with fund-raising activities.

As the director of an agency, it is important that you build positive working relationships with the directors and staff of other programs. These relationships may develop out of the efforts to help a particular child or family in your program. They may grow from your casual conversations with another agency director at a community meeting. You may be asked to serve on another agency's board because of your knowledge about children. You may meet others through social or cultural events in your community.

Building these relationships is important for your agency. You may have a child in your program whose family needs more help than you can provide. Knowing what services other agencies offer can be important. Knowing who to talk to can be useful in getting that family linked with these additional community services. Your help to another agency when needed may very well result in that agency providing help to you sometime, 11-6.

Being a Community Resource

Every community has local groups that need speakers for their meetings. If you are a willing guest speaker, you can help people get to know your program. You are also building community support for your agency. A person who has heard your presentation will feel welcome to call your agency. Follow-up questions allow you to clear up misunderstandings that members of the audience may have regarding your center. A summary of your discussion could easily be sent to the local paper. This provides positive publicity for both the service organization and your program.

Being a guest speaker usually requires that you give up some evening and weekend hours. It also requires preparation and the ability to be at ease before a group. It is, however, an effective way to build community awareness and support for your program.

Many community organizations need volunteers for various activities. This may include helping to clean up a community park or helping to coach a children's sports team. Your willingness to help support another group's fund-raising activity may very well result in additional volunteers from that group when you need help.

Other Human Service Agencies That May Need Your Support	
Area agencies on aging	Big Brothers/Big Sisters
Shelters for victims of domestic violence	Group homes
	WIC/prenatal care programs
Parent education programs that meet the needs of special parenting groups, such as, teen parents, single parents, new parents, parents of children with disabilities, etc.	Community action agencies
	Food pantries

11-6 Directors of human services agencies need to work together to provide coordinated support for families and to bolster each other's programs.

All the activities you would do as a good citizen of any community can help build support for your program. Any activity that builds your reputation as a good, decent, caring, trustworthy, hard-working individual also benefits the reputation of your program. Behavior that causes others to question your judgment reflects negatively on your whole agency. You and your staff represent the program to others in the community. Their impressions of you strongly influence their attitudes toward your program.

Networking

Networking means developing a group of professional colleagues with whom you can communicate. It also involves keeping track of the people you meet in various situations. You will become acquainted with many people throughout your professional career. Someone you have met at a previous meeting might have the answer to an important question or be able to suggest a solution to a problem. Another director might have been faced with a similar situation and could be a source of valuable information for you.

Networking takes place on many levels. Locally, you need to know the directors of other programs. Whether your program is a proprietary or not-for-profit one, other directors of similar programs will be faced with the same administrative issues with which you deal. Talking with each other individually, forming a luncheon group, or finding other ways to communicate can help you gain useful information, 11-7. You can also take advantage of various professional meetings and conferences. They provide an opportunity to meet directors from a broader geographic area, such as other parts of the state or country. Major professional leaders in the child care field may also be available to meet and converse with you at these conferences.

Director's Dilemma

Several human service agencies in town have decided to participate in an informational program at the local mall. The mall will give each organization a booth and space to conduct activities designed to inform the public about the agency's services. How would you decide whether to participate? If you do participate, how would you use your booth and space? What support would you expect from your staff?

11-7 E-mail provides directors with a good way to communicate with one another.

Some simple suggestions can help you network successfully. Meet people in a friendly manner. Approach them with a smile. Make sure you have heard their names correctly. After a brief conversation, exchange business cards for future reference. It is also helpful to jot down some information after your conversation that will help you remember each person. Keep in touch with these acquaintances at future meetings and when circumstances warrant.

While nobody likes to feel "used," most people like to be appreciated for their information and skill. They are often willing to offer advice or give help if what you are asking doesn't require too much time or effort. By the same token, you become a part of the network of others. You may be called upon for help or advice. Networking does not mean using or manipulating people. It simply means creating a group of colleagues and friends who can share common concerns and, on occasion, help each other.

Become an Advocate

Advocates are people who speak out or act on behalf of their beliefs. Your belief in the importance of quality care for children will lead you to work for improvements in the laws, regulations, and decisions that affect child care agencies.

As you work in child care, you will become more familiar with the issues that are important within the field. Your opinions and knowledge are of interest to legislators and politicians who are concerned about children. As a child advocate you might

- meet with legislators to discuss child care issues

- write letters giving your opinion on pending legislation

- send informational articles to legislators

- attend town meetings sponsored by local legislators

- encourage others to become more active in contacting legislators

- invite your representatives to visit your center for a tour

- work with local, state, and national elected representatives

Meeting with Legislators

When meeting with legislators and officials, be sure to bring accurate information. If you mislead them, they will not trust you the next time. If there are several people going to the meeting with you, be sure that you have coordinated your ideas ahead of time. Even if the person you are meeting with does not share your concern for children, maintain a respectful tone. Anger and threats will only hurt your efforts.

Trust that the legislators are trying to do their best, but they may not be well informed about your topic. Many groups feel that it is helpful if you can "adopt a legislator." This means that you build a relationship with that legislator based on trust and respect. The legislator knows that you will provide good information, and that you will be back. He or she also knows you can be contacted for further information if needed. If you meet with a legislator one time, and then are never heard from again, there is little likelihood that you will be influential.

Presenting Testimony

There may be opportunities for you to present information and opinions in a formal setting. *Hearings* are meetings held to receive public reaction to proposed regulation or legislative changes. If you become well known as a director, you may be invited to present testimony at hearings. Even if you are not specifically invited, there is usually an opportunity for you to give your thoughts on the topic. Your professional organization, other directors, and newspaper announcements can alert you to the time, location, and format of hearings.

Building Coalitions

Whenever you are trying to influence the passage of legislation or public policy, it is helpful to have as many people on your side as possible. Legislators and public officials take notice when they get numerous letters or visits on the same topic. Many groups that work on behalf of children and families have found it necessary to "stick together" in order to present strong support for a bill or program. Look around your community. Which other groups or agencies share common interests with you? On what topics can you work together?

Building coalitions with other groups to work together can strengthen your position. There is power in numbers. There may be some issues on which coalition groups may not agree. That does not have to stop you from working together on areas of common agreement. These cooperative efforts to promote common interests can often be surprisingly effective.

How Can I Be a Good Model for My Staff?

As the program director, you set the tone for the general atmosphere within your program. Hopefully, you will be a model of professional and ethical behavior in your administration of the center. Others will follow your lead. In turn, your program will be one that commands the respect and trust of families and your community.

Professionalism

You should feel proud of being a child care director. Because you have taken courses involving child development and child care administration, you have had specific training in your field. This means that you possess knowledge that the general public does not. Because of your training, you have the opportunity to join with others in your field through membership in professional organizations. These organizations provide many benefits, 11-8.

Opportunities for Additional Training

One goal of most professional organizations is to improve the skills and the quality of services that their members provide. They often provide training workshops that focus on new information or techniques in the field. Some organizations provide regular training meetings throughout the year. Annual conferences usually include a mixture of the organization's business meetings and training sessions. Membership in one organization frequently places you on the mailing lists of other related organizations. This gives you an opportunity to find the right educational opportunities to meet your needs.

Benefits of Membership in Professional Organizations
Opportunities for additional training
Meetings with other directors
Legislative alerts and guidance on working with public officials
Special packages of group insurance opportunities
Reduced fees for conference attendance
Newsletters, journals, or access to "members only" Web sites.
Listings of job openings

11-8 Membership in the major child development/early childhood professional organizations helps you keep up to date and can provide many useful benefits.

Meetings with Other Directors

The membership of a professional organization, such as NAEYC, is made up of persons like yourself. Members usually work in a similar field and, often, in similar positions. The professional organization can serve as a catalyst to bring people together. You, as an individual, may not be aware of all of the programs and their directors in your region. The professional organization is most likely to have a complete listing of programs and key personnel. It also will have the money to send out mailings, organize meetings, and provide a worthwhile program. During those meetings, you can gain valuable information and get to know other directors.

Legislative Alerts and Guidance for Working with Public Officials

Professional organizations, especially those whose membership is affected by public policy decisions, usually keep an eye on current legislative activity. They have personnel who understand the legislative process. They also can spot trends in pending legislation and provide educated guesses regarding the impact of a bill. Some professional organizations have lobbyists. Others depend on the advocacy activities of members. The professional organizations keep their members alert so they can react to legislation that could be harmful to children and families.

Special Packages of Group Insurance Opportunities

Insurance costs for programs or personnel can be very expensive. Since professional organizations represent similar individuals, they can often arrange special insurance packages. As an individual director of a privately owned program, you may not be able to obtain any group rate on insurance if you tried to organize it on your own. As a member of a group representing many oth-

Director's Dilemma

As the director of a new child care center, your salary is not very high. You usually have to be quite careful about your budget in order to live comfortably. Another director of a nearby program has encouraged you to join a professional organization representing those who work with young children. You agree that membership would benefit you and your agency. What are the pros and cons of joining the organization?

ers like yourself, the professional organization often can offer less expensive insurance as a part of your membership in the group.

Reduced Rates for Conference Attendance

As a member, you are usually eligible for reduced rates on conference registration fees. At a national conference, this can be a substantial reduction. The cost of a major conference may also include reductions on airline tickets, hotel rooms, and sightseeing tours. Many professionals find that attending a national conference is not only a good way to keep current in the field, but also a less expensive way to visit another city.

Newsletters, Journals, or Web Sites

Most organizations use newsletters, journals, or Web sites to keep in touch with their membership. Each format may include advertisements from businesses that serve child care programs. The newsletters are usually brief and let members know of current activities and events. Journals often have articles to educate on subjects of interest within the field. These may be practical articles for program improvement, philosophical articles related to issues in the field, or research articles. Web sites are a popular way to communicate quickly with members. Web sites can be designed for two-way interaction.

Listings of Job Openings

Many professional organizations offer listings of job openings. These may be included in the newsletters, journals, or on the Web site. Often bulletin boards at meetings or conferences are devoted to notices of open positions. Occasionally, a person looking for a job may be able to meet with the recruiter at the meeting. This can be a good way to make a first impression on the recruiter or to find out additional information about the position. Posting job openings on a bulletin board at a professional meeting is a good way to bring the position to the attention of persons with the training and experience necessary for the job.

Your Code of Ethics

Professionals share a common *code of ethics*. This code is a guide for your behavior. It is valuable in helping you make hard decisions involving the needs and rights of children, families, and staff.

The National Association for the Education of Young Children (NAEYC) has defined the code of ethics for those working with children. It clearly spells out whose rights and needs must take priority. The code of ethics is a guide to ethical decision making that you share in common with other child care professionals.

Your behavior and leadership influence the general atmosphere for your entire program. You

Director's Dilemma

You have been the director of a small, but growing, child care program. You and your agency are well known in your community. An old friend from high school has just returned to town for a brief visit. He wants to get together with you and suggests an evening of partying. You are aware that this person doesn't always use good judgment about the amount of alcohol he consumes. You are worried that the evening's activities could get out of hand. How would you handle this situation?

are a role model for the rest of your staff. Professional, mature behavior on your part is essential if your program is to offer a quality service to families.

☼ Summary

The director of a child care program has responsibilities that are different from any other staff member. The director must have an overall view of the program and a vision for the future of the center.

Certain duties must be performed by all managers. These duties include functions that contribute to planning for the future as well as providing for day-to-day operation. There are differing opinions on which type of management style works best. Most administrators in child care believe in the potential of their staff to become committed to the goals of the program.

There are some types of situations, decisions, or problems that call for group efforts. In those cases, your role may become that of a group leader. You can develop leadership skills to help groups who are working to clarify goals and consider alternative solutions to problems.

You will also find that your job as director is often hectic and almost overwhelming. Improvement of time-management and decision-making skills can help you become a more effective manager.

It is important to build support for your program among community leaders and other agency directors. There are many ways that you can help establish your program as a valuable addition to the community. Your interactions with other administrators, legislators, community leaders, and public officials all contribute to the reputation of your child care center. Your professional and ethical behavior influences the actions of others on your staff. It also builds your personal reputation and supports the actions you take on behalf of your agency.

☼ Terms

planning	reflective listening
controlling	empathy
organizing	goals
staffing	values
directing	hearings
interpersonal skills	code of ethics

☼ Review

1. Explain how the role of the director differs from that of any other staff member in the center.

2. Identify the five basic essential tasks that must be carried out by persons in administrative positions.

3. What factors will have an influence on your plan for organizing the program?

4. Describe the difference between Theory X and Theory Y types of management.

5. What are three components of successful interpersonal skills?

6. Identify the four steps that are useful in conflict resolution.

7. As a group leader, what is your role?

8. Identify the six components of careful decision making.

9. What are some ways you might provide support to other community organizations?

10. What does it mean to be an "advocate" for children?

⚙ Applications

1. Invite your state legislator to discuss the process by which a bill is passed and funded within your state. Find out what bills relating to children and families are currently being considered in your legislature. Ask whether your legislator supports these bills and the reasons why. If there is a piece of legislation pertaining to child care agencies, request that the legislator send you a copy of the bill.

2. Read a book that identifies time management skills for administrators. Give a report on the book to your class. Identify some ideas that seem especially useful.

3. With a small group of class members, identify the duties of a director. Also make a list of the duties of a classroom teacher. Compare the lists. Ask a director and a teacher to each discuss a typical work week. See how closely your list matches with their actual duties.

4. Role-play the appropriate behavior for a director in the following situations: a reception sponsored by your program, a dinner in honor of a retiring director of another community organization, an open house for parents and community members at your center, a group meeting at which you must preside over a discussion about whether your community needs a youth curfew. With your class, identify other social or leadership situations to role-play.

5. Identify a decision that you must make or have recently made in your own life. Write down each of the steps recommended for making a decision. Analyze your decision using the decision-making process. Consider whether working through this process would affect the outcome of the decision.

Maintaining staff morale and stability is an important goal for a director.

Chapter 12
Maintaining Staff Morale and Stability

After studying this chapter, you will be able to

- ⦿ evaluate and improve working conditions for your staff.
- ⦿ design fair and affordable personnel policies that are communicated to staff in written form.
- ⦿ develop a plan for ongoing supervision and evaluation of staff.
- ⦿ recognize and support positive job satisfaction for the program's employees.

A good child care program depends on having good staff. A beautiful building or new toys will not mean much if the people in the center don't work well with children and each other. Employees come with a variety of backgrounds and experiences. Develop a plan that helps each employee get off to a good start. Staff who have been with the program for awhile should receive encouragement and recognition for their efforts. Nothing is more important to providing a quality program than the people who work there.

What Are Personnel Policies?

Personnel policies spell out the nature of the agreement between your agency and its employees. The policies should be in printed form and distributed to every staff member. When all staff members know what the policies are, each person can feel confident about being treated equally and fairly. Staff understand what is expected of them and what they can expect from employment in the program. Written policies support a sense of security in new staff. They can feel comfortable knowing what they are supposed to do. All staff can use the personnel policies to identify their opportunities for advancement and recognition, grievance rights, benefits, and to plan their leave time, 12-1.

It is the responsibility of the board of directors to determine the policies for not-for-profit programs and to amend them when appropriate. As the director of the program, you will be responsible for seeing that these policies are carried out. You may also be asked to explore new policy options and make recommendations to the board. When you are the owner/operator of a proprietary program, you will need to review personnel policies with a legal counsel or a personnel consultant.

12-1 These staff members are pleased about some changes that have been made in the program's personnel policies.

Programs change over time. You may find that it is appropriate to modify the organizational structure as your program becomes more complex. Labor laws and licensing regulations may be revised. As a result, personnel policies should be reviewed by your personnel consultant or the personnel committee of the board of directors on a regular basis. Ideally, this should be done at least once a year. If changes should be made in the policies of a public agency, the committee would recommend action to the full board. If the board approves the revisions, you, as the director, would be responsible for the implementation of these changes.

Some standard items should always be included in personnel policies. Other topics may or may not be included depending on the nature of your program. Some sections are mandatory for not-for-profit agencies but not for proprietary programs. The following are topics commonly included in personnel policy manuals:

- statement of nondiscrimination
- description of benefits
- employee responsibilities and conduct
- grievance procedures
- health and safety
- emergency procedures
- transfers and promotions
- probationary employment
- evaluation procedures

Statement of Nondiscrimination

A statement of nondiscrimination provides assurance that your agency's personnel policies are nondiscriminatory and provide equal opportunity. The specific wording of this statement may vary according to local or state requirements. It must also be in compliance with federal regulations. The statement should appear in your personnel policies as well as your job announcements and applications. If you are not sure how to word it, check with your local employment office or Human Relations Commission.

Description of Benefits

The description of benefits section outlines the benefits staff members receive as a part of their employment. The benefits for which your agency is responsible are, in part, determined by law. As an employer, you must provide such items as workers' compensation and Social Security. Other benefits are determined by what your agency is able to afford.

Typical benefits offered by agencies may include

- Leave days—These may include leave for vacation, sickness, bereavement (for death of a loved one), education, jury duty, and military service. Leaves of absence for other miscellaneous reasons may also be granted. Indicate procedures by which employees must request these leave days. Indicate if you require a note from a doctor when an employee misses an extended period of work time. Specify when an employee is eligible for bereavement leave.

- Health insurance—This may include full or partial payment for health insurance. It may cover the employee only, or it may include family members.

- Dental, vision, or prescription coverage–These benefits are usually purchased separately from basic health insurance.

- Lunches—These may be offered to your staff if you are providing lunch to the children.

- Parking—This won't mean much to employees if your center has no parking problems. However, if your center is located in an urban complex, daily parking can be both expensive and troublesome. A guaranteed space might be highly valued.

- Child care—Many of your staff may have their own child care needs. You may allow them to bring their children to the center or offer a discounted rate for child care. This benefit may have tax consequences for the staff member.

- Dues payments for professional memberships.

- Tuition for additional classes, training, or conference attendance.

The inclusion of such a list lets all employees know what benefits they have. Staff can see they receive more for their work than their paycheck indicates.

Employee Responsibilities and Conduct

The employee responsibilities and conduct should include information that clearly tells employees what is expected of them. It should include such items as

- timeliness in arriving for work

- confidentiality in regard to agency information

- description of agency dress code, if applicable

- expectation of respectful attitude toward children, families, and other staff members

- requirement of commitment to the center's philosophy and practices

- expectation of employee's participation in training opportunities

- adherence to agency's policies and requirements

Methods of communication should also be addressed in the policy. If all staff are expected to read daily notices on a staff bulletin board, they should be aware of this expectation. If there is a method through which staff can make suggestions or communicate with each other, include this also.

Grievance Procedures

The *grievance procedure* spells out the process by which employees can complain if they feel they have been unfairly treated. The procedure should be written in such a manner as to attempt to first solve any problem at the lowest level of administration. This usually involves informal attempts to discuss and resolve the problem with the immediate supervisor. For example, an aide who is unhappy about treatment from an assistant teacher should first discuss the issue with the head teacher of that classroom. If the issue is not settled at that level, the employee would be advised to put the concern in writing and present it to the director. If the employee is still not satisfied with the director's handling of the problem, a written complaint could be presented to the board or owner of the program.

Health and Safety

Issues related to health and safety of employees should also be included in the personnel policies. There are two areas of concern in this category. One concern is for the health and safety of all who work in the center. The other concern is the impact that the health or safety practices of employees might have on the well-being of the children in your care.

Employees should be assured that you are concerned about their welfare. They need to know that the center is in compliance with all laws and regulations that apply to the workplace. Child care licensing regulations are written to protect the children, so the center should be basically safe for the adults who work there as well. Government agencies that have responsibility for the workplace, will have additional regulations designed to protect the welfare of the adults who work there. The Occupational Safety and Health

Director's Dilemma

One of your most highly trained, long-time teachers has developed complications from a serious chronic disease. Her doctor has told her that she can no longer work in the center directly with the children. She is extremely upset about this. What ideas could you explore to help her and your program in this situation? How would the size and complexity of your program influence your decision?

Administration (OSHA) sets and enforces job safety and health standards for workers. The center should be in compliance with these standards, and staff should be trained in health and safety procedures, 12-2. An OSHA office is located in each state.

Current laws require the posted notification to staff of any potentially hazardous chemicals, such as industrial cleaning fluids, or materials used in the center. Notification of staff rights in regard to a safe workplace must also be posted. The federal Right to Know laws require that this information be easily visible to employees. This information may be included in the personnel manual, or you may simply list the locations in the building where such information is posted.

12-2 This quiet outdoor patio gives staff a place to take their breaks on pleasant days.

Policies outlining when an ill staff member should not come to work should also be included. Many people pride themselves on not ever missing a day of work. However, they may not consider the fact that they could spread disease to others. Open, oozing sores, an undiagnosed skin rash, fever, or a severe cold are all conditions under which an employee should stay home.

Emergency Procedures

Personnel policies should include the basic emergency procedures for the center. Staff members must understand their responsibility to follow these procedures if the need arises, 12-3. The procedures must include the following:

- evacuation plans to get everyone out of the center

- universal precautions necessary when dealing with potential blood-borne pathogens

- methods for securing the center should a violent situation arise

- basic CPR, First Aid, and Heimlich Maneuver

You may also develop additional procedures in relation to your particular location, hours, or clientele. One center, located near a busy railroad track, identified a specific set of procedures to follow in case a train carrying hazardous chemicals derailed. Another center served several families with drug and alcohol dependency problems. Plans were developed to

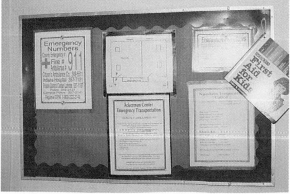

12-3 Emergency information is posted in every classroom and every major area of this center.

ensure the safety of both staff and children in case an out-of-control adult entered the center.

Transfers and Promotions

The personnel policies should also address such issues as transfers within the program. How will you handle a request by an employee who wants to be moved to a different classroom or center? What is the policy regarding an employee who wants to be considered for a higher level position?

Probationary Employment

Your program may also require a probationary period of employment to determine whether a new employee is going to work out well. The amount of time should be standard and made clear to new employees. During the probationary period, it is important to monitor the work of the employee. This is an important time for helping employees improve deficiencies in their performance. Guidance at this point can keep a new employee from falling into patterns that are undesirable or unacceptable. If an employee is not able to carry out the requirements of the job adequately, dismissal must be considered. This is less complex during the probationary time than it is after an employee is given permanent status.

Evaluation Procedures

Within every agency, there must be a plan for evaluation of employees. Many states require this as a condition of funding and licensing. It is also a necessary part of the "controlling" function of management. You must know how well staff members are performing their responsibilities in order to understand how well the agency is functioning. These evaluation procedures should be included in the personnel policies. A sample evaluation form is shown in 12-4.

An evaluation plan should include the following components:

- a timeline that identifies when formal evaluation will occur

- procedures that will be followed for the evaluation

- a hierarchy that identifies those staff members who will have responsibility for evaluation

- selection of items to be included on the evaluation

- a procedure for communicating the results of the evaluation to the employee

- safeguards to ensure that unauthorized persons do not have access to completed evaluations

- a list of training options that could be offered to employees who need to improve specific areas of performance

Evaluation Form for Classroom Staff

Name: _____

NA-if not applicable

Staff	1 Very Poor	2 Poor	3 Average	4 Good 5 Very Good	Total
Planning	Work indicates lack of planning and preparation	Work indicates some planning and preparation		Work indicates exceptional planning and preparation	
Dependability	Is not dependable, reliable, or punctual		Is usually dependable. Has occasional lapses in dependability.	Is always ready and prepared on time. Can be counted on.	
Awareness of total group situation	Generally seems unaware of total group situation.		May be aware of, but does not react to total group. May work well in small group.	Is aware of and reacts appropriately to total group situation.	
Safety	Does not know or ignores established limits.		Attempts to maintain established limits, but is not consistent.	Knows and consistently maintains established limits.	
Knowledge of children's needs	Does not recognize needs and abilities of this age group, or does not make use of this in planning		Work indicates limited knowledge of needs and abilities of this age level.	Uses knowledge of needs and abilities in planning and working with children	
Awareness of group routine	Poor techniques in helping children with routine (either too rigidly involved with routine or not enough).		Indicates awareness of routine, but has some difficulty assisting children in making transitions.	Is aware of group routine and directs children easily in making transitions.	

(Continued)

12-4 This is a sample evaluation form that might be used for classroom staff. Another type of form would be used for staff who do not work directly with the children.

Name: _____

NA-if not applicable

Staff	1 Very Poor	2 Poor	3 Average	4 Good	5 Very Good	Total
Encourages desirable behavior	Uses threats, bribes, shame or competition; states directions negatively.		Alternates between positive and negative directions.		Uses positive guidance.	
Involvement	Is passive or disinterested.		Generally positive but sometimes seems uninvolved.		Appears to enjoy experience with children. Works with enthusiasm.	
Cooperation	Does not aid other teachers; shows little interest or enthusiasm for other's projects or ideas.		Helps others if they are doing something which interests him/her. Occasional enthusiasm for other's ideas.		Active cooperation in whatever capacity he/she is needed. Displays enthusiasm and encouragement to others.	
Emotional quality	Demonstrations of affection and sympathy are unobservable or extreme.		Demonstrates affection and sympathy when need is obvious.		Almost always cheerful; good sense of humor; happy.	
	Often gloomy, or depressed		Usually displays pleasant disposition; some sense of humor.		Appropriately affectionate, sympathetic, responsive.	
	Resents suggestions. Rationalizes. Reluctant to change.		Accepts suggestions; makes an effort to adapt them to teaching.		Seeks suggestions and evaluations; profits from them.	
Language and use of voice	Uses poor English, slang or difficult to understand or inappropriate vocabulary.		Usually uses appropriate vocabulary and speaks clearly; occasionally hard to understand.		Consistently uses good English; appropriate speech; easy to understand.	
Involvement in conflict situations	Does not step in to direct children or to prevent a conflict situation. Intervenes only after children are deeply involved; or not at all.		Usually steps in before control is lost; but rarely acts to prevent problems.		Intervenes at appropriate time to avert difficulty; foresees and acts to prevent trouble as appropriate.	
Preparation of materials	Not prepared; or does not know how to prepare various materials.		Usually prepared for general use.		Correctly prepared for optimum use without help.	

12-4 continued

Name: _____

NA-if not applicable

Staff	1 Very Poor	2 Poor	3 Average	4 Good	5 Very Good	Total
Takes full advantage of teaching/learning opportunities	Interactions do not promote active learning on part of children.		Occasionally asks leading questions or points out interesting phenonmena.		Uses questioning techniques and models behavior that stimulates development of inquiry skills. Po nts out relationships. Encourages problem-solving. Uses appropriate vocabulary.	
Uses techniques to help children become involved in play/activities	Minimal interaction other than behavioral guidance when trouble erupts. Usually limited to reactions to negative behavior.		Occasionally takes an active role in helping children become involved. Inconsistent. Limited skills in encouraging children's interest in activities.		Uses techniques that actively assist children as they become involved in play. Suggests activities. Models social skills. Aids in a ranging environment.	

What areas of train ng were completed last year? _____

_____

What areas of trair ing would be most helpful this year? _____

_____

Recommended training: _____

_____

Comments: _____

_____

Signatures: _____

Date: _____

12-4 continued

It is helpful to develop standard forms that identify the major aspects of successful performance for each job category. The evaluation forms, such as the example in 12-4, should be consistent with the job description and should be available to the employee. It also includes definitions of behaviors that indicate a need for improvement. Additional space for comments, suggestions, or commendations can allow each person's evaluation to be individualized. The completed evaluation must be shared with the individual staff member. It should become the basis for discussing individual and program goals and identifying ways to meet those goals.

Most supervisors do not like to do evaluations of staff members. It is a difficult task. One way to help supervisors feel more confident in this role is to go over the evaluations with them before the evaluations are presented to the staff member. If the supervisor can clearly explain the ratings to you in advance, it will be easier for that supervisor to present them later to the person who has been evaluated. This also ensures that you know what is being suggested to the employee and lends your authority and support to the evaluator.

What Kinds of Personnel Actions May Be Necessary?

When staff members are performing their duties satisfactorily, decisions regarding personnel actions are relatively simple. There may be no action taken at all except to file the evaluation in the personnel file. If the opportunity exists for a promotion or salary increase, the evaluation may become a part of that decision. When a staff member is in a probationary status, a favorable evaluation may result in permanent employment status, 12-5.

When an evaluation has not been satisfactory, it indicates that a person is not working out well in a job. As the director, you will need to consider options in regard to this situation.

If it appears this person needs additional training, your actions may include the development of an individualized training plan. If the staff member is habitually late, unprepared, or irritable and unresponsive to the children, these concerns must be addressed. An unsatisfactory employee may be placed on probationary status for a set period of time. Improvement in the deficient areas should be required for continued employment.

Disciplinary Action

An employee who evades responsibilities or violates the conduct code may be subject to

12-5 All children need to be cared for by well-trained staff who genuinely like being with them.

disciplinary action. A procedure should be in place in case a problem arises. Disciplinary action may involve a simple verbal or written warning. This may be sufficient to serve as a warning that an employee's behavior is unacceptable. An employee who is always late may simply need to be reminded of the inconvenience this causes everyone else. More serious or repeated violations must be handled with stronger action. A temporary suspension or actual termination of employment may be necessary. Discipline at this level will require approval by the board or owner of the center.

Director's Dilemma

You have noticed that the center seems to be using more paper products than in the past. Costs have increased. One day, a teacher alerts you that she suspects a center employee of stealing the items. The next day, as you walk past this individual's car, you spot, what you believe are some of the center's paper products on the floor. What would you do?

Any discipline steps taken should be documented. When you become aware of a problem with an employee, keep a record of the infractions. Also, keep a written record of any disciplinary actions, even verbal warnings, in the employee's personnel file. If stronger action is required, be sure that you have documented both the reasons and the action taken. The evaluation reports will normally be among those items that provide documentation and rationale for the dismissal action. It is not uncommon for a disgruntled employee to claim unfair treatment. You must be able to explain the rationale for your actions. You must also demonstrate that your actions were not discriminatory or the result of a personal dislike for this employee. Be sure that all actions you have taken are consistent with your personnel policies.

Laws vary from state to state regarding termination of employees. It is important that you have legal advice when setting up personnel policies in relation to dismissal of unsatisfactory staff members.

When an employee's conduct is not satisfactory, there should be several levels of warning given before the individual is terminated:

- Level 1—a simple verbal warning that alerts the employee of unsatisfactory behavior.

- Level 2—a written warning given to the employee that documents unsatisfactory conduct.

- Level 3—return to probationary status for a particular amount of time. (This carries with it the expectation of dismissal if additional evaluations do not indicate improvement. At this level, suspension may also occur. This means the employee is on leave without pay as a disciplinary measure.)

- Level 4—termination of employment.

All disciplinary action at any level should be documented in the employee's personnel file. Actions at levels three and four should be backed up by approval from the board of directors or the owner/operator of the center. It is also a good idea to have the disciplined employee sign and date the documentation of the disciplinary action.

As the director, you must determine the appropriate response to more serious disciplinary problems. An employee who abuses a child, violently threatens a co-worker, or commits some other serious offense must be dealt with immediately through a higher level of disciplinary action.

How Can I Support a Positive Working Environment for All Employees?

People choose to work in child care programs for many reasons. Most employees work because they need the money. Doing something worthwhile and helping others are also common reasons people seek employment in human service agencies. Since high salaries are not the norm, and since the work can be both physically and emotionally exhausting, the child care director must find other ways to create a positive working environment and to help personnel find satisfaction in their jobs. Many caring staff members remain year after year in their jobs. When asked why they stay, they often mention how they love their jobs and how they feel they are doing something important for children, 12-6. Your job, as director, involves seeking ways to build job satisfaction among your employees.

Compensation

All employees are interested in the amount of their salaries unless they are independently wealthy. While some may work to supplement household income, others

12-6 Helping children as they grow and learn can be very satisfying for staff members.

may be the sole support of themselves and dependents. Both the amount of the paycheck and the assurance that the paycheck will be received on a regular basis are important to employees.

The process of determining how much you can afford to pay personnel is a difficult one. Almost everyone who is involved in child care feels that salaries for staff should be higher than what they currently are. The reality of budgeting is that you cannot pay salaries with money you don't have. Whatever your wages are, they must be realistic in terms of the income of the program. Wishful thinking won't pay the bills.

In our society, a person's worth is often measured by a salary. In the child care field, salaries do not reflect the significant influence that preschool staff have in the lives of children. For too long, our society has taken the position that "anyone can do it." As a result, many children are in situations where the care is inadequate and indifferent. As an administrator, one of your hardest jobs will be to figure out how to pay adequate salaries to your hard-working staff, while keeping the programs financially secure. Most professional staff in child care are aware of the salary picture in the field. They will appreciate your efforts on their behalf as you work to advocate for improved wages.

As part of your budgeting process, you will have already considered how many children you expect to enroll, how many staff you will need, approximately what your tuition will be, and the amount of fixed expenses such as rent and utilities. By talking to other directors, you can also get a sense of what salaries are paid in other nearby programs. Financial benefits, sometimes called *fringe benefits,* may be included in compensation in addition to salary. These benefits would cost the employees money if they had to pay for them independently. When they are offered as a benefit, the employees don't receive cash, but do receive the service or benefit, in most cases, without taxation. Your program pays the cost of these benefits. When determining what benefits you can afford to offer, you must consider their cost as a part of each employee's compensation package and its impact on your program budget.

When considering how to establish salary ranges, keep the following points in mind:

- All salaries must be at or above minimum wage.

- Your program may not be up to full enrollment all of the time.

- Jobs that require more training and have more responsibility should also have higher salaries.

- Some salary increase should be offered each year to encourage staff to stay.

- Financial benefits are calculated in addition to salary and must be included in the cost of each employee.

- Staff members who are doing similar jobs should be on a similar pay scale.

- Salary increases raise the employee's salary for every year following the increase.

- Bonuses can be given when money is available, but do not raise the base salary.

In addition to monetary compensation, many programs offer a variety of financial benefits.

Cost of a Benefit Package

In planning a benefit package, consider the cost of each item. If you allow each employee to take five paid vacation days, you will have to pay for those days. You will also have to pay for substitutes who must be called in to cover for vacationing employees. Benefits will vary from agency to agency. When considering various kinds of benefits, keep in mind the following:

- leave days—These cost the program money when replacements must be hired to keep the center fully staffed.

- insurance—Often, if your agency can participate in a group plan, the cost per employee will be less than it would be if purchased individually.

- lunches—This would not be a reasonable benefit to offer unless you have some simple way to provide it. If your center is housed in a hospital complex with an employee cafeteria, or if your center has its own cook, this would be a reasonable benefit. If this benefit requires that you "order out" everyday, it would probably become too costly an item to provide, 12-7.

- parking—If your center has lots of space for parking, this benefit would cost you very little. However, if your center is in a city where employees must pay to park in a lot every day, the cost could be high.

- child care—This benefit can also become costly if employees' children are filling positions that could be filled by tuition-paying families. Since you must stay within licensing regulations regarding the number of children in the groups, you cannot simply add employees' children unless you are at less than full capacity. This benefit may also have tax implications for the employee. Check with a lawyer or personnel specialist to determine all of the consequences of offering this benefit.

- dues for professional memberships—The cost for this benefit is usually not much for the agency. It does have the positive effect of linking the staff to outside sources of training and information. This may also help each staff person feel more like a part of a larger group who work in the same field.

12-7 If your program provides meals for children, lunches for staff could also be offered as a fringe benefit.

- tuition for additional classes or training taken—Staff can be encouraged to further their training when this benefit is offered. If additional coursework is a condition of employment, this benefit can help ensure the employee follows through with that commitment. Some programs provide reimbursement for the cost of the class after the employee completes it successfully. It can become expensive if several employees are seriously working on advanced degrees. It would probably cost very little if there were few opportunities for coursework or training available. You may have to set a limit on the amount of reimbursement available for each employee.

- updating of CPR and first aid training—This is another benefit that would not cost your program very much. It would also help encourage employees to take or update this training.

- HIB (Hepatitis B) immunization—It is recommended that personnel working with children be immunized against Hepatitis B. The three injections necessary for full protection are expensive. If your program can provide for the cost of this immunization, it demonstrates clearly your concern for the well-being of your program's employees.

When calculating the compensation your program can afford, consider the cost of the benefits you want to offer. You may have to revise the benefit plan if your program cannot afford the desired plan.

Working Conditions

The atmosphere where a person works is often just as important as the wages that person earns. Many staff members stay in jobs that don't pay well because they love what they are doing. Pleasant working conditions are more important than money for many people. As a director, there are many steps you can take to create a positive working environment.

Positive and Respectful Climate

Creating a positive, respectful climate is an important part of building a good working environment. Staff members need to feel they are valued in their workplace. They must be treated with respect and consideration. You are a role model for this behavior. You set the tone for the center as you treat staff with the same consideration you expect them to show families and children. Greet staff members each day. Let them know you are glad to see them. Encourage a sense of inclusion that helps all persons feel they play an important role in providing good care for the children in the center.

A positive climate also involves an open mind toward new ideas. If staff members' ideas are always met with a "No, we can't do that here!" response, new ideas will not be shared. If things are done a certain way simply because they have always been done that way, stagnation sets in and the work can become boring.

Classroom Assignments

As you make personnel decisions, try to place each person in the particular position where they will work best. For example, certain staff work well with infants, but dislike the more assertive characteristics of preschoolers. Others prefer working with two half-day groups rather than a full-day class. Some may relate better to three-year-olds rather than four-year-olds. If you can place your staff with the age group or classroom where they seem to "click" with the children, things will be smoother for them and you.

It is also important to pay attention to the interactions among staff members. Putting two adults who can't stand each other together in a room all day long is guaranteed to lead to trouble. Even if the two staff basically like each other, personality characteristics should be considered in organizing work groups. Two strong-willed, assertive individuals may not work well together for long without clashing. Likewise, two mild-mannered, nonassertive individuals working in the same classroom may not make the best team. Staff members with complimentary personalities often are the best match if they balance and support each other.

Schedule Preferences

Staff members also have preferences regarding their schedule. Some like early morning hours and feel invigorated by an early shift. Others may have their own children to get off to school and prefer starting later. When staff are able to request their preferred shift, you may be pleasantly surprised that all shifts are chosen. While you may not always be able to accommodate individual preferences, the staff will appreciate your efforts to do so when possible. Scheduling decisions can signal the staff that you view them as individuals and that you are trying to meet their needs. For some staff with complicated family responsibilities or special health considerations, scheduling decisions may make a difference in whether or not they can continue in the job.

Physical Environment

The physical environment of the center is also important. A clean, pleasant classroom with adequate ventilation and lighting will help staff enjoy their workday. Sanitary bathrooms and kitchens not only present a more impressive environment, they also are important in protecting the health of staff and children.

Within your facility, try to find a space where staff can have a few quiet moments away from the children. Interesting magazines, soft chairs, coffee or juice, and a brief chance to talk with other adults can provide a relaxing break. Many valuable ideas can be passed between staff during these casual conversation times. A staff bulletin board could be developed to share training opportunities, sign-ups for shared equipment, or humorous cartoons. Available professional journals or a folder containing successful ideas for field trips can stimulate new activity ideas, 12-8.

Working conditions play a significant role in building staff loyalty to your program. Staff members who feel that you are concerned about their well-being have a greater commitment to the program. While there will always be some staff turnover, many child care agencies have staff who have remained with their program for many years. Even if you cannot afford to pay the salaries you would like to pay, you can create a center where people feel comfortable, safe, and appreciated.

Motivation and Recognition of Efforts

People who choose to work in child care usually do so because of their love for children and commitment to the field. The work is often physically hard and emotionally exhausting. The pay is usually low. Extra effort is often unappreciated by parents who are, themselves, exhausted. As director, you must provide a nurturing and supportive atmosphere that will motivate staff and help them grow. They need to feel their efforts are valued by those who understand the nature of the work.

12-8 Staff members appreciate a pleasant room where they can talk over ideas or events of the day.

Several things can be done to recognize staff who have been with the program a long time. A staff appreciation banquet can give tired personnel a time to relax and visit with each other. Certificates, award pins, plaques, or other small gifts can be given to those who have been with the program for many years. If you have a regular newsletter, you could feature a different employee with a brief description in each issue. Some centers with limited parking offer an "employee of the week" reserved parking space. When the center has an open house, you can usually arrange for local newspaper coverage. Staff can be featured in publicity photos as they work with the children, 12-9.

An important way to recognize staff efforts is for you, as director, to acknowledge them personally. A brief note of appreciation, stopping by the classroom to say "thanks" or a more formal letter of commendation that is placed in the personnel file are usually gratefully appreciated by the staff. Mentioning outstanding effort at a board meeting ensures that the commendation will also appear in the formal board minutes as a permanent record of staff effort.

In-Service Training

In-service training refers to training that a person receives while already employed. Pre-service education, such as vocational school, college, special courses, etc., occurs before employment. Participation in in-service training is usually expected while an individual is employed.

Director's Dilemma
The center staff has worked hard throughout a difficult year. They have endured a long winter, center renovations, and a financial crisis with patience and good humor. You cannot afford to give them all raises or meaningful bonuses even though you know that they deserve them. What kinds of things could you do that would recognize the extra effort they put forth? What could you plan that would be fun and meaningful for all?

12-9 A plaque awarded for many years of service brings a smile to this teacher's face.

The purposes of in-service training may include the following:

- updating knowledge with new information

- providing in-depth information on topics covered briefly in earlier training

- improving specific areas of on-the-job performance

- presenting new activity ideas

- providing an opportunity to share ideas and concerns

- meeting required training hours mandated by funding or licensing agencies

- giving staff the opportunity for personal advancement

- strengthening staff understanding of child development principles

- renewing enthusiasm and providing motivation and encouragement for staff

Many states require that child care personnel participate in training sessions or workshops each year, 12-10. The requirements for this training vary from state to state. States receiving federal money must require at least 12 hours of training every

12-10 The staff enjoys the casual nature and refreshments that are a part of the training session.

two years. Although, from a child development specialist's point of view, this is a very low training requirement, some staff will still be unwilling to participate.

In determining whether your staff is improving their skills, it is appropriate to consider their willingness to participate in training. Are they open to new ideas? Do they choose workshops or training sessions that address their real needs? Do they incorporate what they have learned into their daily work with children?

Staff who do not work directly with children need to have an opportunity to participate in appropriate training also. If you are purchasing a new computer system, it will be necessary for your administrative and clerical staff to have training and support while learning how the new system works. A new receptionist may need training in phone etiquette or how to handle difficult people.

Staff members' needs for in-service training will differ according to their previous training, particular job, and experiences on the job. Lilian Katz, a former president of NAEYC, has identified four stages of professional development that teachers typically experience. At each stage, their needs for support and training are different.

- Stage 1: According to Katz, brand new teachers in their first year on the job are finding their way through the new experience of being responsible for their own classroom. Training needs usually involve suggestions for more effective classroom work as well as information necessary to do the non-teaching part of the job. New staff members will need support as they experience the ups and downs of the first year on the job 12-11.

- Stage 2: As teachers move into the second year of their jobs, they have a better sense of what to expect. They know when reports are due, which types of activities seem to work well with the children, and what to expect as the year progresses. They move into a stage of consolidation. This stage lasts for several years. Teachers in this stage need opportunities for sharing ideas, successes, and frustrations with other experienced teachers. They need an opportunity to refine their ideas through stimulating training. New activity ideas are welcomed as well as ways to help children who have unique needs or behavioral problems.

- Stage 3: By the time teachers have taught for several years, they may begin to experience burnout. They often begin to question whether they are doing any good. They may find themselves discouraged and bored. This is the stage when new challenges are needed. In-service training at this point may focus on helping teachers to prepare to take on new responsibilities. Learning to handle some administrative duties, providing training to others, or serving as a mentor to a new teacher can provide renewal of enthusiasm.

12-11 Most teachers don't mind having observation windows in their classrooms. These can be helpful when determining the appropriate types of training and support to provide.

- Stage 4: The final stage has been identified as maturity. At this point, teachers have the classroom elements of their job mastered. They have experienced a renewal that leads them back to enthusiasm for their field, but there is little in the everyday classroom experience that continues to challenge them. At this point, many teachers begin to ask deeper questions about their profession. Cross-cultural issues and philosophical discussions become invigorating.

These stages were developed specifically with teachers in mind. However, all staff who care about their work, probably experience similar stages to some degree. As the director, you may experience the same stages yourself. The stages are not good or bad. They simply are a reflection of a progression through the professional life cycle. Once you are aware of them, you can use that information to help in planning appropriate in-service training.

Helping Staff Avoid Burnout

After a few years in the child care field, staff members may begin to experience symptoms of burnout. They are mentally tired. They feel unappreciated and bored with the day-to-day routine, and they are easily overwhelmed by the latest problems. These feelings can drain the energy of the individual and discourage all who work around that person.

The basic nature of working with children cannot be changed. It is absolutely necessary to be actively alert when caring for children. Emotional availability and involvement are a part of what makes the relationship between children and caring adults work well, 12-12.

Interactions with many people on many different levels go on continuously. It often seems that no one notices these efforts.

Literature on preventing burnout stresses the need to find ways to renew enthusiasm. Many of the suggestions focus on restoring a sense of playfulness in people's lives. For many, being an adult means putting away childish dreams and delights. Yet, being able to maintain a gentle sense of humor can be a powerful stress reliever. Taking a few minutes each day to do something just for the fun of it, can make routine things more bearable. Exercise or relaxation techniques such as meditation, can all help to renew energy and relieve stress.

As director, you cannot make a person have fun. You cannot restore a sense of playfulness if a staff member was never allowed to be playful. However, you can help the staff to plan activities for themselves that are fun in nature. An agency bowling team can build a camaraderie among staff who don't necessarily know each other well. Picnics or pot-luck dinners for staff can set a relaxed tone. Even refreshments at training sessions can help.

It may be helpful to form a committee to plan these staff activities. Craft classes, aerobics, or flea market shopping expeditions can all help staff become more com-

12-12 Working with children requires alertness and emotional involvement.

fortable with each other. No one activity will interest everyone, and no one should ever be forced to participate. Nor should activities be scheduled in such a way that they take time away from the children.

Once again, your attitudes and behaviors set the tone for the center. If you can maintain a sense of humor and keep things in perspective with a touch of lightheartedness, others will feel free to do the same. If you are gloomy, frantic, or overwhelmed all the time, others will pick up that tone. When you participate in activities that renew your own energy, you can encourage others to do likewise. Many of the concerns facing classroom staff are serious, and their importance should not be minimized. At the same time, being able to "look at the bright side" can help staff address problems more creatively and effectively.

Maintaining a well-qualified staff for the program is one of the director's most important responsibilities. The quality of the program and the day-to-day experiences for children are dependent on the staff. No other component of the program is more important. Many directors find that this is the hardest part of their job. Motivating staff, helping them get along with each other, and supporting their efforts to do a good job are not easy tasks. As the director, you must accomplish all of this, with a good sense of humor and a "thick skin."

⊙ Summary

A good child care program depends on maintaining a committed, well-trained staff. Printed personnel policies help individuals understand their place within the organization and inform them of basic program policies. Staff members need to know what their duties and responsibilities are as well as how to carry out basic job requirements. The personnel policies also let staff know of their rights and the expectations that the agency has of them.

The agency must have some procedure for evaluating staff. The evaluation should be based on the job description of the individual being evaluated. The format should be made clear to the employee ahead of time. Results of the evaluation must be shared with the individual, but maintained in confidence from curious staff. The evaluation should be used as a basis to help the employee grow in the job. If the staff member is not performing satisfactorily, the director may have to take action that may lead to dismissal.

Evaluations are also useful in helping plan training sessions for the staff. At different stages of their careers, staff will have different training needs. A good training program builds teachers' skills and self-esteem and can help them avoid burnout. It helps to improve the quality of care in the center.

Attention also must be paid to staff compensation and overall working conditions within the program. Many child care workers stay in their jobs because they love what they do. Pleasant working conditions, in-service training opportunities, and recognition of efforts encourage staff to stay with the program. The director's support and commitment to a positive work environment can be a crucial factor in maintaining program stability.

⊙ Terms

personnel policies
grievance procedures
fringe benefits
in-service training

Review

1. Why are written personnel policies important to your staff?

2. Why is it necessary to review and possibly change personnel policies over time?

3. What is the purpose of the Right to Know laws?

4. What types of basic emergency procedures should be considered to keep staff and children safe?

5. What is the purpose of a probationary employment period for a new employee?

6. What components should be included in an evaluation plan?

7. Why is it important to document any disciplinary action at any level in an employee's personnel file?

8. What kinds of financial benefits are often a part of employees' total compensation package?

9. How can classroom assignments affect the morale of staff?

10. What are the purposes of in-service training?

Applications

1. Visit a child care center. Look at the area surrounding the building. What dangers exist in that environment that might present a safety hazard to staff? Would the dangers change depending on whether it was daylight or dark? What kinds of ideas would you have to ensure the safety of staff?

2. Contact several center directors and ask to look at a copy of their personnel policies. Examine the policies to see what types of information are included or not included. Report to the class on the differences you found among programs. Discuss how the different policies might affect employees.

3. Role-play with another student a situation involving a director and an assistant teacher. Evaluations of the assistant teacher support the concern that the assistant has not been doing the job in a satisfactory manner. The assistant has been placed on a probationary status, but the work has not improved. You are dimissing the assistant from the program. What documents and materials do you need to back you up? How will you discuss this? How will you handle the reaction?

Management skills and efficient support staff are essential in carrying out the administrative tasks of a child care center.

Chapter 13
Administrative Concerns

After studying this chapter, you will be able to

○ explain the relationship between program organization and cost.

○ describe the types of records that must be kept.

○ outline the role of the computer in supporting administrative functions.

○ name the factors to consider when purchasing a computer system.

As director, your responsibilities include organizing the center so the necessary work gets done in an efficient, accurate manner. How many support staff are needed? What records must be kept? Is it worth buying a computer? Administrative costs can vary a lot from one program to another. Two programs may serve the same number of children, but one may be much more expensive to operate. The additional cost may be fine if you have the finances to afford it. A very inexpensive program, on the other hand, may skimp so much that it eventually collapses under the pressure of heavy workloads, low pay, and lack of administrative support. In small programs with just a few staff, there may not be many options in regard to administrative organization. In larger agencies with multiple sites, numerous classrooms, and many staff, the organizational choices become much more complex.

How Should I Manage the Administrative Part of the Program?

There is no one right way to manage the administrative work of the center. An efficient system for one center may not work as well for another program. Your job, as director, will involve creating a structure that allows the administrative functions of the program to be carried out in an efficient, cost-effective manner.

Director's Dilemma
Your program has had several small centers at sites around the edges of a small city. You now have the opportunity to rent a large, centrally-located building that will comfortably house all of your classrooms. The location will not inconvenience the families who use the program. You believe that a substantial amount of money could be saved through more cost-efficient administrative and support services by this move. What possible advantages could you predict from this consolidation? What are some possible disadvantages?

277

The administrative work of the program usually involves the following types of tasks:

- bookkeeping and financial records
- supervision and evaluation of staff
- enrollment and monitoring attendance
- supporting classroom program development
- obtaining substitutes for the classrooms when needed
- monitoring the program according to specific guidelines of funding
- maintaining records on staff, families and children, and facilities
- answering the phone and responding to requests for information
- locating and maintaining facility sites
- securing and monitoring use of funds
- preparing program documents and communications
- coordinating purchasing decisions for the program
- assessing community need and determining future plans for the program
- marketing and public relations

These tasks are important in building and maintaining a strong program. They cannot simply be ignored or added onto the job of the teachers.

Hiring Administrative Staff

The staffing pattern for the center's classrooms will be determined primarily by licensing regulations. You will not have much flexibility when deciding the number of staff needed in each room. Your choices involving the number and job descriptions of administrative positions are more varied. You must also make choices within the limitations of the budget of the program. It may be difficult to realize that you can't hire all of the administrative help you would like to have. Until a program is financially secure and has been in operation a while, many directors find that they must do most of the administrative work themselves.

When deciding how many administrative staff to hire, consider the following points:

- What administrative tasks must be done in your specific program?
- Are there groups of tasks or parts of the program that fit together logically?
- Within these logical subdivisions, are the workloads even and fair?
- What level of training and expertise is needed to carry out each aspect of the work?

- Which tasks must you do yourself, and which ones can be delegated to other staff members?

One agency providing care for about 500 children is organized around the major age groupings within the program. Three supervisors report directly to the program director. One is responsible for the infant/toddler classrooms, and the affiliated family child care homes. One is responsible for the preschool sites. The third one handles responsibility for the school-age program. Each of these positions has similar responsibilities in regard to enrollment of children, selection and monitoring of staff, and program development.

Each position also has aspects that are unique. For example, the school-age program has more children than the other parts of the program. It operates part-time during the school year, but full-time during the summer. Transportation of children from their schools to the program sites must be coordinated. Because this particular supervisor has extensive computer experience, she is also responsible for training other staff who must use the computer network. The infant/toddler supervisor must recruit and visit the affiliated family child care homes and coordinate the food reimbursement program. The preschool coordinator is also responsible for kitchen operation, general staff training, coordination, and marketing . A financial coordinator handles monitoring of the budget and maintenance of the financial records. The secretary answers phone calls and requests for information along with general secretarial duties.

The director is responsible for overall supervision of the entire program, 13-1. This includes planning, budgeting, and evaluation of the total agency. It is the director who has the understanding of the total program and its role in the broader community. This division of tasks works well for this particular mid-sized program. A small program will not be able to afford the supervisory/coordinator level. In a more complex program, you cannot afford not to have adequate administrative personnel. One administrator and one secretary would not be able to handle the work without additional support.

Hiring Administrative Support Personnel

It is necessary to determine the number of administrative support personnel you will need. Administrative support positions, excluding the executive director, may include the following types of personnel:

- supervisors without direct classroom responsibilities

13-1 This director has established her own system of tracking equipment that must be shared by several different classrooms.

- health and safety

- maintenance

- kitchen and/or food preparation

- transportation

- financial

- training and program development

- secretarial

Large programs with complicated financial packages involving grants, tuition, and government subsidy may need to hire an accountant. A program with simpler finances may operate smoothly with a bookkeeper or data entry clerk. Some programs function well with a financial manager, clerk assistant, and the occasional advice of an accountant paid only on a consulting basis.

Special purpose grants often allow the hiring of additional personnel for the purpose of carrying out the grant activities. For example, a large grant designed to organize training for several different agencies, would normally include money to hire a coordinator. If you write a grant that will involve additional work for the agency, you must be careful to consider who will actually do the work of the grant. Simply committing the program to more work without adequate personnel to get the work done will cause major problems.

The decisions regarding support personnel must be made carefully. Remember, support staff do not work directly with children. Their positions must be paid for out of the tuition or subsidy from children in the program. Additional support personnel do not generate additional money. On the other hand, records must be kept, the phone must be answered, and staff must be supervised. If these tasks are not done, the center is likely to become chaotic and unable to meet future demands.

What Kinds of Records Does the Agency Need to Keep?

Your position, as director, involves having an overall perspective on the total program. This is a part of the management function of controlling. However, you must have information in order to do your job wisely. If you do not have an accurate record of attendance, you will not be able to project anticipated income for the next year. If there is no inventory of equipment, you may spend money on a new rocking boat or tape player when the program already has one that no one is using. If there is no record of a warranty for a copier that won't operate, the agency may be charged unnecessarily for repairs.

Some information must be kept to satisfy licensing requirements. Other records are required by law or by various funding sources. The program must maintain these carefully and accurately. Severe penalties may be incurred if adequate records are not kept in an organized and accessible manner. Some information kept in the program is confidential and must be protected from curious examination. Some information should be tracked simply because it gives you a more accurate picture of what is happening in the program.

The types of records that must be kept may seem endless. Indeed, a major task for the director is to identify the types of information that must be collected. Once you know what types of data to collect, design forms that make keeping track of the information simple and consistent. Jotting bits of information down on a scrap of paper is not a good idea, even for a small program.

Financial Records

Detailed financial records are necessary to satisfy government and funding regulations. If your program is privately owned, these records must be kept to document personal income tax. If the program is a not-for-profit entity, it will be subject to audit by an outside professional. When determining the types of records to maintain, it is a good idea to obtain the advice of a certified public accountant who is knowledgeable about your type of program structure. Establishing the right kinds of records at the beginning can save you a lot of trouble later.

Journal/Ledger

The *journal* is a type of record similar to a checkbook, but is a bit more complicated. All income and expenses must be maintained in chronological order. A balance is kept that shows exactly what amount is available in the program's bank account at all times. The *ledger* is a series of separate journals that track each major category of the budget. For example, if you have planned your budget to include $10,000 for the cost of utilities, you will need a separate column or category to track how much has been spent out of this category. You will have additional ledger categories for supplies, food, staff salaries, rent, and other costs of operating the center. If you have several centers, you may have separate ledger accounts to examine the comparative costs of each center. The categories you establish in your ledger should match the main categories you have identified in your budget. Through the use of the ledger, you can review how much has been spent from the budgeted amount in each category.

You may keep a separate page in a ledger book for each of these categories. It is also possible to purchase preprinted bookkeeping systems that include a spread sheet where all this information can be put on one wide page. These records must be kept carefully. They will become a part of the program's audit or income tax documentation.

Monthly Financial Summary

A *monthly financial summary* is a monthly summary that is kept primarily to provide you with a current picture of the program's finances. It should be designed to list each main category of the budget. The amount allocated to this category and the amount spent to date should be indicated. This type of summary is useful in alerting you if too little income is coming in, or if too much is being spent, 13-2. The summary should be reviewed in relation to the fiscal year. For example, if you are six months into your fiscal year, approximately 50 percent of your income should have

Monthly Financial Summary as of ___(date)___					
Fiscal Year Expenditures					
July 1- June 30 as of percent of Year Completed					
Category	Description	Budgeted	Disbursed	Remaining	Percent Spent
100	Administrative and General	$xxxxxx	$xxxxxx	$xxxxxx	
200	Building and Maintenance	$	$	$	
300	Child Care and Education	$	$	$	
400	Food and Nutrition	$	$	$	
500	Staff Training	$	$	$	
600	Transportation	$	$	$	
700	Health	$	$	$	
Totals		$	$	$	

13-2 The monthly financial summary helps you to monitor the program's spending patterns in relation to the budget.

been received and 50 percent of your expenses should have been spent. If you are nine months into the fiscal year, roughly 75 percent of your financial plan should be completed. If you are six months into the fiscal year, but 75 percent of your food money has already been spent, you can predict that this category of expenditures will run out of money before the end of the year. You can use this information to help you decide whether to increase income, reduce spending, or look for categories with extra money to transfer into the food budget.

Keep in mind that expenses in all categories may not be evenly spread out throughout the fiscal year. For example, you may pay all of your insurance premiums during the first month of the fiscal year. That will eliminate all of the money in that category right away. However, since no additional money must be paid out of this category until the next fiscal year, it is all right to have spent 100 percent of the money budgeted for this cost. You may have certain months in the year when enrollment is lower than normal. At those times, monthly income will be reduced. There may also be certain months when utility or food costs are higher. Months when furnaces or air conditioners are not needed will result in reduced costs.

The monthly summary of expenses is one useful tool that can guide you when making financial decisions. It will allow you to monitor the spending pattern in each budget category in order to determine if adjustments must be made.

Payroll Records

As an employer, the agency must keep detailed records regarding the income paid to each employee and taxes and benefits paid by the program. All information necessary to provide the program and the employee with accurate reporting forms for income tax purposes must be maintained. This includes information on social security showing clearly the program's and the individual's contributions. The income tax that is withheld by the program for each employee must be sent quarterly to the Internal Revenue Service along with a year-end summary form. This may be true for state and local taxes as well. Reporting forms must be prepared in duplicate so there is a copy for the employee and one for the program. These forms are based on the payroll records that your program has been keeping on each employee. Year-end financial reports verifying wages and taxes withheld must be prepared for each employee.

Records must also be maintained regarding the benefits provided for each employee. All employees may not have the same benefits. For example, some employees may be covered by a spouse's health insurance plan and may not participate in the plan that your program offers. Some may choose to receive extra dollars in their paycheck rather than participate in a retirement plan. Your program must accurately record the benefits of employees. The costs of each benefit for each employee must also be paid for by the program and recorded on the employee's records. If the benefit is one where the employee and the employer share the cost of the benefit, the payroll records should keep track of the contributions of both.

Fee Payments

The payments made by each family for child care service must be recorded. When special arrangements exist, such as reduced rate for additional children from the same family, these must be documented. If payments are overdue, and late fees are assessed, this information should be included in the records. These fee payment records are also used to prepare the Report for Tax Credits form needed by families to document their annual child care expenses for tax credits. As with payroll records, a copy of this report should be made for the program.

Child/Family Records

A file for each child should be kept in the center. A method of cross-referencing information related to that child's family and other brothers or sisters in the program should be used.

File on Each Enrolled Child

A file on each child enrolled in the program should include a variety of information to help the teacher and to ensure that the child has the best possible experience in the center. Files on each child should contain:

- current health screening

- enrollment forms

- immunization records

- emergency information

- list of persons authorized to pick up the child

- parent consent forms, such as photo, trip permissions, etc.

- attendance

- court order forms, if there are custody issues the center must know about

- developmental records

- records of parent conferences

- samples of work the child has done over the year

In small programs, there is usually just one file on each child containing all the above information. In larger programs, the teachers may keep the work samples, parent/teacher conference records, and notes on interesting classroom events in a separate file. This is kept in the classroom for easy access by the teacher. All files must be kept confidential, but must be available for parents to review at any time.

Records on Each Enrolled Family

The family data file includes a copy of the contract/enrollment form between the family and the agency that specifies the type, time, and cost of service the program will provide. It should also include information regarding who is responsible for paying the bill. If the family is eligible for a subsidy for part of the cost of care, documentation of eligibility for that subsidy should be kept in the file. Basic information such as home and work addresses and emergency numbers for reaching the parent or other authorized adult should be maintained. If the parent has received any notices warning of possible disenrollment for lack of fee payment or late payment notices, copies of these should also be included in these family records. As with information on each child, these records are confidential. These are not for general examination by curious members of the staff. However, they are open to the family for their review, 13-3.

Registration and Waiting List Records

As a program becomes more popular, the requests for enrollment may grow. Often, there are more children needing care than there are spaces available in the program. It is necessary for you to maintain records that allow you to keep track of the families who have applied for enrollment. You must also be able to identify their place on the waiting list. For parents, the need for child care can be a critical factor in whether they can accept a job. For your center, swift placement of children into the program as space becomes available means that you minimize the loss of income that occurs when the classes are not full.

Attendance Records

Attendance records may be required by funding sources. They provide important information that is used to document payments from subsidizing sources. They also verify attendance for fee payments by families and for reimbursement from food subsidy programs. Records should be maintained on each classroom and for each individual child. They should be kept so attendance patterns for all children in a particular age category can be analyzed. Attendance patterns can provide valuable information that will be helpful in planning for the next year's classroom needs.

13-3 Records must be kept for children and their families as well as your staff. Licensing regulations determine a good bit of the information that should be kept in each child's file. Payroll and benefit records must be accurately kept for each employee.

Personnel Records

Personnel records must be kept on each staff member. Personnel records include:

- verification of each employee's credentials, training, and pre-employment references

- copies of I-9 forms verifying employability including copies of driver's license, social security card, and/or birth certificate

- criminal background clearance, if required

- dates of leave taken

- personnel actions such as promotions or disciplinary actions

- evaluations

- dates of probationary status

- date hired

- CPR and First Aid certification and renewal data

- current physical exam form

- emergency information

- salary and benefit status

- record of in-service training participation

Director's Dilemma

One of your classroom teachers is angry at another teacher for not cleaning up the workroom. This teacher demands that you let her look at the other staff member's yearly evaluation. A parent has had a disagreement with a teacher and is demanding the right to look at the teacher's personnel file. How would you handle your obligation to maintain confidentiality of files and, at the same time, address the concerns of these two individuals?

Inventory

Inventory records help you keep track of various items purchased by the program and where they are. These items have a dollar value, and they are assets of your program. You don't want to purchase things that you already have tucked away somewhere, 13-4. Items, such as food, must be monitored to be sure that it is fresh and is being used for the children in the center.

Inventories should be kept of the following:

- major pieces of classroom or playground equipment

- major pieces of office and kitchen equipment

- food purchased and served

- supplies and materials received

- items donated to the center

Will a Computer Help Me?

The computer is a wonderful tool for tracking the information you need to maintain. As your child care agency grows, you will be dealing with larger numbers of children, families, staff, sites, and funding sources. Computerized management information systems can save substantial amounts of time and effort. It's a good idea to purchase a management systems program that keeps track of all the records you need. A management systems program will also allow you to move back and forth from one set of records to another. For example, it is possible to examine attendance records for an individual child and look at family fee payment records at the same time. Payroll information can be easily located for inclusion in summary financial reports.

The computer is of primary value to your program through its streamlining of office functions. It can give you easy access to the information you need to make important decisions.

13-4 Keeping an accurate inventory of items in the center can avoid waste and unnecessary purchases.

Using Computers on the Job

The computer is useful primarily for administrative tasks. It can free office personnel from copying the same information repeatedly. Calculation of financial data can be completed efficiently and accurately. A computer makes communicating instantly with other centers or programs possible. It can also be an interesting addition to the classroom. In today's world, familiarity with a computer is essential.

Record Keeping

Management systems programs can aid you in keeping track of all the records necessary in the center. These records can include

- attendance
- licensing data
- payments received and disbursements
- family and child data
- inventories
- scheduling
- accounting reports
- payroll

A computer printer can also print out checks and W-2 forms for employees. Data can be copied from one type of record or report to another. There is less risk of error since the person entering the data only has to do so once. Time is saved when the bookkeeper or data entry clerk can simply push a key to copy or move information.

Word Processing

Word processing is the computerized form of typewriting. However, word processing allows you to do much more than is possible on a typewriter. When you are preparing a letter or document, what you have typed appears on the monitor screen. It is not printed onto paper until you direct the computer to do so. It is possible to correct mistakes and move sentences without typing the whole document again. You can also print many copies of the same document.

By using a *database*, you can quickly address copies of the same letter to different people. The personal information is entered into the database fields; the fields are then merged with the main document. You can also use database information to make mailing labels and envelopes. Once the information is entered, you can use the data over and over without retyping the same information, 13-5.

Payroll and Billing

The computer can save time by performing the calculations necessary for the financial components of your program. Some programs can calculate the correct taxes to be withheld and recalculate the information quickly when an employee receives a pay raise. If some staff members are paid on an hourly basis, the computer can figure the amount earned from the hours worked. It can print checks and pay stubs as well as copies of records for file purposes.

Attendance Log														For Month of _____																	
Student Name																															

13-5 Computers can create forms that can be copied and used as needed.

The computer can also calculate bills for clients who may be paying on an hourly basis. Discounts, fee increases, late payment fines, and changes in subsidy status can all be quickly adjusted into the calculations. Once the calculations are made, the computer can print out the bills, receipts, and envelopes.

Computer Networks

A *computer network* allows several staff members to have computers on their desks yet have access to the same information, 13-6. The information that is stored in a central processor is available to everyone whose computer is linked into the network. Data only needs to be keystroked into the computer system once, then it can be available to all who need to use it. For example, a family might have several children enrolled in different parts of the program. All the staff members who supervise those program components would have access to information on the family. The person responsible for the financial records can access the information as well.

A network system is primarily useful for large programs, where several staff members must work regularly with the same information. It is possible to set up a network so persons using it only have access to data they need to know. Confidentiality is protected while the benefits of the computer network are still available.

Communications

Computers are useful in enhancing communication. If your computer has a modem or cable connection you can access the Internet. The *Internet* is a worldwide computer network. It consists of thousands of smaller, local computer networks. Through the Internet, you can access information stored in another computer in another location. If you have centers in several towns, information can be shared easily over the Internet. Data typed into one computer can be rapidly available for use on another computer in another location.

Through *e-mail,* or electronic mail, you can send information that can be read on a monitor or printed out on another computer. Electronic pictures, certificates, and messages can all be sent to others in your network or on the Internet.

Some companies provide a variety of services in addition to connection to the Internet. These services are usually available for a monthly fee. Their offerings may include access to special bulletin boards, information services, computer usage tips, job search information, and e-mail. You may want to investigate what services each provider offers. This will help you determine if it is worthwhile for your program to subscribe.

Desktop Publishing

One valuable use of the computer is for desktop publishing. Work that used to require the services of a printing company can now be easily done in the office. Written information, pictures, backgrounds, and fancy borders can all be included in a document.

Desktop publishing can be used for the following:

13-6 For large programs, computers can be networked to save valuable time and enhance communication.

- newsletters
- publicity flyers
- invitations
- birthday cards
- parent or staff booklets
- certificates and awards
- posters and banners

The computer can save your program a substantial amount of money if you have previously paid for professional printing services. Of course, you will still have to pay for the copying of your items, but the cost of design and layout can be greatly reduced.

Other Uses

New uses for the computer are being developed every day. You can play games, design a room arrangement, and calculate the cost of a mortgage on a computer. You can also teach yourself keyboarding, find out how to repair a broken item, and communicate with someone who has the same interests or concerns as you.

Computers in the Classroom

Computers have become increasingly common in preschool and school-age classrooms. Many children today are familiar with computers in their homes and schools. Games, learning packages, and stories are all available for use on the computer.

The primary value for young children is they can become comfortable with the computer. Many adults are fearful of new technology and remain afraid they will "blow up the computer" if they push a wrong button. Children, on the other hand, are eager and curious about technology. Seeing the computer as a natural part of the environment prepares them for more serious use of it later on in life, 13-7.

Computers in the classrooms add an interesting dimension to the program. If your agency has old computers that are no longer needed in the offices, or if you can obtain them inexpensively, consider using them in the classroom. Keep in mind that you will also have to purchase the learning packages or games to be used on the computer.

Purchasing a Computer

When purchasing a computer system, there are several factors to consider. Be sure to check the expandability of the system. This means the computer has been designed so it can be updated as technology improves.

Compatibility is another factor to consider. If you already have a computer and now want to add to it, you must be sure the new equipment will work with the old. If the two pieces of hardware are not compatible, they won't work with each other.

Computers and software can be purchased with varying capabilities and complexity. Consider the abilities of your staff. If you purchase a complicated system, will you hire someone to train your staff? Will you need to hire someone especially to maintain records and work on the computer?

The array of choices to make when you are purchasing computers and software can be overwhelming. Technology increases rapidly, and many brands are available. The best way to shop is to write a list of what you want the computer to do for you. Which of those tasks are the most important? What do you see as being the future needs of your program as well as its current needs? Also consider the amount of money you can afford to spend.

Hardware

Hardware is the term used to refer to the actual pieces of computer equipment you will need to utilize the software. Hardware includes the central processing unit, memory, output devices, and input devices.

Central Processing Unit

The *central processing unit*, or *CPU*, is the heart of the computer. It contains the *processor*, the electronic circuitry that controls what the computer can do and how fast it can work. It also houses the computer's memory.

13-7 While not a necessity, computers in the classrooms are of great interest to preschoolers.

Memory

The computer's memory is used to store applications and files. *Read Only Memory (ROM)* is the instructions the computer follows when it is first turned on. *Random Access Memory (RAM)* stores data temporarily. This data must be saved on a permanent storage device.

The speed of the processor and the amount of RAM affect the cost of the computer. Processor speed is measured in megahertz, or MHz. In the past, processor speeds of 166 MHz were sufficient to run most software. By today's standards, many programs will not run without processors of at least 300 MHz. Therefore, you will want to make sure to get the highest speed processor you can afford.

RAM is measured in megabytes, or MB. There is usually 64 to 128 MB of RAM in most personal computers. Software packages will list the amount of RAM necessary for the program to run. You will need to make sure any software you buy will run on the amount of RAM your computer has. Additional memory can be added to most computers if needed.

Output Devices

Users obtain information from the computer through *output devices*. Output devices include monitors, printers, modems, fax machines, and voice messaging systems.

The *monitor* is a screen similar to a television. It is connected to the central processing unit so you can watch what you are doing on its screen. Monitors are available in different sizes; the larger sizes are more expensive.

The *printer* copies information from the computer onto paper. There are various types of printers available, each with different capabilities. Many centers find inexpensive ink-jet printers are suitable for their needs. The ink-jet printer uses tiny bursts of ink to print copy. A more expensive printer is the laser printer. It prints an image that is of the same clearness and quality as work coming from a print shop. The printer must also be compatible with the type of computer you have chosen.

The *fax machine* and the *modem* are two pieces of equipment that can be bought as one unit. They allow your computer to communicate with other computers or fax machines. This is useful if you need to send or receive information quickly to or from another office in a distant location. These items may be purchased at the time you buy the computer or later. If you buy them with your computer, they can be built into the central processing unit and simply connected by a cable to your phone line.

It is also possible to purchase a *voice messaging system*, or answering machine, that is installed internally in the computer. You may want to consider this option if your center does not have an answering machine already.

Input Devices

Input devices are used to enter information into the computer. Common input devices are the keyboard, mouse, and scanner.

The *keyboard* includes all the keys found on a typewriter, as well as function keys. Function keys control specific functions in different types of software.

The *mouse* is a small device designed to be rolled around on the desktop. The mouse can make much of the work that must be done on a computer easier and faster. Both the keyboard and mouse control the *cursor*, which indicates on the screen where input will take place. However, the mouse moves the cursor in a more fluid motion than the keyboard. The mouse also has two buttons which, when clicked, will control different functions.

The *scanner* acts like a copier. You can put a picture or a document on the scanner and it will read the information into the computer. This can save a considerable amount of time.

Storage

Because data is not often stored permanently on the computer, you will need different types of storage devices. These include floppy disks, large capacity disks, and compact discs. In order to use these methods of storage, your computer must have a disk drive for each of them.

A *floppy disk* is a 3.5-inch case of sturdy plastic encasing a small flexible plastic sheet. The data is stored on this internal sheet. High-density disks usually hold 1.4 MB of information.

Large capacity disks, including zip disks, hold up to 100 MB of data. These disks are thicker than the floppy disks, so they will not fit in the floppy disk drive. You should be sure the software you want is available on a disk that can be used on your computer.

Compact discs hold even more data. CD-ROMs (compact disc-Read Only Memory) were the first CDs available. You cannot save information from your computer on CD-ROMs; you can only access the software on it. However, new rewritable CD drives are available. By using this drive, you can save approximately 800 MB of data on a rewritable CD.

Software

The term **software** is used to identify packages of instructions that you can buy and load onto your computer, 13-8. It is software that guides the computer's functions. If you want the computer to maintain financial records, you will need to select and buy software that will do those tasks. Software packages are also called *applications*. Common applications include word processing, financial record keeping, and graphics. There are even applications that are designed to speed up the work of other applications.

Before you buy software, you will need to make sure your computer meets the system requirements. Check to see how much RAM is required to run the software, as well as the processor speed. If your computer will not run the software you want, it may be time to upgrade your system.

At the present time, there are a number of companies that are designing and manufacturing management information systems for child care programs. Choosing software can be a difficult task. Conduct research on the different packages available before making a purchase. Many of the software companies have demonstration packages that they will send to you. If you already have access to a computer, you can run these to see how they work. It is also a good idea to talk with other directors from similar programs who use computers. Often word-of-mouth can alert you to good deals or software to avoid.

Where to Shop for Computer Products

It is possible to buy computer systems from stores that specialize in specific brands, large discount stores that carry many brands, or mail order firms. Each has advantages and disadvantages. The smaller specialty stores frequently offer individualized service and assistance. The larger stores give you the chance to compare several different brands. Mail-order firms often have good prices. You will need to think about the options.

13-8 A variety of software is available on CDs.

You should also consider the cost of various software applications. Professional magazines such as *Child Care Information Exchange* or *Young Children* carry advertisements for software designed specifically for child care agencies. If you attend professional conferences, you will usually find software company exhibitors displaying their newest products. You can often obtain a conference discount on the price of the items you wish to buy. In addition to computer stores, many discount electronics stores carry different types of software. Shop around and get the software you want for the lowest possible price.

Technical Support

One final consideration is the availability of **technical support**. This refers to the ease with which you can obtain help if something on the computer doesn't work. It also means having someone available to help if your staff has trouble learning to use the software.

There are many books on the market about computers and software. These can be helpful if your office staff has a basic understanding of computers. If all your staff are beginners at using the computer, technical assistance can be essential in saving time and frustration. You may be able to hire someone locally on a consulting basis to train your staff and provide trouble-shooting for the computer systems. You may also find that your local vocational school or community college

Director's Dilemma

A friend has told you about a small business that is closing. The business is selling its office computers at a great price. You know that you need to buy computers to keep up with all of the records that must be kept in your office. Before deciding to buy these second-hand computers, what factors should you consider? What could be the advantages of buying this way? What are the disadvantages?

offers courses that provide instruction in computer usage. Even the most sophisticated computer user can occasionally run into trouble, so it is important to have access to technical assistance for your program.

⚙ Summary

Programs can be organized in many different ways. The larger your program is, the more choices you will have regarding its structure. There is often a relationship between program organization and the cost of operating the program. As your program grows, consider what positions are necessary to handle the administrative work of the center.

The licensing agency, the government, various funding sources, and internal program policies all require that various records be maintained. You should also keep certain types of information to help you in making important decisions. Records must be kept regarding families and children enrolled in the program, employees, financial activities, attendance, inventory, and other information.

The computer is a valuable administrative tool. It can reduce the amount of time it takes to maintain center records. It can also be used for preparing letters, documents, flyers, and publicity materials. When purchasing a computer, you should consider what you want the computer to do for your program. Identify the software that you need, then find a computer system that will work with that software. Consider the compatibility and expandability of any system you are considering purchasing.

⚙ Terms

journal
ledger
monthly financial summary
inventory records
word processing
computer network
Internet
hardware
central processing unit (CPU)
software
technical support

⚙ Review

1. How are the jobs of administrative and support personnel different from jobs of the teaching staff?

2. What types of positions are considered administrative or support positions?

3. List three categories of records that must be kept by a child care center.

4. Why is it necessary to maintain records?

5. Why is it important to maintain an inventory of various items owned by the program?

6. Describe ways that a computer can help with administrative tasks.

7. What is the value of putting an old computer in the classroom for children to use?

8. What is the difference between computer hardware and computer software?

9. What are the advantages of buying computer products from the following vendors?

   a. large discount stores

   b. small specialty stores

   c. mail-order firms

10. Why is it important to consider the availability of technical support when purchasing computer hardware or software?

◉ Applications

1. Identify the software companies that have applications available for child care program management from ads in journals such as *Young Children* or *Child Care Information Exchange*, etc. Write to the companies for advertising literature and prices of their products. Consider what your program would need. Compare the software ads from each company and what each application would cost.

2. Visit a computer store to examine the hardware. Ask a salesperson to explain the differences among the various types of computers available. Examine the printers and compare the difference in the look of a dot matrix printer, a ink-jet printer, and a laser printer. Ask about technical support provided by this company.

3. Make arrangements to visit a large program that has a fully computerized office. Ask the person who is in charge of record keeping to show you examples of forms that are available on the software used by the program. Find out if the program uses a network among several different offices. How does this affect the efficiency of the administrative staff?

Financial management skills can help in making decisions about purchasing and support services.

Chapter 14
Decisions on Purchasing and Support Services

After studying this chapter, you will be able to

◎ analyze your program's finances in order to make purchasing decisions.

◎ identify the most cost efficient forms of purchasing.

◎ decide whether to offer a food service program.

◎ determine program transportation needs and how to meet them.

Keeping track of how money comes into and flows out of the program is an important part of managing the various financial aspects of the program. You have already carefully prepared a budget and obtained promises of adequate funding for the center. Careful financial monitoring and decisions must still be made. The money you are counting on is not necessarily available when you are ready to use it.

The spending patterns of the program may need to be adjusted. Those purchases or expenditures that are not essential may have to be postponed until the expected income actually arrives. As the end of the fiscal year approaches and back income has arrived, you can reconsider any optional expenses.

Decisions must also be made about food service and transportation. Your program does not have to provide meals or transportation. However, if you are going to provide them, you must meet additional licensing or regulatory standards. Consideration must be given to how you are going to make these services available and what it will cost your program.

What Do I Need to Know About Financial Management?

As a director, you will face many financial decisions throughout the year. However, no book can tell you exactly what those decisions will be or exactly what to do.

When making financial decisions for your program, there are certain economic realities that you must take into consideration. Being promised money doesn't mean that you will get it. Planning a budget based on full enrollment doesn't mean that your program will always be full. Occasionally, money may even become available that you didn't anticipate. Your decision-making process should take into account both positive and negative influences on your program's money supply.

Understanding financial management terms and financial realities can help you in making these decisions.

Cash Flow

Cash flow is a term that refers to the movement of money into and out of your program's bank account. Child care programs receive their money in several basic ways. Parents pay tuition. The program may receive subsidy money from the state to supplement the cost of care for eligible children. Fund-raisers, special project grants, and interest on checking accounts may also provide income to the program. As you plan the program budget, consider the total amount of income from all of these sources. Then map out a spending plan that is in line with your expected income.

Throughout the fiscal year, you are committed to making certain payments. Staff salaries, utilities, and insurance are among the items that must be paid on time. However, you can only pay out money if you have received the money that others owe your program. You cannot spend money without monitoring the receipt of money. Ideally, money flows into your program as expected. In turn, you are able to pay your obligations in a timely manner.

Cash Lag

Cash lag refers to situations where money is owed to your program, but you have not received it yet. You cannot pay bills because this money is not actually in your checking account. Cash lag can be a major problem for a small program. There may not be enough money in reserve to cover expenses. While the program may be owed large sums of money, debts cannot be paid.

Unfortunately, cash can be a common problem. Many programs that depend on state subsidy, find that there is a cash lag at the beginning of each new fiscal year. There may also be a time gap between receiving approval for a special grant and actually receiving the money. In large programs, the amount of money owed to your agency may be thousands of dollars. In small programs, the cash lag is more likely to result from parents who don't pay their fees on time. If an entire community is experiencing financially troubled times, the stability of your program's income can be seriously affected. On paper, everything looks fine. You are expecting enough money to cover all of your debts. However, the reality is that until the money is actually in the program's accounts, it can't be used to pay bills.

Cash Reserve

Cash lag problems must be considered when making financial decisions. Some of your expenditures cannot be delayed. To cover these expenses, you should begin to build a *cash reserve*, 14-1. This means that the program sets aside some money each year, or whenever possible, to cover times when money is not flowing into the program. If you know that state subsidy checks are always late in the summer months, you will be able to dip into the cash reserve to pay salaries. When the subsidy money comes in, use part of it to replace what you had to draw out of the reserve fund.

Bad Debts

Unfortunately, every program, sooner or later, has some experience with bad debts. These occur when someone simply doesn't pay the program for services already received. Parents represent a cross section of the community. As is true in the larger society, individuals vary in their ability to manage their monetary resources. Occasionally, a parent who fully intends to pay the child care bill gets so far behind in payments, that the debt becomes overwhelming. The parent may see no other way out except to withdraw the child and disappear.

There are also occasional individuals who have no intention of paying. They resent any effort to collect the fees. There are some who feel that the obligation belongs to a divorced spouse. Stepparents sometimes resent paying for the care of children of their spouse. Even the state may occasionally determine that a child is not eligible for subsidy and refuse to pay the amount that the program had, in good faith, expected. There are as many reasons why bills don't get paid as there are bad debts. As a director, you may feel sympathy for a parent who has just left an abusive spouse and has no money. You may feel angry if you feel that a parent with an adequate income is simply trying to beat the system. You may resent the parent who takes advantage of the program and its hard-working staff.

14-1 Building a cash reserve can help to avoid cash lag problems.

No matter what the causes of the bad debts, they hurt your program financially. The unpaid bills represent money the center had counted on that is not available. The new swing set, a staff bonus, or needed repairs to the roof will have to wait. A program that allows bad debts to accumulate, is shortchanging itself.

There is no sure way to prevent an occasional bad debt from occurring. One helpful policy is to require payment from all families in advance. Some centers assess late payment fees to discourage missed deadlines. At some point, if fees are not paid, the family will have to be discharged from the program.

Your agency must have specific, printed fee payment policies. These should be a part of each family's contract. The policies need to be explained to families as they enroll their children. If a parent misses a payment or begins to fall behind, reminder notices should be sent out quickly. The farther a parent falls behind, the harder it is to catch up. The larger the amount owed, the more likely it is that the center will lose its money.

At some point, you will have to decide how far to pursue an overdue account. Taking the family to Small Claims Court or hiring a collection agency are two ways to try to force payment. Each of these will cost money. Neither approach offers any guarantee that the bill will be collected. If a parent has left town, lost a job, or undergone a severe financial crisis, it may not be reasonable to pursue the payment.

Unpleasant though it may be, you probably will have to accept the fact that your agency will eventually experience some loss of income due to bad debts.

Encumbered Funds

When reviewing the amount of money available for use at any given time, you must also consider the amount of *encumbered funds*. This is the money for which you have made a commitment, but may have yet not paid out. If you have ordered several pieces of new equipment, you have made a commitment to pay for those items. However, there is a time period between when you placed the order, when the items arrive, and when you receive the bill. During that time, you may hear staff refer to the order as being "in the pipeline". This means that the action has been initiated, but not completed yet. Even when you receive the bill, there will probably be some time before the payment is due. Until the bill is actually paid, the money remains in your bank account. The balance doesn't indicate the amount that your program has promised to pay for the equipment. It is important to keep in mind how much money has been committed or encumbered to pay for these items. If you forget that you placed the order and continue to spend money based on your checking account balance, you will overspend and not have enough money.

What Financial Services Will I Need?

Not all banks and accounts are equal. Some banks charge a service fee for each check the program writes. Others charge no fee unless the balance in the checking account drops below a certain amount. Some banks pay interest on checking accounts. Other banks may offer no interest on checking, but higher interest on savings accounts. Some banks may give better rates on loans to customers, but pay little in interest.

Shop around to find the bank or financial institution that offers the best deal for your program's needs. As the program grows and large sums of money are involved, the interest that is accumulated on program accounts can be substantial. An accountant can offer advice on the best types of accounts or other forms of savings to pursue.

Line of Credit

If you have not been able to accumulate money in a reserve account, you may need to make arrangements with a lending institution, for a *line of credit*. This is a short-term loan. As you repay it, the amount becomes available to you to borrow again. Try to anticipate this need so you can work out details in advance. Most directors dread having to take this step. It seems unfair when the program is owed money to have to borrow funds and pay interest. On the other hand, the consequences of missing paydays for staff can be devastating if good staff members decide to leave the program. The likelihood of having to pay late fees on payments can also be costly to the program.

Credit Cards

Credit cards can serve two purposes in regard to child care. One use is to enable the program to receive payments from parents who wish to charge the cost of their child care. Once the parent pays by credit card, the program will receive its money. This is true even though the parent may skip paying the credit card company. In order to have this guarantee of payment, the center will have to pay a substantial fee for the use of the credit card company's service. Before deciding to offer credit card service, consider the following:

- What are the fees to the program associated with the credit card service?
- Have parents been asking for this convenience?
- Has the center had a lot of bad debts?
- Will the service attract more families?

Many parents like the convenience of being able to pay by credit card, 14-2. It can be quicker and more convenient than other forms of payment. The center can also benefit from the guaranteed payment of bills placed on the card. This can help to reduce amounts lost through bad debts.

The agency, itself, may need to have a credit card. Many purchases can be made over the phone, by fax, or through the Internet if the center has a credit card. Without a credit card, phone purchases will usually not be accepted. Ordering by mail and enclosing a check is a slower process.

If the program does use a credit card account, it will have to be monitored carefully. Only authorized staff within the agency should have access to the account number and card. The card should be kept in a safe place where it cannot be stolen or misused. Since credit card accounts charge high interest rates, the payment schedule must be carefully planned.

What Kinds of Purchasing Decisions Must Be Made?

Managing a center means that equipment, materials, and supplies must be available as needed. Can you imagine arriving at the center one morning and discovering that there is no toilet paper or paper towels? This could quickly become a major crisis.

Purchasing for the agency will include items for the following:

- classroom supplies and materials
- office supplies and equipment
- indoor and outdoor play equipment
- cleaning supplies and equipment

14-2 Many parents like the convenience of paying for child care by use of a credit card.

- kitchen supplies and equipment

- paper products

- repair and maintenance items

- insurance

Purchasing responsibility includes making sure that items are available as they are needed to keep the center functioning. This function of the director's job is often delegated, in part, to other staff members. It makes sense, for instance, for the cook to develop the list of needed groceries. The secretary or office manager is the logical person to develop the order of office supplies. A larger program might have an administrative staff member, responsible for purchasing, who coordinates orders and checks for the best deals.

Often, staff, particularly teachers, need a great deal of input in choosing the materials for their classrooms. When each teacher has a budget out of which to order small classroom supplies, you can be sure that they are getting exactly what they want. If teachers have to stay within a classroom budget, they must set priorities.

As director, you will need to review all orders in light of the financial status of the program. A new copier might be needed, but you may not be able to authorize the purchase until you are sure that enough income is coming into the program.

Small programs will have less complicated purchasing decisions. It is easier to determine the amount of paste needed for one classroom than it is to decide how much to buy for 10 classrooms with varying age groups.

Choices must be made about where to purchase needed items. The term, *vendor*, is used to refer to all of the sellers of the various supplies and equipment that the center will need. Small specialty stores, large discount chains, department stores, and mail order firms may each offer the items that you need. Some are willing to discuss price discounts with you. Others have a set price that is non-negotiable. Some will give special deals to not-for-profit programs. Others will not. Some have sales at certain times of the year. For example, one local hardware store sold all leftover sleds at a sale price at the end of the winter season. Buying the sleds ahead for the next winter saved the center a lot of money.

Wise purchasing practices will save the program money. Comparison shopping can reveal price differences from one vendor to another. There are also strategies that can help you get the best deals.

Bulk Purchasing

Many vendors of food, paper, art, or other types of supplies will give discounts to programs that buy large quantities of the same item. Buying 30 reams of red paper will probably cost less per ream than buying five reams each of red, yellow, green, blue, orange, and purple. Buying 20 gallons of bathroom disinfectant will often cost less per gallon than buying five. Larger programs that use more supplies usually have a price advantage over programs that need to purchase less.

Bulk purchasing may save the center money, but only if the center has enough storage space to handle the large quantities being ordered, 14-3. One center got a great deal on a large amount of construction paper. The paper was all stored in the center's basement. Unfortunately, during the rainy season, the basement flooded and all of the paper was ruined. The program had to buy more paper. It actually ended up spending more money than if it had bought several smaller orders of paper throughout the year. Another program had to turn down a local grocery store's offer of sale-priced frozen turkeys because it didn't have enough freezer space.

Bulk purchasing only saves money if the program is buying items that it will actually use. One center bought 15 gallons of paste at a great price. But, over the next year, the classrooms only used 10 gallons. The rest sat on a shelf, taking up needed space. A year later, when staff went to use the paste, they discovered that it had dried up and was not usable. More paste had to be purchased. Any cost savings is likely to be wiped out if supplies are bought that the center doesn't need or want.

Director's Dilemma

A local butcher has offered your program a great price for the purchase of a side of beef. The meat would be cut into usable portions and wrapped for freezing. Your program would save money by buying the beef this way. However, you do not have freezer space to store the purchase until use. You would have to spend the money you saved plus an additional amount to purchase a freezer. What are the benefits and disadvantages to your program of making this purchase?

Cooperative Buying

One way that smaller programs can obtain some of the advantages of bulk purchasing is to work together. If there are several small centers in the same area, they will probably need many of the same types of supplies. Forming a cooperative buying arrangement means that only one order is sent. It is made up from each of the individual orders. For example, if five small programs each need 10 boxes of dishwashing detergent, an order could be placed for 50 boxes. This should result in a lower cost per box than the five smaller purchases. Each of the programs saves money.

Cooperative buying only works if there is someone available to coordinate the orders. It takes time to rewrite the order to include each of the co-op members individual orders. Each of the individual programs must also be financially stable. If a program's purchases are included in the group order, but that program goes out of business, the rest are left "holding the bag."

Deliveries of items purchased through a co-op are usually made to only one location. This means that all of the other programs will need to have someone available to pick up their orders. For large amounts of supplies, a truck or van may be necessary.

14-3 Adding storage space allows a center to take advantage of bulk buying opportunities.

Seasonal Buying

Sometimes money can be saved by paying attention to the time of the year when items are purchased. The geographic location of your program will have some effect on whether you can benefit from the changing of the seasons. Fresh fruits, vegetables and other produce is least expensive to buy during its harvest season. When the produce you want is grown locally and "in season," it will cost less, 14-4. The same items, purchased out-of-season, will have to be bought in canned, frozen, dried, or irradiated forms. These are all more expensive.

Some outdoor equipment can be bought on sale at the end of its usable season. Beach toys and wading pools are more likely to be on sale at the end of summer. Occasionally, stores even put seasonal items on sale at the beginning of the season. They are hoping to sell out quickly before the customer shops elsewhere. Vendors don't want to have to store seasonal items until the next year. The next year, a new style or design might be popular.

It is also helpful to be aware of certain patterns in store sales. If you watch carefully, you can predict when certain types of items will be going on sale. Children's toys frequently go on sale right after the big gift-giving holidays. Linens usually go on sale in January. Whenever new models of office equipment or vans are introduced, the prices on old models are usually reduced.

In order to take advantage of seasonal specials, keep a "wish list" of items that you need for the center. Watch for sales or special promotions. Think ahead. Consider what the center will need a year from now. If an item is a program priority, the classrooms need it right away, and the center can afford it, you probably should go ahead with the purchase. It's a good idea to get an item on sale if you know that the center will need it in the future. Even though you may have to store it for awhile, you will have saved the program money by buying during the sale.

Bids

Another way to save money on expensive items such as carpeting or a new furnace, is to obtain bids from several vendors who sell equivalent items. Many programs have a policy regarding major purchases. Any time the program needs an item that is more than a preset limit, such as $500, bids from several vendors must be obtained. Before seeking bids, you must be clear about what you want. If you are planning to buy an appliance or other major purchase, be sure that you have compared several different brands. Give the bidder a "spec sheet," the common name for a specific description or detailed specifications of the product you want.

When you receive bids from vendors, examine the bid and the merchandise carefully. You must be sure that the bidders have quoted prices for equal products. Be sure that the specifications are the same as those on your request. Check the model year, the features of the item, its size, and options. Also be sure to determine whether the bids include the same services. For example, does the carpet price include padding and installation costs? Does the refrigerator price include delivery, set-up, and removal of the old one?

Private child care agencies can choose how and where to purchase items. Publicly funded agencies or those that receive grant money may be required to seek bids and accept the lowest when purchasing costly items. The choice of vendors may be limited.

Petty Cash

Petty cash is cash you keep on hand for small, unexpected expenditures. These items, such as extra stamps, are usually paid for by some authorized member of your staff. This person will need to be reimbursed for this cost. Receipts for any money spent this way should

14-4 This cook tries to buy fresh, local produce to make the meals taste better and to save the center some money.

be kept, as well as a journal of overall expenditures. While there is usually only a small amount of money designated for petty cash expenditures, it is easy for that money to be "frittered" away. Over time, a substantial amount of money can be spent without adequate monitoring, if you don't have a system for tracking it.

You must be sure to have a way of keeping track of petty cash. It is easy for staff to "borrow" money for a cup of coffee or other small expense. Even if petty cash only amounts to $10 per month, it still represents $120 by the end of the year.

Procedures for the use of petty cash should be established. This includes determining which staff members are authorized to use it. All use of petty cash should be documented by receipts from purchases. Any item over a preset limit, such as $5.00, should have to go through regular purchasing procedures. While these procedures may seem elaborate, they can discourage casual, unnecessary use of the fund.

Other Purchasing Considerations

Cost is not the only factor to consider when making purchasing decisions. Although the price of an item is important, there are other hidden costs that must be kept in mind.

Warranty/Guarantee

The terms *warranty* and *guarantee* mean the same thing in regard to purchasing items. They mean that the item you purchased is backed by the manufacturer or vendor to do what you expect it to do. They also mean that the item is expected to last for at least a certain period of time. Warranties/guarantees typically cover repairs if the product is defective or if it breaks under normal use. They may also provide for a replacement if the item breaks within the specified time frame. When you are considering the purchase of an expensive item, be sure to check the warranty/guarantee. Repair bills on an inferior product can wipe out any savings you may have gotten in the initial purchase.

Return Policies and Trial Offers

Vendors also differ in their return policies. Some vendors have generous return policies. If the program is dissatisfied with the purchase for any reason, the vendor will take it back. Other vendors refuse to handle returns, so your decision to purchase is a final one. Some will allow exchanges for other merchandise, but will not give money back.

Some items come with a free or minimal cost trial offer period. The program is able to use the item for a period of time. If the item is not satisfactory, it can be returned unpaid. These offers are very helpful when considering the purchase of an expensive item with which you are unfamiliar. Tricycles, indoor climbers, and office copiers are examples of the equipment that can often be obtained on a trial basis. After using an item during the trial period, the staff may agree that they want to purchase it. The staff may also decide that they don't like the item. In that case, you can return it, and the program is not stuck with something no one likes.

Delivery and Service

The ease with which you can have an item delivered and/or repaired can represent a cost to your agency. Every day that you need an item and don't have it can be an expense. If you have to take time out of your day to go somewhere to pick up an item, your time is being taken away from your other duties.

In the search for the least expensive item, it is easy to forget the cost of staff members' time. This is easy to see in relation to the administrative tasks. If the computer breaks, the people using that computer will be stopped. You will be paying for their time when they can't do their work. If you have to drive a distance to pick up a cheaper vacuum cleaner, the cost of your travel and time must be considered. If you pay a delivery fee, it must be viewed as part of the cost of the item.

Vendors also differ in their ability to provide service for the items they sell. If a truck is available to your program for picking up orders, it may be best to purchase wherever the basic cost is least. If you must rent a truck and pull a staff member away from other tasks, paying a delivery fee makes good sense. Sometimes there is a local person who is able and willing to make repairs. Then, you can buy from any vendor and not worry about service.

Support for Local Businesses

One factor you may want to consider is whether to purchase from local businesses. If your center is located in a city, the whole city is your shopping center. If your program is based in a small town area, it may be considered disloyal by local merchants to shop elsewhere. You may have little choice if what you need is not available nearby. Often purchasing needs can be met locally at almost the same cost as from a distant supplier. Local vendors may be more willing to establish charge accounts for your program since it is part of their community. The decision to buy locally may be seen as support for the hometown. It can be a positive public relations decision that strengthens your program's position as a "team player."

Should the Program Offer Food or Transportation Services?

Food service and transportation of children are additional services that parents frequently request. Some programs offer both of these services. Many centers do not offer either. Children in those programs bring their own lunches. All transportation is the responsibility of the parents. Most centers do provide breakfast as well as mid-morning and afternoon snacks. Parents are responsible for providing a nutritious lunch. Although Head Start centers are required and funded to provide hot lunches to children, there is no state that requires child care centers to provide meals.

If you are thinking about offering food or transportation services, you need to be aware of the commitments as well as the costs involved. Both of these services involve elements of care that play an important role in supporting children's well-being. A decision to provide food service must also be a commitment to providing healthful, nutritious meals. Establishing a transportation service involves hiring qualified drivers and having safe, properly equipped vehicles. Both of these services are costly.

Food Service

Many parents like the idea of not having to prepare box lunches. When lunch is served at the center, the parents don't have to worry about it. They can feel comfortable knowing that their children are eating good food in a familiar, comfortable environment, 14-5. Unfortunately, parents are often reluctant to pay the increased cost that food service adds to their weekly bill.

While some food reimbursement funds are provided through the U.S. Department of Agriculture's Child Care and Adult Food Program, they only cover part of the costs involved in center-based programs. Government surplus food may be available for eligible programs. Food obtained this way usually is offered to the program in large quantities. Appropriate storage space is needed to take advantage of this supply source.

Frequently, there is a lot of paperwork that must be maintained when the program participates in government food programs. Only certain types of food are

14-5 These children enjoy their hot lunches served at the center.

eligible for reimbursement. Careful inventories must be kept. Food audits must be able to track and match

- the amount of food purchased

- the type of food purchased

- daily menus

- the number of eligible children in each classroom

- the attendance days of eligible children

- the amount of food portions served each day

- the amount of food left over and still on the shelves

Because of the paperwork and low rate of reimbursement, many programs have had to give up on plans to offer hot meals. Some programs that have offered the service have dropped it. In some states, food from the food reimbursement programs cannot be used to feed non-eligible children. The program must bear the full cost of providing food for these children. In turn, the programs typically must pass the cost on to parents in the form of higher fees.

On-Site Meal Preparation

If you decide to prepare meals in a kitchen at your center, your program may be subject to additional regulations and monitoring in most states. Product liability insurance will also be needed. Many states require that the kitchen facility meet the same standards as a restaurant. The kitchen must pass regular inspections for sanitary conditions, 14-6. This means that the center may be required to have a commercial dishwasher and a three-bowl sink. Heavy duty appliances and a sprinkler system may also be necessary. Storage facilities, including cabinets, freezers, and large rolling carts will all be necessary to accommodate large quantities of food.

Additional staff will be needed, at least on a part-time basis. Those persons preparing meals must be trained in proper sanitation procedures. Preparation, serving, and storage methods designed to minimize any possibility of food poisoning must be strictly followed.

Establishment of a kitchen will require the purchase of the following items:

- dishes, eating utensils, and serving dishes

- cups and glasses

- pots and pans, casserole dishes, and mixing bowls

- measuring spoons and cups

- cooking utensils

- small appliances, including toasters, mixer, microwave oven, griddle, waffle maker, etc.

- large appliances, including range, refrigerator, freezer, and perhaps a dishwasher and washer/dryer for linens

14-6 The kitchen in this center must pass regular safety inspections.

The space that will be necessary to set up a kitchen must be considered. Every center needs a small kitchen area for the preparation of snacks. A large food service program for many children will require space for more staff and larger quantities of food. You must decide whether this space is best used for a kitchen, or if there might be some better use for it, such as another classroom.

Menu Planning

Menus designed for large groups must be developed or identified. This may require the services of a nutrition consultant or food service specialist. Meals and snacks served in the center should provide two/thirds of children's minimum daily requirements of nutrients in order to meet school lunch program criteria. In response to current health concerns, many centers are making an effort to use low-sugar recipes for meals.

Menu cycles should be planned to cover at least six weeks of meals. After six weeks, the cycle can be repeated. This helps centers get away from the "if it's Wednesday, it's spaghetti day" boredom that occurs when foods are repeated too often. In areas where climates vary, centers should develop "warm weather recipes" and "cold weather recipes." This allows for the use of seasonal produce. It also takes into consideration seasonal preferences. The hearty stews that simmer for hours in the cold weather can be replaced by cool pasta salads in the hot weather. Nutritional needs are still met.

Regional foods should also be the base of the center's recipes. Each part of the country has foods that are native to those areas. Children are comfortable with foods that are familiar to them. It helps to give them the feeling that the center is an extension of the home environment. Introducing new foods once in awhile, can interest children. However, using recipes all the time from books featuring the foods of different regions of the country, may meet with resistance from the children.

Catered Food Service

Some programs have opted to have meals catered by an outside food service organization. These programs sign a contract with the outside agency specifying the terms of the agreement between the two parties. Successful food service contracts have been developed with private restaurants or catering companies, or with the food service departments of schools, hospitals, and/or nearby office buildings or factories.

Available options should be reviewed carefully. The following questions must be answered:

- What quality of service will the caterer provide?

- What types of facilities will still be required in the center to allow for unpacking, set-up, serving, and clean-up?

- Will the caterer prepare menus and recipes that are appropriate for the center?

- Is the caterer sensitive to the qualities that make food appealing to young children?

- Can the food be served in an attractive manner, preferably family style?

- What will the cost be?

- Does the caterer have a good reputation in the community?

- Has the caterer been in business for awhile, or is this a new company without a "track record"?

Each of these aspects is important to review when you are making decisions about contracting with a food service provider.

Mealtime Practices

Children's attitudes toward food are influenced by the mealtime atmosphere. Staff must be careful at mealtimes to help children develop positive attitudes that will lead to good nutritional choices, 14-7. Just as children are "beginners" at learning colors, numbers, and other concepts, they are also beginners at learning about eating. It takes testing and practice to learn how much food to take when serving yourself. It takes trial and error to discover what you like and don't like. It takes time and patience to learn how to handle knives, forks, and spoons. Pouring juice or milk into a cup is tricky business. It's hard to get it right without spilling or tipping the cup.

Staff members often come to the center with outdated ideas about appropriate food behaviors. Nutritionists believe that many of the old demands that insist children eat more than they really want, contribute to the current weight problems of many adults. The "clean plate club" that staff often demand, discourages children from paying attention when their stomachs are telling them that they are full. Serving food cafeteria style, with proportioned servings already on the plate can create problems. Children may neither need or want the amount served to them.

Another negative mealtime practice is the comment, "You took it! You eat it!" Children, as many adults, occasionally have "eyes bigger than their stomachs." When a food looks good, they take a giant helping, only to discover that it is more than they can eat. A better approach is to use small serving spoons and to help children learn how to start with smaller portions. Staff must be trained to help children learn about portion sizes in positive, helpful ways, rather than with harsh, inappropriate demands.

Children often resist new foods or casseroles where several foods are mixed together. It can be difficult to get them to try new foods while, at the same time, respecting their preferences. Some staff insist that children try "just a taste" of everything. Even this can be inappropriate if it leads to harsh threats of "no other food" or "no dessert."

Withholding the "good stuff," or threatening loss of dessert, is another negative approach that works against good nutrition. Dessert should be planned and presented as a part of the meal. If it becomes a reward or punishment for other behaviors, it takes on inappropriate importance. Since many desserts are sweet, children begin to associate sweet items with rewards and pleasing others. The temptation to reward ourselves with sweets often lingers into adult behavior with undesirable nutritional results.

14-7 Children need snack and meal times that are relaxed and encourage conversation.

In general, children are most likely to try new foods enthusiastically if they see others eating and enjoying the strange items. Curiosity and their desire to be like their friends and beloved teachers will usually motivate them to try something new. Children need a relaxed, comfortable mealtime atmosphere where they feel safe from ridicule or harsh demands. This will usually produce a greater willingness to be more adventurous with food.

Transportation Service

Some programs offer transportation services to get children to and from the centers. This may include picking children up at home and returning them there at the end of the day. Some centers limit this service to only one part of the center's enrollment. For example, transportation may be provided for school-age children only. It brings children from school to the after-school program. Most parents cannot leave work in the middle of the day to drive children from school to the center. This service is necessary to support enrollment in the school-age program.

Providing transportation can be costly for the program. A careful analysis must be done to be sure that there really is a need for it. Most programs will have to charge extra for this if it involves door-to-door service. If parents are unable or unwilling to pay for the convenience, the program will not be able to afford to provide it. If arrangements can be made for children to ride their regular school buses from school to the after-school program, there may be no extra cost. Head Start and other special purpose programs may receive money to support transportation services, including home pickup and return. Child care programs rarely receive any support or reimbursement money for it.

Most often, centers provide transportation primarily for field trips. Trips to a nearby park, museum, or pool can enhance the daily program, 14-8. This type of service is easier to organize than is a full-scale daily operation.

Legal Responsibilities of Providing Transportation

Your program must meet additional state regulations if you are providing transportation for young children. Child safety seats, seat belts, specially licensed drivers, and additional staff for supervision may all be required. Vehicles must meet state inspection requirements and be carefully maintained. Additional insurance must also be purchased.

Care must be taken in the hiring of drivers. You must see that applicants have the appropriate licenses and verify any special training they have had. Previous employers should be contacted to verify dependability and accident-free records. It is particularly important to determine that potential drivers do not have histories of drug, alcohol, or child abuse.

Contracting with a Transportation Company

Many program directors have found it is more convenient and cost-efficient to contract with a transportation company. That company is responsible for meeting all licensing and insurance requirements, hiring qualified drivers, and maintaining the vehicles. Private transportation, school bus, or community transit services may all be willing to work with you.

Most contracts are based on a cost-per-mile. This cost must take the following factors into account:

- cost of fuel

- wear and tear on the vehicle

- insurance

- maintenance

- cost of driver and other adult supervision

- cost of administrative paperwork involved in maintaining the service

14-8 Some centers provide transportation service for special events such as field trips, whereas others provide transportation on a daily basis.

You will need to work with the company to carefully plan safe, efficient routes that do not involve a lot of unnecessary miles.

Lease or Buy Vehicles

If you decide not to contract with a transportation company, your costs may be affected by the same factors. You will need to decide whether to purchase or lease vehicles. When you purchase vehicles, they are owned by your program. The program is totally responsible for their care and operation. After several years, the program will own old vehicles that will require more maintenance. You must consider whether the program will have the resources to replace the vehicles as they get old.

Leased vehicles are not owned by the program. When the lease is over, the program owns no vehicle. If the program decides to move to a new leasing company, it will have no used vans or buses to use as a down payment.

When the program operates its own transportation service, vehicle maintenance is a daily responsibility. The staff person in charge of transportation must make sure drivers take responsibility for checking the vehicles daily. Checking fuel and oil levels, maintaining current inspections, and taking the vehicles for regular servicing must be part of the job description. Drivers must check each vehicle to be sure that tires are properly inflated, seat belts are working properly, and the engine sounds normal. A vehicle checklist should be developed to help drivers remember all the things they need to check, 14-9. Regular maintenance schedules should be included so routine care is not overlooked.

Each vehicle should have a first aid kit and a list of children with emergency information for each. Emergencies sometimes happen while on a trip. If all emergency numbers are back at the center, they will not be quickly available if needed. Many transportation services are now including cellular phones or two-way radios for driver use in case of an emergency.

Transportation Precautions

Transportation of children involves additional responsibilities and liabilities for the center. It must not be undertaken without careful thought and planning. Many directors have reluctantly come to the conclusion that it is not a good idea to use volunteer drivers and private cars for even short field trips. Eager, willing parents may have hidden drug or alcohol problems, or may simply be bad drivers. Their cars may not be properly equipped with safety features. Any of these factors pose unnecessary risks for the children.

Vehicle Check List

Driver's Name _____ Vehicle # _____

Inspection Due _____ Beginning Mileage _____ Ending Mileage _____

Under the hood:
_____ Oil level
_____ Coolant level
_____ Belts: tension & condition
_____ Power steering fluid
_____ Battery water level (if appropriate)
_____ Windshield washer fluid
_____ Check for leaks

Inside the vehicle:
_____ Seat adjustment
_____ Clean windows
_____ Mirror adjustment
_____ First aid kit
_____ Fire extinguisher pressure
_____ Reflector/flag kit
_____ Emergency phone numbers
_____ Washer/wipers
_____ Heater/defrosters
_____ Clean floors
_____ Horn
_____ Spare fuses
_____ Emergency door buzzer
_____ Emergency door
_____ Interior lights
_____ Check brakes

Check gauges: (motor running)
_____ Oil pressure
_____ Fuel
_____ Water temperature
_____ Air pressure
_____ Ammeter

Walk around vehicle:
(engine and lights on)
_____ Headlights - high and low beams
_____ Parking lights
_____ Clean lights and mirrors
_____ Check turn signals
_____ Check condition and pressure of tires
_____ Check exhaust system
_____ General appearance of vehicle

Under the vehicle:
_____ Leaks
_____ Loose parts

Final checks as vehicle moves out:
_____ Seat belts fastened
_____ Brakes - stop and hold
_____ Steering feels correct
_____ Any unusual sounds
_____ Transmission shift feels correct

Fire Drill Record:
Date: _____
Door used: _____
Time: _____
Notes: _____

14-9 Transportation safety is a major responsibility. A vehicle checklist can help to keep track of necessary vehicle maintenance and inspections.

⊙ Summary

Wise financial practices can save the program money. Understanding the realities of how money flows into and out of the program can help you use financial resources more carefully. Money that is owed to the program might not necessarily be there when you need it. Purchasing decisions must consider the cash flow pattern of the program.

There are many strategies for purchasing that can stretch the money available. Bulk buying or cooperative buying, trial offers, and awareness of warranties, all help to save the program money. Some purchasing decisions must also take into account storage capacity, delivery charges, and ease of service, if needed.

Some centers offer food service that include full lunches as well as snacks and breakfast. If there is a demand for this service, you will need to consider if and how to offer it. Choices must be made between preparing meals on-site or contracting with a service that will cater the food. The benefits and drawbacks of each should be analyzed.

Some programs also offer transportation service. This is a serious responsibility for the program to undertake. The service may be limited to providing transportation from school to the center for school-age children. Field trips are also a reason for considering transportation service. Decisions must be made regarding whether to contract with a transportation company or to purchase vehicles and have the program operate them. The safety of the children must be the prime consideration in transportation decisions.

⊙ Terms

cash flow
cash lag
cash reserve
encumbered funds
line of credit
vendor
petty cash
warranty
guarantee

◉ Review

1. Why is it necessary to monitor the actual receipt of money into your program even though you have sufficient income projected to cover the costs of the program?

2. Why is it a good idea to build a cash reserve?

3. What can you do to try to minimize the problem of bad debts?

4. What does it mean when a program has encumbered funds?

5. What factors should you consider before making arrangements to allow parents to pay for child care by credit card?

6. Besides classroom supplies and equipment, what other kinds of supplies must be ordered to keep the center functioning well?

7. Give an example of cooperative buying.

8. What is a way to save money on expensive items such as carpeting or a furnace?

9. When considering offering food service for children, what should you consider?

10. If a center provides transportation, what are the director's responsibilities in the hiring of drivers?

◉ Applications

1. Invite an auditor to speak to the class. What kinds of certification or training does this individual have? What does the auditor look for when conducting a financial audit? What "red flags" or inconsistencies signal to an auditor that there may be problems with the program's financial records?

2. Visit local banks and/or financial institutions to find out what services they offer. What are their fees? Do they pay interest on checking accounts? Do they have automated teller machines, lines of credit, and savings accounts? Are there penalties if your program's checking account falls below a certain limit? Are there penalty fees for late repayment on a line of credit? Compare the costs, services, and convenience.

3. Determine when various fruits and vegetables grown in your area are available for purchase from nearby farmers. Make a calendar that shows the best weeks of the year for purchasing large quantities of these fruits and vegetables. Ask an extension home economist to discuss seasonal food purchasing, processing, and storage information with your class.

Chapter 15
Making the Center a Safe and Healthy Place

After studying this chapter, you will be able to

⚙ design a safe and healthy environment for children and staff.

⚙ explain the role of licensing requirements in establishing a safe and healthy program.

⚙ identify appropriate health and safety policies and practices for the center.

⚙ discuss the need for a health and safety committee.

Child care programs are faced with serious concerns regarding the health and safety of children. The number of children entering child care grows each year. Likewise, the number of adults working in child care jobs continues to grow. Health and social issues that had little impact on child care a decade ago have become major factors in the establishment of center policies and procedures.

Concerns over health and safety issues and their resulting legal implications have made this area of administration more difficult. Health-related issues are changing rapidly. There is a need for a program to develop clear policies that can guide staff and parents through difficult decisions. Policies must be designed to protect both children and staff. As a director, you must be aware that mistakes in judgment or behavior in this area can have serious consequences. Plans for ongoing policy revision and staff education are essential.

As the program director, you must ensure that the center's policies reflect appropriate health and safety practices. The center must be a safe place for children and staff. It is somewhat ironic, however, that in an effort to ensure safety, many of the risks that help children grow in their own confidence must be eliminated. For instance, a tree to climb, a creek to jump across, a gate to swing on, all typical pleasures of childhood must be limited at the center. One of the most difficult judgments for staff is how to let children be children. Children need the excitement of exploring, the joy of running free, and the exhilaration of climbing. At the same time, as adults, the staff must make decisions about what can and cannot be allowed, 15-1. What are the acceptable risks that allow for growth and, yet, provide for safety and well-being?

15-1 Most teachers consider working with real tools an acceptable risk as long as appropriate safety guidelines are met.

How Do You Assure a Healthy and Safe Environment?

Children and staff will be spending a large portion of their day inside the center. Care must be taken to make the environment a safe, secure place.

Avoiding Safety Hazards

Many potentially hazardous objects and materials are present in any child care center. It is the responsibility of the director and staff members to protect children from these hazards. Continually be on the lookout for possible dangers. The following are suggestions that can help to avoid some common safety hazards:

- Be sure there is no cracked and peeling paint or plaster in the center. Use only nonlead based paint.

- Do not use toxic materials in the classrooms.

- Keep all medicines and cleaning fluids in locked cabinets.

- Keep electrical outlet covers on all unused electrical outlets.

- Avoid extension cords. If they must be used, be sure they are not run under rugs or placed where children could fall over them.

- Do not use small throw rugs on slippery floors.

- Install the type of hinges on toy chests that will prevent the lids from falling.

- Keep water or wet items away from electrical appliances.

- Ban all weapons from the center.

- Maintain developmentally appropriate toys in each classroom.

There is no totally complete list that will help you avoid all possible hazards in the center. Careful thought and alertness are necessary to spot potential trouble spots. If your center is on a second floor, be sure to consider safety hazards related to stairs and windows. If your center is in an old building that was not designed for child care, you may have additional potential hazards to identify.

Provide Clean Air

Children are more vulnerable than adults to the effects of unhealthy substances in the air they breathe. Because their bodies are smaller, breathing the same amount of smoke or insecticide as an adult can have greater consequences. They are easily susceptible to respiratory diseases. To protect the health of everyone in the center, policies regarding air quality should be developed.

The entire center should be designated as a nonsmoking area. Posted signs should clearly alert all staff, parents, and visitors of this regulation.

It is important that children have opportunities to play in the fresh air. Many newer buildings have windows that don't open. The ventilation systems may be inadequate to provide sufficient air. This condition can increase the potential for respiratory diseases. Disease breeds in dark, damp, warm, unventilated areas. Children need the opportunity to play outside in the fresh air every day, as long as weather permits, 15-2. Rooms should be aired out on a regular basis.

Activities such as pesticide applications and painting should be scheduled for evenings or weekends when the center is empty. Efforts should be made to plan construction or renovation for off-hours or days when the center is closed. If this is not possible, the construction area should be sealed off so plaster dust and other construction-related air pollution are confined to the work space.

15-2 Playing outside every day, when weather permits, can help keep children healthy.

Test for Radon

Another area of concern in some parts of

the country is the presence of radon gas. Radon can seep into the center from the ground. Testing kits can be obtained to check for this gas. If radon is present in dangerous levels, hire a company trained in the proper methods of reducing this hazard.

Keep the Center Clean

Arrangements must be made for the regular cleaning of the center. The size and complexity of the center should be considered when planning the schedule for custodial care. Some centers will need full-time custodial help. Others may be able to hire part-time custodians or contract with a cleaning service, 15-3.

Some elements of maintenance, such as garbage removal and bathroom cleaning, must be completed every day. Other tasks, such as dusting, may be done every other day. Carpet cleaning may need to be done only every six months. A checklist should be developed to ensure that elements of cleaning are not missed. Items can be scheduled on the list and checked off as completed, 15-4.

Centers may also have other custodial needs. Centers with swimming pools must have provisions for pool maintenance. Some centers will require yard work that includes raking leaves in the fall. Custodial help also includes having someone who can fix loose doorknobs, oil squeaky hinges, and take care of basic maintenance of equipment.

Check for Outdoor Safety Hazards

A playground safety inspection should be made on a regular basis. This task should be specifically assigned to one staff member. Equipment must be carefully inspected for:

15-3 Careful cleaning of the center is necessary to prevent attracting bugs or rodents and to help minimize the spread of germs.

- rotting wood or splinters

- weakened S hooks or fasteners on climbers or swings

- bolts with protective covers missing from the exposed ends

- rusted parts

- vandalism

The outdoor areas should also be examined for wasp nests, dead tree limbs, animal burrows, or holes in the ground. Also check for insect-infested areas, animal remains or deposits, standing water where insects could breed, and uncovered manholes or wells. Remove or correct any hazards you find. As with the indoor environment, the outdoor area should always be kept in compliance with licensing regulations.

Suggested Cleaning Schedule			
Daily	**Twice per week**	**Weekly**	**As needed**
Floors mopped or vacuumed	Clean mirrors in bathrooms	Dust classrooms and offices	Refill towels and toilet paper
Toilets and sinks cleaned and sanitized	Wash garbage cans	Spray crib mattresses with bleach solution and wipe	Wash windows
Water fountains sanitized	Examine vacuum cleaners–empty bags and check belts	Clean refrigerator	Wipe bathroom walls
Chalkboards wiped clean		Change and wash crib sheets and blankets	Spray changing table with bleach solution and wipe after every diaper change
Stove Wiped			
Wastebaskets and garbage cans emptied			
Plastic toys washed with bleach solution and rinsed (infant/toddler/rooms)			
Wipe crib bars with bleach solution (infant/toddler rooms)		Check inventory of cleaning supplies for re-order if necessary	Lawn care
Clean entrance and exit areas			

15-4 Prepare a schedule so the cleaning staff know how often each task should be done.

Outdoor Environmental Hazards

Young children sunburn easily. They should not be exposed to the sun for long play periods during the late morning and early afternoon. You may want to discuss the use of a sunscreen with parents. Other forms of protection can allow children to play outside safely. Hats with brims, unbreakable sunglasses, T-shirts instead of halter tops, umbrellas, awnings, and tops for strollers provide protection from the sun. If your program has no shaded place to play, think about how some shade can be added. Picnic shelters, fast growing shade trees, party tents, and covered porches can all make it possible for children to play safely outside.

Centers in certain areas of the country may have higher risks of insect-borne diseases. Any use of insect repellent should be discussed with parents and medical advisors.

What Health and Safety Policies and Practices Should the Center Follow?

Many children, parents, and staff come together daily in a child care center. Children interact with more individuals every day than they would normally be exposed to in their homes. Careless health practices can result in the spread of disease at the center. Emergencies can arise that require actions on the part of staff members to keep children safe. Children must also be protected from potential child abuse. Security that is designed to prevent entrance of unauthorized individuals adds to the physical and emotional well-being of those inside the facility. It contributes to the caring and nurturing atmosphere your program should provide for both children and adults, 15-5. The center is obligated to support the health and safety of the children and staff.

Safe Food Practices

Even if you don't provide meals for children, there will still be food in the center. Snacks, beverages, and bag lunches hold the potential for food contamination. Sanitary conditions and proper storage of food items are essential to minimize any danger of foodborne illnesses. The following safety precautions should be followed regarding food in the center:

- Keep refrigerated items at 40°F or less. Keep frozen foods at 0°F or less.

15-5 The security system in this building helps keep unauthorized persons from entering.

- Do not allow refrigerated foods to sit out. Place leftovers in the refrigerator promptly.

- Be sure all meats and eggs are thoroughly cooked.

- All unrefrigerated foods should be stored at least six inches off the floor. Use containers that will prevent contamination by insects or rodents.

- Keep counter areas and utensils washed. Do not allow contamination from one food to spread to another.

- Surfaces should be washed with soap and hot water, and sanitized with a universal bleach solution.

- Do not use food from dented, leaking, rusted, or bulging cans. Avoid using home-canned foods.

- Refrigerated foods should be covered or wrapped to prevent contamination.

- Garbage containers should have tight-fitting lids. These containers should be clearly labeled, out of the reach of children, and emptied daily.

- When dishes are washed by hand, a three-bowl sink or three separate basins should be used. These steps must be followed: 1) wash dishes in hot (170°F), soapy water; 2) rinse and then dip dishes in sanitizing bleach solution; 3) rinse dishes; and 4) air-dry.

- Keep all food preparation areas clean.

Director's Dilemma

The grandmother of one of the children in the center is getting ready to move. She has graciously offered to give the center a large quantity of food that she canned but has not had time to use. You know that her donation could save the center some money in its food budget. What would you need to think about in regard to her offer?

Be sure food for children is cut into small bites. Infants and toddlers are particularly vulnerable to choking. Their food should be cut into ¼-inch pieces. Thick peanut butter, round slices of hot dog, nuts, grapes, popcorn, hard candy, and stringy cheese are potential hazards for young children. These foods should not be served.

Safe food practices are essential in the center. Food poisoning caused by contamination at the center is a serious health threat. An outbreak of food poisoning would also be a major threat to the reputation of the center. Your local extension home economist can help you with food preparation concerns.

Practices to Prevent the Spread of Disease

Staff members must understand the need to automatically follow certain health procedures when working with children. These procedures are necessary to prevent the spread of disease. It must be clear in center policies that these practices are not optional. They are required!

The Centers for Disease Control has developed a set of health practices called **universal precautions**. These practices require that all staff treat every situation as having the potential to spread disease. Uniform sanitation and protective behaviors have been identified. Because of the seriousness associated with blood-borne diseases, these precautions are primarily focused on situations that might involve the handling of bodily fluids, such as vomit, diarrhea, blood, or mucous.

Handwashing

Careful handwashing is the best protection against the spread of germs and disease. The hands of children and staff should be washed upon arrival at the center and when coming in from outside. Hands should always be washed after diapering, toileting, and nose-wiping. Additional need for handwashing includes before and after cooking activities and snack or mealtimes, 15-6. Staff should also wash before administering medication or first aid.

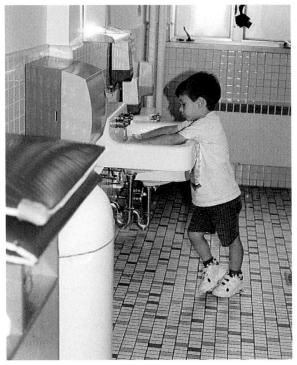

15-6 Careful handwashing is an important defense against the spread of disease.

The following procedure should be followed:

1. Wash hands under running water with liquid soap.

2. Rub hands together well. Work the soap into a lather.

3. Rinse hands well and dry with a paper towel.

4. Turn off the faucet with the paper towel to avoid recontaminating hands.

Using Disposable Gloves

Disposable gloves should be available in every room of the center. Staff should use these gloves when changing diapers. They should also be used when cleaning up bodily fluids such as vomit, diarrhea, blood, or mucous. After use, the gloves should be thrown away. Staff must understand that the use of gloves does not remove the need for handwashing. After throwing gloves away, hands should be washed.

Disinfecting

Like handwashing, disinfecting is an essential part of maintaining a healthy, safe environment. It is not expensive, but it does take a little extra time. A sanitary disinfected facility is required for a quality child care program.

A bleach solution should be used to disinfect

• tables, before and after eating or an activity

• changing tables, after each diaper change

• toys that children have mouthed or otherwise contaminated, 15-7

A standard bleach solution should be made fresh daily and kept in every room, out of reach of the children. A large amount can be made at one time and divided into quart-size spray bottles for individual rooms.

The standard bleach solution is ¼ cup bleach to a gallon of water. If made in quart containers, the amounts are 1 tablespoon of bleach to 1 quart of water. A stronger solution of one part bleach to 10 parts of water may be used for more heavily contaminated areas.

Diapering

Changing diapers requires a safe and appropriate place. An easily accessible area that can be kept clean should be designated as the diapering area. All diapering should occur in this area.

It is essential that food handling areas and diapering areas be kept separate. The diapering area should have a storage area where each child's personal items, such as powders or lotions, can be kept out of reach. The surface of the diapering area should have some type of disposable pad or leakproof paper placed on top. A plastic bag or plastic-lined container should be available for disposal of diapers. State licensing may require that staff use disposable gloves when changing children, 15-8.

Follow these steps when changing diapers:

1. Soiled clothing and the dirty diaper should be removed.

2. The diaper should be folded in on itself, retaped, and discarded.

3. Moist towelettes should be used to wipe the child from front to back. Each towelette should be used only once and new ones used if necessary.

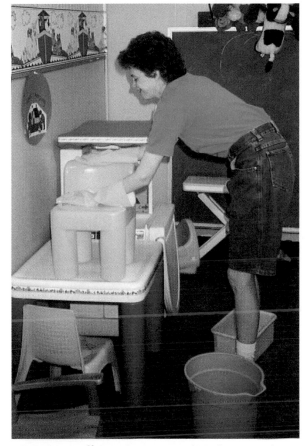

15-7 This staff member uses a disinfectant solution to keep the center clean.

4. If gloves have been used, they should be removed at this point.

5. The adult should use a towelette on his/her own hands.

6. The new diaper and clean clothes should be put on the child.

7. The dirty clothes and nondisposable diapers should be put into plastic bags and then into a larger plastic bag to be sent home.

8. The child's hands should be washed at this point.

9. Sanitize the diapering area with a bleach solution.

10. The staff members' hands should be washed.

Toothbrushing

Each child should have an individual, labeled toothbrush. Teeth should be brushed daily after lunch. After use, toothbrushes must be stored upright and exposed to the air so they can dry. There must be sufficient space between

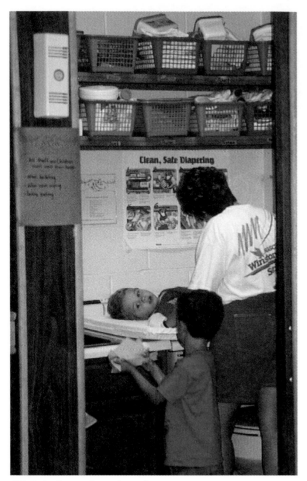

15-8 A chart showing the correct steps to change a diaper is posted right above the changing area in this center.

toothbrushes so they are not touching each other, 15-9. A separate, inverted, disposable cup with a hole in the bottom for each toothbrush is a good way of holding the brushes between uses.

Napping

Children should have their own mats and blankets with their names on them. Mats/cots should be placed head to toe and with open space between each mat. The position of the mats/cots should include enough space to prevent children from coughing and breathing on each other. Each mat should be placed at least three feet from any other mat. Linens should be washed each week. Cots/mats should be stored so the sleeping surfaces used by different children do not touch each other. It is possible to buy cots that stack without allowing any surface areas to touch. Racks on which mats can be hung also can provide suitable storage.

Policies Concerning Illnesses

No matter how careful the child care providers are, children will still get sick. The staff must have specific procedures to follow in case of illness.

Signs of Illness

All staff should know the typical signs of illness. Children can become seriously ill very quickly. Each staff member should take responsibility for alerting the responsible teacher or senior staff if a child appears to be ill. Fever, vomiting, rash, and/or diarrhea are relatively easy to spot. Changes in behavior, internal injuries, or a sore throat might not be so obvious. Often children who are becoming ill show few symptoms other than unusual irritability. Once you have determined that a child is sick enough to be sent home, a parent should be called. The center should have an isolation area where the child can rest comfortably until the parent arrives.

Policies Regarding Administering Medications

Parents may request that center personnel administer a medication to their children. This is a serious responsibility. Care must be taken the right dosage is given on time. Center policy on medication should include the following:

- All medication, over-the-counter and prescription, must be in the original, labeled container.

- Medication must be in the locked first-aid kit in the classroom or the refrigerator.

- Staff must wash hands before and after giving medicine.

- All necessary information, such as times for dosage, should be given to the staff in writing by the parent.

- Staff member should record time when medication was given and sign initials.

- No medication should be given without parental consent.

- Permission from the prescribing physician is sometimes required by licensing regulations.

15-9 This toothbrush holder allows brushes to dry without touching each other.

- Staff should notify parents if the child has refused to take the medicine or has gotten only part of the dose.

- The medicine must be kept at the appropriate temperature.

Meeting the Special Health Needs of Children and Staff

Many children have special health needs that must be met. Allergies, disabilities, chronic diseases, and compromised immune systems all must be taken seriously. It is necessary to develop an individual care plan and provide for the education of staff who will care for each child with special health needs.

Staff members should work with parents to learn as much as possible about a child's particular condition and needs. The child's doctor may recommend books or materials that could be helpful. Often, service and research organizations such as the American Lung Association and/or the American Cancer Society can provide up-to-date educational materials for staff education. These organizations may also be able to provide the special equipment and staff training needed to ensure each child's safety and full participation.

Sometimes it is necessary to assign additional staff to classrooms with children with special needs. An extra adult may be necessary to ensure that the needs of all the children are met.

Adults are usually immune to the typical childhood diseases that occasionally circulate through the center. Those who have received all appropriate immunizations are reasonably well protected from most serious illnesses.

HIV/Acquired Immune Deficiency Syndrome (AIDS)

The Americans with Disabilities Act specifically forbids discrimination against or exclusion of children or staff members who have tested HIV-positive or who have developed AIDS. It is illegal to ask a prospective employee or family about HIV/AIDS status.

All staff must be trained to understand that the risk of transmission of this disease in the center is minimal. Staff must also be trained to assume that any individual in the center could be infected with a contagious disease. The use of universal precautions is essential as an ongoing part of staff basic procedures.

All staff must also understand that the "Right to Privacy" is guaranteed to everyone in the center. Any child or staff member's HIV status is not a topic for casual conversation. If a parent or staff member chooses to share that information, it should be only known by those immediate staff who have a need to know in order to look out for the best interests of the child or staff person.

Because HIV-infected individuals have a weakened immune system, they are susceptible to the typical illnesses that may circulate around the center. If the family has shared information about the disease with the center, it may be possible to obtain guidance and help from the child's doctor. Special efforts will have to be made to ensure the well-being, as much as possible, for the HIV-affected individual.

At some point, extra support may be necessary for the staff and children who work and play with the affected individual in the center. Because there is currently no known cure, those who care for an AIDS-infected child or are friends with an infected staff member may eventually have to deal with the loss of that child or friend. No amount of preparation can ease the emotional pain of this loss. The special support of a psychologist may be needed for staff, children, and families.

Hepatitis B

Hepatitis B is a contagious blood-borne disease that may be present in the center. It is another reason the use of universal precautions is essential. There is a vaccine to protect against Hepatitis B. Many children are now receiving this as a part of their immunizations. Child care staff are among the groups of workers who are being encouraged to get this vaccine, which is administered in three doses.

Cytomegalovirus (CMV)

Cytomegalovirus (CMV) is a disease that causes concern for women who are pregnant or considering becoming pregnant. Because this virus is common in children under age three, it

Director's Dilemma

It has recently become public knowledge, through sources outside of your center, that one of your staff members is HIV-positive. Several frightened parents have called to withdraw their children from the program. The local TV station, looking for a dramatic story, has called to set up a visit and interview. Staff members are talking among themselves and probably discussing the situation outside of the center. How would you begin to get the situation back under control? What might you have done to prepare staff and parents for the possibility that eventually someone with AIDS would be in the center? What kinds of training and policies should staff have had? How should the media and parents be addressed? How can you protect the dignity and the rights of the HIV-positive individual?

may frequently be present in the center. The affected child usually has no symptoms, yet the virus can still be spread through saliva and urine. This infection in a pregnant woman could cause fetal damage. All staff who are pregnant or considering becoming pregnant should be screened to determine CMV status.

Other Children with Weakened Immune Systems

Other children in the center may also have weakened immune systems. These include

- children with cancer who have received chemotherapy
- children with asthma who have recently been treated with certain steroid drugs
- children who have one of a variety of immune deficiency diseases

Children with weakened immune systems are more susceptible to diseases than most children. Their bodies cannot fight off illness easily. Diseases that are usually mild may be serious for them.

Alerting Parents to Contagious Diseases

Chicken pox, fifth disease, CMV, and other typical childhood diseases may cause serious complications. They could also be dangerous for parents who may be pregnant or have weakened immune systems themselves. Whenever children in the center have been exposed to these highly contagious diseases, parents should be alerted by letter. Typical symptoms of the disease should be described. Because of the minimal risk for the spread of HIV in the center, parents do not need to be informed if an HIV-positive child is enrolled or an HIV-positive staff member is hired.

When Children Must Be Excluded from the Center

Knowing when to exclude children from the center for health reasons is not always easy. Many children are contagious with a disease before they show any symptoms. For example, by the time the chicken pox breaks out, the child has already been contagious for several days. In general, the following conditions make it necessary to exclude children from the center:

- open, oozing sores that cannot be covered
- diarrhea
- high fever
- unidentified rash
- untreated lice
- forceful vomiting

These are usually signs of contagious conditions that cannot be ignored. Children may be able to come back to the center before all signs of the condition have gone away. A doctor's recommendation should be followed in regard to re-entry to the program. Often, a public health nurse or clinic can be consulted by both parents and staff to provide information and advice.

Confidentiality

Many aspects of work in the center require a commitment to confidentiality. The health status of children, families, and staff are among those topics that must not be discussed by anyone who is not directly involved. Only those who must know in order to do their jobs should be communicating about the health status of anyone affiliated with the program. It should be quite clear to all staff this is an area of employee conduct that is taken quite seriously. Consequences for breaching this confidentiality should be included in the center's personnel policies, 15-10.

Policies Concerning Emergencies

No matter how careful you have been to maintain a safe, healthful environment, an unexpected emergency will probably occur at some time. The best way to handle an emergency is to anticipate it. Plan ahead for what you and your staff would need to know and do if an emergency would arise.

Keep Emergency Numbers Posted

Emergency numbers for fire, ambulance, police, and the nearest poison control center should be posted beside each phone. In an emergency, there is no time to search for a phone book and look up numbers. Staff who are frightened and upset may find it difficult to find the correct numbers. Valuable time could be lost. When numbers are clearly posted where they can't be missed, help can be obtained more quickly.

Emergency numbers and e-mail addresses for parents should also be clearly marked in a nearby file box or posted on a list. The only exception to this would be if there is a need to protect confidentiality regarding a parent's information. In this case, be sure the information is available and the appropriate staff know how to get it quickly. All classroom staff should know emergency procedures and have assigned roles in carrying out emergency plans. Keep in mind that emergencies may occur when a substitute teacher is in charge of the classroom. Make sure substitutes are aware of the emergency procedures.

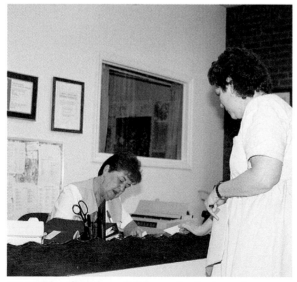

15-10 The director of this center has made sure all employees are aware of their responsibility to maintain confidentiality.

Administering First Aid

Many states have no requirements regarding first aid training for child care providers. Other states require that there be at least one

Red Cross certified adult in each classroom. Even if it is not required, it makes good common sense to have several staff members who have been trained to provide first aid if needed. Appropriate care can be provided quickly. Having a certified person on staff also reassures parents that their child will be well-cared for if an accident were to occur. It may also reduce the center's risk of charges of negligence and potential lawsuits.

A first aid kit should be available in each classroom. It must be easily accessible to staff, but out-of-reach of the children. These kits should be checked on a regular basis to be sure that they are fully stocked. Items inside with expiration dates should be checked to determine that they are not out of date.

Alerting Other Staff to Emergencies

A procedure should be established for alerting additional adults in the center if an emergency is occurring. It may require several adults to care for the non-involved children, provide first aid, make emergency phone calls, and guide emergency medical personnel to the location of the emergency. If anyone must be taken to the hospital, at least one familiar adult should go along to stay with the child until a parent arrives.

Plan and Practice Evacuation Policies

There may be times when it is necessary to get everyone out of the center quickly. Fires, floods, power outages, chemical spills, intruders, bomb scares, and other emergencies may require immediate evacuation of the building.

Emergency exit plans should be worked out carefully before any need arises. Regular practice drills should be held on a monthly basis. Staff in each room should know which exit to use and an alternate route if necessary. Diagrams of exit routes should be posted in every room and in the hallways. One staff member should be designated to check the building quickly to make sure that all children are out.

Once outside, to make sure all children are accounted for, one staff member from each classroom should be responsible for taking attendance. Plans should be made in case children need to be transported to another location. One program made arrangements with the local Head Start and the school district. Buses and vans, properly equipped with seat belts and safety seats, would be sent to the center for emergency transportation if necessary.

Plans should also be made to notify families, if necessary. Local radio stations can broadcast messages. Specific staff can be designated to call parents according to an organized phone list or phone tree.

If an emergency has occurred at the center, children may be upset. Even though they have practiced evacuation drills, they are likely to sense the tension produced by a true emergency.

Teachers of one center who experienced a bomb scare during naptime found that many children had difficulty taking naps for days afterward. Staff members should provide extra support and reassurance to children who may be badly frightened. In some cases, professional counseling may be needed.

Policies Concerning Child Abuse

Those who work directly with children may be the first to suspect that a child is being abused outside the center. This is a sad, painful discovery for staff members. Child abuse can occur in any neighborhood. Sooner or later, most programs will have to deal with this situation. Staff training and center policies regarding suspected child abuse are essential in order to take appropriate action.

Recognizing and Reporting Suspected Cases

All staff should be trained to recognize signs of possible child abuse, 15-11. As children arrive and throughout the day, staff should note any unusual bruises or other injuries. Children's comments should also be noted.

Symptoms of Possible Child Abuse	
Physical abuse	Visible bruises, burns, bites, welts, or other injuries
	Wears clothing that covers injuries, even if it is inappropriate for the weather
	Fear of adults
Emotional abuse	Unpredictable behavior
	Unusual or excessive clinging or crying
	Destructive behavior
	Withdrawal from center activities and people
	Unwilling to talk
	Underdeveloped muscle coordination skills
Sexual abuse	Trouble walking or sitting
	Itching, bruising, or pain in the genital area
	Pain when going to the bathroom
	Refusal of help in bathroom
	Behavior indicates sexual knowledge beyond that of typical age group
	Regressive, disruptive, or aggressive behaviors
Neglect	May be dirty and wearing inappropriate clothing for the weather
	Seen unsupervised when away from the center
	Thin, often hungry
	Constantly tired
	Poor dental hygiene
	Slow development

15-11 Teachers should recognize patterns in children's appearance or behavior that may indicate child abuse.

In most states, child care staff are classified as ***mandated reporters***. This means that if child abuse is suspected, the center is legally obligated to report it to the proper authorities. The program must have specific procedures in place to support staff in meeting this obligation. You, as the director, or a member of the senior supervisory staff, should be alerted to staff concerns. One person on the supervisory staff should be designated to evaluate the situation and make the report. When one person has responsibility to make the report calls, that individual will become familiar with the questions that will be asked. That staff member can also help classroom staff understand what investigative procedures will occur and what will be expected of them. A written report should be made that documents

- the date and time of the observation

- the observed injuries

- any comments made by the child or parent

- the staff consultation with the program's designated reporter

- the time the report was made

Parents should be aware of the center's obligations and policies regarding reporting suspected abuse. They must also understand that telling the classroom staff that they "lost it last night" does not release the staff from their obligation to report abuse. It is best to include information on this policy in the parent handbook or during the enrollment orientation.

Minimizing the Risk of Hiring Child Abusers in the Center

Both parents and directors alike fear the possibility that someone who wants to deliberately hurt children could get into the child care system. ***Pedophiles***, individuals intent on the sexual abuse of children, are known to seek employment in jobs or activities that bring them into daily contact with children. Research indicates that most children who are subjected to sexual abuse, are abused at home or in their neighborhoods. However, several well publicized cases of alleged abuse in child care centers, have had the serious effect of frightening both parents and center staff.

Hiring practices must have certain built-in safeguards to minimize the possibility of hiring a staff member whose intentions are to harm rather than to help children. Review applications carefully. Look for unexplained gaps in employment history. Look for a pattern of brief employment in several different places. Check references of previous employers carefully. Call and speak directly with previous employers and colleagues. Be alert for hesitations and comments that indicate previous problems. Insist on seeing original copies of all state-required clearances and criminal background checks. Be particularly cautious about individuals who seem to appear in your community "out-of-the-blue" or who have relocated from other states. Also keep in mind that criminal background checks will not reveal anything about abuse crimes an individual may have committed while still a juvenile.

Protecting Staff Against Unwarranted Charges of Abuse

Many staff and parents have been frightened by several widely publicized situations involving allegations of child sexual abuse in child care centers. Parents may look upon staff with suspicion, especially male staff. This can result in staff members feeling untrusted and uncomfortable when providing the basic comfort and care that young children need.

Center policies must include procedures designed to protect both children and staff. Suggested policies include:

- The supervision of nap room and bathroom areas should be handled by two staff members.

- Two staff members should be present whenever a child has to change clothes for any reason.

- No child should be taken alone to an isolated area of the center. The isolation area designed for sick children should be easily observable and the door should stay open.

- No child should ever be left unattended.

The best way to ensure the safety of both children and staff is to be extremely careful in staff hiring procedures. Also, be sure that parents and staff understand that parents are allowed to visit the center at any time. An open-door policy for parents helps to reassure them that the staff has nothing to hide. There is nothing secretive going on behind closed doors.

Other Safety Precautions

Additional precautions must be taken to ensure children's safety and well-being. As with other emergency or health situations, it is best to plan ahead. Establish policies and procedures that will help to prevent potential problems.

Authorizations for Adults Picking Up Children

During the enrollment process, parents should identify those adults who are authorized to pick up the children from the center. A form should be developed on which a parent can identify by name, phone number, and address, those authorized persons. The parent should be informed that the child will not be allowed to leave the center with any person who is not on that authorized list. In case of unforeseen circumstances, verbal permission from the parent by phone, along with positive identification of the person trying to pick up the child, will be acceptable. Adults who bring children to and from the center should accompany them to their classroom door. Sign-up sheets should be posted for adults to sign children in and out of the center each day.

Unauthorized Intruders

Centers must take security precautions in order to prevent entry by unauthorized intruders. Many programs have a policy of locking the doors after children have arrived. Anyone coming later must ring a doorbell to enter. Additional security measures may be necessary in some areas.

Dealing with Intoxicated Adults Attempting to Pick Up a Child

When an intoxicated parent (or one who appears to be under the influence of drugs) arrives to pick up a child, these steps should be followed:

- The teacher should confront the parent while another staff member alerts the director.

- The parent should be asked to leave and send another authorized adult to pick up the child. The teacher should offer to call a substitute for the parent, if that is requested.

- If the parent insists, you will have to let the child go. You cannot hold the child against the parent's will, even if you are rightly concerned. Inform the parent the police will be called.

- If the parent leaves with the child, call the police immediately. Be prepared to describe the car, license plate, home address, and probable route home.

- Contact the person the next day, when he/she is sober, to arrange a conference to discuss the problem.

Although staff may disagree, this situation is not considered child abuse in most states. Therefore, it is not an incident requiring a child abuse report.

How Do Licensing Requirements Affect Health and Safety?

Many possible sources of danger for young children are covered by licensing regulations. While states vary in their requirements, all states make an effort to ensure that the physical surroundings are safe for children. As director, you are responsible for making sure that the center complies with all licensing regulations. This includes compliance whether inspectors are present or not!

Some programs are careful to meet all standards when an inspection is scheduled, but become less careful at other times. Such things as keeping medicines in a locked cabinet or taking care to make sure all unused outlets have outlet covers, can seem less important when the inspectors are gone.

You must demonstrate support for maintaining these licensing regulations. They have been established to help keep children safe. Your staff will be more careful themselves if they sense your commitment, 15-12. Plotting with staff to deceive inspectors by hiding safety violations puts children at risk and undermines your ability to lead your staff. If a child might be harmed because your center is not in compliance with safety regulations, resulting lawsuits could destroy your program. They could also result in severe penalties for you and your staff.

Director's Dilemma

A young mother arrives at the center with her boyfriend to pick up her child. Both are obviously intoxicated. The biological father of the child is divorced from the mother, but is listed as an authorized individual to pick up the child. What should your staff say to the mother? How would you handle the situation?

15-12 When using small electrical appliances, such as this popcorn maker, extra effort must be made by the staff to ensure the safety of the children.

Why Does the Program Need a Health and Safety Committee?

Because centers are faced with an array of both legal and ethical concerns, the center's health and safety practices must be taken seriously. Genuine thought and effort must be put into making the center as safe as possible for all those who spend their days there. As the director, you may work independently to try to figure out every possible hazard in the center. You may then be the person who develops the health and safety policies. However, rapidly changing knowledge about disease, as well as increasingly complex legal issues, have led many centers to establish special committees on health and safety.

It is strongly recommended that your program have an established preventive health and safety committee. This may be established as an ad hoc committee reporting to the board of directors. It may be an advisory committee that provides advice for your decisions. However it is organized, the committee can help ensure the center is a safe and healthy place, 15-13.

Membership

Membership on this committee should include individuals who are in a position to provide helpful information to the group. Ideally, this committee should include

15-13 Keeping children safe and healthy is a primary goal of all quality centers.

both a doctor and a lawyer. Many concerns involving contagious diseases and the legal impact of the Americans with Disabilities Act are still unknown. As the director, you may need help in remaining up to date on judicial decisions, changing interpretations of the law, and medical practices relating to blood-borne pathogens and contagious diseases.

It is also necessary to have a staff person on this committee. This person must be able to represent the staff's concerns. She/he should also be able to communicate clearly with the staff regarding the concerns and recommendations of the committee. Membership on this committee will be a time-consuming part of this staff person's job. It should not just be added onto other responsibilities. With time specifically assigned away from other duties, this staff member can serve as a resource person for the committee. Keeping current on the latest information is a big job. The staff member can then present that information to the committee. She/he can also develop training programs and materials to educate the entire staff in up-to-date information and procedures.

Parents should also be included on the committee. They have a commitment to quality care for their children and a desire to make sure the center is a safe place. Parents who work in health

Director's Dilemma
You have decided to establish a health and safety committee to advise you on center policy. You have already identified one staff member who can be given some release time to work on finding resource information for this group. A local pediatrician has declined because of lack of time. What other people might you try to enlist to help with this committee?

professions can be particularly helpful in spotting potential trouble spots. A representative from the board of directors should also be included on the committee. It may be possible to request that members of the board who fit into the categories needed, also serve on this committee. For example, parents on the board may also be nurses or lawyers. They may be more willing to put in the time and effort needed than someone else who has no direct involvement with the program.

Responsibilities

The committee should be charged with several specific responsibilities. This will help to keep it from getting off-track. These responsibilities should include:

- periodically inspecting the center to look for potential hazards
- identifying and categorizing infectious diseases
- advising on procedures to minimize the risk of spread of contagious diseases
- identifying and addressing educational needs of staff and families in regard to contagious disease
- advising the director regarding center compliance with state and federal laws
- identifying an official agency spokesperson to represent the program to the news media.

The committee should try to anticipate as many potential health problems that may occur in the center as possible. Different categories of health concerns should be established. Guidelines can be set for dealing with these different categories. For example, all centers will eventually have to deal with an episode of impetigo, lice, or pinworms. These are unpleasant health issues, but common ones in child care. They can be dealt with in a fairly routine manner. Centers may also have to deal with Hepatitis B, AIDS, or other more serious diseases. Obviously, policies and staff training for these two types of contagious illnesses will have to be different.

◉ Summary

A center must be a safe, healthy place for children to be. It is the responsibility of the adults to make sure that licensing standards are followed. Equipment must be regularly inspected to ensure that it is safe. When food is prepared and served, practices established to minimize the risks of choking and/or food contamination must be followed carefully.

Policies must be established to ensure children's safety while they are at the center. These include the use of universal precautions to prevent the spread of disease. Guidelines regarding other health-related aspects of the center must also be established. Parents need to be informed of these policies when they enroll their children at the center.

Concern for the health and safety of the staff must also be considered. Many child care staff may be in their child-bearing years. If there are pregnant staff or those who are considering becoming pregnant, they will need to be aware of the health risks involved in working daily with young children. Appropriate training to help staff in dealing with health and safety issues should be provided.

A health and safety committee should be established to assist in the development of center policies. Issues related to both wellness and liability must be considered.

⚙ Terms

universal precautions
mandated reporter
pedophiles

⚙ Review

1. What does the concept of *acceptable risk* mean?

2. Identify three actions you can take to minimize safety hazards in the classroom.

3. Why is polluted air more of a problem for young children than for adults?

4. For what kinds of problems should outdoor equipment be inspected?

5. What types of foods present potential choking hazards for young children?

6. Explain what is meant by the term *universal precautions.*

7. What is the best defense against the spread of disease and germs?

8. When must children be excluded from the center due to illness?

9. Why is it important to plan and hold practice evacuation drills?

10. How can a director minimize the possibility of hiring a staff member who's intentions are to harm rather than to help children?

⚙ Applications

1. With permission, plan and conduct an evacuation drill for your classroom. Make signs showing appropriate exits, assign any tasks that must be done to specific individuals, and check the amount of time it takes to empty the classroom to the outside of the building. Afterwards, discuss factors that might cause confusion or delays in evacuating a child care facility.

2. With two other classmates, role-play a situation where a parent arrives intoxicated to take a child home. Assign the roles of director, parent, and child.

3. Offer to be a member of a health and safety committee for a local child care center. Share your knowledge of these issues to help the committee develop appropriate policies. If this is not possible, form a similar committee in your classroom for this course. Prepare policies to be followed in your own classroom to minimize the spread of disease.

Some child care programs that primarily serve preschoolers are expanding to serve infants, toddlers, and school-age children.

Chapter 16
Programs with Special Administrative Concerns

After studying this chapter, you will be able to

- identify areas of administrative concern associated with special purpose programs.
- outline the benefits and disadvantages of offering these programs.
- describe special services that programs may offer to families.
- describe factors to consider when deciding whether or not to offer special services.

In the past, most people thought of child care as serving primarily children in the three- to five-year-old range. Services were usually limited to these preschool years. If parents needed infant care or care for a school-age child, they called on neighbors, relatives, or the parents of their children's friends. School-age children were frequently left to care for themselves.

Today, many more parents return to the workforce while their children are still young infants. The schools keep hours that can create a hardship for working parents. As a result, child care agencies have been called on to provide care for both younger and older children. Families also have need for drop-in care, sick child care, weekend care, all-night care, and child care in emergency situations.

Many child care programs have had to expand to meet the needs of families. Each of these new types of services has certain administrative concerns of which you should be aware. School-age care is not the same as preschool care. Infant/toddler care has special areas of concern. In order to offer each of these types of care successfully, you must be aware of the pitfalls and plan carefully, 16-1.

You cannot assume that there is a real need for the service based on one or two requests. As you consider offering additional types of services, you will need to get a sense of the actual demand for such services. Once you have established that the need exists, you must explore the costs, staffing, space, licensing requirements, and equipment necessary in order to operate the program component successfully.

16-1 An open bathroom can work well in toddler and preschool rooms, but would not be acceptable for school-age children.

What Do I Need to Know About Infant/Toddler Programs?

A dramatic increase in the need for infant/toddler care has led many states to support the development of group settings for infants and toddlers. Infant/toddler programs are good ways to introduce families to your program. A family who is happy with the care provided for their infant or toddler is likely to stay with your program as long as there is a need for child care. If you cannot provide care for very young children, families will go elsewhere. You may have lost them to a program that provides comprehensive infancy through school-age services.

Each state has licensing regulations for these programs. Unfortunately, in many states the licensing regulations are far less demanding than what child development experts think they should be. Often, centers that are meeting the minimum licensing requirements, are not providing the number of qualified adults that experts believe are necessary to operate a quality program.

Staffing

In order to have a good program for very young children, you must have a low adult-to-child ratio. Ideally, the center should have one adult to every four children. (Many experts think that one-to-three is a better ratio.)

The more adults you have and the better their training is, the higher the cost for care will be. As a result, infant/toddler care is the most expensive form of care to provide. It is often costly for the center.

Very young children require smaller group sizes. They simply cannot relate to all of the children and adults who are normally found in a bustling preschool classroom. Too much noise, confusion, and people can become overwhelming for young children. They may respond by becoming fussy, tuning out, or not building a special relationship with anyone. None of these are healthy patterns for them.

Continuity of Care

Children in child care should have consistent caregivers with whom they can build a sense of trust and emotional attachment. This is particularly important for very young children. Staffing patterns should be developed that will allow children to build attachments. Frequently changing or rotating caregivers is detrimental to children. It will not help to develop the sense of trust that is the basis for a healthy personality.

Many staff do not like working with babies. Others love it. You will need to find a match between those adults who love the infants and their placement in infant classrooms. Often, as staff members receive additional training in the developmental characteristics of infants and toddlers, the children become more interesting to them. As staff learn to recognize the importance of developmental milestones, they begin to view development as a fascinating process to be supported with enthusiasm. This leads to better care and to more satisfaction for the adults providing that care.

Grouping

The placement of infants and toddlers in specific groups is an important consideration. Toddlers who have just learned to walk are thrilled with themselves. They are so busy practicing this new skill, that nothing in their way will stop them. Unfortunately, it may be a baby on the floor who gets in their way! Toddlers, who have no sense of themselves as a force, are likely to walk right over anything on the floor. The baby has no way to get out of the way, and the toddler has no sense of obstacles in the way. This is a dangerous combination. Toddlers are unsteady. They can be doing just fine, and then suddenly fall over their own feet. A 20-pound toddler falling on top of a 10 pound infant can cause serious injury. Think of yourself being landed on from above by a 250-pound squirming weight. Not a pleasant thought!

Most experts feel strongly that walkers and nonwalkers should be in separate groups. While safety is one reason, another reason has to do with cognitive development. The ability to walk is often viewed as a signal that children are ready for more active exploration of the world. This new-found freedom opens the doors for greater exploration. The ability to walk is also followed quickly by a desire to climb, 16-2. Toddlers need these expanded opportunities. Babies need to be protected from the enthusiasm of the toddlers.

States vary in their licensing requirements regarding this age group. Some states specify that walkers and nonwalkers cannot be in the same area. Other states have no restrictions.

Director's Dilemma

A staff member who has been hired to work with a small group of infants, decides that she doesn't like working with this age group. She finds it boring. She has suggested a rotation system for staff. Under this system, every month, the staff would switch groups. At the end of the next month, the staff would switch again. She feels that with this system, the staff would have a chance to work with different age groups and would never get bored. How would you react to this suggestion? How do you think child development experts would respond to this idea? What kinds of things could you do that might help this staff member find her job more interesting?

16-2 Toddlers love to climb, so many centers are now using lofts that give toddlers a safe way to climb stairs.

Location of the Infant/Toddler Program

It is best to locate the infant/toddler rooms away from the rest of the center if possible. A separate wing of the building would be ideal. This placement can help to reduce the spread of illness from the older children to the younger ones. It can also reduce the noise level reaching the infant/toddler classroom. Nearby preschoolers or school-age children need a lot of physical activity and often engage in loud play. This can be stressful for infants or toddlers who need a calmer environment with few startling noises. It is also important, however, to be sure that the infant/toddler staff doesn't feel isolated from the rest of the program. Staff who are working with these youngest children often feel a great need to see and speak to adults periodically throughout the day. This may be a difficult need for you to address since you also want to encourage the staff to devote their attention to the children.

Infant/Toddler Equipment

Equipment in the infant/toddler areas must be designed for this younger age group. Simply moving preschool toys into this classroom can lead to injuries. Many of the toy companies that specialize in sturdy toys for child care centers now carry a line of equipment designed for younger children. The equipment is smaller in scale. It is designed to be sturdy so it will not tip if a wobbly toddler grabs onto it for support.

The basic toys needed for younger groups include the following:

- push-pull toys
- soft, cuddly toys
- small scale climbers
- toy telephones

- dolls

- busy box-type toys that respond to children's actions

- sturdy books

- rattles for infants

- unbreakable mirrors

- rubber or sponge balls

- puppets

- soft blocks

- stacking rings

- toy cars and trucks

- easily washable chew toys

Because young children put almost everything into their mouths, a simple method of washing toys should be developed. A conveniently placed laundry basket, out-of-reach of the children, can be a collecting point for toys that have been in someone's mouth.

Additional equipment will be needed for the classroom. Items needed will include

- several rocking chairs

- a tape or CD player

- plastic storage bins for each child's diapers and supplies

- small storage trays for each child's food or formula in the refrigerator

- shelves that can be closed off when not in use

- foldable gates to close off hallways or other areas

- step stools and toilet seat inserts

- strollers, preferably the type designed for child care centers that hold six children

- high chairs

- cribs, 16-3

- changing table

16-3 Sturdy, safe cribs are a necessity for infant care.

Daily Schedule and Activities

The daily schedule of infants and toddlers must reflect their needs. While there should be some general pattern and sequence to the day, the schedule should be flexible. Rather than following a rigid minute-by-minute preplanned routine, caregivers must be sensitive to the individual needs of each child in their care. If one child gets hungry early, he or she should be fed. If a child is not quite sleepy at the usual time, he or she should be rocked and quietly helped to relax.

Caregivers need to be actively and emotionally involved with the babies in their care. Every interaction is important as the infant begins to recognize the warm, caring faces of the staff members and the predictability of their behaviors. These interactions, whether they take place during routines such as diapering, or during play time, are an important part of the program in a quality center.

Activities should always be developmentally appropriate. As with preschoolers, this means that the activities should be matched to the developmental levels and individual interests of the children. Infants need items they can grasp, mouth, and examine. They like simple patterns and bright colors. Safe, interesting objects to look at, hear, and touch fascinate them and help them learn. As they learn how to reach, they need items to grasp. They need toys that they can control. It is a wonderful discovery for infants and toddlers to find that when they pull, or squeeze, or shake, something in the toy responds. They also need to see themselves. Mirrors in several spots around the room will fascinate young children.

Toddlers need even more items to help them develop muscle control and coordination. Kiddie cars, beach balls, toy trucks and cars, and large, soft blocks are valuable additions to the toddlers' toy supply. They need the opportunity to run, roll, jump, and laugh heartily. Cruising around the room, looking at the adult to confirm the names of objects, is also a valuable use of a toddler's time. A simple game of "Ring Around the Rosie" can be a fun way to encourage balance and coordination. Toddlers also enjoy soft stuffed toys and dolls as they begin to develop an interest in pretend play. For both older infants and toddlers, walks around the center or outdoors expand their awareness. In a developmentally appropriate program, children are never bored.

Health Concerns

Infants have immature immune systems. The immunities they inherited from their mothers are beginning to break down. They are beginning the slow process of building up their own immune systems. Part of this process involves getting their proper immunization shots as specified by the American Academy of Pediatrics. Center policy should require that infants have these shots on schedule. Immunity to other disease comes as a result of having caught the disease and building up antibodies against it. Because infants are young, they are susceptible to many diseases. Respiratory diseases, rashes, and gastrointestinal diseases are particularly common in infants and toddlers. Staff must be trained to follow health policies carefully.

Health policies established for the entire center, as identified in Chapter 15, are particularly important for infants and toddlers. Diapers and food are not a good combination, yet each is a part of the infant/toddler program. Staff must be reminded of the importance of universal precautions and handwashing as steps in the prevention of disease.

Safety Concerns

Infants and toddlers have no judgment in regard to what is safe and what is not. Their care is fully in the hands of the adult caregivers. Special consideration must be given to keeping them safe. Young children have a developmental need to explore their environment, but this also means that staff must be constantly vigilant. There must be constant awareness of what each child is doing. Staff must make sure there are no objects on or near the floor that could be dangerous to crawling infants or pushing, pulling, climbing toddlers. The following guidelines can help prevent accidents:

- No toys smaller than one inch in diameter should be available for play. If an item fits into a 35-millimeter film container, it is too small for children under age three.

- Toys should be checked for small parts that could pull off and be swallowed.

- Large motor toys should be checked to ensure that small fingers cannot be pinched in moving parts.

- Dolls should be checked to ensure that eyes are not attached with pointed parts that could be pulled out.

- Bulletin boards that are placed low should not have items attached by thumbtacks.

- Shelves should be balanced or anchored so that they cannot be pulled over by a climbing child.

- Low-level storage areas should be locked.

- No child should go into the bathroom unsupervised.

- Evacuation plans should take into account the fact that children cannot walk themselves out of the building. (It's a good idea for each classroom to have at least one crib with castors that is small enough to go through the doorway. In case of an emergency, several infants could be placed in the crib and wheeled out to safety. This would help to avoid the situation of one caregiver trying to carry several children.)

Communication with Parents

Staff in infant/toddler programs have an increased responsibility to communicate daily with parents. A daily report with certain kinds of information is vitally important in telling parents what they need to know about their child's day. For example, parents have to know the amount of food or formula the child had.

A simple form can be developed for the staff that will cover information to pass on to parents. Items covered on the form should include:

- amount and type of food or formula taken

- amount of water or juice taken

- number of wet diapers changed

- texture, color, and frequency of bowel movements

- temperature, if child seems to have a fever

- nap information

- interesting things the child has done during the day

- any cause for concern noted by the staff

With a simple form, most of this information can be recorded quickly, 16-4. It may seem like a bother to staff, but it is necessary to ensure the child's well-being.

What Your Child Did Today!

Name: —————————— Date: ——————

Ate or Drank: Ounces

Formula ———— Juice ———— Baby food ————

Other ——————————

We changed wet diapers ———— times.

Number of bowel movements ——————————

Consistency and color of bowel movements was

——————————————————————

Any fever? Yes   No

Napped from ———— to ————

Went to sleep easily? Yes   No

Interesting things your child did today.

——————————————————————

Concerns ——————————————————

Signature ——————————————————
            (staff member in room)

16-4 A simple form like this one provides an easy way to share important information with parents of infants and toddlers.

What Do I Need to Know About School-Age Care?

Working parents frequently find that the hours of school do not match the hours when they must be at work. While elementary schools typically start at 8:00 or 9:00 A.M., parents must often go to their jobs by 7:00 or 8:00 A.M. They worry about their children who may have trouble getting breakfast and getting to the bus or school on time.

The same problem occurs at the end of the day. Schools are usually out by 3:00 or 4:00 P.M., yet parents frequently work until five. Some parents must work evening or night shifts, while others have shifts that change every few weeks. Some children come alone into an empty house, try to fix their own snacks, and watch afternoon soaps or talk shows with adult themes. This situation is cause for worry for parents. Many young school-age children are on their own for several hours each day. On days when school is out, they may be on their own all day long. This can create a stressful situation for both children and parents.

Concern about *children in self-care* (commonly called latchkey children) has grown.

There have been some educational attempts to help children learn to manage on their own. However, children in self-care are often lonely and frightened. They may not have the maturity of judgment to handle emergency situations that could arise. Most parents and child development experts feel that self-care for children under 12 years of age is not a good idea.

School-age care programs are currently the fastest growing component of child care. Many school-age programs are bursting with enrollment. There are waiting lists, especially for the full-day summer programs. School-age programs also tend to be cost-effective for centers. Because the groups of older children can be larger, the cost of providing staff is not as high as it is for other age groups. Programs can often coordinate with other school-age services in the community to provide varied activities, 16-5.

Many child care centers have expanded their programs to include school-age children. The children, however, may be reluctant to attend child care if they feel that the program will not be suited to their age group. The center should work carefully to create an atmosphere and program that is appealing to older children if it is to be successful.

16-5 Children in after-school programs need nutritious snacks. They also enjoy participating in organizations such as Scouts.

Location and Facilities

Locating a suitable facility for school-age care may be difficult. In many cases, elementary schools have been reluctant to have these programs in their buildings. The licensing requirements for school-age programs are sometimes in conflict with school procedures and safety regulations. Only recently, primarily in response to parent requests, have schools become more willing to allow their facilities to be used for after-school child care programs.

If school rooms are not available, it may be difficult to find rooms suitable for school-age programs. Often churches or community centers have rooms that meet licensing standards. The facility must have running water, bathrooms, a small kitchen area for fixing snacks, access to an outdoor playspace, and ideally, a gym for indoor active games. Transportation may be necessary to transport the children to and from school.

Hours

School-age care hours must be established around the school schedule and the needs of parents. Some children may need care for an hour or so before school starts in the morning. Because they have to be up and out of the house so early, there will probably not be time for a healthy breakfast at home. For this reason, breakfast is often provided in before-school programs. Early morning activities should be quiet ones that give the child a chance to prepare for the school day.

After-school hours are also necessary. Children may arrive from several different schools. They will need a snack and time for activities. Most of these programs do not extend beyond the dinner hour. Most children are gone by about 5:30 or 6:00 P.M. However, if your community has a factory or other major employer with hours that extend into the evening, there may be a demand for later evening hours. Parents who commute long distances to their jobs may also need extended evening hours. In the summer or on days when the schools are closed, the program must be open all day.

Staffing

Hire trained staff who enjoy working with school-age children. Staff must also be willing to work a split-shift schedule. This may include several hours in the early morning and several more hours in the late afternoon. Some staff may be willing to work part-time, working one shift or the other.

Some programs create full-time jobs for school-age staff by using them as assistants in preschool classrooms. They may help prepare snacks for the whole center or serve as part-time office staff. For some staff, being employed full-time is important. For others, part-time work with the school-age program is ideal.

Most school-age programs expand substantially during the summer. You may need to hire additional staff for the summer only. These staff will not be needed when the program goes back to its fall schedule. This is a good opportunity to work with nearby colleges and work training programs. There are a number of work-study opportunities, internships, and job training programs, that may be looking for summer placements for qualified college students or high school graduates. In most states, these employees will not be able to take full responsibility for groups of children, but they may be able to serve as assistant group supervisors or aids with the groups. You may be able to hire elementary school teachers who would like summer employment when elementary schools are closed, 16-6.

Program

The needs of school-age children are different from those of preschoolers. Because they have been in school all day, they are ready for lively after-school events. An outdoor playtime, organized games, and a nutritious snack are essentials for an after-school program. Some children will be tired after a long day. They need opportunities for quiet activities. Crafts, board games, opportunities for dramatic play, and quiet reading may appeal to them. Centers also need to provide quiet working space for those children who have homework. If a child needs the help of a tutor, this may be arranged through coordination with a local tutoring agency. Because the after-school program usually is only open for a couple of hours, activities must either be short or must be ones that can extend over several days time.

During the summer, or when school is closed, most programs expand into full-day service. The summer can offer lots of opportunities for more involved projects and activities. One large center divided the children into age groups. The counselors then had children sign up in advance for particular project areas. One group dismantled an old discarded engine, another group designed and decorated house plans using a computerized program and lots of old magazines. There were groups who spent the week exploring colonial crafts, making jewelry, taking bowling lessons, learning the fundamentals of cooking, and preparing a play for the whole group. The next week, children could change their choices. New activities were constantly being added. In addition, each group had several days a week when their group got to go to the local swimming pool and park. There was always lots of time for outdoor play.

16-6 These elementary school teachers spend their summer working at a center that provides school-age care.

Director's Dilemma

Your program operates a large after-school program at one of the local elementary schools. Several of the staff members are school teachers who stay on with your program at the end of the day. Some of the families and children have complained that the after-school program seems to be run like an extension of the school day. The teachers are tired and expect the children to sit quietly and do their homework. What kind of after-school activities do you think the children need? How could you address these concerns with the teachers?

Working with the Schools

It is important to develop good communication with the school district personnel for your program to run smoothly. Be sure you are on the school's mailing list and receive a copy of the school year calendar. You must be able to plan ahead for your program to be open on teacher in-service days, parent conference days, or vacation days when the schools are closed.

You will also need some way to be alerted if the schools are unexpectedly closed. In areas where snow days are common, announcements are usually made on the radio or TV. However, in order to have your staff ready to go, you may need to request an early morning phone call from the school district administrator in charge. One local center director always gets a phone call at 5:00 A.M. on snow days as an advance warning that the school-age program will need to be open all day.

Coordination with Other Agencies

Many communities have other organizations and agencies that provide services and activities for school-age children. It is helpful to develop cooperative relationships with these agencies. Many times, their offerings can enhance or enrich those you provide. Organizations such as Scouts, Boys and Girls Clubs, the local library, Y's, community centers, 4-H, museums, or local dance or karate schools, frequently offer after-school programs and lessons, 16-7. Some require a fee, while others are free. Many of these programs have great appeal to children. School-age children want to be where their friends are. They may resent coming to your center if their friends are all swimming at the community center. You may be able to work out agreements with some of these other services so children at your center can participate.

What Do I Need to Know About Family Child Care?

Many family child care providers operate independently. They have no contact with other family child care providers or child care centers in their area. Family child care providers, however, may also affiliate with other child care programs. If carefully planned, this can provide benefits for both the child care agency and the family child care providers.

16-7 Some centers make arrangements with community centers so school-age children can take swimming lessons.

Benefits to the Agency

When the agency has a network of affiliated family child care homes, there are several benefits. It gains some flexibility in the placement of children. For instance, many families prefer the more family-like structure of the home setting. Some children have great difficulty adjusting to the more complex settings of a center. They may be more comfortable in the coziness of the family child care home environment. When the center has a network of affiliated homes, it can offer families a choice of homes that meet the program's standards for quality care.

Family child care providers often have more flexibility in hours of operation. Because the children are cared for in the provider's own home, a parent may be able to arrange for later hours than would be possible at the center. Many parents in professional positions have the types of jobs where they must stay until the work is done, no matter how long that takes. Doctors, for example, cannot leave surgery to go pick up their child from the center. The family child care home setting is often more adaptable for parents with irregular schedules.

The family child care home may also provide the best choice for a child with special needs. The needs of the child to be with other children can be met, yet the setting usually has fewer children and confusion than in a center classroom. Interesting activities can be provided, but within a more limited setting. This is a choice that parents, the center staff, and the provider should consider. The ability of the provider to meet the special needs of the child must also be a consideration.

Benefits to the Provider

Many family child care providers find the benefits of affiliation with a child care agency to be of value. The agency can help to ensure that the home provider's enrollment is always full. Parents may be reluctant to use a provider who simply advertises through the paper. Providers who are affiliated with your child care agency are more likely to be considered reputable by families who are looking for care.

The providers can also obtain appropriate insurance for their child care operation through group policies coordinated by the center. Help in meeting state licensing or registration requirements can also be obtained from the center. One large agency arranged for discounts on the smoke detectors and fire extinguishers that each provider had to purchase. Individual providers were saved a substantial amount of money by purchasing as a group.

Providers may also be eligible for partial reimbursement of the cost of the food that they serve to the children. Many providers do not know this. Many don't want to be bothered with keeping the necessary records to claim the money. The child care agency can provide the forms and the help that these providers need in order to claim the reimbursement. Although the reimbursement is not a lot of money, it can amount to several dollars a day. Over a year's time, this can represent several hundred dollars of additional income. Most providers who participate have found that it is worth the effort. Providers may be able to participate in the food reimbursement program without fully affiliating with your program. Since this helps the provider get to know your center and its staff, it may eventually lead to full affiliation.

Director's Dilemma
Your program has about 25 affiliated family child care providers. Several of the providers have requested some opportunities to get together with each other and other center staff. They complain about feeling isolated since they are not a part of daily center activities. What kinds of activities could you plan to provide more support for them? How could you help them feel more a part of the center program?

Affiliated providers have access to training and resource materials that may not be available to others. They can find support by getting to know others who are doing the same work and have similar experiences as they do.

Family Child Care Affiliation for Agencies—Factors to Consider

Some agencies have decided not to establish any affiliation with family child care providers. Other agencies have large networks of 40 to 50 homes and few center-based classrooms. If you do decide to work with family child care homes, you will need to hire some additional staff to recruit new providers, offer training, and monitor those who represent your program. You will be responsible for helping the providers obtain and fill out various forms correctly. Providing these services to the providers will cost your agency additional money.

In some programs, family child care providers are considered full employees of the program. They are on the regular payroll and receive benefits. This is very costly, but it may be required by state regulation. In other programs, family child care providers are independent contractors. They are self-employed and contract to provide specific services (care) to the program. Neither party has any obligation to the other beyond the terms of the specific contract. When that contract is over, there is no further relationship unless a new contract is established. Under this arrangement, the family child care provider is free to provide care for other children who are not enrolled through your agency.

A major source of concern with family child care homes is that they operate in locations away from your center. Therefore, they are difficult to supervise. It is impossible to know what is going on in the homes at all times. Insurance companies that are willing to insure center-based care may be less likely to insure the home provider component of the program because of its lack of supervision. The fear of potential child abuse from family members or guests of the provider have made insurance companies wary. The high cost of liability insurance for home care providers has resulted in some centers dropping family child care affiliation altogether. It has also forced many independent family child care providers to operate without insurance or to stop providing care.

In some locations, recruitment of new family child care providers can be a problem. Many existing providers would rather continue working without a license or certification. They resist bringing their activities under the scrutiny of the center staff or state officials. Most home-based child care providers have no formal training or background in child care. They can be an "unknown quantity" in terms of their ability to provide quality care that is consistent with your program's philosophy. A program director must carefully consider the pros and cons of offering family child care as an option.

What Other Types of Special Programs Might Be Offered?

In addition to the types of services already described, there are other special programs that your program might consider operating. The need for each service must be determined. Each will involve benefits and costs to your program that you must analyze before making a commitment.

Drop-In Care

Another service that is popular in some areas is drop-in care. **Drop-in care** is provided occasionally for a child whose parent may need a day to take care of personal business, 16-8. The child is not enrolled on a regular basis and may only come to the center several days out of every month. Health clubs, shopping malls, and resorts often offer this type of care. If your center has the space to offer a drop-in group, you may decide to offer it, too.

There are several things to keep in mind about drop-in care. All of the health and safety precautions you keep in place for the regularly enrolled children must be followed for drop-in children as well. You must always be certain that there is enough staff assigned to the drop-in group to always comply with licensing regulations. Group size cannot grow beyond the number allowed by the licensing standards. Because of these regulations, you will need to establish an advance sign-up procedure that will allow you to schedule the appropriate number of staff and to maintain limits on the number of children who can attend on any given day. You will also need to collect proof of immunizations, health forms, emergency information, and names of authorized adults to pick the child up.

Drop-in care has become very popular with parents who need an occasional day away from their children. In a well-equipped, interesting classroom with good teachers, it can offer a positive experience for the children. There are some factors that can make drop-in care difficult. These include

- the ever-changing group of children who must adjust to the setting and may be distressed

- mixed age groups

- teachers having little opportunity to build a relationship with the children

- difficulty in establishing routines with the changing "mix" of children from day to day

Because drop-in care is a specialized service, the center can usually charge a higher hourly rate for it than can be charged for full-time care. It can provide additional income to help support other parts of the program.

Part-Day Groups

Part-day nursery school programs are usually easy for a child care center to offer. If your

16-8 Drop-in care can provide a flexible service for families who don't need full-time care.

community has a population of families who do not need full-day care, but would like the advantages of a preschool program, a part-day group may be a good idea.

The part-day groups can be offered without concern for meals or naptime. They normally operate for two to three hours per session. Some programs offer these classes every day of the week. Others may have sessions only on certain days, such as Monday, Wednesday, and Friday mornings. If there is an unusually large demand, you may want to offer afternoon sessions for additional groups. Fees charged for the part-day groups are usually prorated higher than those charged for full-day service. Additional money brought in by this part of the program can help to defray the cost of administration or the other more costly components of the program.

Weekend and All-Night Care

In some areas there is a demand for weekend or all-night care. In areas where shifts of employees must be available all the time, such as hospitals, resorts, factories, or round-the-clock businesses, families may need that type of care. Weekend care is not particularly different from the care provided during the week.

The greatest difficulty may be in finding staff who are willing to work on weekends. Someone from the senior administrative staff must also be present to handle administrative decisions that may have to be made. Provisions should also be made for the safe handling of any money that is received by the center during the weekend.

Overnight care usually involves additional licensing regulations. These vary from state to state. They usually involve requirements regarding sleeping arrangements, bedding, use of nonflammable pajamas, and other safety features. There may be additional requirements regarding food, snacks, and health practices. It may be necessary for on-duty staff to remain awake all night even though all children are sleeping.

Overnight care is difficult to provide. The children may be upset by having to sleep away from their own beds. The usual bedtime routines that they are used to may not be possible in the center. If you try to offer this type of care, it is important to work closely with parents.

Sick Child Care

Child care arrangements often fall apart when a child is ill. A sick child cannot go to the center, yet the parent may face serious hardship if forced to take a day off of work. Some centers have been started for the sole purpose of caring for sick children, 16-9. Most of these programs will only take children who are not seriously ill.

Hospitals with unused rooms may provide sick child care as long as there is space available. The child is not admitted to the hospital, but is enrolled in the sick child care program for the day. Hospitals providing this service often try to provide a playroom type atmosphere for children. Hospital personnel may be used to staff the program.

Sick child care may also be provided by a single purpose program that only cares for sick children. In order to survive financially, the program must be located in an area with lots of children. Otherwise, there usually will not be enough attendance to keep the center open.

Sick child care may be offered at a regular child care program. Some centers have special rooms devoted to children who aren't feeling well. This allows the children to stay in the center with which they are familiar. Separate rooms are necessary to keep children with different illnesses from infecting each other. Other programs may have several staff hired specifically to go out to the home of a sick child to provide care. The child does not have to go outside and is not in contact with other children.

16-9 Sick child care is expensive to provide. This type of care is sometimes offered by hospitals or child care centers that can provide a one-to-one adult/child ratio.

Sick child care is very expensive to provide. It often requires a one-to-one adult/child ratio. The price of the service must be enough to cover the wages of the caregiver and the administrative costs involved with the program. For this reason, even when sick child care is available, parents may be reluctant to use it unless they have no alternatives. Some employers have been willing to share the cost. This usually happens when parents are in highly skilled positions. The employer may lose money if the parent misses work. The cost of a substitute employee or lost production may be more than the cost of the sick child care.

Crisis Care

Some programs offer a service usually referred to as *crisis care*. As a part of this service, several spaces in the center are held open for use in emergency situations. If a family's house has burned down or a single parent has been taken to the hospital, young children in the family may have nowhere to go. The center can provide temporary care during the day until permanent arrangements are made.

This type of program is usually funded through a special grant. The center cannot continually have vacant spaces without losing income. To offset this loss of income, agencies such as the child welfare agency or other service organizations that work to meet emergency needs may pay for the vacant spaces. This can keep the spaces available when needed.

Information and Referral Support

After your center has become well established, you will probably have more requests for enrollment than you can handle. In many parts of the country, waiting lists are so long that children will be too old for the center before an opening occurs for them. Parents who call your center may think they will be able to enroll their child right away. When they find out that is not possible, they are often frantic to find some other source of care.

Many areas have no central referral service to help match families who need care with centers that may still have available space. Parents who are new to an area usually have no idea where to go to find good care for their children. Your agency can serve a need by providing an information and referral system. This may start out informally by simply telling parents where other licensed centers are located. If you are in a metropolitan area, your service may grow into a major component of your agency, complete with a computerized matching system, 16-10.

One information and referral program discovered over 2,000 licensed providers and programs in its medium-sized city. It became a full-time job for one staff member to keep a current list of the providers, and the families needing care. The staff member also began to use major road maps to track primary routes to major work and housing locations. This allowed a more accurate way to recommend centers that were conveniently located near the parent's route to work.

You must make sure the programs or providers you are recommending are licensed and meet state standards. Parents will assume that if you have a center included on your list that it is OK. They may do little other checking except to find out the location, price, and if there is an opening. If there is a problem with the center, your program could be at risk of additional liability.

Parents must understand that you are not recommending any particular center. You are simply giving them a list of programs that meet licensing standards. Most information and referral services also give parents a list of points to look for when choosing a center. Ultimately, it is up to parents to choose what is best for them. Most appreciate having some guidelines to follow to help them identify quality care.

Some programs have a full-time person who does nothing but help to match families up with child care providers. A method should be developed to pay for this service. In some cases, parents pay a fee to get a list of nearby programs or providers. Some centers have received grants to fund the staff member's salary and administrative costs to keep the service in operation. Other information and referral services charge a fee for providers to be listed in your directory. Employers may also be willing to pay part of the cost of the service if their employees are having trouble finding child care.

A number of states have established information and referral systems statewide. The state funds the cost of the service. These have been especially useful in urban areas. Rural areas may have so few providers that everyone knows who and where they are. Information and referral services do not increase the number of spaces available for child care. They simply serve a function of helping to match families needing care with providers.

16-10 Often, administrative staff can be helpful by making referrals to other programs when their own program is full.

What Other Services Might Be Offered by My Program?

Centers often look for other ways to meet family needs besides basic child care. Many families are willing to pay for services that save them extra time and effort. By serving as the coordinator who makes these opportunities available, the center can simplify life a bit for busy parents.

Special Classes, Lessons, or Services

Many parents would like their children to have the opportunity to take swimming, dance, piano, instrumental, or other types of lessons. The center may be able to arrange these lessons. One school-age center had a piano available. Arrangements were made with a local piano teacher to be at the center certain afternoons to provide lessons for those parents who wanted to sign their children up for them. Another program organized gymnastics and dance classes at a nearby dance studio. The studio provided a van to take the children to and from the lessons. Parents were delighted because their children had opportunities that they would not have had time to provide.

Parents also like individual or group pictures of their children, 16-11. You may be able to arrange with a professional photographer to take portraits of the children. Packages of pictures could include a class photo. Your program could charge a small administrative fee to the photographer for organizing the space and providing clients.

16-11 All of the children in this program were brought together for a group picture that parents could purchase if they wanted.

Take Home Food Service

If your center has a full kitchen and prepares meals for the children each day, you may be able to offer a take-home food service. You kitchen will already have had to meet state standards regarding food service. These may be the same standards as those required of restaurants. If so, it may be fairly simple to upgrade the kitchen in order to be able to sell additional food to parents.

Many parents would rather spend time with their children than on preparing the evening meal. They may drive through a fast-food take-out window, or stop at a local deli, rather than cook themselves. Some centers have established a dinner take-out service where meals are prepared in the center's kitchen. Menus are posted. Parents sign up and pay for the food ahead of time. Then, the correct number of meals can be prepared and wrapped for pick up when the parent comes for the child.

This has been a popular service at some large centers. However, you would have to be certain that a fairly large number of families want the service on a regular basis. In order to offer it, the working hours of the kitchen staff would need to be expanded. Additional cooking utensils, storage facilities, and disposable containers for take-out would be needed. Local zoning laws would have to be checked. There may be regulations against this type of service. Other local restaurants may complain that you are affecting their business. All of these factors must be considered if you are thinking about offering this service.

Special Events Child Care

Some centers offer care on weekends or evenings when special events are occurring. Many communities, especially in resort areas, have special events planned that are appropriate for adults, but not for children. Rather than having to search for a babysitter, many parents would prefer to bring their children to the center. This is a familiar atmosphere where both parent and child feel comfortable. The center should have appropriate staff to meet all licensing requirements. Higher fees can be charged since this is a special service not normally provided. If children who are not normally enrolled in the center are to be included, the procedures for drop-in care should be followed. This will ensure that emergency numbers and information are on hand.

Family Excursions

Another service provided by some programs is the planning of family excursions. The center may organize a trip to an amusement park, an interesting historical site, a museum, or some other place that families would like to take their children. Many families are reluctant to go on their own to some places, but would like to go with a group. The idea of not having to drive, look for parking, choose an eating place, or read maps is appealing to families who want a hassle-free outing with their children. Your staff would have to plan and organize the outing. The fees for families would include the actual costs plus an additional amount to cover the administrative costs of planning the event. As with the take-out food service, this type of event will only work if there are enough families interested to make the effort worthwhile.

Many of the extra services that your center provides can bring extra income into the program. Since basic child care services always operate on a tight budget, the extra services can be a valuable asset.

⚙ Summary

Besides basic child care for three- to five-year-olds, there is also a need for infant/toddler care and before- and after-school care. Centers should consider offering these program components to meet the needs of families. Each of these special types of care has unique administrative concerns.

Many child care agencies also have affiliated family child care homes. Both the center and the home care providers can benefit from the cooperative arrangement. Part-day nursery school type programs, drop-in care, and crisis care are other services the center may choose to offer. Some centers also provide information and referral services, take-out food service, special events care, and organized family excursions. Often, these services can bring additional money into the program to help defray the cost of the basic child care service.

⚙ Terms

children in self-care
drop-in care
crisis care

⚙ Review

1. Even though infant/toddler care is expensive to provide, how can it be beneficial to your program to offer it to families?

2. Describe the concept of continuity of care as it relates to young children.

3. In infant/toddler care, walkers and non-walkers should be separate groups. Why?

4. List five types of equipment that are needed for infant/toddler programs.

5. How can you determine whether or not a toy is too small to be safe for infants and toddlers?

6. What are the typical hours of operation for school-age programs? How might this change in the summer?

7. What are the benefits to your program of having affiliated family child care providers?

8. Identify five other special types of children's programs that your center might be able to offer.

9. Explain what an information and referral service does.

10. What factors should you consider before offering a take home food service for families?

○ Applications

1. Arrange to visit an infant or toddler care program. Report to your class on the types of equipment and activities you observed. How did the staff work to meet the individual needs of each child?

2. Interview a director or program supervisor regarding the operation of a before- and after-school-age program. Find out what had to be done to get the program started. What were the difficulties in setting up such a program? How does this service fit into the structure of the overall program?

3. Develop a list of licensed child care programs in your area for use as a simplified form of an information and referral service. Include the ages of children served, the hours when care is available, and the program's address and phone number. Obtain permission to use mall booths, pediatrician's offices, and other means to make the list available to parents.

Chapter 17
Parents and the Child Care Program

After studying this chapter, you will be able to

- determine various ways to communicate with parents.

- describe ways of providing understanding and support for parents.

- organize parent meetings and educational workshops.

- identify ways that parents can be actively involved in the center.

Children will get the most benefit from their child care experience when the center staff and their families are comfortable with each other. This comfort level is directly related to the type and quality of communication you have with parents. Ideally, the center works in partnership with parents and provides a support to the whole family. As with other aspects of atmosphere in the center, you, as director, set the tone. Your warm, respectful greetings and responses to parents are noticed by all. Staff orientation and training should stress the need for respect for families. Ideally, if you have been able to hire caring and compassionate staff members, respect for families will come easily. Consideration for families is an extension of your care for their children.

Not all of the parents will be pleasant and polite to you and the staff. This makes your job harder. It is important to try to treat even these parents politely. You do not have to give into their demands. You do not have to give them special favors. However, you must maintain a respectful demeanor. This is where it helps to have official center policy on which to rely. If someone wants a special discount or favor, you can easily say, "I'm sorry, but our center policy is… We feel it is a fair policy for all." Few people are willing to argue that center policy should be broken just for them, even though they might like it to be.

How Will We Communicate with Parents?

There are many ways to communicate with parents. Most will welcome information about the program and their children. Parents appreciate a variety of communication methods, 17-1.

17-1 This bulletin board is an effective way to communicate with parents about center activities and announcements.

Parent Handbook

A handbook explaining basic center procedures, policies, and philosophy is important in helping parents understand how the center works. Any program working for NAEYC center accreditation must have a *parent handbook*. It is a basic tool of written communication to which parents can refer. Among topics you might want to include are:

- types of programs offered by your agency
- statement of nondiscrimination policies
- program philosophy
- program objectives
- admissions policies and procedures
- fee policies
- arrival and departure policies
- general procedural policies
- health policies and concerns
- program history and governance
- calendar
- general staff qualifications and training
- program address, phone numbers, and center addresses
- typical full-day schedule and summer school-age schedule

The parent handbook is a useful reference for parents. It also helps them to know that they have entered into an agreement with a well-organized and stable program. It is not absolutely crucial to develop a handbook of this type in the early stages of opening your center. However, it is something to work on that will enhance the image and professionalism of your program.

Home Visits

Home visits used to be routinely done by teachers. Home visits give teachers a chance to meet with parents in a setting where the parents feel more comfortable. Teachers are also more easily able to recognize important elements of the family's cultural, religious, and ethnic heritage and lifestyle by visiting the home. They can get a sense of the reading materials in the home as well as the types of entertainment the family enjoys. The better the teachers know the families, the more likely they are to feel comfortable with each other. When teachers know the families, they also gain a better understanding of the children.

Unfortunately, teachers in many centers no longer make home visits. Working parents may not have the time or energy to welcome visitors. Teachers have more paperwork and responsibilities than they did when most programs were half-day nursery schools. Some programs, such as Head Start, continue to have home visits as a part of their program. Head Start programs usually have specific staff members designated as home visitors. These staff members, not only serve as a link to the program, but they also play a role in helping to improve parenting behaviors.

When home visits occur in child care, it may be because a child and family have become friends with the teacher. The teacher may be invited to a birthday party, summer picnic, or special dinner. These can be pleasant occasions. The teacher, must be careful, however, that a special friendship with a family does not lead to favoritism of that child in the classroom.

A home visit may be especially helpful when a child is having difficulty adjusting to the center. A chance to show off meaningful things from home life can help a child feel more comfortable with the teacher. Children seem to adjust to the center more easily when they feel that they have a special, one-to-one relationship with the teacher. While home visits are no longer considered necessary in most programs, they can be helpful in supporting that special relationship between child, parent, and teacher.

Parental Visits to the Center

Parents should feel welcome at the center any time. This is important in reassuring them that their original impressions of the center are correct. It confirms that the center is a safe place for their children to be. Many centers try to have an area that serves as a parent reception room. It can be an informal meeting place, a waiting area, or just a place to sit and have a cup of coffee. It is the ideal place to set up a lending library of books, magazines, or pamphlets that may be of interest to parents, 17-2. Some centers also have organized a clothing or coupon exchange. Parents can exchange clothing or coupons they don't need for others that they can use. Parents may drop in at inconvenient times for your staff. When the children have settled down for nap, or in the middle of cleanup time, a parent may arrive. As parents become more familiar with the schedule and secure with the center, they become more sensitive about the best times to visit.

17-2 Parent reception areas can include a lending library that provides parenting resources.

The center can also plan special events to encourage parents and even grandparents to visit, 17-3. One center plans a Thanksgiving Dinner each year on a day late in November. The staff, with the help of the children, prepare the turkey and main dishes, while parents bring desserts or salads. The dinner attracts a big crowd. Children are proud of the meal they've helped to prepare. Parents are delighted to have an evening off from cooking. Although it's a big job for the staff, it has been a major factor in helping parents and staff feel comfortable with each other.

Parent Conferences

Some centers make it a regular practice to schedule a conference at some point during the year with each parent, 17-4. Licensing requirements in some states require parent conferences. Parents are aware that this is a routine conference and are usually not too concerned about it.

Occasionally, additional conferences must be scheduled. Perhaps the parent or teacher has some special concerns about a child. Often these conferences are related to behavior problems, possible developmental difficulties, or special concerns about vision, hearing, speech, etc. In many cases, it is the child care teacher who first notices that a child may have a problem. Parents who are used to their child's mannerisms or who may be unaware of normal developmental patterns may not notice that their child is in need of special screening.

These types of conferences may be more difficult. Parents may come in frightened or upset. They may feel that something is wrong. The teacher may need your support, as director, in meeting with the parents. It is a good idea to prepare for the conference by reviewing the teacher's concerns ahead of time.

Set up a conference time that is convenient for the parent. Find a location where you can talk without interruptions. The following suggestions may be helpful:

- Express your appreciation to the parent for coming.

- Share some of the positive characteristics and strengths of the child. Let the parent know that the staff like and care about the child.

- Have examples of child's work in all developmental areas to show parents.

- Express the concerns the staff has about the child. Give specific examples.

- Ask if the parent has noticed these behaviors or characteristics at home. Invite the parent to come in to observe the child in the center.

- Listen to the parent's concerns and comments. Let the parent know you understand those concerns.

- Don't be drawn into criticism of the child's teacher or the program. Don't become defensive if the parent begins by attacking some aspect of the program.

17-3 A special "grandparents visiting day" draws a big crowd at this program.

- Offer some suggestions of ideas for both the staff and parent to try. If the child seems to need further developmental testing or screening, offer to help the parent arrange for this.

- Reassure the parent of your staff's commitment to work with him/her for the child's best interests. End the meeting positively with a restatement of the goals for helping the child.

- Thank the parent for coming and walk him/her to the door.

- Follow-up later with a progress report and plan for the next meeting.

17-4 Sometimes a conference is necessary to address concerns of parents or teachers.

Helping Parents Find Support

Your center may play an additional role in the lives of families beyond providing child care. As your staff and parents get to know each other, they naturally begin to communicate more freely. Those parents who have few resources and no support system to help them, may begin to share their problems with the staff. Staff members, as sensitive human beings, will vary in terms of how well they can cope with sharing in someone else's troubles. Though most of your staff will not have training in social work or counseling, they may want to help these families.

As the director, you will probably have contact with other human service agencies in your area. You should be familiar with the types of services they provide and the needs of the people they serve. Be prepared to advise your staff about services they can recommend to families. It is important that you provide support for your staff when they are working with families with problems. It is sometimes necessary to remind caring staff that they cannot solve everyone's problems, no matter how much they want to help. Point out that the best support may be to help the family find the right agency or service to meet their needs.

When your program is not in a large metropolitan area, families may depend on your agency to help them get in touch with needed services. Your agency, working together with local medical or educational personnel, can help families find the more sophisticated services that are available in a city. Children's medical centers, family guidance clinics, and rehabilitation agencies are examples of services that may be available, but are outside of the local area.

Newsletters

If your program has a regular newsletter, you may have a good way of distributing helpful information to families. You may be able to feature a different social service in each issue. This way, a family may identify their own source of help without feeling that their need is obvious. Including snack or meal menus lets parents know what their child will be eating each day. This helps parents to avoid serving the same food at home on the day that it has been served in the center.

Many centers are also including grandparents and noncustodial parents on the mailing list. This gives the whole family a feeling of involvement with the center. Be sure to have the custodial parent's permission before adding other family members to your newsletter circulation. Sometimes this is not a good idea because of custody issues.

Newsletters may cover the whole center or may be developed by each classroom. With desktop publishing capability, you may be able to develop a newsletter from each classroom without too much difficulty. The basic heading and major articles could be the same for each room's newsletter, but articles related to the activities and children of each room could be interchanged. In this way, all parents would get the major articles, announcements, etc., but each classroom's parents would get the articles specific to their child's classroom. You may want to subscribe to a newsletter service. This service provides a prepared newsletter for parents on a regular basis. You can distribute it as is, or take parts of it to use in your own newsletter. These services can be very helpful in saving time and are not too expensive.

Other Methods of Communication

Child care parents are often a very diverse group. In order to reach them, it is wise to have several different forms of communication. A study done with a group of Pennsylvania child care parents found different forms of communication useful. Among these communication methods were:

- a center newsletter
- center bulletin boards
- periodic letters or flyers
- notes sent home with the child, 17-5
- regular parent/teacher conferences
- group meetings and workshops
- informal conversations with the teachers when the parent picks the child up
- telephone calls
- home visits

Interestingly, parents from different sections of the state had different preferred methods of communication. All agreed that expecting a child to give a verbal message to the parent was not a good idea. Some centers are now adding surveillance cameras to each classroom so parents can watch their child's room on the Internet. This can be a valuable tool in helping parents feel confident that their child is happy and receiving good care. As a director, your best strategy is probably to use a combination of communication methods and stick primarily to the ones that work best with your group of parents.

How Can I Help Teachers and Parents Understand Each Other?

Parents and teachers do not play the same role in children's lives. Ideally, they complement each other and work together for the best interests of the children. Problems sometimes arise when parents and teachers don't understand each other.

Some parents have little understanding of child development or developmentally appropriate programming. They may not understand why the teachers allow children to play at messy activities. They may be concerned when boys and girls both play with dolls and trucks. They may expect workbook sheets and strict discipline. It may be a surprise for them to see children freely moving around the room in busy activity.

17-5 One way of communicating with parents is to send information home with the child. Announcements may be placed in each child's cubbie for parents to pick up at the end of the day.
....

Teachers, on the other hand, may not have considered the factors that influence parental attitudes and behavior. They may assume that all parents trust them and understand the classroom activities.

Influences on Parent Behavior

Teachers can be more supportive when they understand some of the factors that influence parental behavior. You may find it useful to schedule some staff training designed to help your staff become more sensitive to parents.

Each parent is a unique individual. Just as each child has special characteristics, so will each parent. Part of working effectively with parents includes getting to know them as individuals.

Parents may not have the same level of energy. A parent with a chronic illness, a recent surgery, or a disability, may be willing to get involved with center activities, but may be limited in the scope of that involvement. Some parents may be both mentally and physically tired after long and demanding work days. Other parents work long days and still have energy to jump into evening activities. They volunteer to help with flea markets, center picnics, and fix-up projects.

Parents will differ in terms of their intellectual abilities. Some are easily able to grasp basic child development concepts and understand the impact of their parenting behaviors. Others may have great difficulty understanding the connection between their own behaviors and their child's development and behavior. Parents with intellectual abilities bordering on retardation may have great difficulty meeting their children's basic needs without help. Efforts by the center staff to provide parent education must consider the abilities of the parents to grasp the information presented.

Social Influences on Parents' Behavior

Parents usually do not live in total isolation. They interact with neighbors, belong to religious groups, and join social clubs. They identify with a particular ethnic or cultural group, and are a part of other informal social groups. While they may or may not realize it, these groups play a role in influencing their behavior. Religious, social, and cultural groups can be very strong influences in how parents choose to raise their children. Ideally, the advice of these other forces in a parent's life are consistent with the advice of the professional child care staff. In some cases, however, the advice is not consistent. This can create added stress for the parent, confusion for the child, and discouragement for the staff.

Parent Values

Social and religious group membership, past experiences, and their own beliefs influence the values that are important to the parent. Sometimes these values are a close match for the teacher's own values and for the developmentally appropriate philosophy. Other times, there may be conflict between the values of the home and the center. For instance, parents who expect their children to be quiet and obedient and who consider play a frivolous activity may not appreciate the typical busy center.

Sometimes the value conflict can be easily resolved. A parent may take great pride in sending her daughter in a very fancy "best" dress to the center. She may not understand that the child cannot participate freely if worried about messing up her dress. The mother may need to be reassured that she will not be considered a "bad" mother if her child comes to the center in old clothes. On the other hand, if the mother feels strongly that children should be dressed in their best clothes for the center, the teacher may have to figure out a thoughtful solution. Special care will need to be taken with smocks and protection for shoes to allow the child to participate in messy activities.

A special effort must be made to ensure that value differences of this type don't become battlegrounds between parents and the center. Often, as parents and teachers get to know each other, areas of disagreement can be resolved. Sometimes the parents' values and/or expectations of the center are impossible to accommodate. For example, a parent who feels that a child should be denied lunch for misbehaving must be clearly told that the center cannot do that. When a request by a parent is in violation of licensing regulations or in opposition to the standards of appropriate and ethical care identified by the profession, the center must maintain its obligations to the child's welfare. The parent must be told in a respectful, but firm manner.

Ideally, as parents become familiar with the philosophy of the center, and as teachers come to understand the values and concerns of parents, reasonable agreements can be reached. Occasionally, a parent's values and the center's philosophy are in serious, irreconcilable conflict. When this occurs, either the center or the parent may feel it necessary to suggest looking for another placement for the child.

Past Experiences

Parents' previous experiences may influence how they view the center and its staff. When earlier experiences with child care have been positive, parents are likely to approach your program with a positive attitude. If earlier experiences have not been good, parents may be suspicious, angry, and quick to criticize. On the other hand, they may be thrilled to find a center that is obviously better than the one they used previously, 17-6.

Parent behavior is also influenced by childhood experiences. For instance, a parent who, as a child, was severely punished for lying, might become extremely agitated at the normal exaggerations and wishful stories of his/her child. Parents often react negatively to those children who behave in ways that were forbidden to them. These negative feelings may be in response to their child or another in the center.

An additional influence on parent behavior is their experiences with other social services or schools. Those parents who did not have a positive school experience may look on child care as "another school." Some who have had experiences with government bureaucracies may see the required paperwork for enrollment as just another intrusion into their lives. Parents bring both their positive and negative attitudes and experiences with them as they enroll their child in the center. The center staff may have to go more than halfway to establish open communication with these families.

Substance Abuse

Unfortunately, substance abuse has become a major factor in the lives of many American families. Drug and alcohol abuse lead to inconsistent and often inadequate parenting. Money needed for basic necessities, such as like food and clothing, may have been spent to support the parent's addiction. Drug and alcohol abuse often leads to violence. Young children in the home usually see both the substance abuse and the family violence. Often, young children, who need to be nurtured themselves, have to take on roles as nurturers to their parents. One of the center's greatest contributions is that it is a safe and secure place for children to be. Parental substance abuse problems are beyond what most staff have been trained to handle. Staff must work with the appropriate social service agencies to try to support the child and family in finding the help they need.

17-6 This mother was delighted to find a center where she could spend a few extra moments each morning playing with her son.

What Kinds of Parent Education Would Be Helpful?

Parent meetings and workshops are a valuable addition to any children's program. Planning and organizing these meetings can be a time-consuming job, but it adds an important dimension to the work you are doing for children. You may need to try several different meeting times or formats to see what parents respond to best. Planning programs for parents is not the same as teaching school. Parents don't come to your class because they want good grades. They don't come because their own parents make them. They come because they believe that what you have to offer may be helpful to them.

Many parents are eager to get all the help they can to become better parents. Most American parents have little formal preparation for parenthood beyond their family living classes in school. When they are actually faced with making the decisions that parenting demands, they often feel unsure of themselves. They may not realize that many of their concerns are shared by other parents with children of the same age. Opportunities for parent education and the chance to get together with other parents for support are usually welcomed.

Adult learners are interested in topics that are immediately relevant to their needs. If they have a child who won't eat, they are looking for advice on feeding. If they have a toddler who has grown increasingly negative and independent, they want information that assures them this is normal behavior. Child care parents who choose to participate in parent meetings are giving up precious free time. They are not as interested in abstract theories as they are in suggested solutions for current problems.

The following is a list of topics that might be of interest to parents:

- typical age characteristics, for instance, "what toddlers are like"

- what is normal behavior and what are signs of developmental problems

- activities to interest different age groups

- guidance and discipline

- gifts and toys that parents can make

- how to childproof a home

- nutritious snacks and lunches

- how to encourage a "picky" eater

- potty-training

- rainy day activities

- getting a child ready for school

- how to choose appropriate toys

- how to create a positive home environment

- dealing with the stresses of parenting

Part of the value of parent workshops or classes is the opportunity for families to meet others with children of similar ages. Parents often can relax when they discover that their child's "difficult" behavior is perfectly normal.

Programs must be enjoyable in order to attract parents. If parents feel uncomfortable, out of place, or bored, they are unlikely to come back. However, if at the end of the program, they have had fun, met some interesting people, and picked up some good ideas, you have a good beginning for a series of programs.

Be sure to make the environment pleasant when planning a parent meeting. Consider the following guidelines:

- Choose a comfortable, pleasant room.

- Be sure lighting is bright and cheerful, but check seating to see the sun is not in anyone's eyes.

- Have nametags so people can call each other by name.

- Serve simple refreshments to help keep the environment informal.

- Check the seating arrangement. Chairs in straight lines are fine for watching a video, but discourage interaction and discussion. Chairs in a U-shape encourage discussion.

- Organize the meeting so there are several different parts to it, such as, a short presentation, a video, questions, discussion, and refreshments. This breaks up the time so the participants don't become bored or tired from sitting in one position.

- If appropriate, provide paper and pencils for notes.

- Keep the discussion moving. Don't let one person dominate.

- Offer child care during the meeting or help arrange carpools for parents with transportation problems.

- Give parents a chance to tell you what topics they would like to explore. This helps parents know that you want to address their interests. It also can give you new ideas for programs. Parents also enjoy actually making something, such as play dough, to take home for their children. Workshops on simple gifts to make are popular before holidays.

- Trying out the activities of the center may also be of interest to parents. A parent who has never finger painted may be fascinated by the process. Experimenting with the children's activities may give the parent more understanding of its value.

Director's Dilemma

You have been working with one staff member who is primarily responsible for organizing staff training. You have asked her to also begin to plan some education and support programs for parents. You both understand that simply setting up a series of meetings will only have limited success. What are some other ways that you could begin to communicate with parents?

Don't be discouraged if attendance at initial meetings is low. Sometimes it takes awhile for an idea to catch on. As the word gets out that the meetings are interesting and worthwhile, more parents will come. Sometimes getting a group of parents to serve as an advisory board can give you new ideas for programs to pursue.

Some centers offer parent education programs as a separate component of their agency. Parents may enroll in the classes even though they do not have children in the center. This may be done at the center or could be arranged with other local educational institutions.

How Can I Get Parents Involved with the Center?

Research indicates that children are likely to gain the most benefit from the center if the parent is also involved with the program. Children will profit from their child care experience when the center staff and their families are comfortable with each other. Ideally, the center works in partnership with parents and provides a support to the whole family. Because many of the traditional center parent activities have focused primarily on mothers' and/or women's interests, it is important when planning to remember the interests and talents of the men in children's lives also.

In Head Start programs or parent cooperatives, each parent usually spends time in the classroom helping out or observing, 17-7. In child care programs, this is rarely possible because the parents are employed. When parents have worked a full shift, they may have little enthusiasm for center-based activities. It is often a challenge to get families involved with the center. It is a continuing challenge to keep them involved.

The center should plan opportunities for parent involvement. A staff member can coordinate activities and help match them to suggestions and requests from parents. It is also valuable to keep track of parent involvement in program activities. Head Start programs and many grant-funded projects require documentation of the numbers of people participating in various activities. Other programs have also found that keeping a record of participation is useful. It helps to identify those activities that parents prefer and those parents who want to be more involved. By keeping track of participation, you know which parents are likely to be available and willing to make a time commitment to the center.

17-7 Many centers welcome parent visitors and encourage the parents to observe how teachers work with the children.

Activities for Families

Most families are looking for activities they can enjoy with their children. The center has staff with the expertise to plan family activities that will be successful. They can plan simple outings or events that will not take a lot of energy, money, or time commitment from the parents. Examples include the following:

- swimming parties at a local pool

- potluck picnics at a nearby park

- spaghetti dinners where the school-age children help

- organized group trips to a children's play or child-oriented amusement park

- children's fun fair or carnival

Often, group rates can be arranged if the activity involves an entrance fee. Amusement park or show tickets might be very expensive for an individual family when added to the cost of parking, gas, and meals. The center might be able to arrange a cheaper package by coordinating group ticket sales, chartering a bus, and making box lunches for the trip. With this help, families who would not go on their own could participate.

Sharing in Center Activities

Parents have a variety of talents, hobbies, and backgrounds. There is much that they can share with the center. Children are elated when their parents come to the classroom with some special experience their friends can all enjoy. It helps to build pride and self-esteem for both child and parent alike. It also helps the child to see that the center and the parents are working together.

Below are some ideas for ways that parents might bring their interests into the classroom.

- cooking ethnic recipes with the children

- modeling clothing from other countries

- teaching the children their favorite dances

- demonstrating a hobby, such as wood carving

- sponsoring a field trip to a place familiar to the parent

- playing and demonstrating a musical instrument

- reading a favorite story

- bringing in a family pet

Most parents feel great pride when they can contribute something to their children's classroom.

Volunteer Opportunities

In addition to providing special activities, there are many important volunteer jobs with which parents may be willing to help. Most

Director's Dilemma

Many of the typical center parent activities tend to be oriented around mothers and children. You are interested in getting men more involved in center activities. What are some ideas of activities that might be more appealing to the men in children's lives?

directors try to make sure they never turn down an offer to help. Most are usually delighted to get some extra workers for special projects. Many times, there are opportunities to have information booths at a nearby mall or community center. Staff who have worked all day cannot be asked to give up evenings or Saturdays to handle the booth. However, a parent may be willing to help.

Extra help is always needed on field trips and to supervise any transportation. Repair or "fix-up" activities at the center may also be handled by volunteers. Volunteers can help to organize the workroom or center library. If you operate a lending library of books, magazines, and videos for parents or children, a parent volunteer may be willing to handle the check out process, 17-8.

Keep in mind that most child care parents are working parents. Most will not be available for projects that occur during the day. Some who can volunteer for limited projects cannot commit themselves to long-term or time-consuming activities. Some may need child care or transportation if they are requested to help on weekends or evenings. Above all, be gracious if the parent must say "no" to a request. And, express appreciation in ways that sincerely let volunteering parents know you appreciate their help.

Fund-Raising

Parents are a major force in any fund-raising activity of the program, 17-9. Candy sales, car washes, flea markets, and/or raffle sales all depend on the participation of parents. This is another aspect of the program where a good relationship with parents plays an important role. Also, a variety of fund-raising events gives parents choices about how they want to participate. A parent who might not be willing to sell raffle tickets, might be happy to donate items to a flea market. A parent who might be delighted to participate in a sponsored golf tournament might dislike the idea of selling candy bars.

Sometimes, parents need an evening away from their children to relax and have fun. One successful activity has been to raffle tickets for a "Night on the Town". The winners are treated to an evening of free child care, dinner, and a movie.

17-8 A parent volunteer operates this lending library.

Parents as Board Members

If your program is organized with a board of directors, you may want to have some parents included as board members. Licensing may require the inclusion of parent members. Board positions are important because it is the board that sets official policy for the center. The parents who are, in a sense, the consumers of the service, have a significant interest in the policies and the overall well-being of the center.

The *nominating committee* of the board is the group that nominates potential parent representatives. As director, you may be asked to

17-9 Fund-raising activities require the support of parents. These parents are selling decorated T-shirts to earn money for playground equipment.

recommend parents who have shown an interest in the program. It is important to find parents who will be able to commit the time and energy necessary to participate in the board process and who can work cooperatively with others. You may also want to recommend those who are concerned about the well-being of all children, not just their own.

Parents as Advocates

Parents can be an effective and powerful voice speaking out on behalf of quality child care. Whether it is your program alone, child care in your state, or even national child care programs, parents who have benefited from having good child care can work to gather more support for programs. Politicians and government leaders pay attention when they get letters or calls on particular topics. When a group of your child care parents feel strongly about an issue affecting families, they can organize their efforts to get their message across.

Whenever issues of importance to child care are being debated in a governmental body, be sure your parents are informed of the debate. For example, if a change in zoning laws would affect your affiliated family child care homes, be sure program parents know about it. While it is important for staff to be advocates for family programs, it is even more important for the parents' voices to be heard.

Director's Dilemma

A group of parents, with staff support, have been actively involved in raising funds for the center. The funds were to be used to buy new playground equipment. Now, one of the parents has suggested the program use the money for a parent dinner party at an expensive local restaurant. How do you feel about this? What would you say to this parent?

When parents are pleased with the care their child is receiving and when they feel valued and respected, they will be willing to support your requests for help. Most parents are eager to have their choice of child care validated. Receiving or working toward accreditation supports their feelings that they have made a good choice for their child.

Parents are the most important influence in their children's lives. Child care staff and parents working together can create a powerful partnership on behalf of children.

☼ Summary

Parents are the principal influence in their children's lives. Child care center staff play an important role in providing support to families. This support can take on different forms. Some parents need help figuring out what type of care will best meet their needs. Others need help filling out paperwork or helping their children get a successful start in the center. Parent orientation programs, handbooks, and other forms of communication help parents feel more involved and comfortable with the center.

There are many causes for parents' behavior. It may be difficult for staff to understand the choices that some parents make. Parent education, support programs, and referral to other family service agencies may be helpful to many families in the program. It takes coordination and effort on the part of staff to help families find the support they need and the level of involvement that is right for them.

Parent involvement can take on many forms. Some parents like to volunteer to help in the center. Others have good ideas for fund-raising activities. Those with a deeper level of commitment to the program may want to serve on the board of directors or participate in the accreditation process. Parents who are happy and satisfied with the program can be effective advocates for child care.

☼ Terms

parent handbook
nominating committee

☼ Review

1. Why is a parent handbook a valuable communication tool?

2. What are some advantages of having teachers do home visits?

3. What are some ways you can encourage parents to visit the center?

4. List at least three ways to communicate with parents.

5. Identify factors that can affect parent behavior.

6. What are adult learners most interested in when they come to an educational meeting?

7. Why is it better to have a parent meeting that is made up of several short segments as opposed to a meeting with one long presentation?

8. Why is it useful to keep a record of participation in the various activities offered to parents by the center?

9. When recommending parents for the board of directors, what factors should you consider?

10. How can parents serve as advocates for your program and for child care in general?

❂ Applications

1. Plan a parent meeting to role-play in class. Consider how you would rearrange your classroom to make it more comfortable. Create an invitation that could be sent to parents and plan the content of the meeting. Determine your method of presentation, such as discussion, workshop, etc., and plan snacks. Identify other things that could be done at this meeting to help parents feel welcome and relaxed.

2. Prepare a parent newsletter for the center you would like to have someday. Include articles that you have written, a heading, and information about one of your classrooms. Make the newsletter professional and attractive in appearance.

3. Develop a list that includes the names, addresses, and phone numbers of human service agencies or organizations in your area. Identify the types of services provided by each group. Discuss in class situations where you might need to refer a parent to one of these groups.

The ongoing evaluation of a child care program helps to ensure quality care.

Chapter 18
Program Evaluation

After studying this chapter, you will be able to

- ⚙ assess children's progress while participating in your program.

- ⚙ analyze your program's effectiveness in meeting family and community needs.

- ⚙ monitor staff growth in their knowledge and skills of child care.

- ⚙ evaluate your program's status in regard to state licensing, fiscal stability, and national quality standards.

Good care for children doesn't happen by accident. It takes hard work, commitment, and an ongoing evaluation of program quality. As a director, you want to know that your program is a good place for children to be. You need to know that your program is meeting family and community needs. It's also important to be aware of your program's status in regard to the "ideal" program as represented in accreditation standards.

Evaluation is a planned process of studying the components of your program in a systematic way in order to determine their quality and effectiveness. The information that is collected from the process provides feedback on what is working well and what is not.

Evaluation is part of the controlling duties of an administrator. Through the evaluation reports, the director has information that might not otherwise be apparent. This knowledge can then be used in making decisions about the program. Without a regular evaluation process, you might miss changes that need to be made to improve the program. Many sponsors, funding sources, and licensing regulations require that your program have a formal evaluation system.

An evaluation strategy should be made when you are first planning and organizing your program. As you consider how each component of your program should function, plan how to monitor and evaluate its status. Evaluation should include all aspects of your program. This includes determining whether attendance is benefiting the children and that their needs are being met. It also requires a review to assess parental satisfaction with the program and the program's support for their families. Since your program is also a part of the community, it is helpful to know whether or not your program is seen by the community as an asset. Your evaluation plan should also include provisions for staff evaluation and determination of the accuracy of all records. NAEYC accreditation standards provide guidance in identifying how well your program matches those quality standards identified by experts in the child care field.

Are Children Benefiting from the Program?

Children are the reason for the existence of your program. A quality program should support their growth and development, 18-1. There are many ways to evaluate children's progress. Some are informal and based on the judgments of you and your professional staff. Other methods are more formal and must be done in a more organized manner. Observations of children and samples of their work collected in a portfolio throughout the year can be an effective way to determine the child's progress. Various checklists and rating scales may be developed by the teachers or purchased. Developmental screening tests are also available commercially and may be useful. It is a good idea to consider use of a combination of methods when looking at the changes that occur in children as they progress through your program.

It is useful to pay attention to the general atmosphere when you walk into a classroom. Do you hear the busy hum of children actively involved in a variety of activities? Do you hear the shrieking, raucous noises of a classroom that is out of control? Are the teacher's voices warm and supportive, or harsh and demanding? Is it absolutely silent as children work at teacher-directed activities without talking? Is the general tone from children and teachers unhappy and tense?

Above all, you want the center to be a happy, joyful place for children to be. As you evaluate children's progress, it is important to not lose sight of the fact the center should be a place where children can feel safe, where they can relax and play. It should be a place where they can feel secure in the presence of caring adults who understand their needs and who can guide with gentleness and a warm sense of humor.

Most centers, however, go beyond this intuitive level of evaluation. Parents want to know that their children are making progress. Licensing may require ongoing records of children's development. Funding or research requirements may expect the keeping of more detailed developmental changes. If a program is affiliated with the public schools, Head Start, or diagnostic centers, there may be a need for the use of more structured types of assessment.

A great concern among child development specialists is children are subjected to too many formal types of testing situations. These cause stress for the children, and their results are questionable. Teachers frequently feel pressured to "teach to the test" in order to be sure their children do well. There is a strong movement today to limit the use of these formal assessment methods in the early childhood years. The challenge has been to identify other satisfactory forms of determining a child's abilities and needs.

18-1 Children are the focus of a quality program.

Evaluation of children's progress is currently focusing on the use of developmentally appropriate forms of assessment based on careful, systematic observations conducted by the staff. Well-trained teachers who work closely with the children on a regular basis can provide accurate descriptions of what each child can and cannot do, 18-2. Samples of children's work collected throughout the year can also be used to document change.

Methods of Assessing Children's Progress

Teachers who work each day with the same group of children usually know quite well how each child is doing. Good teachers know each child as a unique individual. They are aware of children's development throughout the year.

In order to more accurately assess each child's progress, however, child development specialists recommend the use of several types of assessment tools. These include typical samples of each child's work from the beginning of the year. A variety of written observations can add to the development of a portfolio or profile for each child. Teachers use written observations to give a richer, more complete look at children's behavior than can be achieved through the use of a checklist.

The following observation techniques are discussed below: narrative observations, anecdotal records, specimen descriptions, time sampling, and event sampling. Developmental checklists, rating scales, work sampling, portfolio development, and developmental screening tests are also discussed.

Narrative Observations

Narrative observations are observations where the teachers write down what they have observed. There are several formats for observing a child or a group's behavior. These include anecdotal records, specimen descriptions, event sampling, and time sampling. Each type of format provides slightly different information. Teachers who are looking for patterns or changes in behavior might use a combination of observation formats over a period of time.

All meaningful observations must be done by trained staff who are able to keep a clear distinction between objective information that is observable to all, and subjective opinions or inferences. **Objective information** can be seen, smelled, felt, heard, or touched. Everyone who perceives the situation will agree with everyone else in describing it. For example, if one child walks away from another, every observer will see it. All will agree about what occurred and who did it. **Subjective interpretations or inferences** reflect each observer's feelings, guesses, and judgment about what happened. One observer may feel that the child walked away in anger. Another may believe that the child sadly walked away because of not being

18-2 Teachers can assess many different areas of development as they observe children's growing abilities and skills throughout the year.

allowed to play. Still another observer may simply see this event as a play episode concluding and one child moving on to another activity.

Anyone who is observing children must make a careful distinction between objective and subjective information. Many observers use a paper folded in half lengthwise. They keep all objective descriptions on one side of the page and all subjective interpretations on the other side, 18-3. Some types of observations require a more elaborate coding system to keep separate facts and interpretations.

Anecdotal Records

Anecdotal records are a common form of observation through which teachers write down brief descriptions of children's activities and/or behaviors. This is the simplest type of observation. Teachers simply keep a small notebook handy. The teacher jots down some key words relating to an observed incident. Later, when there is more time, a more detailed description of the behavior or situation can be written.

Anecdotal records are done informally. They usually involve only several paragraphs. There is no set time or place where an observation must occur. The teacher may or may not be a part of the action taking place and does not intentionally have to be uninvolved with the group. Anecdotes may involve several children or just one child.

There are limitations as to the usefulness of anecdotal records. Often, teachers jot down only funny or unusual situations. They may not record common behaviors that can demonstrate a child's progress. Anecdotal records without a date and time on them offer little information regarding how behaviors have changed over time. It is also easy for teachers to forget significant details since they may be writing the record from a few brief words on a notepad.

Specimen Descriptions

Specimen descriptions are used to study some predetermined aspect of the classroom or children's behavior by providing detailed examples of what is observed. Specimen descriptions require that the observer step back from direct involvement with the children. The observer must be in a position to write the observation as it is occurring and not interfere with the progression of the behavior episode. Before doing the observations, the observer must determine guidelines that will bring more structure to the observation. For example, the observer may decide to watch every day at the same time, or to spend time concentrating on the behavior of one particular child. The observer may also decide to concentrate on one area of the room or one type of activity, such as the block building area or large muscle activity.

It is the purpose of a specimen description to record as much detail as possible about the behavior or activity being watched. The observer spends the designated time for the observation writing down as accurate and detailed a description of behavior as possible. Ideally, specimen descriptions include

- events leading up to the situation

- child or children involved

- interactions of the children

Child's Initials or Code:_____

Date: _____ Time: _____

Setting: _____

What You Observed (Objective)	Your Interpretation (Subjective)

18-3 When observing, it is important to separate the exact actions you have seen from your reactions or opinions.

- any input from or interactions with teachers

- the general context within which the activity is occurring

- how the situation comes to an end

To be useful, specimen descriptions must be dated and identify the children and the setting. It is also helpful to develop a coding system where particular behaviors or situations are identified. This way, when reviewing the observations later, it is easier to identify similar situations and to see the frequency with which they occur. For example, one teacher coded a child's hitting behavior with a small blue check mark in the margin of the observation sheet. Six weeks later, when reviewing the observations, it was clear from the check marks, that the child's hitting behavior had decreased. Specimen descriptions are often lengthy and may involve a great deal to review. Coding such information as the following can be helpful in identifying particular areas of interest:

- patterns in a child's behavior

- a child's usage of certain areas of the room or certain activities

- the impact of particular teacher-child interactions

- a child's interpersonal skills

The observer of a specimen description should attempt to collect such detailed information so a stranger reading the description at a later date would have no trouble understanding what happened.

Specimen descriptions have a number of drawbacks. They are expensive in staff time. Whenever a staff member is observing, he or she must not be involved with the children. That means that other staff must be alert to additional children or areas. The specimen descriptions also take time to review and code.

Time Sampling

Time sampling is an observation method devised to determine how often a particular behavior or situation occurs. It is a useful technique for studying behaviors that are easily observable, occur often, and occur on a regular basis, 18-4. Over time, you can then determine if a child has increased or decreased this behavior, i.e. hitting or biting, social play, or following simple directions. You can also tell if a child has progressed in some area of development.

Time sampling also requires that the observer remain uninvolved with the children. A space is required where you can see a clock and take notes quickly. Time sampling takes a written snapshot of a child's behavior at regular intervals. For example, you may decide to observe three minutes out of every 20-minute time period. If you started at 9:00AM, you would observe and write down everything the child does for three minutes. Your sample would end at 9:03 AM. At 9:20, you would do another three minute sample (9:20-9:23). Sampling again at 9:40-9:43 would give you a time sample spread out over an hour. If you wanted to observe for two hours, your second hour would begin at 10:00 AM.

Time sampling over several days or throughout the year can tell you if the frequency of a child's particular behaviors has changed. A child who spent all of the time at the water table early in the year may be using the equipment all over the room later in the year. A child who cannot get along with others when new to the center may be playing well in a group as the year goes on.

Time sampling is not a good approach when you are trying to look at how children flow through activities throughout the day. It picks up only isolated bits of behavior. Time samples rarely provide any useful information on events leading up to the sampling time. The overall classroom environment and behaviors that lead up to or occurred after the sample are not included.

In spite of these shortcomings, time sampling focused on individual children can give you a sense of the changing nature of their behavior over a period of time. As with all narrative observation techniques, it is time-consuming on the part of the observer, but not as much as some of the other methods.

18-4 One observer is watching, on a daily basis, to see how often this child chooses to play alone and under what circumstances.

Event Sampling

The *event sampling* technique requires recording certain types of behaviors any time they happen to occur. For example, you may choose to focus on a child's large muscle coordination. Then, you would record any time the child is trying to pump on the swings, ride a trike, play with a ball, hop, or participate in other large motor activities. There is no time limit on the event sample. You record as much of the complete event as possible. Ideally, each event sample will include information on the setting, the activity, and what factors bring the event to a close.

You may watch only briefly, or over a several hour time period. However, recording is only done when the predetermined behaviors are occurring. As with specimen descriptions, a coding system can simplify your efforts to find key points in your observation notes at a later time.

Event samples are supposed to focus on one type of behavior, for instance, ability to listen to stories, fighting, or playing with other children. It is important to clearly define what behavior your teachers are researching. It is easy to become distracted by other interesting behaviors. Many teachers who are spending time doing formal observations find it useful to develop a form on which they keep the event samples, 18-5. Another form can be available nearby to record anecdotal records when the specific event behavior is not occurring. That will give additional information about the child. It will also make it possible to jot down information on other children as well as the specific child you are observing.

Child's Initials: _____

Date: _____

Area of development being studied: _____

Time	Description of Event	Code
_____	_____	_____
_____	_____	_____
_____	_____	_____
_____	_____	_____
_____	_____	_____
_____	_____	_____
_____	_____	_____
_____	_____	_____
_____	_____	_____
_____	_____	_____
_____	_____	_____
_____	_____	_____
_____	_____	_____
_____	_____	_____
_____	_____	_____
_____	_____	_____
_____	_____	_____
_____	_____	_____

18-5 Event sampling can be used to study a particular type of behavior that occurs often during the day.

Over a period of time, event samples can give you a picture of a child's progress in specific areas. By reviewing event samples periodically, you will be able to determine if a child has developed improved coordination and strength. You can also identify and evaluate such skills as the child's ability to participate comfortably in group activities, enter into cooperative play with others, or work creatively with blocks.

Event sampling, like other observation techniques, is time-consuming. To do it, the teacher or other observer must be free of classroom responsibilities. This is so attention can be focused on the observation process. The observer must develop the ability to anticipate target behavior. In other words, if the target behavior is cooperative play with others, the observer must be alert to catch the times when the child approaches others and whether he or she is accepted into play. Simply recording a situation where a child is already engaged in cooperative play doesn't give a full picture of how the child became involved in the situation.

Developmental Checklists and Rating Scales

The progress of the children can also be monitored by the use of *developmental checklists* or lists of behaviors and abilities specific to the child's age group. The teacher can check off that a child can perform a certain behavior anytime that it is observed. Checklists may be developed by the teachers or are available in standardized form in books and reports on child development.

It is important that the checklists are appropriate for the age of children who are being observed. A checklist that identifies abilities normally expected in four-year-olds would be useless to use when observing two-year-olds or six year olds. Checklists must be specific, taking broad categories of behavior and breaking them down into more specific, easily observable behaviors.

The checklist should also be organized in a logical way. For example, when looking at large muscle skills of four-year-olds, the checklist might include such items as

- ability to walk on a balance beam without falling off

- ability to gallop

- ability to pump on a swing

- ability to climb to the top of a developmentally appropriate climber

If the checklist is organized around muscle skill abilities, it would not include behaviors that fall under the social skills or other developmental areas.

Checklists can be set up in different formats. Some are more complicated to develop and use than others. In the simplest checklist format, the observer may only have to check off *yes* or *no* according to whether the child has been seen performing the behavior.

Rating scales require that the observer make a value judgment regarding how well the child can perform the target behavior. The observer may have to rate a child's skill on a scale from 1 to 3 (or 5). Generally, higher rankings indicate greater skill in performing the behavior.

There are also more complicated types of rating scales on which two opposite conditions are listed, such as shown in 18-6. The teacher must decide which number

Sample Rating Scale		
Has difficulty following simple directions from the teacher.	1 2 3 4 5 6 7 8 9	Able to follow simple directions from the teacher.
Dramatic play is mainly solitary or associative in nature.	1 2 3 4 5 6 7 8 9	Can play cooperatively in sociodramatic play.
Seems unaware of schedule and has difficulty following daily routines.	1 2 3 4 5 6 7 8 9	Is aware of and follows center routines and schedule.

18-6 Teachers often make up simple rating scales to help them assess a child's progress throughout the year.

best indicates the child's ability to follow directions. If this type of scale is used several times throughout the year, it can help the staff see where the child is making progress.

Work Samples

Work samples include examples of children's classroom activities in a variety of areas. Teachers should agree early in the year about what types of samples should be collected for assessment purposes. Care should be taken that all developmental areas are covered. If samples of work, such as an elaborate blockbuilding, cannot be easily saved, photographs or sketches of the constructions can be used. Videotapes can be useful in documenting children's improvement in large muscle coordination or in capturing a child's portrayal of a complicated role in dramatic play. Audio tapes can document children's language skills. Examples of children's creative work throughout the year also help convey a sense of each child's uniqueness, 18-7.

Portfolio Development

Many programs use children's portfolios as a method of showing how a child has developed and what has been learned throughout the year. A *child's portfolio* is an organized collection of information about a particular child. It may include

- samples or photos of the child's creative work (art, block building, etc.)
- written observations made of the child over the year
- checklists indicating the teacher or other staff member has seen the child perform certain tasks, for instance, name colors while playing a game or demonstrate an awareness of the concept of high-low while climbing on a climber, etc.
- video tapes of the child developing improved muscle skills throughout the year
- audio tapes of the child describing a story
- work samples that document abilities in predetermined areas

18-7 Teachers can document children's progress in the use of creative tools and the growth of their ideas by keeping samples of their artwork over the year.

At the beginning of the year, teachers must plan what types of information they will try to collect for each child. These generally relate to basic concepts and skills that are developmentally appropriate for the age group, 18-8. Additionally, teachers should brainstorm about what other types of information might be useful to gather. Each classroom teacher should also determine unique characteristics or needs of every child in the group and collect information related to them.

To be useful, the contents of the portfolio should be summarized at least twice a year. These summaries then become the basis for

- recognizing and documenting children's progress

- identifying special needs that a child may have

- developing plans that meet children's needs

- preparing for conferences with parents

- documenting the program's effectiveness for licensing or grant purposes

The staff should develop a form that can be used to summarize the information in each child's

Director's Dilemma

In your center, the teachers have decided to develop portfolios for each of the children. This will be a way of documenting the children's progress throughout the year. What kinds of items would you encourage them to collect in the portfolio? How will your scheduling decisions be affected by the plan to include a series of observations on each child? How could the portfolios be useful in preparing for parent conferences?

18-8 Photographs and teacher observations provide useful documentation when reviewing the growth of a child's large muscle control.

portfolio. This is particularly helpful when talking with parents. Any of the following can be used to store the portfolio:

• large folders

• photo albums

• plastic bins

• boxes

Any container that can hold reports, videos, photos, and samples of children's artwork can be an appropriate portfolio. Whatever method your staff uses, there must be some way of keeping the contents of the portfolio confidential. As with other records in the center, the portfolios must not be wide open for everyone to inspect.

Developmental Screening Tests

Child care teachers work with many children. Often, they are the first ones to notice if a child's development or behavior is not following normal patterns. Sometimes a teacher senses a child may have some special problem that needs further diagnosis. This is where the use of *developmental screening tests* may be appropriate. These tests are designed to detect whether a child has needs for additional help or further testing.

Developmental screening tests can indicate the presence of developmental delays, vision or hearing difficulties, or other concerns that require attention. These tests may be necessary to help parents and teachers make plans to address a child's special needs.

Developmental screening tests are usually administered to children on a one-to-one basis by a trained professional. They are used only when there is an indication of a problem. If a teacher suspects a special need, parents must be involved in the decision to pursue developmental screening. You and your staff can help parents identify the most appropriate source for the screening. The staff can help make arrangements and even accompany the child if the parent cannot. Sometimes developmental screening can be done right at the center if a private setting is available.

Sometimes the observation and screening process leads to the conclusion that a child needs therapy or a special service the center cannot provide. In this case, it is appropriate to help the parents find a qualified, reputable provider of the service. The center can play an important role by maintaining a current list of other community agencies and specialists that can be recommended to parents.

The whole process of evaluating children's progress is a complicated, but important one. Observations and portfolio development take time, training, and effort on the part of staff. Without a formal evaluation system that the staff is committed to and able to carry out, it will be difficult to ensure that children are benefiting from their time in your program.

Are We Meeting the Needs of Families?

To attract new families and continue to provide service to enrolled families, the program must meet the needs of the families it serves. If enrollment demand increases, you know your program must be doing well. If parents withdraw their child from your center, this, too, is an evaluation of your program.

Often, your staff is able to assess whether or not your families' needs are being met. When staff members have a friendly, warm relationship with parents, they also have an opportunity to become aware of what parents need and want. They will know when parents are dissatisfied with your program in any way. You may wish to use more formal parent evaluation tools. Written questionnaires can be used to solicit parents' viewpoints and suggestions. If your center has a parent newsletter, it may be easy to include a questionnaire regarding services or needs that parents have themselves. Parents may also be aware of needs of other families in their neighborhoods. Parents can be asked to evaluate your program. Some of the questions you might ask include

- Is the center open at hours that are convenient with your work schedule?

- Are there additional times you would use the center if it were open?

- Are there other services, such as weekend care or sick child care, that you would like the center to provide?

- Do you know of other families that are having trouble finding child care?

- What kinds of additional services from our program would benefit other families in the community?

Of course, many programs serve a more narrowly defined group of children and are able to maintain a successful program. Your program may be limited to preschoolers only or some other age group. As long as there continues to be a large enough population of children in this age group, your program can remain full. If, however, there is a large demand for school-age care and little need for preschool care in a particular year, you will need to find some way to adapt your program to the changing family needs.

Are We Meeting the Needs of the Community?

It is important for your program to be recognized as a "good place for children to be" by the general community. When your program is viewed as an asset to the community, it is easier to get community leaders to serve on your board of directors. It can also result in referrals of new families to your program. Community acceptance and support are important. They help to build your reputation and strengthen your ability to attract new families and recruit staff.

By building relationships with other community agencies and leaders, you can work cooperatively with them. For example, the Chamber of Commerce in any community is eager to attract new businesses and industries. By supplying them with program brochures and taking the time to explain your program, you are actually giving them another tool that helps them do their job.

Over the past 20 years in child care, there have been major shifts in the services that parents need. In the 1970s, most of the demand was for preschool child care. By the mid-1980s, concern over the well-being of school-age children in self-care led to an increased demand for before- and after-school programs. By the 1990s, infant and toddler care had also become a major need.

All of the factors that you considered in determining if there was a need for a child care program must be evaluated on a regular basis. Additional programs, such as a group of parents and their infants or toddlers might serve as a support group for young parents. Knowing that a community has no half-day preschool might lead you to consider offering a half-day group. A cooperative effort with the local schools might result in support services and parent education for parenting teenagers. Support groups for single parents, parents of special needs children, and purely social activities that include all families and staff, can enrich the child care experience.

You must be aware of trends within your community. Are there new businesses coming to town that will offer new employment? How will that possibly affect the demand for enrollment in your program? Does your community have an aging population, or is it successfully attracting new, younger families with children? Have you talked to other directors of similar programs in other communities? Often, they can help you with ideas for adapting your services to changing community patterns or needs. For example, in some communities, intergenerational programs have been designed to meet the needs of both children and older adults.

Your program's waiting list can give additional information on the need for child care services. If you have a long waiting list, particularly for certain age groups, you might consider adding an additional group in this age range.

It is a good idea to keep a record of inquiries that parents make about your program. People often call to seek information, but may not actually enroll their children. While you may have only limited information about the caller, you can learn what the caller's needs might be. For instance, if you have had numerous calls from parents who are searching for infant care, you can determine that a need exists for this type of service.

Keeping a record of inquiries about your program may give you valuable information about locations in the community where demand is high, 18-9. If you are considering opening an additional center in a new location, this knowledge can be a part of your needs assessment.

As your program becomes a more integral part of the community, community leaders and businesses are more likely to rally support for your program in times of need. When your program is seen as a valuable part of the community, the commu-

Telephone Log			
Month of:			
Date	Time	Caller Information/Request	Response or Action Taken

18-9 A record of phone inquiries can help you identify trends or needs for child care in your community.

nity has an interest in helping to support its viability. When callers feel that your staff is sincerely interested in helping them find appropriate care, they will be more likely to recommend your program to their friends and neighbors.

Is Our Staff Continuing to Grow in Their Skills?

Ideally, you will have been able to hire trained, competent staff members who come into the program well-prepared to do a good job. In many areas of the country, persons who are trained specifically to work with young children are in short supply. It may be very difficult to hire the quality of staff that you want at the salaries that you can afford to pay. As a result, you may have to rely on various types of in-service training to improve the abilities of your staff.

Staff Evaluations

Even though your program may not be required to conduct regular staff evaluations, it is necessary for some form of staff evaluation to take place, 18-10. Otherwise, you have no systematic way of knowing which of your staff members are carrying out their jobs well, and which ones are barely carrying out the minimum requirements of their jobs.

Staff evaluations, as described in earlier Chapter 12, primarily give you information on individual employees. They are also useful in determining the needs for additional training and the relative strengths and weaknesses of each classroom. Specific training sessions or workshops can be designed to help improve the skills of particular staff members. Staff should maintain a commitment to the philosophy of the center. They should also continue to grow in their ability to carry out that philosophy in the daily activities and interactions within the program.

Formal evaluations and informal interaction with staff should also give you information regarding each employee's ability and willingness to follow center policies. Committed, mature staff will be able to support the organizational structure, policies, and informational needs of the program without feeling resentful.

Ideally, your staff will be enthusiastic about their work and committed to the field of child care and development. That enthusiasm and commitment result in an eagerness to learn and a willingness to share knowledge with others. While these are difficult characteristics to evaluate on a checklist, they are not difficult to determine from regular observation of staff. Excitement about attending a conference, either as a participant or as a presenter, is contagious. Interest in training others who are new to the program can help to keep teachers fresh and up-to-date about new information in their field.

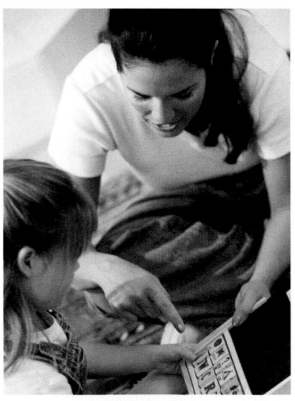

18-10 Licensing requirements in some states require a regular evaluation of each staff member who works directly with children.

Are Our Fiscal Affairs and Reports in Order?

The paperwork of a center must also be looked at as a part of the evaluation process. A good program maintains adequate and correct records to meet the requirements of funding sources, the government, and licensing regulations. Accurate, complete records maintained on all aspects of the program not only meet legal requirements, but also provide additional information about the center.

Yearly Audit

Most funding sources will require that your program have a thorough financial audit once every fiscal year. An *audit* is a detailed review of your program's income and expenditures. It is similar to having a teacher check your homework. The auditor will also make sure that your financial activities meet all legal requirements.

The auditor will check various financial aspects of your program as needed. If you have children who are subsidized (for whom you receive government money), the auditor will check to make sure that all these children are from families that are financially eligible for the subsidy. If your program participates in the Child Care Food Program, a separate audit may be required to determine that the proper amounts of food in each food group are being purchased, prepared, and served to eligible children in your groups. This will probably involve matching attendance records with the number of meals served and the amount of food inventory on hand.

Some programs, such as the Child Care Food Program, send their own auditors out to review your program's records. To satisfy other funding sources, you may need to hire an independent auditor. Preferably, the auditor should be someone who is familiar with the type of financial structure that you have, 18-11. Not-for-profit agencies or any of those that receive money from various government or charitable sources must often meet more stringent requirements for record-keeping than do proprietary programs that receive no public funding.

Many states or funding agencies require that the auditors be Certified Public Accountants. Their fees may be quite high. You should be sure that adequate money is included in your budget to handle the audit fees for your program.

Licensing monitors or inspectors may also visit your program to make sure that all safety, program, and personnel requirements are being met. In addition to visiting classrooms, they often examine records kept on personnel, children, adult/child ratios, and fee collection.

When an auditor or licensing monitor comes to carry out an audit or inspection of your program, it can be a disruptive and stressful time for center personnel. The audit for a large program with many different classrooms and funding sources may take several weeks. You can try to minimize that disruption. It is usually helpful to prepare for the visit by considering the following factors:

- The auditor/monitor will require a private, comfortable place to work. This area should include a desk, chair, provision for coffee or ice water, and adequate lighting.

- All records to be audited should be accurate, up-to-date, and easily available. Time is wasted when you have to go searching for attendance, immunization, or other records.

Director's Dilemma

An auditor at the state licensing department has sent you a letter stating that your program received more money for subsidized children than it should have during the fiscal year that occurred three years ago. The state wants your program to repay $15,000 of money that it received. You are sure that the state auditor is wrong. Who would you contact to help you prepare a defense against this charge? What documents would be most helpful in proving that your program should not have to return the money?

18-11 The auditor for this program also works for other child care centers. He is knowledgeable about the specific auditing practices appropriate for these programs.

- Staff should all be reminded that, even though the audit is an inconvenience, the auditor is there to do a job that is important to the center's existence. As with all visitors to the program, the auditor should be treated with good-natured respect. Any staff support or information that is needed by the auditor should be provided.

Upon completion of the audit, the auditor will prepare an official report of findings. This report is usually formally presented at a board of directors meeting. You will probably have discussed the report with the auditor in advance. If your program has kept all required records accurately and has carefully met all licensing requirements, you should have nothing to fear from the audit report.

The final audit report is a legal document. Copies of it are usually sent to funding sources and licensing agencies. It assures them your program is operating in compliance with sound financial practices and licensing regulations. It also assures them your program is maintaining adequate records to document its compliance.

Other Reports to Be Filed

Most funding sources require your program to file periodic reports throughout the year. These reports may provide attendance, financial, enrollment, or other types of information. They allow the funding agency to see your program is progressing throughout the year. The mid-year reports may also be helpful in spotting negative trends before the center has too many problems to solve.

Local Evaluation

Most funding sources require some type of overall program evaluation as a requirement for the next year's funding. You may be called upon to develop an evaluation plan using people and resources in your community.

Many centers use the program committee from their board of directors to perform this function. The program committee is usually made up of people who are particularly interested in the philosophy and daily activities of the center. They are the group most likely to have the training or to have taken the time to learn about quality programming for children, 18-12.

The members of the program committee may have the expertise to develop their own evaluation system. They may need your help in providing books or other

18-12 Each classroom should be evaluated in order to determine the quality of the program.

resource materials regarding what to look for in a good program. The committee members also need to be able to spend some time visiting the center and talking with staff.

Your program's reputation will benefit if all reports are filed accurately, neatly, and in a timely manner. This conveys an unspoken message to licensing or funding agencies. It tells them that the program staff is careful and professional in carrying out their activities. This reputation also reflects on you, the director.

Do Other Professionals Think We Are Doing a Good Job?

Your program's reputation among other professionals who are trained in child development and care is also an evaluation of the center's value to children and families. While your program might not be as perfect as you want it to be, there are some forms of evaluation that can tell you that you are on the right track.

Meeting All Licensing Standards

Although licensing standards vary from state to state, they still identify the basic, minimal standards that are acceptable for operation in each state. Your center should voluntarily meet those standards. The standards should be maintained consistently even when you know that licensing inspectors will not be around. If your state has relatively low standards, you should try to make it possible for your program to meet higher standards than the minimums.

Independent Consultant

Many programs use independent consultants to evaluate their programs. *Independent consultants* are recognized experts in their field who are hired to provide additional knowledge and expertise. Child development experts may be university professors, successful teachers or administrators from other programs, or individuals who have gained expertise from advanced levels of training or unusual work experiences. Programs located near a college or university with a program in the child development, family and consumer sciences, or early childhood education areas may have an easy time finding an expert who can help evaluate your program. If you attend professional conferences, you may be able to meet potential consultants through workshops or other conference activities.

Consultants are not regular employees of your program. They are not on your regular program payroll and cannot be counted in any adult/child ratios. Consultants are hired for a brief period of time to provide a specific service to your program. Evaluation, training, and general overall advice on programming may be jobs that consultants are typically hired to do.

Usually, consultants are considered independent contractors. In that respect, the financial arrangements with them are not different from hiring an electrician or plumber to fix a problem. Your program must pay the appropriate fee to the consultant, but your program has no responsibility for fringe benefits or withholding tax. You may also have to pay travel expenses if the consultant is from out of town. You have no further obligation to the consultant after the task is completed. Likewise, the consultant has no further obligation to you or your program.

Many programs find a knowledgeable, likable consultant who does a good job. The program may continue to hire this person for specific jobs, such as program evaluation, as long as the arrangements are mutually agreeable.

Working Toward NAEYC Accreditation

The most prestigious award that can be given to programs for young children is accreditation by the National Association for the Education of Young Children. *Accreditation* is an honor that programs must work hard to achieve. It means that a center that receives accreditation has reached a high level of excellence in its program for young children.

Accredited centers must meet standards that are above and beyond the minimal standards that usually characterize licensing. A fully licensed center may still not meet the accreditation standards. Accreditation standards have been developed by a large group of experts in the child development and early childhood education fields. The standards bring together the research

Director's Dilemma

You and your staff have been discussing the idea of applying for center accreditation. Everyone is in favor of the idea, but hesitant to begin the process. Which people, outside of your center, might you consult who could give you additional information? What other things could you do to bring more information to the decision-making process?

about how children develop and how programs can best support optimal development. The accreditation standards represent the best information available on how to provide quality programs for young children.

It is not easy to earn accreditation. It involves

- careful planning

- extra work

- forms to fill out

- teamwork on the part of staff, administration, and parents

- an ongoing daily program that consistently meets the NAEYC standards

- the financial resources to pay for the accreditation process

In order to begin the process of accreditation, you must order the appropriate information and application materials from NAEYC. Your program's name will also be entered on a list of programs that are working toward the award. A program may spend a year or more in preparation for submitting the required paperwork and preliminary study. In order to receive accreditation, a program must participate in a three-part process. This process is the same for all programs seeking accreditation. NAEYC oversees the process to ensure that it is fair and accurate. The actual application process involves these three basic steps:

- self-study

- center profile

- validation visit

The Self-Study

The self-study is the first step in the accreditation process. This part of the process involves an extensive examination of your program on the part of your staff, parents, and yourself. You study the program itself to see how well it is currently matching up with the NAEYC standards. This is also a time to work toward correcting problems that your self-study may identify.

The staff and administrators of the program must consider whether their program meets each of the criteria. Components of the program are ranked according to whether the criteria are *fully met*, *partially met*, or *not met*. This process is designed to ensure that the staff takes an honest, critical look at the program. It also helps staff become familiar with the criteria that are expected of an accredited center.

The forms provided for the self-study are detailed and cover every aspect of the program. Each classroom must be observed and rated according to quality criteria by both the head teacher and the program director independently. Often, the head teachers use the opportunity to improve their classroom program before you, the director, come to observe. According to NAEYC materials, each observation in each classroom will take about two hours. After the director and teacher agree that appropriate changes have been made if necessary, a ranking for the classroom is determined. If multiple classrooms are included in the process, the overall program ranking in each category is an average of the rankings of each classroom.

The self-study materials also include questionnaires to be completed by all staff who work directly with the children, and parents of enrolled children. The responses to these questionnaires give a look at how staff and parents view the program. These responses may also lead to some improvements. This self-study must be completed and submitted to NAEYC.

Each of the following areas must also be examined as a part of the self-study process:

- program philosophy

- staff qualifications and development

- staffing patterns including work hours and adult/child ratios

- administrative policies

- staff-parent interactions

- appropriate maintenance of records

- health, safety, and nutrition components of the program

- adequacy of physical space and developmentally appropriate equipment

- ongoing evaluation procedures

A primary concern in the process is a close look at the quality of the interactions among individuals, 18-13. The day-to-day relationships between staff-child, child-child, staff-staff and staff-parents are extremely important in determining the day-to-day quality of the program.

Parents as a Part of the Accreditation Process

If your program has decided to pursue accreditation status from the National Academy of Early Childhood Programs division of the National Association for the Education of Young Children, parents must be involved in that process. An important part of the accreditation criteria involves the quality of staff-parent relations and the support for parents as the principle influence in their children's lives. NAEYC's criteria recommend annual parent conferences, a variety of forms of written and verbal communication, and the assurance to parents that they are welcome in the center at any time. Staff are urged to make an effort to support continuity between the home and the center.

Part of the self-study includes input from parents. The parents of children in the program are asked to add their evaluations and comments. Parents can provide information about how the program has met their children's needs. They also evaluate the quality of the interactions between staff and parents. Sample parent questionnaires are offered, but centers may use other methods of collecting input from parents. These may include such methods as having a team of parents interview other parents or having a group meeting to discuss points on the NAEYC questionnaire. The results of the parent input must be current. It cannot be several years old. It must be submitted as a part of the self-study documentation.

Center Profile

A program description is developed, usually by the director, that includes a *center profile*, an overall description of the program. Results of both the administrative report and the classroom observation report are included in the program description. The program description, which includes information from the self-study, is to be sent within one month to the National Academy of Early Childhood Programs, the accrediting division of NAEYC. This deadline ensures that the information in the program description is not out-of-date.

Some programs may decide to delay seeking accreditation until a later time. There is no obligation to submit the program description and proceed with the process if you feel that the center is not ready for a successful outcome.

The Validation Visit

When the center has completed its self-study and the parent evaluation, it can proceed with the validation visit. Arrangements are

18-13 The NAEYC Accreditation process includes examining the quality of the interaction among individuals in your program.

made with NAEYC for a trained team of validators to visit the program. *Validators* are professionals in the early childhood/child development field who have worked directly with children. They have received special training in the validation process. It is the validators' responsibility to verify the information in the program description.

The validators visit classrooms, talk with staff, review the results of the parent and staff questionnaires, examine appropriate program documents, and discuss any concerns or discrepancies with the director. The number of validators assigned to visit your program and the length of their visit will be determined by the number of children enrolled in your center. Larger centers require more validators and a longer visit. At the conclusion of the visit, the validators submit the results of their findings and verify that procedures have been followed correctly.

The report from the site visit is submitted to a committee at NAEYC. This committee, after reviewing the report, determines whether the program should receive accreditation. Programs receiving the accreditation are permitted to use the designation in advertising and press releases.

The Accreditation Decision

The actual decision to award accreditation is made by a committee at the Academy headquarters. The members of this committee, called Commissioners, are specialists in the area of early childhood programs. They review your program's validated program description without knowing the program's identity. This committee makes the decision regarding whether your program sufficiently meets the criteria to receive the accreditation award.

Accreditation by NAEYC is a significant honor. It should be celebrated by staff and parents alike. Press releases, publicity documents, open house events, and posters available through NAEYC all contribute to the recognition that a successfully accredited program deserves. Accreditation identifies those programs that meet the highest standards of quality and commitment to children and families.

⊙ Summary

Part of a director's responsibilities include establishing a regular evaluation process that will provide information on the program's strengths and areas that need improvement. Most important is to develop a method for determining how children are benefiting from enrollment in your program. The current direction most experts are recommending is based on both formal and informal observations of children during the day. Samples of children's work and activities can be collected to form a portfolio that shows how children have developed through the year at the center.

It is also important to evaluate how well the program is meeting the needs of families and the community. There may be a need for new services or additional classrooms that your program could provide.

A yearly audit, required for most programs that receive outside funding, is used to determine that all financial affairs are in proper order. Appropriate records must be maintained and available for the auditor to review. The audit report serves to assure funding agencies that your program has been using its funds properly.

One characteristic of competent program management is that reports are turned in on time and prepared in a professional manner. Sloppy reports with many errors may give your program a bad reputation with regulating and funding sources.

Program evaluation must include making sure that you are meeting all licensing standards consistently. Evaluation requirements for future funding may be conducted by a committee from the board of directors, a committee including staff with advanced levels of training and parents, or an outside consultant.

The most outstanding award of excellence that a program can receive is to be accredited by the National Academy of Early Childhood Programs, a division of the National Association for the Education of Young Children. Achievement of this accreditation requires that a program meets standards of quality that are above the licensing requirements in most states. Much work and a lot of preparation are involved in applying for the accreditation award. Programs that receive the accreditation have earned a special place of honor among programs serving young children and their families.

○ Terms

evaluation
narrative observations
objective information
subjective interpretations or inferences
anecdotal records
specimen descriptions
time sampling
event sampling
developmental checklists
rating scales
work samples
child's portfolio
developmental screening test
independent consultants
center profile
validators

○ Review

1. Why is it important to develop and carry out an evaluation plan?

2. On an intuitive level, what is the first thing you should be aware of when you walk into a classroom?

3. What is the value of using the time sampling technique of observing children?

4. What is the purpose of event sampling?

5. Explain the purpose of developing a child's portfolio.

6. Why is it important to evaluate your program's role and reputation in the community?

7. What is the purpose of an audit?

8. What services do independent consultants often provide to a program?

9. What does accreditation by NAEYC mean about a program?

10. Describe how accreditation standards differ from licensing standards.

○ Applications

1. Review the characteristics of the different types of narrative observation formats. Spend several days observing in a child care center, preferably a laboratory center with an observation booth. Use each type of observation format. Later, compare the types of information you have obtained from each method of observation.

2. Examine child development and child care books and discuss typical activities that preschoolers are likely to do over the year's time. Identify items from those activities that could be included in a portfolio designed to show the child's involvement and the changes in the child's abilities during attendance at your program. Decide what type of container you would use to hold the items collected for the portfolio.

3. Read some articles about developmental screening tests designed for young children. When do you think the tests are appropriate for use? Why do you think NAEYC is opposed to their routine use with every child?

4. Interview an accountant to find out what types of records and documentation would be needed for a financial audit of a child care program. What does the accountant check? What problems frequently show up in an audit? Report the information from your interview to your class.

Glossary

A

abstract. a summary of a proposal, providing an overview of the proposal to the reader. (4)

accessibility. safe, easy access to and throughout the building. (6)

accreditation. a form of official recognition. This means that the program meets certain standards of quality. The program has also gone through a specified evaluation by an organization that represents the professional field. (5)

administrative staff. those employees with organizational and planning skills who provide direction for the total program. They seek funds, pursue licensing, recruit and enroll children, and handle other managerial duties. They do not usually work directly in the classroom. (8)

adult to child ratio. the number of adults who must be in the classroom with the children. (8)

advisory board. a board that can study issues and make recommendations, but cannot require that those recommendations be carried out. (5)

anecdotal records. a common form of observation through which teachers write down brief descriptions of children's activities and/or behaviors. (18)

appendix. the part of a proposal that is a variety of items that lend credibility or support to a narrative. These are items that cannot be included easily in the body of the narrative, yet, may add important information that can support the funding of a project. (4)

audit. a verification done to examine the accuracy of records and to verify expenses. (3)

B

behaviorist programs. programs developed from a psychological theory known as the scientific analysis of behavior which focuses on observable behavior and does not identify stages of development. (2)

block-building area. provides space that children can use for creating arrangements built out of blocks. (6)

break-even point. having enough money to cover basic expenses. (3)

budget. projected spending plan based on expected income. (3)

business plan. a plan written to convince a bank or lending agency that the program you want to start is needed, is realistic, and that you have the skills necessary to carry it out. (4)

bylaws. a set of rules that identify the official structure of the board. They also specify the rules by which the board will conduct its business. (5)

C

carpet. a floor covering made from natural or artificial fibers. (6)

cash flow. refers to the movement of money into and out of a bank account. (14)

cash lag. situations where money is owed to your program, but you have not received it yet. (14)

cash reserve. setting aside some money each year, or whenever possible, to cover times when money is not flowing into the program. (14)

center-based care. care for larger groups of children in settings that have been organized specifically for their use. (2)

center profile. an overall description of the program. (18)

central processing unit (CPU). the heart of the computer. It contains the processor, the electronic circuitry that controls what the computer can do and how fast it can work. It also houses the computer's memory. (13)

child-initiated activities. activities that allow children to have some control over their activities which helps them feel responsible for their actions. (1)

children in self-care. children who care for themselves when parents cannot be there (commonly called latchkey children). (16)

child's portfolio. an organized collection of information about a particular child. (18)

chronological groups. groups of children of similar age who have similar developmental characteristics and similar needs. (9)

classroom staff. those people who work directly with the children. (8)

code of ethics. a guide for behavior. (11)

computer network. a network that allows several staff members to have computers on their own desks, yet have access to the same information. The information that is stored in a central processor is available to everyone whose computer is linked into the network. Data only needs to be keystroked into the computer system once, then it can be available to all who need to use it. (13)

concrete experiences. experiences where children can touch, smell, see, taste, or hear. (10)

contact person. a person from your agency who is most knowledgeable about a proposal and to whom a funding agency would direct requests for more information. (4)

contract. a legal agreement signed by the new employee and director, that commits each to the terms specified in the agreement. These terms usually include starting salary, starting date, commitment to personnel policies, and an ending date when the contract expires. (8)

controlling. a function of management that includes regular monitoring and evaluating your program as well as taking action, when necessary, to maintain and improve its quality. (11)

co-pay. the amount still needed to pay the tuition and is the family's responsibility. (3)

cost coding. identifying each major budget category with a number code. (3)

cost per child analysis. an identification of the costs of providing service to each child on a monthly or daily basis. (3)

cots. resting surfaces held off the floor by a frame with legs. (7)

crisis care. a service in which several spaces in the center are held open for use in emergency situations, providing temporary care until permanent arrangements are made. (16)

cubbies. a commonly used term for lockers that hold children's coats and possessions. (7)

custodial programs. programs that do nothing more than keep children safe. (1)

D

dramatic play area. an area designed to encourage and enhance children's pretend play. (6)

drop-in care. care provided occasionally for a child whose parent may need a day to take care of personal business. The child is not enrolled on a regular basis and may only come to the center several days out of every month. Health clubs, shopping malls, and resorts often offer this type of care. (16)

developmental checklists. lists of behaviors and abilities specific to a child's age group. (18)

developmentally appropriate practices. the concept that equipment, activities, and guidance are carefully tailored to the developmental characteristics and needs of each group. (1)

developmental screening tests. tests designed to detect whether a child needs additional help or further testing. (18)

directing. the part of a job that involves providing leadership for a program and influencing others to successfully meet their responsibilities. (11)

E

early childhood programs. according to NAEYC, all programs for children from ages birth to eight. (2)

easel/art area. an area for creative art activities and easel painting. (6)

empathy. the ability to understand how others feel and to recognize their point of view. (11)

employment at will. refers to hiring an employee without using a contract. This means that the employee or the program can terminate the employment at any time. No reason is needed. (8)

encumbered funds. the money for which you have made a commitment, but may have yet not paid out. (14)

enrollment. process that occurs when the center has an opening for a child and the parent(s) or guardian make a commitment that the child will attend. (9)

entrepreneur. a person who is willing to take the risk that opening a new business involves. This person also expects that the new business venture will be successful and will earn a profit. (1)

evaluation. a planned process of studying the components of a program in a systematic way in order to determine their quality and effectiveness. The information that is collected from the process provides feedback on what is working well and what is not. (18)

event sampling. a technique that requires recording certain types of behaviors any time they happen to occur. (18)

F

fiscal year. reflects a period of time during which a particular budget or source of grant money is in effect. (3)

fixed expenditures. expenses to which a program is committed. (3)

fluorescent lighting. lighting usually found in public buildings. It is energy-efficient because it does not generate heat, gives off more wattage, and can last almost seven times longer than other bulbs. (6)

for-profit programs. programs operated to make a profit for the owners. (3)

free play time. the time of the day when children can make choices about the things they want to do. It is a time when they can work on those things that have meaning to them. (10)

fringe benefits. financial benefits included in compensation in addition to salary. (12)

G

goals. what you are trying to achieve. They define future directions and/or desirable achievements for your program. (4, 11)

governing board. a legal entity that is authorized to actually operate the program. Decisions requiring legal and financial commitments must be made by this board. (5)

grievance procedure. a procedure that spells out the process by which employees can complain if they feel they have been unfairly treated. (12)

guarantee. a warranty that the item you purchased is backed by the manufacturer or vendor to do what you expect it to do and that the item is expected to last for at least a certain period of time. (14)

H

hardware. the term used to refer to the actual pieces of computer equipment needed to utilize the software. Hardware includes the central processing unit, memory, output devices, and input devices. (13)

hearings. meetings held to receive public reaction to proposed regulation or legislative changes. (11)

home-based care. care that is provided in a home setting, particularly for infants and toddlers. (2)

home visits. when teachers visit with parents and children in their own home. This allows the family to get to know the teacher within a familiar environment. (9)

I

incandescent lighting. light from the normal lightbulbs found in homes. They are available in different brightnesses and they produce the warm colors of the light spectrum. These bulbs also generate heat. (6)

incorporation. affects how your agency will be treated by the law. It establishes that your program is eligible for tax-exempt status and certain types of government funding. It also provides legal protection for those persons who are willing to serve on your board. (5)

independent consultants. recognized experts in their field who are hired to provide additional knowledge and expertise. (18)

in-kind support. refers to items or services that received from another source without having to pay for them. (3)

in-service training. refers to training that a person receives while already employed. (12)

Internet. a worldwide computer network. (13)

interpersonal skills. refers to an ability to get along with others and to help them feel at ease. (11)

inventory records. records that help you keep track of various items purchased by the program and where they are. (13)

isolation area. a space where sick children can be kept away from others. (6)

J

jargon. particular words, phrases, or abbreviations that are known to those who work in the field. (4)

job descriptions. these spell out the duties as well as the qualifications and experience needed for each job classification. They help to clarify in the director's mind the purpose for each job. (8)

journal. a type of record similar to a checkbook, in which all income and expenses must be maintained in chronological order. A balance is kept that shows exactly what amount is available in the program's bank account at all times. (13)

L

laboratory schools. those programs that exist for the primary purposes of training future teachers and studying children. They are affiliated with colleges, universities, vocational schools, high schools, community colleges, or other training and research institutions. (2)

labor -intensive. "people power" is the most important part of the program structure. (8)

latch-key children. children in self-care. (2)

ledger. a series of separate journals that track each major category of the budget. (13)

library area. provides children with a quiet space that contains an interesting selection of age-appropriate books. (6)

line of credit. a short-term loan. As you repay it, the amount becomes available to you to borrow again. (14)

M

mandated reporters. child care staff who are legally obligated to report suspicion of child abuse to the proper authorities. (15)

matching grant. a type of grant in which for every dollar you provide, the granting agency will match it with additional money. (3)

mats. provide a padded, vinyl resting surface that comes in one- or two-inch thicknesses. (7)

mentor. a person who serves as an advisor, a role model, and a friend. (8)

monthly financial summary. a monthly summary, listing the main category of the budget, that is kept primarily to provide a current picture of the program's finances. (13)

music area. an area where rhythm instruments, tape or CD players, and, possibly, even a piano are usually found. (6)

N

narrative observations. observations where the teachers write down what they have observed. (18)

negative guidance. guidance often based on unrealistic expectations of children's behavior. It is often harsh and makes children feel worthless and incompetent. Shame, humiliation, embarrassment, threats, and physical punishment are examples of negative guidance. (1)

networking. creating and maintaining lines of communication with people who have similar interests, jobs, or goals who can provide information and support. (2)

nominating committee. a group that nominates potential representatives. (17)

not-for-profit programs. programs legally organized to operate without making a profit. (3)

O

objective information. information that can be seen, smelled, felt, heard, or touched. Everyone who perceives the situation will agree with everyone else in describing it. (18)

objectives. goals or what teachers want the children to gain from class experiences. (10)

open areas. areas in a classroom that can be used for lively movement or full group participation. (6)

optional expenditures. expenditures for nonessential items or services. (3)

organizational capability. proof of your agency's ability to carry out a project. (4)

organizational chart. a chart that shows how the staff positions are related to each other and what the lines of authority are in the organization. It can present a visual image of the organization that can be understood more quickly than a presentation of the same information in paragraph style. (4)

organizing. determining an appropriate arrangement of time, people, and space, in a plan that will support the achievement of goals and the efficient operation of a quality program. (11)

orientation meeting. a meeting that gives new parents in the program a chance to learn more about the center. (9)

orientation plan. a plan that includes both formal and informal ways to help new staff become acquainted with the center and their role in it. (8)

P

parent cooperatives. child care programs, usually owned by a group of parents, that use parents as assistants in the classroom. By volunteering their time, parents can reduce the cost of the care. (2)

parent handbook. a basic tool of written communication to which parents can refer. It often includes center rules, policies, and procedures. (17)

pedophiles. individuals intent on the sexual abuse of children. (15)

personnel policies. policies that spell out the nature of the agreement between your agency and its employees. (12)

petty cash. cash kept on hand for small, unexpected expenditures. (14)

planning. a function of a job that involves setting goals for the program and identifying methods or strategies for reaching those goals. It involves considering what the priorities of the program should be. (11)

portfolio. a container including samples of an individual's previous work. (8)

positive guidance. guidance that helps children learn what behaviors are acceptable. It is matched to the age level and understanding of the children with an understanding that children need gentle guidance to help them grow. (1)

positive self-esteem. the knowledge that you are a good and worthy individual. It supports your sense that you can be a successful person and that what you think and do matters to others. (8)

probationary employment period. a time to get to know the new employee before a permanent commitment is made to hire someone. (8)

project methodology. the section of a proposal used to describe clearly to the reader exactly what you are going to do. It may also be called the "management summary" or "work plan." (4)

proposal. a document explaining what you want to do, why there is a need to do it, why you think you can do it, and what kind of help you need. (4)

proprietary. privately owned, and operated for a profit. (5)

public relations. refers to an awareness of, and a positive attitude toward, a business or program. (9)

Q

quorum. the number of board members who must be present in order to conduct legal business. (5)

R

rating scales. evaluations that require that the observer make a value judgment regarding how well the child can perform the target behavior. (18)

reflective listening. a technique in which you repeat a person's statement back again only using slightly different words. (11)

registration. a written expression of interest telling you that parents are seriously interested in having their child attend your program. (9)

resilient flooring. refers primarily to linoleum, and vinyl or asphalt tile. (6)

resume. a summary that includes name, address, phone, educational background, professional certifications, work experience, honors, special talents, and the name and addresses of references. (8)

S

sand and water area. an area that allows children to participate in activities involving sand and water. (6)

science and nature area. an area where interesting science items are available for children to explore. (6)

separation anxiety. fears children experience about being away from their parent(s) or primary caregiver. (9)

software. packages of instructions that you can buy and load onto your computer. It guides the computer's functions. (13)

specimen descriptions. used to study some predetermined aspect of the classroom or children's behavior by providing detailed examples of what is observed. (18)

sponsor. a commitment to provide ongoing support through donations of money, space, equipment services and/or supplies. (3)

staffing. the recruiting, hiring, and retaining of the skilled individuals needed to operate a quality program. (11)

start-up costs. expenses incurred before you receive any income from a program. (3)

subjective interpretations or inferences. interpretations or inferences that reflect each observer's feelings, guesses, and judgment about what happened. (18)

subscriber services. services that print newsletters on a regular basis to identify new grants that are available, government allocations that will result in more funding, or a condensed version of new information of interest to center directors. (4)

subsidized care. care provided for a reduced fee for families who meet certain guidelines. The state or other agency, through various formulas and financial mechanisms, pays the remainder of the child care cost. (9)

support personnel. staff that includes secretaries, bookkeepers, receptionists, cooks, van drivers, and maintenance staff. Their work provides essential support to program activities. They help others do their jobs. (8)

T

table activities area. an area in the classroom for special activities, mealtimes, or general daily use. (6)

target population. who will actually be helped by a proposed project. (4)

tax-exempt. do not have to pay taxes. (3)

technical support. refers to the ease with which you can obtain help if something on the computer doesn't work. It also means having someone available to help if your staff has trouble learning to use the software. (13)

time line. a visual display of how you will complete the project. (4)

time sampling. an observation method devised to determine how often a particular behavior or situation occurs. (18)

tuition. the amount paid for child care. (3)

U

universal precautions. A set of health practices developed by the Centers for Disease Control that requires all staff treat every situation as having the potential to spread disease. (15)

V

validators. professionals in the early childhood/child development field who have worked directly with children. They have received special training in the validation process. It is their responsibility to verify the information in the program description. (18)

values. represents beliefs about what is important and significant as the center accomplishes its activities. (11)

variable expenditures. costs that are paid on a regular basis, but the amounts may vary. (3)

vendor. refers to all of the sellers of the various supplies and equipment that the center will need. (14)

vertical grouping. occurs when mixed ages are present in a classroom. This type of grouping is also called family grouping, since the varying ages in the room are closer to what children would experience in their own homes. (9)

voucher. the promise to pay a certain amount of money. (3)

W

waiting list. a list of children who are registered but waiting for an opening to occur. (9)

warranty. a guarantee that the item you purchased is backed by the manufacturer or vendor to do what you expect it to do and that the item is expected to last for at least a certain period of time. (14)

word processing. the computerized form of typewriting. (13)

work samples. examples of children's classroom activities in a variety of areas. (18)

Z

zoned areas. areas broken into smaller areas, with each zone focusing on a particular type of play. The entire space is divided like a collection of smaller rooms, yet the barriers are low in height, so teachers can always see the children. At the same time, the children can always see the teacher. (6)

zoning codes. rules that specify the types of land use that are permitted. (5)

Index